Benjamin Franklin
Butler

Benjamin Franklin
Butler

The Damnedest Yankee

Dick Nolan

PRESIDIO

Published by Presidio Press
31 Pamaron Way, Novato, CA 94949

Library of Congress Cataloging-in-Publication Data

Nolan, Dick, 1918–
    Benjamin Franklin Butler: the damnedest yankee/
    by Dick Nolan.
        p.   cm.
    Includes bibliographical references and index.
    ISBN 0–89141–393–6
    1. Butler, Benjamin F. (Benjamin Franklin), 1818-1893.
2. Generals—United States—Biography. 3. United States.
Army—Biography. 4. New Orleans (La.)—History—Civil War,
1861-1865.
I. Title.
E467.1.B87N65   1991
973.7′092–dc20
[B]   91–6460
                                                   CIP

Cover and frontispiece photos:
Lowell Historical Society

For Ida

Maps

Illustrations

Acknowledgments

I received much assistance in preparing this book and would especially like to acknowledge with thanks the help I received from the following:

Carol Kuzdenyi, my wife, who designed the book, diligently searched out reference sources and photographs, and prepared the maps

the staff of the University of California Library at Berkeley, especially Kevin Burke at that library's Northern Regional Facility

the staff of the San Francisco Public Library

the staff of the California State Sutro Library

Louise Hunt, historian of Saint Anne's Episcopal Church Library and Archives, Lowell, Massachusetts

Susan Boone, curator, Smith College Archives

Martha Mayo, archivist at the University of Lowell

Suzanne Welker of the Annapolis Area Library

Laura S. Rice of the Maryland Historical Society

and Anne O'Brien and Peter Alexis, who in my behalf rummaged the newspaper archives of the Pollard Memorial Library in Lowell—an institution whose Children's Room, many, many years ago, introduced the author to the wonderful world of books

Introduction

Historians have not been kind to Maj. Gen. Benjamin Franklin Butler. As an important military man in the great Civil War, he has been overshadowed by the glamorous Robert E. Lee and the relentless Ulysses S. Grant, not to mention many other monuments on horseback only slightly less fabulous, whose nicknames echo like trumpet calls down the long years: Stonewall Jackson, Uncle Billy Sherman, Little Mac McClellan, Fightin' Joe Hooker, Jeb, Jube, and Old Bory Beauregard, and all the immortal rest.

As for Butler it is still considered a kindness when, in rare and fleeting references, the general is referred to merely as Ben. Often enough, in an enduring triumph of Confederate propaganda, he wears in print the name embroidered on him by the outraged ladies of New Orleans. They called him Beast Butler, and in the Confederacy that tag stuck fast. The other rebel nickname, the sibilant one, hailed him as Silver Spoons, or sometimes just Spoons. That slur was used by postwar political enemies, but it rather lost currency as time went by and the mythology of Ben's plundering ways died away unsupported by fact.

Perhaps none of this is surprising, since so much of the literature is framed in the lyrical prose of Southern writers who thrilled to the clash of arms, saw glory in the cavalry charge, reveled in early Confederate successes, and wept bitter tears over the ultimate defeat of their heroes by the sheer weight—as they perceived it—of the unchivalrous hordes of the industrial North. Nevertheless, taken all in all, and with poetical bias aside, it can certainly be argued that Ben Butler was one of the brightest generals of his time. In many respects he was also the toughest, since at all times he had to cope both with the honest enemies before him and with far less scrupulous enemies to the rear.

Butler was combative from his very infancy when, as a puny child, he had to fight hard just to survive. In school he fought to be top scholar. He fought poverty to achieve competency as a lawyer and to be admitted to the bar. Once admitted he fought with learned judges and prosecutors on stubborn points of precedence, and in the process got a reputation as "sharp"—meaning he was wily and not easy to beat.

As a Democrat in Whig-Know-Nothing Massachusetts, he fought the ruling political establishment. In his early career he fought the textile corporations that owned and operated his hometown of Lowell, Massachusetts. When the slavery issue brought civil war ever closer, Democrat Butler in abolitionist Massachusetts did not shun the unpopular view. Deaf to the clamor, he pointed to pertinent language of the Constitution which, in so many words, did indeed protect the slave states from Federal interference in their "peculiar institution."

But when secession was in the air and many moderates in the North were in a mood to let the South depart the Federal Union in peace, Fighting Ben Butler was aggressive as ever. States, he said, might legally do as they liked with the issue of slavery, but they had no right whatever to dissolve their ties to the Union. Butler scared poor old President Buchanan half to death by urging him to try secessionist negotiators before the Supreme Court for treason, thus to settle the issue of secession that way and at once, either with a finding favorable to the South or else a proper number of hangings.

When war finally came Ben Butler was first in line as a brigadier general of Massachusetts militia, a commission he had fought a Know-Nothing governor to retain. Massachusetts troops under his command were the first to rush to the defense of Washington. Thereafter he entered history.

The tragic quirk of fate that made Andrew Johnson president of the United States might have cast Butler in that role. It is largely overlooked that Abraham Lincoln offered Butler the vice presidency on his reelection ticket and that Butler refused the offer, preferring to remain with his troops.

Perhaps Butler himself best summed up his career as a commander when, late in life, he dictated a terse and proud paragraph for his memoirs:

"In all military movements I never met with disaster, nor uselessly sacrificed the lives of my men."

Very few if any of the "greats" in copious Civil War literature could make that statement, least of all Ulysses S. Grant and certainly not Robert E. Lee.

In the postwar period Ben Butler resumed fighting at the bar and in rough-and-tumble politics. Always, whether he won or lost, his opponents were left with reason to know they had been up against a formidable battler.

1

Benjamin Franklin Butler had a theory that stress, conflict, alarm, struggle, and the lurking presence of deadly threat were all factors leading to a long and healthy life, particularly when accompanied by a routine of hard physical labor. In Butler's view, benefits accrued not only to those who were forced to undergo such perils and hardships; they were also passed along in the genes as a boon to descendants of the stressed and pressed.

Ben also included a dash of illicit sex in his prescription for longevity, praising it especially for the stressful nature of the exercise and noting its excellent effects upon the hardy yield from such adventures. The best of European aristocracy, he argued by way of proof, were its bastards. According to Butler's hypothesis, the more nervous and physical excitement that went into their begetting, the tougher those fortunate begotten emerged. For much the same reasons, he thought, the first child of the newly wedded tended to be the best of the bunch.

All of these musings went to explain the hickory hardness of the born-and-bred Yankee, of whom Butler considered himself a splendid example. In his view it was no accident at all that among early settlers in his region William Scovy lived to the age of 104, and James Wilson to 100, and James Shirley to 105. For one thing, they had the Indians to thank for it.

In frontier times, not all that distant when Butler flourished, there were the incursive Indians, first egged on by the sly French and later by the perfidious Brits. The mission of the Indians, not to say their pastime, was to harass the Yankees in their fields, their villages, their rude homes, and even in their churches. Edgy New England forebears routinely went about packing guns and knives while constantly looking over their shoulders. All this, according to Ben, when taken along with hard work and freezing winters, was splendid conditioning for the early settlers and genetically beneficial to their descendants.

Butler in time forgave the French for their mischief, since they had aided the colonies in the War of the Revolution, but he never absolved the British, against whom he nurtured a lifelong hostility. Ben came from feuding stock, the North Irish Presbyterians who, after decimating as much of the native Irish Catholic population as they could reach, turned their rage upon the popish Church of England and then, unable to resolve that conflict in satisfactory massacre, gathered their rude gear and headed for America.

Curiously enough, in view of Ben's genetic theories, Butler himself was not the firstborn of his father, but rather the sixth. He was, in fact, the third and last child of John Butler's second marriage, that to Charlotte Ellison, who was John Butler's July bride in 1811. Little Ben, presumably packing his rugged genetic heritage, entered the world at Deerfield, New Hampshire, on November 5, 1818, at 4:00 in the afternoon.

In any case Ben's father, John, was not one of those prototypical frontier farmers, but rather an adventurer and a rover. When the War of 1812 broke out, he hastened to raise a company of dragoons and head for the Canadian frontier. While on field service he suffered a broken left leg, which was set so badly that he was no longer fit for cavalry duties or for much soldiering of any description. Still restless, however, John got some of his friends together and financed a privateering venture that he led, sailing out of Portsmouth to harry British shipping.

Nor did eventual peace with Britain return John Butler to the hard, dull routine of farm life. He became a trader, sailing among the Caribbean islands and along the coast of South America. And from this period came a whiff of scandal that continued to outrage his son well into the latter's middle years. Was John a pirate? Ben's political enemies delighted in raising the old rumor.

What's known is that John Butler sailed under letters of marque signed by Simón Bolívar, The Liberator. These purported to authorize him to plunder the shipping of Bolivar's enemies. The line between out-and-out piracy and actions authorized under letters of marque, always thin, was especially tenuous in this case because Bolivar's republic existed only on paper, in the paragraphs of Bolivar's proclamation at the time. Bolivar orated and proclaimed, but to the rest of the world he was no more than a rebel in arms against a legitimate government.

Pirate or not, while careering about bearing Bolivar's credentials, Capt. John Butler sailed his ship to the British island of Saint Kitts for trading and refitting, where he and many of his crew were promptly stricken with yellow fever. The wanderer died there, and his ship and all proceeds of his venture were totally lost—possibly confiscated, possibly stolen. His family, back in New Hampshire, was left destitute. It was now up to the widowed Charlotte Butler to raise her children alone. And fatherless little Ben, who was one day to expound on the benefits of a rugged genetic inheritance, was in fact a weak and puny child.

2

Ben was about one year old when his father died in far-off Saint Kitts and when, as a result, the Butler children were parceled out among relatives. His elder brother, Andrew Jackson Butler, went to live with an Uncle Benjamin. Ben's mother, her daughter Charlotte, and baby Ben sought shelter with Uncle William Butler and Grandma Abigail Butler, who had a small farm in Nottingham, New Hampshire. There the frail infant survived to become a spindly child. Ben was undersized and skinny, with lank sandy hair and a sprinkle of freckles. Moreover he had a cast in one eye, producing a permanent squint that in later life was to become something of a trademark as well as a source of delight to hostile caricaturists.

Whatever his physical misfortunes, however, Ben was luckier than most in the benefits he derived from the character and abilities of his remarkable mother. She took him in hand, as the saying goes, and she loved him dearly. At Nottingham he responded to the healthful effects of clean country air and solid farm diet. As soon as he was able, his wise mother assigned him the chores of herding the cows out to pasture early each morning and each evening driving them back to the barn. Since the field in which the cattle grazed was a good mile away from the house and by the end of the day they had scattered considerably, the task involved a lot of activity. The result was that little Ben's frail physique benefited from a couple of miles of vigorous running every day.

Nor did Mother Butler neglect stretching and shaping Ben's mind and character. She taught him the alphabet, so that by age four he had mastered the rudiments of spelling. And then there was astronomy. On cold, clear winter nights, wrapped warmly, Ben and his mother scanned the skies, and she picked out for him the planets and the constellations, lore she herself had acquired in childhood from her father. She, a devout Calvinist, read to him regularly from the Bible. Ben and his mother were very close for as long as she lived, and Ben revered her to the day he died.

Late in life, while compiling his memoirs, Ben Butler would recall his mother's standing fearlessly by an open window during a particularly wild thunderstorm. It was her way of teaching by example. As the lightning crashed around, Charlotte Ellison Butler reminded her earnest little boy that he was never to fear, since the lightning, like everything else in the universe, was in God's hands, and if it was intended to strike him, it would find him no matter where he went to hide. Whatever the lesson may have lacked as a measure of scientific probabilities, it was effective as a builder of character. Notably enough, in the long years to come, not even his enemies seriously questioned Butler's personal courage, although bitter rebel lampoons sometimes attempted that libel.

In the summer of his fourth year Ben was sent to the village school at Nottingham where, during the six-week session, he learned very easily to read well. Like his farm chores, the experience was physically healthful, since it required him to trudge at least two miles each way between home and school. Nor was it easy strolling. The road traversed a particularly steep hill that was legendary among teamsters of the time. To negotiate it the drivers of the laden wagons had to use double hitches.

Summer drew to a close and the New Hampshire hills began to blaze in their usual autumn glory, but Ben's mind was focused on distances at once much closer and much farther away. He had discovered books. He was hungry for all the wonders to be found in print, although at home there was scarcely any choice at all. There Ben had access to an almanac and the Bible. The first he devoured, poring over the astronomy it contained. The second he scanned dutifully (although without much comprehension) because it pleased his mother that he should do so.

The village shoemaker, of all people, came to sense Ben's craving for the printed word, and it was he who gave him his first and most prized volume. The little boy had become an old man—a rich, powerful, and famous old man—when he recalled softly in his memoirs the wonder of that gift, which he termed "the book of all books for boys, *Robinson Crusoe.*"

Ben was scarcely to be separated from his new book, but his mother imposed a measure of Calvinist discipline. She read along with him in *Robinson Crusoe*, but he had to agree to read the New Testament as well. It was an even deal. So many pages of Testament earned him so many pages of *Crusoe*. To please her, though, he went further: he learned large sections of the Old Testament by heart, and ever after could recite them from memory.

Perhaps encouraged by Ben's scholastic leanings, the family enrolled him for the winter session of the town school at Deerfield, arranging for him to board in town at the establishment of a spry and well-loved old lady who was known to everyone as Aunt Polly Dame. Aunt Polly was not really a relative, but she took good care of Ben, seeing to it that he was well fed, warmly clad, and off to school on time each morning.

At school he was well behaved and generally well liked by his teacher, although that overworked and harassed man became exasperated now and

Capt. John Butler
Sophia Smith Collection

Charlotte
Ellison Butler
Sophia Smith Collection

then at Ben's inquisitive turn of mind. Ben asked questions incessantly. Often, instead of getting an answer, he was simply told to sit down and be quiet. The boy did so well in the winter session, though, that he was allowed to attend the summer school at Deerfield as well. He continued to read avidly, and he demonstrated that whatever he read he retained in a memory that was proving to be no less than phenomenal.

By the time he was six, Ben was attending the winter session of the village school back in Nottingham, trudging the miles again and carrying his lunch in a little package. Against the hazards of the severe New Hampshire winter, arrangements were made with the town tavern keeper: if heavy snow made the hike impossible, Ben could stay in town until the road was cleared, a process that sometimes took days. Warm and well fed, Ben didn't mind being snowed in. He had his schoolbooks for company. Besides, he had made what seemed to him a wonderful discovery: the town of Nottingham had a little library, and he was free to make full use of it.

Ben haunted that library, exploring the wonders of ancient history as a kind of specialty. He remembered all he read about the ancients, although much of it he did not understand. The chronology tended to baffle him. He was fascinated by all those exotic peoples—the Medes and the Persians, the Egyptians, the Greeks, the Romans. But in his untutored mind he saw them as occupying fixed periods in history, one race appearing as another totally disappeared. When he came to references about their fighting wars with one another, he was puzzled as to how this could come about.

At school his retentive memory continued to serve him well, but as with ancient history full understanding tended to elude him. A standard textbook of the time was a heavy tome known as *Whelpley's Compend of History*, which sought to teach history by posing questions and providing the answers. Ben's teacher would take a pencil and tick off questions and answers for Ben to learn, and the boy would do so unfailingly; before he was seven he could reply smartly to every question in the book. But that was not to say that he knew what the answers meant. For example, one of Whelpley's questions asked, "What would the American states be if the Revolution had failed?" And the answer provided was "Little better than British provinces." Ben knew the answer by rote and could recite it on demand, but he had no faint notion of just what a British province might be. When he asked for enlightenment, he was told to sit down and be quiet. The harried teacher, dealing with seventy pupils of varying age and intelligence, had neither the time nor the patience to explain such details.

History of a more immediate nature Ben learned by the fireside at home. Two elderly neighbors, pensioners of the War of the Revolution, were in the custom of warming themselves inside and out by the cozy Butler fireplace. When they took their place of an evening, hard cider would be brought up from the capacious barrel in the cellar. Peppers, hung drying on the mantelpiece, were added to the cider, which was then heated by the blazing logs to a satisfactory temperature for drinking. After a few swallows of mulled cider, the old boys' memories stirred and their tongues loosened.

They told tales of Indian raids, of shootings and scalpings and burnings at the stake, and of atrocities encouraged first by the French in their war with the king and later incited by the king's own officers as punishment for his rebellious Yankee subjects. The veterans relived old battles against the hated redcoats, whose ferocity and treachery lacked no detail in the telling.

To all of this the wide-eyed boy listened in delicious horror and fascination. His childhood games and dreams of derring-do revolved around scenarios in which he was fighting the hated redcoats. In later life he was to recall that the emotions stirred in him by the old soldiers' tales were so firmly implanted that he always bristled when meeting an Englishman and had to remind himself to exercise ordinary politeness. As a soldier he would have welcomed a clash with the British.

During this childhood time he was, figuratively speaking, adopted by his grandmother. She was an imperious matriarch in her eighties and a pioneer feminist. She took her meals with the family, but at a separate table at which only Ben was invited to sit. At mealtimes she would inveigh against men's unfairness to women—especially their custom of taking care, in drafting their wills, to see that property passed only to the eldest male of the family. Her lack of formal title to the Butler farm was always a sore spot with grandma, although she ruled quite capably without it.

Grandma Butler also voiced enormous contempt for kings, princes, and hereditary nobility in general; at the same time she expressed a curious satisfaction with the concept of aristocracy. She considered herself of that class, proclaiming proudly that her family, the Cilleys, were of the best bloodline in New Hampshire. From this indoctrination, Butler was to say, he came to consider himself both a democrat and an aristocrat.

3

Ben Butler's best-remembered teacher at Deerfield, one James Hersey, specialized in English. Hersey was a fanatic about the exercise of parsing. Hersey's pupils had to be able to pluck any given word out of its context, wrestle it to the floor, and extract from it all pertinent information as to its grammatical credentials. At a crucial time this led to Ben's winning a kind of parsing contest, which in turn secured him a scholarship at Exeter to prepare (at age nine) for college.

The occasion was an oral examination at Deerfield, attended by all the clergy and other bigwigs of the area. It was a kind of public performance, the pupils arranged on stage according to standing, which put little Ben at the foot of the class. Hersey read a bit of ponderous verse whose first line read, "The lamb thy riot dooms to bleed today. . . ." To the bright lad who stood at the head of the class he then issued the terse instruction, "Parse *lamb*."

The boy stammered an answer. Wrong. Eight others seized *lamb* and met defeat. Finally it was Ben's turn, and he responded smartly, "*Lamb* is a noun in the objective case and governed by *dooms*. . . ."

"Right," said the teacher. "Go to the head of the class."

What the other lads thought of Ben at that moment can easily be imagined, but it impressed the assembled dignitaries no end. Then and there they began to consult with one another on how they could wangle a scholarship for the parsing champion of Deerfield, and the following autumn Ben indeed entered Exeter to continue his patchwork education.

At Exeter he was introduced to Latin and Greek, although to somewhat limited effect. His phenomenal memory quickly absorbed the mechanics of the classic languages. Conjugations and declensions were mastered easily, since they were elements that could be learned by rote. But free and meaningful translations were something else again. As he recalled it afterward, "My learning was nothing but memorizing. . . . I was far too young to appreciate the beauties of the *Iliad*."

Religion troubled him at Exeter. He was required there to attend the school's Unitarian services, which clashed with the fundamentalist teachings that had been drilled into him at home. Religion, indeed, was to trouble him throughout his formal schooling, and in the long years ahead he tended to become something of an agnostic. In the end Ben Butler's faith came to be lodged mostly in Ben Butler.

The Exeter interval was brief. When the winter term ended in 1828, Ben found himself in a new home in a very new city, the bustling cotton-mill town of Lowell, Massachusetts. For the rest of his life Lowell would be his power center. All of his future wealth, his political influence, even his military career, would have their roots in the Spindle City that sprang up by the Pawtucket Falls of the Merrimack River.

While he was at Exeter, Butler's mother and sister had removed to Lowell at the urging of a clergyman friend, and with his considerable assistance. There she operated one of those peculiarly well regulated boarding houses which, under strictest of rules, served as dormitories for the mill workers, whose lives were timed and governed by the tolling of the mills' great bells.

In the growing tensions of the times, there were those who were pleased to score debating points by noting that wage slavery in the cotton mills of the abolitionist North was not all that different from out-and-out slavery in the cotton fields of the plantation South. In Yankeedom this smarted a bit, because it certainly was evident that in the model industrial city of Lowell such freedom as the mill workers enjoyed was a closely circumscribed privilege. The mill owners pursued one goal with cold determination, and that was to produce as much cloth as possible as cheaply as possible for the maximum possible return on investment. To this end the work force was regimented, regulated, and ruled.

It is legend in Lowell that Edgar Allan Poe was inspired to sing about the tintinnabulation of the bells, bells, bells by listening to the booming and echoing clamor that emanated from the belfries of the mills. They rang in unison, a mighty brazen chorus. "Get up and go to work," they said. "Break now for your noontime meal," they said. And precisely half an hour later they tolled, "Get back to work." Curfew rang at 9:00 P.M. to warn of the 10:00 P.M. deadline hour, at which time the doors of the corporation boardinghouses were locked and any worker still abroad at that hour was out of luck, out of lodging, and out of a job.

Workers were roused by the bells before dawn so they could eat their breakfast on their own time and not waste any daylight hours. Those productive hours belonged to the mills, fourteen hours each day, six days a week.

Mill workers also submitted to a kind of bondage. If a person hired on at one mill, at that mill he stayed unless the management saw fit to release him. By agreement among the corporations, a worker could not switch jobs as between mills unless the original employer granted him or her a pass authorizing the change. Without such a pass there was no work in any mill. To quit was to quit for good.

Still, heavy thinkers of the time saw the Lowell industrial development as a model social scheme. Matrons in the boardinghouses were charged with overseeing the morals of their boarders, and that was considered a notable plus. And there was the long, free Sunday with a profusion of preachers to uplift the spirit and strengthen the soul. Much of the work force, after all, was drawn from the good farm families of the region, daughters eager to earn a stake for marriage or to help out at home. When the mill owners undertook to see to it that they were returned home pure and godly after a period of years, and with some cash savings as well, this was seen as benevolence untrammeled.

And it must be added that the workers themselves—those who lasted, at any rate—were often infused with pride at their status. This was remarkably demonstrated when President Andrew Jackson visited Lowell in 1833. All the mill workers paraded to greet him, and patriotism was so stirred among them that weavers at one of the mills promptly staged a strike, not on issues but on principle. The management, the workers said, had belittled their status as homegrown Americans by hiring an Irish woman to scrub the weaving-room floor. Management, properly chastened, quickly remedied that insult to the natives.

Butler was to observe all this with general approval, particularly after he had acceded, in later life, to ownership of considerable stock in the manufacturing corporations. The stock paid fabulous dividends. However, that fourteen-hour day did provide him with an issue when he was starting out in politics as a young firebrand lawyer. He campaigned persistently for a mandatory ten-hour day. After all, he suggested privately to such management people who would deign to listen to him, they could always run the machines faster and attain the same production level.

All this was in the far future, though, at the time when Ben left Exeter to live in Lowell. More immediately there was his further education to consider. Ben, still enthralled by those fireside tales told by the old soldiers, thought it would be a great idea if he could get an appointment to West Point. Instead he reluctantly wound up at Waterville College in Maine, a Baptist theological institution that was later to become Colby College. Mother and her preacher friend thought Ben would make a splendid man of the cloth, and Ben, faced with Waterville or nothing, had little choice but to agree.

4

Ben Butler was born in New Hampshire, to be sure, but Major General Benjamin Franklin Butler—lawyer, politician, industrialist, soldier, and administrator—was a product of Lowell, Massachusetts, a vigorous, bustling, brand-new boomtown ideally suited to fulfill his needs and nurture his talents. When Butler and Lowell first came together in 1829, Ben was eleven while the town was only three. The town was to mature first. Only seven years later the town became a city—in fact, the second city in Massachusetts, after Boston.

In a way the city of Lowell was the product of a legal invention that had matured years earlier in the mind of Francis Cabot Lowell, Harvard class of 1793. His invention, looms and spindles aside, was nothing less than a prototype of the modern American stockholder's corporation. F. C. Lowell's financial concept brought practical realization to his other innovation, which was one of technology. Heretofore the textile industry had been comfortably fragmented: spinning mills spun, weaving mills wove, dye plants dyed. Lowell proposed to combine in one factory all the machinery required to process raw cotton into finished cloth. Bales of raw cotton would enter the factory, bolts of cloth would emerge, and all wasted motion would be eliminated.

To finance the first consolidated textile mill, Lowell and his associates (brother-in-law Patrick Jackson and friend Nathan Appleton) had recourse to that innovative investment scheme. Instead of forming an ordinary partnership, they parceled out shares in the enterprise: stock holdings. With the funds thus raised, they built their first mill at Waltham, Massachusetts. As projected, the mill prospered. The shares paid dividends and acquired a cash value in the marketplace, where they could be freely bought and sold.

In 1817, not long after the Waltham mill was established, Francis Lowell died. The city that was to bear his name was as yet just a glimmer in the minds of his surviving associates. At Waltham they had learned in practice how to put a complete textile plant under one roof and how to harness waterpower to run the mill efficiently. But perhaps most important, they now knew how to finance great enterprises through the sale of corporate shares. Small wonder, sentiment aside, that they came to name their new town on the banks of the Merrimack River for their friend and mentor, Francis Cabot Lowell.

Earlier entrepreneurs surveying the Merrimack had largely overlooked its possibilities as a great source of power. Instead they were preoccupied with a dream of taming the river to make it navigable. They saw the sharp drop of the Pawtucket Falls not as an asset, but as an obstacle. To get around the roaring falls and rapids, they constructed a bypass waterway, the Pawtucket Canal. But their project, as it turned out, was never any great shakes either as an engineering accomplishment or as a money-maker.

When Jackson and Appleton began prospecting for mill sites, they saw the canal property in a different light. The two men recognized at once that while the powerful flow of water at Pawtucket Falls and through the canal was wasted on transportation, it was exactly what was needed to run their machinery. Moreover, the canal company, a loser, was anxious to unload its holdings. All the land in the area was cheap and, except for a few scattered houses, unoccupied.

Clearly it was time to launch another corporation. Appleton and Jackson joined with Paul Moody, Warren Dutton, and an autocratic Englishman named Kirk Boott. They formed the Merrimack Manufacturing Company in 1822, and their first mill was in operation a year later. Perhaps even more important, from the standpoint of never ending dividends, they also formed a proprietary corporation (known locally as Locks & Canals), which controlled all the adjacent land and waterpower. Besides operating the Merrimack Mill, the proprietors furnished mill sites and power for additional mills. From their enterprise sprang a city, and for all practical purposes the mill men owned it.

Of all the founders it was the Englishman, Boott, who in a curious way was to figure large in Ben Butler's early years, and by no means as a benefactor. The clash had to do with Ben's educational opportunities—more specifically, whether he would have any. And it provided Ben with an early hero figure, the young rector of Saint Anne's Church, Theodore Edson.

Boott, a former cavalry officer, had absorbed very little of American democracy. He comported himself as a proper British autocrat, both destined and duty-bound to furnish guidance and example to the lesser breed about him. Boott felt that he knew what was good for the artisans and the yokelry, even if they themselves did not. One of the things obviously good for them would be a proper church where he and they could worship together while maintaining, of course, a correct respect for his rank and position. So with corporation funds he founded a church; provided a matching parsonage; staffed it with a proper Episcopalian rector; and assessed his mill workers for all its upkeep through regular deductions from their wages. It was Boott who named it Saint Anne's, and it is still to be seen in Lowell— a very pretty, very English parish church, complete with ivy clinging to its gray granite.

For himself, Boott provided within Saint Anne's a large and specially ornamented personal pew. And nearby he built himself a kind of manor house, from which he could oversee his domain. If Boott made an error in any of this, it was in underassessing the character and fortitude of the first rector of Saint Anne's, that remarkable young man, Theodore Edson.

In 1829, with Ben out of Exeter and somewhat adrift, his education was languishing. He dawdled at home, studying his Latin text in desultory fashion. His mother got him a job in Lowell's only bookstore, and he worked at various chores there for a few months. Then toward the end of the year came a kind of minor miracle: Lowell High School was established, and Ben became a member of its very first class. This came about, as it happened, through Edson's stubborn efforts and over the loud, personal, bitter, and peremptory objections of no less a grandee than Kirk Boott.

Earlier, the young Reverend Edson had begun testing tempers with a modest proposal that the new town of Lowell set aside two large parks, a North Common and a South Common, to provide pleasant open space. Boott, the autocrat, may have harrumphed a bit, but he permitted this, probably because there was plenty of land available and all of it was cheap. However, civic uproar ensued when Edson proposed further that two small schools be built—two solidly constructed brick schoolhouses, in fact—one on a corner of each park. The cost was to be something over $20,000, and this brought Boott to his feet snarling like a treed panther. Since that $20,000 could only come from such taxation as was assessed against the mills, Boott was outraged at the sheer impudence of it all.

When the proposal came before a town meeting, Boott himself appeared, flanked by a posse of mill managers. With Boott as keynote speaker, all argued vehemently against the outrageous extravagance of building public schools—and of brick, no less—at such ruinous cost. Their heavy rhetoric met no disagreement, the assembly being properly cowed as usual, until a quiet, well-modulated voice was heard, a voice that was actually contradicting Mr. Boott. It was the young Reverend Edson speaking, and he was eloquent—and he was alone.

Boott and his mill men responded with bullying questions and with raging argument against the school measure, but Edson, still alone, continued to urge approval of the project. When it became evident that the town meeting might actually adopt the school appropriation, Boott quickly maneuvered for a postponement.

During the interim Boott took Edson to task. He reminded him sternly of their relative status in the community and assured the young clergyman

Kirk Boott
Saint Anne's Episcopal Church Library
& Archives, Lowell, Massachusetts

Rev. Theodore Edson
Saint Anne's Episcopal Church Library
& Archives, Lowell, Massachusetts

that, if he persisted in his foolishness, Boott would withdraw all financial support from Saint Anne's. No more pew rent from Boott himself, no more tithes extracted from the wages of the mill workers. It was of course a raw threat, and nothing in Boott's American experience had given him reason to suspect that it would not prevail.

Nevertheless, when the town meeting reconvened, the Reverend Edson was there to renew his arguments for the new schools, and in a long and eloquent performance against loud opposition from Boott and his henchmen, Edson carried the day. The money was voted. The schools were built. And on the upstairs floor of the new school on the South Common—the little building that was one day to be known as the Edson School—the first class of Lowell High School convened on December 28, 1829. In his mature years Butler was to testify, "Here I received, if not the most part, the best of all my educational teaching in my preparation for college."

It was to prove a happy circumstance that one of his classmates at Lowell High School was Gustavus V. Fox, one day to become assistant secretary of the navy, a man in a key position to help Maj. Gen. Benjamin F. Butler at critical points in Butler's military career.

More immediately, however, Ben's sojourn at the Waterville theological college still lay in his future, and that experience was to be a stormy one. As for the young Reverend Edson, he was to serve as rector of Saint Anne's for a distinguished sixty years, and throughout his lifetime he remained a close friend of Butler and the Butler family.

5

When Lowell High School finished fitting him for college, Ben Butler made one last, desperate effort to escape that Baptist institution in Maine. This attempt put his doting mother in the middle, beset on one side by Ben, who wanted to go to West Point, and on the other by her clergyman friend, who continued to insist that Ben was ideal material for the ministry and that West Point was a nest of infidels who would almost certainly corrupt him.

Ben won the skirmish but lost the campaign. Reluctantly, Mrs. Butler applied to the congressman representing her current Massachusetts district and also to the representative from her old New Hampshire district, asking for a West Point nomination for her son and recalling his father's wartime service as an officer of dragoons. The two politicians, Caleb Cushing and Isaac Hill, promptly replied with the smoothest of regrets, but their answer in both cases was not only no but no way. At this turn of events Ben learned a little something about politics and political influence, and he also acquired a bitterness about West Point and West Pointers that was to affect his judgment all the rest of his life. He simply never got over the snub.

Reluctantly off to Waterville, Ben found himself in the midst of a student body most of whose members were striving for the ministry. Whether out of pique or from a snobbish sense of intellectual superiority, he lost no opportunity to confound the apprentice divines with arguments questioning their dogma. Reveling in controversy, Ben quickly became a proud outcast among the faithful. Perhaps more significant, he argued so well that he even convinced himself; never afterward did he take organized religion all that seriously.

At Waterville Ben also set his own study priorities, neglecting subjects he didn't like and, to others, devoting his attention with the zeal of a hobbyist. He leaped into a largely ignorant pursuit of chemistry, being especially fascinated with the arcane lore of the ancient alchemists and their efforts to turn base metals into gold. As a sideline he found explosives amusing, and with a like-minded confederate he spent some time blowing things up.

In his mature years Butler had little to say about Waterville or its

faculty. He was to recall his adventures in science and pseudoscience ironically: "For nearly two years I pursued my scientific studies substantially
outside of the course, because our professor of chemistry, Dr. Holmes, for
reasons satisfactory to himself, did not think it worthwhile to give lectures
on chemistry."

The mundane study of geometry interested him not at all, and his
neglect of the subject led him into a characteristically impertinent class-
room episode. At the blackboard Ben failed miserably to demonstrate a
theorem, fumbling around until the instructor finally snatched the chalk out
of his hand.

"Butler," said the teacher, "you don't know anything."

"Not about that demonstration," retorted Ben. "But I can tell you a
good many things that *you* don't know."

For that time and place, Butler's impudence was no less than shocking.
He went on from there to challenge the faculty at the very core of their
methods and beliefs: he balked at attending compulsory prayer meetings
and church services. In this, intellectual and religious arguments aside, Ben
was moved both by financial considerations and his standing as a student,
since nonattendance at services not only cost him a fine of 10 cents per
infraction, but also reduced his academic grades. The 10-cent fine was
important to him, since his purse was slim, but the other penalty affected
his pride, which was tender at all times.

In a manner suggesting the care with which in future years he would
prepare a case at law, Ben set about researching the roots of Calvinism. He
concluded that, if the prevailing doctrine at Waterville was correct, his
attendance at services was likely to do him more spiritual harm than good.
According to the doctrine, Ben reasoned, he was either already predestined
to be saved and go to heaven, or else, if he were not among the elect from
the beginning of all things, then he must inevitably go to hell. Moreover, he
contended, hell was destined to be somewhat less painful for heathens
unaware of the Word and designedly worse for those who had been
exposed to the teachings. In conclusion he argued that either he was going
to heaven anyway and the services would make little difference, or else he
was condemned already to the other place, and the more he was exposed
to the teachings of the divines the worse it would be for him, since outright
heathens were so much better off because of their ignorance. Ben put all
this medieval pin peering in the form of a petition that asked the faculty to
excuse him from prayers and services.

The school administrators, in a fine mixture of horror and disgust,
refused to dignify the impertinence of the seventeen-year-old Butler with a
reply. They did consider expelling him, but with truly Christian charity they
decided finally to put up with him for his devout mother's sake.

In any case, as it turned out, the most important event in Ben's college career occurred off campus. He heard that the great Jeremiah Mason, the most famous trial lawyer of the time, was arguing a case in a nearby county courthouse. Ben attended that trial and came away star struck. Suddenly his life's course was clear. No matter what, Ben was going to be a lawyer, a trial lawyer, an argufier, a swayer of juries, a gladiator in the arena of the courts.

Ben stayed on at Waterville, just the same. He especially wanted to continue with his independent study of chemistry. After all, he noted, it might come in handy some day in trying cases of murder by poison.

6

In rugged old snowbound Massachusetts, few boys grew up without being dosed early and often with that ancient and honorable nostrum, cod-liver oil. In softer times it came to be emulsified and sweetened in one patent medicine or another, but in Ben Butler's day it was served up straight and repulsive, and was altogether so revolting that it just had to be good for you.

In Ben's case, as it happened, those healing dollops of cod-liver oil were administered along with a dash of adventure aboard a Gloucester fishing boat. Afterward he even professed to like the stuff, and he credited it with giving him such a sturdy constitution that he was never really sick a day in his life. But in the year Ben finished his stint at Waterville College, he was so emaciated that people thought he was a likely candidate for the graveyard. He weighed just a gaunt ninety-seven pounds and had a hacking cough that made friends and family wince.

Ben came to this condition through an excess of energy and confidence. Somehow, throughout his puny childhood and spindly adolescence, he had never got around to thinking of himself as a weakling. The thought simply never occurred to him. So it was characteristic that when the winter ice on the Kennebec River broke loose in the spring of his final college year, Ben nonchalantly decided to go skinny-dipping in the frigid waters. He had done this before. He took satisfaction in it as a kind of spring ritual. The winds and currents had driven blocks of ice ashore on the banks of the river, so Ben chose a handy one to sit down on while he disrobed. Then he leaped into the river and splashed around, luxuriating in the chill of the water and in the exertions of a hard-driven circulatory system.

After his swim he returned to his icy bench, got dressed, and then set out to run a couple of miles. He had found that a brisk stretch of the legs usually restored a glow of warmth to his chilled body on occasions like this. But now the formula failed. Ben continued to shake and chatter. Shortly afterward he came down with a heavy cold. It left him with that persistent cough wracking his gaunt frame, and it was in that condition he returned home clutching his new diploma.

This time his mother truly feared for his life. Although Ben scoffed at her concern, she determined to take heroic measures. It was arranged that Ben would go on a sea voyage in a fishing vessel captained by an old friend from his father's privateering days. The prescription had a measure of kill-or-cure desperation. But then, the fishermen would be after cod, as usual, so there would be plenty of cod-liver oil as well as hearty food and fresh sea air.

Ben reported to the captain togged out in his sportiest outfit and accompanied by a large box of books. The old man looked him up and down in evident disgust and promptly consigned Ben's portable library to the hold. "There'll be no reading on this voyage," he said. "Now go ashore and get yourself a proper seafaring rig."

The captain assigned the first mate to go along and see to it that Ben was outfitted for rugged, heavy-weather sailing. The mate did his best, but Ben, who both then and later had a taste for finery, managed to hold out for fancy ribbons on his sou'wester, embroidery on his jacket, and a fine pair of trousers more suited to musical comedy than the slippery decks of a New England fishing boat.

The captain surveyed the result sourly and opined that Ben looked like a dressed-up monkey. But he accepted the lad aboard and imparted some practical wisdom. Ben would be well advised, he said, to stand regular working watches with the crew. If he set himself apart, the captain warned, the sailors would make his life a misery. But if he were accepted as one of them, he would enjoy the experience and learn a lot about practical seafaring at the same time. The sailors for their part, the captain added, would no doubt be interested in what the young scholar could teach them out of his store of book learning, and the voyage would be pleasant all around.

And so it went. Ben took the captain's advice and soon was sailoring with the best of them. Fishing was good. The cod were plentiful, and so was the cod-liver oil. It was the practice aboard to store the cod livers in a large barrel on deck, where the cold air sufficed to preserve them. Oil from the livers rose naturally toward the top of the barrel, on the side of which hung a large tin dipper. On passing this barrel, Ben got in the habit of dipping the big ladle into the oil and drinking deeply, smacking his lips over the loathsome stuff. In later years he was to declare, seriously or not, that nothing he drank ever tasted better to him than the fish oil from that shipboard barrel.

In any case, when Ben returned from his voyage, he had gained twenty-five pounds and was never to be scrawny again. His lungs had cleared in the cold sea air, that hacking cough was a thing of the past, and a newly invigorated Ben Butler was ready and eager to begin preparing for his true career. Not as a minister, certainly; he had rejected that almost as soon as he found himself an outlaw among the earnest students at Waterville. Ben was going to be a lawyer for sure. He had made up his mind.

7

Once back in Lowell from his sea voyage, young Ben exulted in renewed health and energy. Shaking the last remaining dust of theology from his mind, he set about at once to cram it instead with the principles of the law. Nor was this just an intellectual exercise. Ben had an instinct for power, and power was evident all around him. The river made power for the mills, and the mills made money, and money put power in the hands of the textile tycoons. Ben sensed that what the river could do for mill owners, the law could do for him.

He observed many lawyers at close range—some of them family friends, all of them prospering admirably. At the same time he burned with a youthful certainty that he was brighter than the brightest of them, and bolder as well. At no time then or ever did Ben Butler find virtue in humility.

In the Lowell office of Attorney William Smith, Ben found the opportunity he was looking for. Not only did Smith possess the most complete law library in town, he was genially absent from the scene most of the time. Smith, originally a New Hampshire man, did most of his work in his Boston office, commuting there daily. Moreover, he was more concerned with his real estate enterprises than his legal practice, although he continued to serve selected clients. To egocentric Ben, reading law under Smith's benevolent absentee sponsorship seemed an ideal way to prepare himself for a legal career.

It went as he expected. Practically speaking, Ben was on his own. Smith directed him to that bible of the law, Blackstone's *Commentaries*, advised him to read it carefully, and then left him to find his own way through the thicket. Although he volunteered very little instruction, Smith was patient and kindly with his apprentice. If the would-be lawyer had a question, Smith would indeed take the time to answer it fully and clearly, but that was the extent of his teaching.

Ben floundered at first. He labored his way through Blackstone, not only studying the text and notes but also looking up the cases cited in the notes and analyzing those as well. This was learning law the hard way, and it took him many months to complete his first assignment even though he put in a long day every day working at it.

His routine was Spartan. Up early every morning, wolfing a quick breakfast, then to the books at 7:30 A.M. Break for lunch at noon, back to the books less than an hour later. Pause for supper at 6:00 P.M., back to the office at 7:30. Knock off work some time between 10:00 and midnight.

At this time he owned a small but spirited gray horse, and it was Ben's custom to saddle up and canter about the countryside on lonely rides after closing his books for the night. He enjoyed the night air and the exercise, and perhaps also the solitude. On these midnight excursions he would purge his mind of Blackstone by recalling and declaiming aloud to the wind some of the favorite poetry he had learned by heart—Byron, Moore, Pope, Scott.

As spring warmed into summer in the year 1839, Ben had mastered Blackstone and digested a number of other basic texts as well. Better to understand commentaries on the Constitution of the United States, he had committed the entire Constitution to memory—that remarkable memory that was always to serve him so well.

In addition to book learning, the young apprentice began an actual practice of law in a small way, although he had not yet been admitted formally to the bar. It happened that Lawyer Smith's real estate holdings included a number of tenement buildings in Lowell, and not all of his tenants were diligent about paying the rent. Smith was all too happy to turn over the troublesome problem of evictions to Butler, who processed them in what was then known as police court. Ben took the job seriously, researching points of law in each case as carefully as though he were practicing before the Supreme Court. In police court he not only learned basic criminal law, but also a great deal about courtroom procedure.

Toward autumn, with his purse slender as ever, Butler seized an opportunity to digress from the law long enough to earn a little money. There was in the adjacent town of Dracut a small academy given over to teaching what passed for juvenile delinquents in those days—unruly pupils who had been kicked out of the Lowell schools for fractious behavior. Ben took a job as the lone teacher there, his predecessor having been utterly routed by the outlaw urchins.

In short order Ben's hard discipline had driven eleven of his twenty-one pupils to leave the academy, "not one of them without a thrashing," as he later recalled with relish. This cost him money, since his fees depended on enrollments. However, Ben worked so well with his diminished flock that the school acquired a modest reputation and attracted new enrollees, not all of them problem students. In the end Ben was teaching five more pupils

Young Ben Butler and friend
Sophia Smith Collection

than he had started with. Meanwhile, he continued to devote six hours a day to his legal studies. At the end of the school term, the trustees asked him to return for another session and even offered him a raise. Though Ben needed the money, he declined the offer, since he felt a pressing sense of urgency to have done with apprenticeship and achieve the status of a recognized professional at law.

So Ben went back to his full-time studies and his police court practice. For additional self-training he attended the sessions of superior court, taking copious notes. After court sessions he would go back to the books in Smith's extensive library, looking up points of law that had been raised in this trial and that, and remembering everything.

Finally, when the September 1840 session of the court of common pleas opened in Lowell, Ben applied for formal admission to the bar, with Smith as his sponsor. Such admission was routinely granted at that time to any applicant who had spent three years clerking in a lawyer's office, whether he had learned very much of anything or not. But since Ben had been reading law in Smith's office for only two years, this meant that he had to pass an examination to be given by the presiding judge of the court, in this case the eminent Judge Charles Henry Warren.

Scanning Butler's qualifications, Judge Warren was kindly but dubious. He quizzed Ben about his education, asked him what law books he had studied, and remarked that Ben seemed to have read very few. Why not forget about the examination, he suggested, and take another year to prepare properly. Ben replied bluntly, with a touch of early Butlerian sarcasm, that he would be delighted to spend another *five* years reading and preparing, but that he couldn't afford even one. He insisted on taking the examination at once.

Judge Warren reluctantly began to quiz him on points of procedure, assuming that Ben's limited book learning would have left him more or less ignorant of courtroom practice. However, Ben had covered this ground thoroughly in dealing with Smith's various eviction cases and in listening carefully to all that went on in the court sessions he had attended.

After about an hour of question and answer, Judge Warren finally asked Ben to outline the points of a case the judge himself had heard that day in court and to discuss the ruling. Ben promptly dissected the arguments in the case (a lawsuit involving a promissory note) and summed up Judge Warren's findings. As the judge nodded approval, Ben went his typical step beyond: he told the eminent jurist that the ruling he had made that day was wrong.

Fortunately for Butler, Judge Warren was a tolerant man. He invited the young upstart to supply the authority for his statement. Ben did so, providing chapter and verse. In court the next day, the fair-minded judge reversed his ruling in the case. Then Judge Warren not only directed Butler's immediate admission to the bar, but credited Ben in open court with the suggestion that had caused him to change his ruling. Somewhat later, the judge's revised finding, in accordance with Ben's reading of the law, was upheld by the Supreme Court. By that time Ben was a full-fledged and busy attorney, and he and Judge Warren had begun a warm, enduring friendship.

In addition to furious energy and ambition, yet another force was driving young Ben Butler in the spring of 1840. Ben was in love. When he told Judge Warren he couldn't wait to qualify as a lawyer, he might well have added that he was also in an all-fired hurry to qualify as a husband. The previous autumn he had met Sarah Hildreth, daughter of a Dracut physician, Dr. Israel Hildreth, and had come away smitten.

Earlier, by great good fortune, he had formed what was to be a lifelong friendship with Dr. Hildreth's only son, Fisher Ames Hildreth. Young Hildreth had invited him to his father's house for the family's Thanksgiving dinner, and there among Dr. Hildreth's bevy of daughters (he had six of them) shone Sarah, the second eldest.

Sarah was nothing like the farm women of Ben's childhood background. She was, in fact, an accomplished professional actress of great charm and polish. Very early in life Sarah had been introduced to the plays of Shakespeare by her father, whose literary bent was toward the great poets of the English language. Dr. Hildreth was so avid an enthusiast that he had remodeled an entire floor of his house as a little theater for family presentations of readings. Thus Sarah's scholarly father was delighted when she chose the stage as a career and set about studying seriously for it.

Ben's acquaintance with the theater was minimal. He had never seen Sarah onstage, although she had performed to critical and popular acclaim before audiences in the major theaters of Boston and New York. At that Thanksgiving dinner in her father's house, he knew only that this young woman was elegant, intelligent, and good looking—a charmer.

Precipitous Ben lost little time in proposing to Sarah, but she was cautious and sensible where Ben was ardent and rash. Their initial meeting led to a warm and intimate courtship and to what used to be known as an understanding. Ben loved Sarah and Sarah loved Ben, but she was having nothing of marriage until the young man had proved himself in his profession and acquired a solid cash standing at the bank.

Their relationship went on in this way not for months, but for the years it took Ben to acquire a reputation at the bar and the money that went with it. Finally, in the spring of 1843, Ben pursued her to Cincinnati, where she was appearing in a starring role onstage. And there, at last, Sarah said yes, and they became formally engaged.

On May 16, 1844, Ben and Sarah were married in Saint Anne's Church, with Ben's old friend, the Reverend Theodore Edson, officiating. It was to

Sarah Hildreth Butler
Sophia Smith Collection

be no ordinary marriage, but a lifetime love affair and an enduring partnership. They were to be inseparable, even during Maj. Gen. Benjamin F. Butler's rigorous campaigning days in the Civil War.

That war then was threatening but distant, like the glimmer of heat lightning on the far horizon. Uncompromising abolitionism was becoming a political force in the populous North. In the South, equally stubborn proslavery sentiment congealed around the proposition that the states, having once freely entered into a federal union, could just as freely withdraw.

But meanwhile, in their new home in Lowell, the Butlers settled in to prosper and raise a family. Their first child, Paul, was born in June 1845, but he died in 1850 before he reached his fifth birthday. Their only daughter, Blanche, was born in 1847. A second son, also named Paul, was born in 1852, and their third son, Ben Israel, was born in 1854.

8

Whiggery was ascendant when Ben Butler, newly confirmed as a lawyer, made his first tentative foray into politics. With the socially respectable and financially powerful Whigs firmly in control of Massachusetts, it was characteristic that Butler chose to campaign for the Democrat, Martin Van Buren, in the presidential election of 1840. When Van Buren lost by a landslide to the Whig candidate, William Henry Harrison, Butler's chagrin was such that he foreswore politics altogether. For several years afterward he turned all of his energies to his growing law practice.

It was a time when the guidelines of national politics were being rearranged in a mad whirl of shifting alliances. Under pressure from a hodge-podge of varied interests, old coalitions were coming apart and new ones were forming. Young Ben may have taken sharp note of this and considered that it might be prudent to sit back and wait for conflicting forces to sort themselves out.

Andrew Jackson's old Democratic party was attracting support from new Americans: immigrants from Germany and Ireland, laboring people, mostly Catholics. Meanwhile the Whigs, conglomerated to defeat the populist financial policies of "King Andrew" Jackson, had become a hodgepodge dominated by bankers, businessmen, and planters. The Whigs' strength was centered among Northern industrialists and Southern slave owners. Whiggery was also gaining adherents among native-born Protestant working men who had somehow been persuaded, against the simple logic of the marketplace, that joining forces with the moneyed interests was a way to dampen immigrant competition for their jobs.

Abolitionism was dividing the Democratic party along sectional lines, North and South. Southern Democrats were solid in their conviction that slavery was protected as a matter of state sovereignty, but Northern Democrats were quarreling among themselves over the issue. Butler himself had to conclude, as a lawyer, that slavery was clearly sanctioned under the Constitution as a matter within a state's right to decide.

Labor unions had appeared on the political scene, sometimes offering their own slates of candidates in local elections. Failing to coalesce into a viable separate force, organized labor gravitated toward the Northern Democratic party, but had little in common with the proslavery Southern wing. More immediately, the unions pressed for pay-envelope reforms. But they also campaigned, sometimes successfully, for social advances, notable among them the establishment and maintenance of free public schools.

In Butler's first active election, the slaveholding planters had it both ways. Southern Democrats, their ranks swelled by Southern Whigs rejoining the Democratic party, dominated platform debate. As a result, Democrat Van Buren was running on a program opposed to further congressional flirting with abolitionism. And as for the Whig candidate, Harrison, he was running on no platform at all, but rather on a magnificent and heavily financed public-relations campaign based on an empty slogan, "Log Cabin and Hard Cider," which successfully pictured him as just a good old boy. That Harrison's log cabin was actually a splendid country estate and that his lineage was sprung from the Virginia aristocracy were items totally buried in Whig propaganda. As the electorate came to see it, Harrison was the honest, rough-and-ready man of the people running against that sharp, sophisticated New York politician. Issues were lost in the carefully contrived din engineered by the Whig insiders.

While noting all this and possibly filing away a few campaign pointers for future use, Ben adhered to his decision to tend to his own law practice for a while. That purely local issue, the grinding long workday at the Lowell textile mills, now began to attract his attention, however.

A physician friend, probably his cultured, gentlemanly father-in-law, advanced the theory that the burden of working thirteen and a half hours a day, six days a week, imposed too great a strain on the ordinary constitution. Moreover, gloomed the doctor, if such conditions were allowed to continue, the strength of the entire working population would deteriorate.

Although Ben took it upon himself to campaign relentlessly for a mandatory reduction in the mills' working hours, it is curious to note that he lived to expound, approvingly, what he called an axiom about wages. Said Ben, "The great men who founded Lowell . . . knew that the unit of the price of ordinary labor, other things being equal, was what a laborer could barely live upon and support his family. That rule has now become axiomatic: the cheaper a laborer can live, the cheaper he will work."

That cold appraisal tends to support the proposition that Ben's furious crusade for shorter working hours was less inspired by humanitarian concerns than by purely personal motives. As a beginning politician he saw an issue and proceeded to make it uniquely his. Butler's ten-hour–day campaign was to make his name known throughout the state and beyond and gain him a loyal band of adherents among a growing segment of the voting public.

It also earned him the immediate enmity of the Whig mill owners and their captive press. The newspapers they controlled carried on a nearly hysterical barrage of editorial insult. The *Lowell Courier* was especially venomous, leading to a long feud between Butler and the editor, whom Ben at one point publicly accused of having contracted a disfiguring venereal disease during the Mexican war by consorting with prostitutes south of the border.

Butler's blast was in response to *Courier* editorials like this one:

> Ben Butler, this notorious demagogue and political scoundrel, having swilled three or four extra glasses of liquor, spread himself at whole length in the City Hall last night. . . . The only wonder is that a character so foolish, so grovelling and obscene, can for a moment be admitted into decent society anywhere out of the pale of prostitutes and debauchés.

Ben got a grand jury to indict the editor for criminal libel, but a Whig judge, Ebenezer R. Hoar, came to the man's rescue. The only evidence, the judge charged the jury, was the article itself naming one "Ben Butler." It was up to the jury to decide, the judge continued, if the "Ben Butler" referred to in the article was *this* Ben Butler or possibly some other fellow of the same name. The sheepish jury, thus shown the way, found for the defendant editor.

Butler marked Judge Hoar down in indelible ink in his little black book. Many years later, Hoar, then attorney general in President Grant's cabinet, was nominated to the Supreme Court. Ben took enormous satisfaction in using all of his considerable influence to see to it that the Senate rejected the nominee. Still later, when Hoar ran against him for Congress, Butler's revenge struck again. "I published an open letter describing him so exactly, both morally and politically, that there could be no doubt of his identity," Butler recalled, "and I beat him so that all the votes he got would be hardly sufficient for mile-stones in our district."

Ben's fight for the ten-hour workday went on for years, without a chance of success. Besides exerting the pressure of the newspapers, mill owners fought the ten-hour–day proposal more directly. They made it known that any worker attending a "ten-hour" rally would be fired. And of course if a worker got fired in one Lowell mill, he never got to work in another. Whig legislators consistently voted down ten-hour measures whenever they got so far as to make it to the floor.

By 1848 the tangle of Northern politics had become more snarled than ever, but Ben at last sensed opportunity in the confusion. The ten-hour proposition was still high on his personal agenda, and now he thought he saw how he just might make headway with it—while advancing his own political ambitions.

The Democrats by this time had split into two main factions:

Barnburners and Hunkers. The Barnburners, because of what was seen as their rule-or-ruin stance, achieved their name from an apocryphal yarn, current at the time, about a Dutch farmer who got so mad at the rats in his barn that he proposed to burn it down to get rid of them. The Hunkers earned their name because of the charge that they "hunkered" (or hankered) after jobs and patronage. Ben was a Barnburner.

In 1847 the Barnburners held a convention of their own in which, among other actions, they resolved in favor of the highly controversial Wilmot Proviso. The proviso, an amendment tacked on to an appropriations bill by Rep. David Wilmot of Pennsylvania, was intended to forbid slavery in any territories gained in the war with Mexico, but the Senate stalled the bill. By supporting the Wilmot Proviso, the Barnburners were reaching out for liberal, antislavery support; the Hunker Democrats took a more conservative, Whiggish position, particularly in matters affecting business and banking.

In the upshot the feud-torn Democrats in 1848 nominated Sen. Lewis Cass of Michigan as their presidential choice. The rebellious Barnburners broke away and nominated Van Buren, with the Wilmot Proviso as their principal platform plank. The Whigs chose Gen. Zachary Taylor and were silent regarding the platform.

And then yet another party appeared on the already confused scene: the Free-Soil party, made up of abolitionists bolting from both the Whig and Democratic parties. The latter insurgents included many leading Barnburners, who plumped hard and successfully for Van Buren as the Free-Soil nominee.

The Whig Taylor won, but out of all this disarray Ben Butler saw opportunity for a coalition in Massachusetts that could turn out the Whigs in his home state. He lent all his energies to a somewhat Machiavellian scheme intended to capitalize on the split in his own Democratic party while catering to strong antislavery sentiment in that Yankee abolitionist stronghold. The proposal was to align Free-Soilers and Barnburner Democrats, so as to sow confusion among local Hunkers and Whigs. The national election was history. What he wanted was control of the state legislature and State House.

Butler contrived a deal. There were two United States senators to be named by the legislature. If the coalition succeeded in winning those seats and ousting the Whigs, the Free-Soilers were to get one Senate seat as their prize, and the Barnburner Democrats would get the other. Butler's Barnburners would also win the governorship and the rest of the state government.

The key to the plan lay in the state constitution, which required that all elections had to be decided by a majority vote. If no candidate for governor got a majority, the newly elected state legislature chose one from a list of the four candidates who received the most votes.

State senators, elected by counties, were similarly chosen by the legislature for counties in which no candidate received a majority vote. Candidates for state representative who failed to achieve a majority in the regular election had to try again in a second election two weeks later.

Free-Soilers and Barnburners agreed that, in counties where their combined strength could elect a senator, they would nominate the same candidate. In counties where their chances were slimmer, they would nominate separate candidates, splitting the vote. Wherever proslavery Hunker Democrats nominated their own man, they would split the vote further, leaving the Whig candidate likewise short of a majority.

In sum, the plan was to throw the election into the hands of the new legislature—while controlling that legislature. In return for getting their man named United States senator, Free-Soilers were to join with the Barnburners to name Barnburners to that other Senate seat and to all the offices of the state.

As part of the deal, Ben insisted that the ten-man coalition slate for representatives from Lowell—five Barnburners, five Free-Soilers—must be pledged to support his ten-hour workday limitation. He campaigned on that, to the great distress of the mill owners and their press.

When word of the coalition scheme got out, there was uproar. One learned judge branded it a criminal conspiracy. The *Lowell Courier* was so incensed that it committed a typographical error, which it solemnly corrected:

> Errata: Yesterday the compositors made the *Courier* say, "By the use of gloves well scented with cologne, or some disinfectant, and a pair of tongues, it may become a duty to handle such a putrid carcass as that labelled B. F. Butler." Of course for "pair of tongues" read "pair of tongs."

On election day, nine of the ten candidates on Butler's slate got majority votes. The tenth, an Irishman, was shunned by militant Protestant voters, and he lost. As planned, no candidate for governor or lieutenant governor got a statewide majority. When the ballots were counted, it became clear that the coalition, especially with those nine representatives from Lowell, would in fact have the votes to fill all the Senate vacancies and all the state offices from governor on down.

But the Lowell Whigs were not ready to quit just yet. It developed that in Lowell's 4th Ward the election clerk had blundered. Since 800 votes had been cast for Butler's ten-man ticket, the clerk, in some kind of dither, had reported the vote as 8,000—or 800 votes for each of ten men.

The mayor and all the aldermen were Whigs, so it was not surprising that they seized on the chance to declare the election void and call for another one. The harassed clerk offered to submit an amended return, but this was refused. The Butler ticket had to do it all over again in a second election nine days away. And this time the corporations were prepared to play rougher than ever.

A large placard was posted on the gate of the Hamilton Mill, one of the biggest textile plants. It read, "NOTICE: Whoever, employed by this corporation, votes the Ben Butler ticket on Monday next, will be discharged." When Butler's committee met that night, it was learned that other corporations were making the same threat. The atmosphere at the meeting was one of gloom. The feeling was that Butler's supporters simply would not dare to risk their jobs. Uncertain what to do, the committee finally voted to leave it up to Ben. He responded by calling a mass meeting to be held at city hall the following Wednesday evening at 8:00.

When Butler showed up to speak, the crowd was so large that he couldn't get through it. Husky workers solved the problem by picking him up bodily, passing him hand to hand overhead, and all but dumping him onstage, rumpled but otherwise ready to orate.

Ben started slowly but worked up to that Hamilton Mill notice, which he read verbatim. Conversationally, he acknowledged the power of the corporations. But he added, still quietly, that there was power, too, in working men united in a cause.

There was a pause for effect. Then he wound up and roared: "As God lives and I live, by the living Jehovah! If one man is driven from his employment by these men because of his vote, I will lead you to make Lowell what it was twenty-five years ago—a sheep-pasture and a fishing place. And I will commence by applying the torch to my own house!"

Uproar followed. Yells and applause broke out. Cries were heard, "Let's do it now!"

But Ben, much in control, called for silence. Perhaps, he suggested smoothly, that notice was just the act of some overzealous employee. Maybe the corporation officers had not authorized it at all. Then he continued:

> We will vote as free men, and not as slaves. We have given them here and now notice of our solemn determination. We must vote on next Monday as free men. . . . They shall have Thursday and Friday in which to adopt or repudiate this threat of theirs to the working men of Lowell. . . . If we must come to blows it must be on their invitation.

Then, speaking as Col. Benjamin F. Butler, to which state military rank he had progressed over the years, he added a grim little joke: "I do not think they will call on the militia of Lowell to suppress us, for you are the militia, and I am its commander."

The Whigs sounded retreat. Next day the *Courier* printed a statement in which the corporations repudiated the Hamilton Mill placard and denied any intention to fire anybody. The second election then went off quietly. Ben's ticket had lost some strength in the interim, but the coalition had won control of the state government in any case. The newly constituted legislature duly seated all the Ben Butler candidates who had won at that first election.

As a proper postscript, Lawyer Ben got the grand jury to indict the Whig mayor and aldermen who had disallowed the results of the first election. But this was just a bee sting; a Whig judge threw the case out of court.

And the ten-hour workday? The Free-Soil–Barnburner coalition did not hold together on that issue. Not until several legislatures later did a half-hearted compromise make it into the statute books. Thereafter the workday in Massachusetts mills was legally limited to eleven hours, fifteen minutes.

In a time then in the far future, a wealthy Ben Butler would come to achieve, himself, a heavy financial interest in Lowell's Middlesex Mill, and it must be added that, in the Middlesex, a ten-hour workday would be the fixed rule, whatever the state law said.

9

When Ben Butler launched his own law practice in the autumn of 1840, he began acquiring almost at once a large and growing coterie of enemies. Cranky old judges considered him an impertinent young whippersnapper. Opponents at the bar labeled him "sharp," the term *shyster* not yet being widespread in the American language. Gentlemanly prosecuting attorneys, failing to land a Butler client in jail where the rascal obviously belonged, complained that Ben made sly use of legal technicalities to defeat the ends of justice. Sometimes prosecutors even begged him to look the other way while they convicted the miscreant on sheer points of fact.

To all complaints of this kind, Butler had a ready answer. A good point of law, he said, was as much the property of his client as a good point of fact, and as an attorney he had no right to waive either one or the other. He was tireless in his search for those good points of law. The more ingenious he found them, the more he was pleased; the guiltier a client appeared, the harder Ben looked.

A typical case of the more desperate sort involved a career burglar, Elijah Record, whose specialty was fashioning skeleton keys out of ordinary door keys, the better to gain access to premises he meant to plunder. As for the basic door keys on which to work his magic, Elijah, practically enough, stole those as well.

Record came to grief one day when he was strolling down the main street in Lowell, adding to his key collection whenever he found one carelessly left in an unguarded shop door. He had garnered several keys in this way and was zeroing in on another when he made a serious tactical mistake. The proprietor of the shop where he paused to snatch the key happened to be sitting right behind the door, perfectly poised to grab him. And, when Elijah turned to run, he fell straight into the outstretched arms of a policeman who had been observing all this.

Elijah was arrested; the stolen key was marked for evidence; and in due course the miscreant came to trial, with Butler for the defense, Elijah's wife having advanced a retainer.

The city marshal himself was so elated at having a slippery thief like Record caught dead to rights that, while they were entering the courtroom, he made Ben a jovial bet. If young Butler got *this* crook off, said the marshal, he'd give up his city job.

At the trial the district attorney produced his evidence, put his witnesses on the stand, and proved beyond all doubt that Elijah had indeed stolen that key. Therefore, he summed up, Elijah was without question guilty of larceny.

"The government rests its case," he said.

Young Ben was nonchalant. "Surely you don't intend to ask for a verdict of the jury in a case like this, do you?" he asked.

"I should like to know why not," replied the district attorney.

"Well, I'll tell the court," Butler drawled.

Whereupon he proceeded to demonstrate that since the key was actually in place in the door when Elijah snatched it, that key, under Massachusetts law, was an item of real estate. Citing book and chapter, Butler proved that Elijah had taken real estate, and that taking real estate simply was not larceny, the crime with which Elijah was charged.

When the district attorney was at a loss for an answer, the judge directed an acquittal. Elijah walked out of the courtroom free. And the legislature, at its next session, took notice of Elijah's good fortune by plugging the loophole through which Ben had arranged his escape. A measure was passed belatedly defining theft of *portions* of real estate as larceny.

Butler didn't leave the court that day without directing a barb at the city marshal. As the judge began to order Elijah turned loose, Ben in deadpan fashion asked him to hold up the proceedings, explaining that he had not yet collected all of his fee.

"I was promised by the city marshal, who sits there, that if I got Record clear he would throw up his commission. I move Your Honor to enforce his promise."

Thus Ben, never easy on an opponent, topped his performance with a quip at the marshal's expense, and when the laughter in the courtroom died away he was able to add majestically, with a glance at the red-faced policeman, "Record may go."

Another of Ben's sharp victories involved a defendant, Peter Moore, who was charged with having committed adultery with one Mary Stuart, "she being then a married woman, and having a husband alive." The penalty faced by the defendant Moore, under the rigorous Massachusetts law of those days, was three years in state prison. Even at the time, Ben was moved to remark that the commonwealth was a bit rough on adulterers. "The laws of some states," he noted, "leave that crime as if it were almost an accomplishment."

Fortunately for Moore, Ben found a technical flaw in the indictment.

When Moore was called upon to plead guilty or not guilty, Butler objected at once. No crime was stated against Moore, he argued, because nowhere in the indictment did it set forth that Mary Stuart's "husband alive" wasn't Moore himself.

The trial judge ruled against Butler. He said that he was rejecting Ben's theory and relying instead on old and well-established case law. If the old texts were wrong, well then, as the judge put it, he was "preferring to err with the ancients"—a jibe at Ben's youth and assumed lack of experience.

Ben promptly took the case on appeal to the state supreme court, which reversed the judge's ruling. Ben received the decision with undisguised glee. To rub it in, the reckless young Butler made a point of sending a copy of the decision to the trial judge, with a covering note expressing the sarcastic hope that he'd read it over and enjoy knowing that he had indeed "erred with the ancients."

A wealthier client, an elderly kleptomaniac of good family, got off free because of Ben's quick mind and sharp eye for details. The zany old man faced trial on four indictments for theft. If found guilty on all four, under the law as it stood, he faced a cumulative prison term of sixty years. But Ben, as usual, had scanned the indictments well.

Just before the trial began, Butler conferred with the prosecutors. The defendant was already well along in years, he said, so why condemn him to end his days in prison for something that was more a mental disease than a crime? Surely one indictment would be enough, he argued.

After some discussion the prosecutors agreed to drop three of the indictments if the prisoner would plead guilty to the fourth one—the one involving the largest monetary value.

When the trial began, the bewildered defendant was all but bullied by Butler into pleading guilty to the major indictment. The prosecution thereupon dropped the other three, as agreed. At that point Butler promptly moved for dismissal of the remaining indictment, to which his client, as agreed, had just pleaded guilty.

Before plea-bargaining, Butler had noticed that the lone indictment he had offered "free" to the unsuspecting prosecutors happened to contain a fatal flaw. It did not properly designate where the alleged crime had been committed; therefore the court had no jurisdiction in the case. The defendant was discharged, a free man.

As Butler's reputation as a winner grew, he naturally attracted a richer class of clients, although he never turned his back on those not so well heeled. Over the course of time, he racked up courtroom victories over all of the leading lawyers in New England. He was not invincible, but nobody could rate him as less than formidable when he undertook a case.

Despite his reputation as a sharpster, Butler by no means confined his preparations merely to those fine points of law. Although he never neglected the book work, he was also remarkably persistent in digging out points of fact, carrying his researches to extremes then rare in the legal profession.

Anticipating by a century San Francisco's famous King of Torts, Melvin Belli, Ben Butler made himself knowledgeable in human anatomy and delighted in tormenting medical doctors when they appeared as expert witnesses in opposition to his clients. In one typical case, a client charged with homicide was acquitted chiefly because Ben so thoroughly confounded a medical witness that he couldn't trace the correct path of the temporal artery. It was a key point in the case, so far as the jury was concerned, because the victim was said to have bled to death from that artery, a circumstance that Ben proved impossible.

Butler appeared as counsel in many cases involving railroad accidents, sometimes for a defendant railroad, sometimes for a plaintiff suing a railroad. In either circumstance he was exceptionally well prepared, since he spent much careful time in shirtsleeve research, either in a nearby railroad repair shop or riding the cab alongside engineer and fireman. He even became fully competent to operate a locomotive and, during the war to come, actually had occasion to do so.

Not all of his growing practice was restricted to courtroom pyrotechnics. Notably, he prepared the patent documents for Elias Howe's invention of the sewing machine. These were so carefully drawn that they stood up under attack from the Singer Sewing Machine company, which was forced in the end to pay Howe rich and continuing royalties for infringements on Howe's basic design.

In 1845, at the age of twenty-seven, Butler was admitted to practice before the Supreme Court of the United States, perhaps the youngest lawyer ever to win that distinction. In the same session, as it happened, another attorney was also admitted to practice before the high court—a gawky country lawyer named Abraham Lincoln, aged thirty-six.

The California Gold Rush brought Butler a Supreme Court client in the person of John Sutter, on whose backwoods sawmill site on the American River gold was first discovered, touching off the boom. Sutter's case (*Sutter v. the United States*) was a complicated one involving his rights to vast California land holdings originally conferred on him by the Mexican government, rights that had been thrown into great confusion when Mexico ceded California to the United States in the Treaty of Guadalupe Hidalgo.

Sutter's original empire embraced nearly 141,000 acres before it was overrun by gold seekers and squatters. By the time he went to Butler for help, his situation seemed all but hopeless. In the outcome of that long-fought case, however, he was awarded certified American grants covering two huge tracts. One consisted of 8,800 acres by the American River, and the other included in toto the site of California's present capital, Sacramento.

Thereafter Sutter himself was more or less the author of his own ruin, although it must be said that the forces he had to contend with were all but unstoppable. Settlers streamed into California in hordes, and Sutter was utterly unable to cope with them. He wound up broke, a victim of history, destroyed by the wealth that others garnered from what had been his enormous domain.

As for Butler, he profited from the gold rush in his own way. His usual studious approach in the Sutter case made him an outstanding expert in Mexican law. This in turn brought him many other California cases of the same kind, all of them lucrative.

Just as he had promised himself when he signed on to clerk in Lawyer Smith's office, Ben had far surpassed all his old mentors and had become at a very early age one of the most distinguished lawyers in the nation.

10

While driving himself without pause in all his activities, Ben Butler also undertook a serious, long-range program to prepare himself for war. He began this well before any particular war had loomed up on the far horizon. Ben was not bracing for a call to the colors. It was just that he was certain that every generation of Butlers was destined to take part in one military conflict or another, and he proposed to be ready. After all, he had Grandpa Zephaniah Butler's powder horn as a souvenir from the French and Indian War; an uncle had fought at Bunker Hill; and Ben's father, John, had commanded dragoons in the War of 1812. Sooner or later it would be his own turn to march. He was sure of it. If he was lucky, he might even get to march against the redcoats.

Having been denied West Point training, Ben chose the only practical alternative, enrollment in the state militia. His own unblushing estimate of his abilities, when considered together with his heritage, led him to sure anticipation that he would eventually hold a post of command. Butler did not intend to fight his war in the ranks. Since a commission in the Regulars had been withheld from him, he proposed to win that commission another way, working toward it for as long as it took.

Thus in 1839, when a new militia company was forming in Lowell, Ben promptly signed up as a private. He planned to start at the bottom and learn everything there was to know about the art of war, from squad drill to grand strategy.

In the years that followed, Butler attended every drill, every encampment, every maneuver, and rose steadily through every rank and grade until finally he was elected colonel of his regiment. This was all the more remarkable in that his rigorous devotion to these military duties occurred in the period when he was also studying law, building a practice, courting and marrying Sarah Hildreth, establishing a family, and vigorously engaging in the highly passionate and frequently hysterical politics of the time.

It was a time when politics alone might have taxed the energies of any ordinary man. After Butler's success with the Free-Soil–Democratic coalition, which wrested control of Massachusetts from the Whigs in 1851, genteel and conservative Whiggery had begun to dissolve. A new force was taking hold: the Know-Nothings were on the rise. Part political party, part pseudo-secret society, Know-Nothingism was unashamedly vicious in the bigotry that energized its sudden rise to power and influence.

In the confusion stirring the major parties, Know-Nothingism spread like a virus. As greater debates raged, the Know-Nothings may not have been entirely in agreement on what they were for, but they were dead certain of what they were against. They were against Catholics and Catholicism. And, as a necessary corollary to this, they were violently against Irish and German immigrants—more so against the Irish, but with plenty of enthusiastic loathing left over to direct against the Germans.

In Massachusetts, tragically enough, a less than adept Catholic hierarchy, more bullheaded and defiant than wise, was fated to play straight into the hands of the Know-Nothings by defeating a constitutional reform in which Ben Butler was deeply concerned. This action by the archdiocese stirred up an immediate backlash, led to the election of a Know-Nothing governor and government, crippled Butler's political career, and even cost him the colonelcy of his regiment. And of course the turn of events exposed the Catholics of Massachusetts to an officially encouraged wave of unabashed religious persecution.

In 1852, at a point just preceding the debacle, Democrat Butler was elected to the state legislature. Almost at once he set about championing a measure that was bound to offend the anti-Catholic forces.

Ben's long memory went back to the night eighteen years before when, as a young man, he had stood at the peak of Fort Hill, Lowell's highest point, and watched the fiery glow in the sky as the Ursuline Convent in Charlestown burned to the ground. The convent, a teaching academy for young women, had long attracted the harassing attentions of the militant Protestant workers in a nearby brickyard. On this night they formed the nucleus of a mob that first set a bonfire on the academy lawn, then drove the nuns and their terrified students to take shelter in a tomb on the grounds. It was an irony, perhaps, that the students were mostly from prosperous Protestant families, who were in the custom of sending their daughters to that school for the superb quality of the education and the social graces they could gain there.

As the mob grew in size and violence, the rioters finally went about torching all the buildings. Fire departments of the area stood aloof and let the structures burn. Destruction was total.

In the immediate aftermath, leading citizens of Boston attended a meeting in Faneuil Hall to denounce the outrage, but the outpouring of oratory accomplished little more than to differentiate, for the record, the behavior of persons of Bostonian refinement from that of their social "inferiors." More significant, as a measure of the true cultural and political climate, the brickmaker who openly boasted of having led the mob was tried in criminal court and, in spite of his remorseless confession, was acquitted. Thereafter, all efforts by the diocese to obtain recompense from the Whig legislature for the heavy loss incurred in the outrage proved fruitless.

Butler, newly elected, set about trying to rectify the old injustice. He offered a bill providing certain compensation for the destruction of the Ursuline Convent; fought it through committee; and won passage of the measure in the House of Representatives, which voted approval on a Friday and sent it to the Senate.

Over the ensuing weekend, however, the militant forces of Know-Nothingism went into furious action. Many of the more bigoted divines preached hellfire-and-damnation sermons against Butler's measure. Heavy nativist pressure was brought to bear on the state senators, and in the upper house Butler's measure was refused passage. The issue was never raised again.

Reform of the state constitution, quite another matter, found Butler and his Catholic-Democratic constituency on opposite sides. The new constitution, drawn by a convention in which Butler was a member, contained a clause providing that no tax money should ever be appropriated "to any religious sect" for the support of its schools. Harmless enough in its context, since it applied universally to all schools maintained by churches, the clause nevertheless had its roots in anti-Catholic sentiment and was seen as such by the stubborn diocesan authorities. The new constitution came before the voters in 1853 and was narrowly rejected at the polls. Its defeat came about when Catholic Democrats, at the urging of their bishop and clergy, voted almost en bloc against it.

Resentment against this display of political power immediately raised anti-Catholic feeling to new heights. To the primitives it seemed like direct proof of their warmly held thesis that American Catholics took their political orders directly from the Pope. As one result of the hotly contested constitutional referendum, the rising Know-Nothings gained enough new adherents to sweep the moderates of Butler's coalition from power. The Know-Nothings elected their man, Henry J. Gardner, as governor, whereupon the state government at once, as of January 1, 1855, set out upon a course of adopting as many stringent anti-Catholic measures as ingenious and angry minds could conceive.

In this context Know-Nothing Governor Gardner and Col. Benjamin F. Butler came into collision almost immediately. Butler's militia regiment included a company calling itself The Jackson Musketeers. The company's members were Irish, Catholic, and Democrats to a man, so it had long attracted the hostile attention of the Know-Nothing element. A threatened riot soon brought hostility against the Musketeers to the point of physical conflict.

In the general surge of anti-Catholic violence, a mob in Philadelphia had burned down a Catholic church there, and word of this brought widespread rumor that a similar plot was afoot to torch a large Catholic church in Lowell. Butler's militia was alerted to preserve the peace, whereupon the Know-Nothings let it get about that, if a confrontation occurred, the Irish militia company would be targeted for stoning.

Butler's response was prompt. Assembling his regiment, he re-formed the members of all four companies according to height rather than by company, so that the Irish militiamen were thoroughly intermingled with the Protestant militiamen. Thus he made sure that, if stones were to be hurled either by Catholics or Protestants in the anticipated melee, neither group of combatants would be able to identify a favored target. In the end, whether because of Butler's foresight and ingenuity or not, no riot took place.

However, Governor Gardner had marked the Irishmen of the Jackson Musketeers for special attention. As commander in chief of the Massachusetts militia, Gardner ordered Colonel Butler to disband the Irish company immediately. Butler refused. Gardner issued yet another order, dismissing Colonel Butler from the state service, and Butler refused to obey that order, either. In both cases Colonel Butler was relying on Lawyer Butler to provide the sound legal grounds required to support his stubbornness.

Gardner consulted with *his* legal counsel, however, and his next act was decisive. He used his executive powers to reorganize the entire state militia, simply disbanding all the existing regiments and then forming them up again as new ones that were differently numbered and assigned to different districts. Since officers of a regiment had to be residents in that regiment's district, Gardner saw to it that in the reorganization Butler's 5th Regiment was assigned to a district in which Butler did not reside. Butler's residence was then encompassed in the district of the 6th Regiment, and of course Butler was not the colonel of the 6th. In sum, Butler had to bow to a sharp point of law and surrender his colonelcy.

However, Butler had unlimited patience as well as a long memory. He waited for a vacancy to occur in the grade of brigadier general, a post to which field officers of the regiments usually elected their senior colonel. When at last the vacancy did occur, the field officers promptly elected Butler. The newly minted brigadier took more than mild satisfaction in receiving his handsome new commission signed and sealed by Governor Gardner, who had no choice in the matter. Another sharp point of law, then check and mate.

J. E. Baker's painting of Butler as a brigadier general of militia
attempts the classical and winds up baroque.

Instead of a regiment, Butler now commanded a brigade, which he took on encampments each year from 1857 to 1860. By that time the great North-South conflict had reached the flash point, and Butler's certainty that his generation would have its war had been proved well founded.

In the maelstrom of politics, finally, Democratic President James Buchanan was waiting out the last months of his term, paralyzed by good intentions while his party was being torn apart by dissension. A new party, the Republicans, had formed around the principle that the Federal Union was inviolable. Clusters of Whigs, Know-Nothings, radical abolitionists, and fire-eating secessionists all milled around, seeking suitable places to roost.

Butler remained a Democrat. As a lawyer, he read the Constitution as clearly providing legal authority for the states to decide for themselves regarding slavery within their own borders. But as a Federalist, he denied that any state had the right to secede from the Union. And as a soldier, he was prepared to urge full military measures against any rebellious state undertaking to attempt secession by force of arms.

11

During the hectic decade of 1850–1860, patchwork compromise on the issue of slavery unraveled at an accelerating rate. In a parallel process a severely stressed Democratic party also began to come apart at the seams. Ben Butler, by now a national figure of power in that party, increasingly found himself applying his influence and energies to damage-control measures.

Later, when outright civil war had finally erupted, Federal General Butler would be the one who would take the first practical steps toward emancipation of slaves, and thereafter it would be Butler who would most notably champion black civil rights. But in that angry prewar decade, Butler's personal attitude toward slavery remained ambiguous. He held no blazing moral convictions on the subject, but rather took a cool and distant view. He contended that where slavery existed it was legal under the Constitution, no matter what the abolitionists preached nor how wildly they inveighed against the Constitution itself. Otherwise, as in the matter of the Fugitive Slave Act, which purported to require all good citizens to help collar escaped slaves, Butler remained aloof, remarking in one speech and another that nobody was likely to find him bounding around his native countryside chasing runaways, no matter what the law said.

What counted with Butler and Democrats of the same stripe was preservation of the Federal Union. The greatest present evil inherent in the institution of slavery, as these conservatives saw it, was in the passions it had come to arouse, North and South. With increasing exertions they tried to cool those passions before they reached the flash point, and up to the very last they thought they might still be able to do it. Butler, attending every Democratic convention from 1848 to 1860, was consistent in promoting tactics of patience and compromise.

While the North-South fracture line of the Democratic party was yielding to relatively clear-cut stress, the nucleus of a new coalition was gathering into itself all the political debris of the period. The emerging Republican party, formed out of political chaos, would finally end the era of compromise and take the nation to war.

The new party included a motley assortment of strange bedfellows. Hard-line Know-Nothings, who wanted to limit suffrage to the native born while suppressing Catholicism wherever they found it, ranged themselves alongside land-hungry immigrant German Catholics pushing for homesteads on public lands. Many discouraged conservative Whigs joined up, along with militant prohibitionists crusading for laws against demon rum. Yet another earnest contingent decried polygamy in the Utah Territory, zeroing in on that as their special target. Prominent in the new Republican party were large numbers of defecting Democrats as well.

While many of the wilder Republican components carried their own flags locally, the Free-Soil abolitionists provided the great national banner under which nearly all could march. The Republicans at this point were less a party than a political conglomerate, but they had numbers.

In 1856 the first Republican national convention nominated a former Democrat, John C. Frémont, for president. Frémont, whose well-publicized explorations in the Far West had won him the glamorous nickname of Pathfinder, was the canny and well-managed choice of eastern power brokers whose abiding interest, slavery aside, was the financing of hugely profitable railroads. After nominating Frémont the party proceeded to stand him firmly upon a platform ingeniously contrived of splinters. The platform was crafted so as to contain a little something for all components of the new coalition and, in particular, to include a call for a railroad to the Pacific.

Those diehard Know-Nothings and inflexible Whigs who still shunned the new Republican party held themselves entirely aloof, rejected Frémont, and nominated Millard Fillmore.

The Democrats, meeting in Cincinnati, nominated James Buchanan, putting him forward as a levelheaded statesman who would continue a policy of compromise, and thus save the nation from the hotheads, North and South. The platform denounced Know-Nothingism. And it endorsed the Kansas-Nebraska Act, with its principle that settlers in new territories should decide in each case for themselves whether to organize as "free" or "slave."

In a close contest, aided by the split opposition, Buchanan won. Even so, Butler and other inner-circle Democrats were inclined to an educated belief that skulduggery with the ballots in Buchanan's home state of Pennsylvania had won that state for the Democrats and decided the election. Naturally they made no issue of this at the time, but they saved the recollection for their memoirs.

But time for compromise had run out. It became apparent at once that neither Buchanan nor anybody else could pacify militant secessionists of the South, certainly not while radicals of the North were howling for outright, federally enforced abolition. It was no longer just a bitter quarrel over the extension of slavery and of maintaining the slippery balance of free states and slave states. Neither side had any tolerance left for concessions.

Buchanan was greeted at once with the Supreme Court's Dred Scott decision (in *Scott* v. *Sandford*) which declared that Congress had no right to prohibit slavery in the territories; that the Missouri Compromise (which had limited extension of slavery) was unconstitutional; and finally that neither Dred Scott nor any other Negro whose ancestors had been sold as slaves had any of the rights of a United States citizen, and that therefore no such persons had any standing whatever in court.

Scott, the petitioner in the case, had been the slave and personal servant of John Emerson, the army doctor who owned him. In 1834 Dr. Emerson took Scott with him from the slave state of Missouri to the free state of Illinois, and then to Fort Snelling in what was then Wisconsin Territory, above the slavery deadline established by the Missouri Compromise. At Fort Snelling Dr. Emerson permitted Scott to marry. Finally, in 1838, Dr. Emerson returned to Missouri, taking Scott and Scott's wife with him.

When Dr. Emerson died, Scott took issue with the notion of being inherited as property by the Widow Emerson. He asserted that, because he had lived in a free state and a free territory as Dr. Emerson's servant, he was no longer a slave but a free man. He sought clear freedom for himself, his wife, and their two children. Lower courts went this way and that, until, in 1856, the case finally reached a Supreme Court dominated by five justices from the Old South, a circumstance which cannot be said to have helped Scott's chances.

Buchanan accepted the Dred Scott decision, in some dim hope that it would at least put an end to wrangling over the issue of slavery in the territories. Instead, uproar increased in volume and bitterness. North and South drew further apart. Resolutions of secession began to be taken seriously, as Buchanan muddled on.

In autumn of 1859 the fanatic John Brown, hearing voices, undertook to invade the state of Virginia and raise a slave insurrection. Mustering his followers on a farm he had rented as a staging area, he marched on Harpers Ferry, seized the Federal arsenal there along with a number of hostages, and had to be pried loose by a detachment of United States Marines directed by Col. Robert E. Lee, USA. Brown was then tried and hanged, achieving martyrdom in the North and his own special place in the demonology of the South.

John Brown's body had scarcely begun a-moldering in the grave before it was time for political conventions again, and Buchanan was looking toward them as eagerly as a man awaiting rescue. The Democrats, still hoping for compromise, chose to meet in the very hotbed of secessionism, Charleston, South Carolina. They convened there in April 1860, with delegate Ben Butler a prominent figure in the proceedings as usual. Also as usual he was playing a sharp game, and this time it was to land him in considerable trouble back home.

Butler's district had sent him to the convention pledged to Stephen Douglas. But Douglas was perhaps the candidate he least wanted to see chosen. Butler did not agree with Douglas's policies, did not think he could be nominated, and believed that if by chance or maneuver Douglas did get nominated he could not be elected.

In a private conversation before the convention formally opened, Butler put that case to Douglas himself in just about those terms. Nevertheless he promised to stay with Douglas for at least five votes once the balloting started.

Playing it close to the vest, Butler was planning to do his best to secure the nomination for James Guthrie of Kentucky, who had been secretary of the treasury in the Pierce administration. However, in the early balloting he voted not five, but seven, times for Douglas, and then switched his vote to Jefferson Davis, another candidate he believed to be without hope of nomination.

What Butler was driving for was a deadlocked convention which, in weary hours, would finally turn to Butler's man, Guthrie. But his plan failed utterly when large numbers of Southern delegates quit the convention in protest over the moderate platform that had been adopted, leaving matters in a state of confusion.

The delegates adjourned to meet again and re-form their tattered ranks in Baltimore. There Douglas did win the nomination, but only after some rejiggering of the rules. Guthrie's candidacy, never prominent, got lost in the shuffle. Finally, to compound the schism, Butler and other conservative Democrats held a convention of their own and nominated Buchanan's vice president, John C. Breckinridge of Kentucky. Touchy Southerners, including those who had bolted the Charleston convention, later also chose to align themselves with the Breckinridge candidacy.

With the Democrats now in thorough disarray, the pegs were well set for a Republican victory in the election ahead. Butler and the other Breckinridge supporters left Baltimore certain in the knowledge that they couldn't win and that, given their defection, Douglas couldn't win, either.

Butler returned home to meet a storm of criticism just this side of lynch-mob fervor. He had voted for Jefferson Davis no fewer than fifty-seven times in his effort to stop Douglas, the man his district had directed him to support. A crowd of more than six thousand angry Democrats showed up, ostensibly to hear his report but actually to boo Butler. They raised such a roar that Butler never did get to speak. The occasion was not just a meeting, it was a public chastisement. Ben was burned in effigy and, as usual, flayed in the ever hostile press.

Outwardly undismayed, Butler postponed his report, since he couldn't be heard above the uproar anyway, and arranged to deliver it two weeks later at a second meeting. By that time mob fever had cooled. Butler's speech, which was more like a lecture, went on for several numbing hours, enough to sedate any crowd. Still defiant, he then proceeded to run for governor on the Breckinridge ticket, an effort that was to net him a paltry six thousand votes statewide.

Butler had just about abandoned his preoccupation with elective politics anyway. He knew as a certainty that the Republicans were going to win. He was equally certain that the South would thereupon break away. He saw that civil war was inevitable, and that it was now time to assert himself in his capacity as a brigadier general of militia.

12

Butler and other leading Breckinridge Democrats had been rather certain that the Republicans would nominate William Henry Seward of New York. They had also expected that Seward would win the election and succeed Buchanan as president. The prospect of a Seward presidency, as a matter of fact, was not entirely disagreeable to many of Butler's faction.

In the usual manner of powerful political insiders figuring the odds, they went on to estimate that Democrats would continue to hold a majority in both houses of Congress. Some of Butler's more optimistic colleagues thought this anticipated dispersion of power might even serve to keep the peace. Butler, however, did not agree. He and the more pragmatic movers in the Breckinridge group reckoned that, after a Republican victory, at least six slave states would defy Federal authority, secede, and bring about a shooting war. In their hard view, the only questions were how serious the war would be and how long it would last.

Their respect for Seward, at any rate, was well founded. Seward was an exceptionally able politician. Some of his policies were of the sort that Northern Democrats of the rank and file readily approved, although his unyielding opposition to slavery won him no friends in the deep South. But policies aside, Seward's career had prospered from the beginning, because of the sheer force of a genial personality. People liked him. And his close and lasting association with Thurlow Weed—the powerful journalist, publisher, and political tactician—was a continuing asset. Weed's skillful management had always kept Seward's public image in a state of shimmering repair.

An attorney, Seward had begun his political career as a leader of New York's spirited Anti-Masonic Party, warmly supported by Weed's Anti-Masonic newspaper. Later, as a Whig, he became a popular governor of New York, sponsoring liberal legislation that, among other things, improved free public education and eased the lot of newly arriving immigrants. With Weed's backing Seward went on to become a United States senator.

When the Republicans met in Chicago, Seward's well-organized forces did their best to stampede the convention with parades, banners, bunting, blaring brass bands, free liquor, free cigars, and a high-decibel cheering section in the meeting hall. But fragmented opposition hardened into a determined "stop Seward" coalition. Since the Republican party was such a ragbag of differing pressure groups, this turn of events may not have been all that remarkable, although Butler's group had not foreseen it while they were crystal gazing.

The anti-Seward coalition rapidly took shape. Seward's popularity with immigrants, especially Irish immigrants, was enough in itself to offend and alienate the Know-Nothing delegates. That peripatetic busybody Horace Greeley, whose editorial opinions tended to waver and turn like a weathervane, was there to argue and connive against Seward as effectively as he was able, taking quite some pleasure in exercising an outsize ego in the cause of an old and cherished enmity.

Then there was the imposing Salmon Portland Chase, senator from Ohio, who strenuously sought the presidency as his due. Chase was a Pooh-Bah whose unblushing admiration of his own abilities would scarcely permit him to consider backing anyone less worthy than himself. Another leader, the rich and powerful Senator Simon Cameron of Pennsylvania, a pioneer wheeler-dealer of easy scruples, sat smug in the convention, holding a large bloc of votes in his pocket. Cameron was prepared to dicker, in this case for a high cabinet post or whatever else might be offered. And then, of course, there was that lanky Illinois politician, Abraham Lincoln, whose main asset (aside from the fact that the convention was being held in his home country, Chicago) was that nobody held very much of anything against him. Lincoln's abilities seemed less than dazzling, but the man was at least acceptable.

What was not so evident at the time was that the bean-pole country lawyer was also a tricky contender. On the night before the balloting, Lincoln's campaign manager had indeed cut a deal with Cameron: a cabinet post in return for those Pennsylvania votes. Lincoln's people had also printed up thousands of counterfeit admission tickets and used them to pack the hall with a well-led cheering section.

The Seward forces put all their effort behind a drive for a first-ballot victory, but they fell short. Seward led with 173 votes; Lincoln was next with 102; Cameron retained his 50 votes; and the prideful Chase, possibly to his astonishment, attracted only 49.

On the second ballot, amid wild cheers from those well-posted Lincoln rooters, that Cameron check was cashed: Pennsylvania went to Lincoln. Others followed, and the tally read Seward 184, Lincoln 181, all others 99. With Seward stopped cold, the third ballot put Lincoln over the top.

The contender whom Butler and his friends had given little consideration emerged as the Republican standard bearer. However, their high estimate of Seward's potential would prove close to the mark. As secretary of state in the Lincoln administration, Seward would all but invent a new job for himself as virtual prime minister to the president. Seward still believed the Federal Union could be saved and that he was the man who could work the miracle.

By the time all the nominations of all the parties had been completed, the ensuing election campaign had become in effect two separate efforts, North and South. The Constitutional Union party, largely made up of recycled Whigs and with strength among conservatives in the upper tier of the Southern states, nominated John Bell of Tennessee, with the famous Massachusetts orator, Edward Everett, as his running mate. Their platform was a simple one: defense of the Constitution and the Federal Union, a last effort to restore sanity in a nation clearly going wild.

In the ensuing brawl regular Douglas Democrats and Lincoln Republicans were to contend mainly for the electoral votes of the North. Unionist Bell and the Breckinridge Democrats vied against each other for the South. Douglas himself, once the tide of the campaign had turned clearly in Lincoln's favor, would take his message courageously to the South also, practically as a loner. Douglas knew it was hopeless to campaign there, but he was driven by a sense of patriotic duty to challenge secessionism on its home ground.

Butler watched most of this remotely. He himself went through the motions in Massachusetts. Although he was running for governor he was not running very hard. In behalf of the Breckinridge ticket, he contented himself with uttering—or muttering—an unemotional, legalistic argument, explaining, if anyone cared to listen, that he was against Douglas because Douglas proposed to leave that burning issue of slavery to the Supreme Court, an unelected body whose decisions were not subject to ready amendment. How much of pure sophistry was contained in Butler's muted utterances proved irrelevant in the campaign, as indicated by the inconsequential six thousand votes he received.

A more or less hidden issue, much in Butler's mind as he sought some common ground with his Southern friends, typically had to do with money. If slavery was to be abolished peacefully in some manner, who was to indemnify slave owners for the immense cash value of all the slaves? Butler's private arguments against secession, questions of constitutionality aside, suggested rather broadly that in choosing a war they could not win the Southern slaveholders were inviting emancipation by edict and the total loss of their investment. Where this line of reasoning was intended to lead was toward some scheme, as yet undefined, for the gradual elimination of slavery, together with universal recognition that the public purse should buy the slaves out of bondage, however long the process took.

This was Yankee dickering at its shrewdest, but it failed to consider the quasi-religious nature of the antislavery movement in the North. Nor did it take into account the inborn fears which Southerners felt for the latent power of that alien race they were holding in subjection. In the South it might be considered all right, even virtuous, to grant freedom to one or two favored slaves from time to time. But state laws often provided that emancipated slaves were subject to immediate arrest and resale if they were found at large in the states where they had been freed. To antebellum Southerners the thought of a huge black population living free and unrestrained in their midst brought nightmare visions of rape, violence, and miscegenation. The only way Southerners might ever consider the buy-out proposition would be on the basis that the purchase price include transportation en masse to somewhere else. And that, besides being clearly impossible from sheer weight of numbers, did not take into account the role of slaves as an indispensable labor force.

The Breckinridge convention had named fifteen of its leaders, Butler among them, to a national committee, and directed the committee to meet in Washington in December to assess the results of the election and talk tactics. Butler showed up as scheduled, but only half a dozen others bothered to attend. Their party was dead, and everyone knew it.

The meeting, however, furnished an opportunity for Butler to exchange notes and notions with his many Southern friends and also to poke around town, gathering useful information. South Carolina had formally seceded from the Union and had sent commissioners to Washington to serve formal notice of this on poor old Buchanan, the quivering lame-duck president. In Butler's committee the only question argued was whether the North would fight, now that the crisis had arrived.

The Southerners told Ben that the South was now united in determination to form a new and separate nation. As an indication of their rancor, they added that even if the new Southern nation should ever agree someday to reunite—on its own terms—with some of the Northern states, New England would forever be barred from the confederation. In their scenario a future damyankee New England would be an alien republic tucked up in a corner and fending for itself.

All of this proud projection was based on the belief that the North would tamely accept secession, as many Northern editorialists, the mercurial Horace Greeley among them, were now suggesting. A Greeley editorial in the *New York Tribune* of December 8, 1860 declared:

> . . . . Whenever six or eight contiguous states shall have formally seceded from the Union, and avowed the pretty unanimous and earnest resolve of their people to stay out, it will not be found practicable to coerce them into subjection; and we doubt that any Congress can be found to direct and provide for such coercion. One or two states

may be coerced; but not an entire section or quarter of a Union. If you do not believe this, wait and see.

That obese and superannuated gourmand, Gen. Winfield Scott, echoed the theme. "Wayward sisters," groaned the weary commander of all United States armies. "Let them go in peace."

Against all this well-publicized wisdom, Butler insisted that the North *would* fight. He warned his Southern colleagues of the consequences, once they found themselves in a subjugated South. Fully aroused and pugnacious, Ben decided it was time to pick up the gauntlet. He proposed a quick, legal, and emphatic decision regarding the status of those South Carolina commissioners.

Jeremiah Black, Buchanan's attorney general, had just delivered a careful estimation to his despairing chief, who was wondering what in the world he should do about South Carolina. Black had tortured the statutes into shaky support for an opinion that the secession convention in South Carolina could be legally defined as a riot. Therefore, Black opined, it was a matter for local authorities to deal with, and to use Federal forces in putting down the "riot" would be illegal.

Buchanan had no sooner breathed a sigh of relief when Butler hove on the scene with a different legal interpretation. He said Buchanan ought to put it to the Supreme Court to decide whether the South Carolina action was a riot or whether it was outright treason. Butler left no doubt that he knew for certain, as an expert in Constitutional law, that what the Carolinians were up to was treason, all right. He told Black:

Let the President say to them, "Gentlemen, you are either ambassadors from a foreign state, and should be received and treated as such, or you are citizens of the United States giving aid and comfort to its declared enemies, which is treason. I must receive you in one of these two characters or not at all. I think your condition is the latter. Gentlemen, you will go hence in the custody of the marshal of the United States as prisoners, charged with treason against your country."

Then, Butler added, let the secessionist commissioners be indicted and tried, and when convicted, hanged. Butler offered to volunteer his services as prosecutor. He made it clear that he expected to win the case.

The startled attorney general, treading carefully, suggested that Ben put his proposition directly to Buchanan, and Butler promptly did so. Some testimony to the Butler-Buchanan meeting suggests there was almost a comic element in the scene, since both Buchanan and Butler were squint-eyed and conducted their talk close up and face-to-face, each scanning the

Benjamin F. Butler, Attorney at Law

other askew. It was also reported that the faltering president, desperately awaiting Lincoln's inauguration and the opportunity at last to flee the premises, blanched and all but fainted dead away. Summoning his wits, however, Buchanan said in effect, "Well, these men do claim to be ambassadors, and they have put themselves voluntarily in our power, so they seem to have a kind of a right to be warned away before we treat them as criminals, don't they?"

Hem and haw, and there the matter ended.

In his heart Buchanan felt he had done all he could to preserve the Union. He had backed the Breckinridge Democrats as the last forlorn hope of continuing his conciliatory policies. In his valedictory message to Congress he blamed the "continuing and intemperate interference" of Northern abolitionists for bringing about the secession crisis. And he proposed, finally, that Congress present a constitutional amendment that would affirm the legality of slavery in states where it existed, uphold in all territories the property rights of slaveholders, and require all states to refrain from interfering with slave owners in the recovery of fugitive slaves.

Northern leaders rejected Buchanan's proposal out of hand, and Southerners now bent on separate nationhood spurned it as well. The outgoing president, whose inner sympathies had always been with the South, continued to temporize in the matter of the South Carolina "ambassadors," although Edwin M. Stanton, newly named as attorney general, seconded Butler's opinion that they ought to be arrested as traitors.

Butler, giving up on Buchanan, went on to arrange a meeting with Sen. Jefferson Davis. They had tea together and talked for several hours. Davis made it clear that when (not *if*) Mississippi seceded, he would honor his allegiance to his state. At the end of their meeting, they solemnly shook hands and parted. Butler was left with no doubt whatever that war was inevitable.

After his talk with Davis, Butler nosed about Washington, listening to gossip, seeing what he could see, gathering intelligence. He was anxious to test the temper of the capital, in view of the impending inauguration of Abraham Lincoln, and he found it an alarmingly hostile city. He noted that the women of Washington seemed more vehement than the men in expressing their hatred of the incoming president. As for Lincoln's male enemies, they were also outspoken and, as a practical matter, somewhat more menacing.

One old Southern acquaintance, after a leisurely dinner with Butler at Ben's hotel, suggested that they take a stroll. "I'll show you something of what we mean to do," he said.

Lighting their after-dinner cigars, the two old friends went on a long walk, fetching up at what looked like a large market shed, dimly lighted. Butler climbed up on a keg that stood against the building and peered through a crack in the rough wooden wall. Inside, he saw nearly 100 armed men performing the basic military drill then commonly known as The School of the Soldier.

"Well, what is all this about?" asked Butler.

"We're getting ready for the fourth of March," said his friend.

"Drilling a company of the district militia to escort Lincoln?" Butler asked, with assumed naiveté.

Butler's friend laughed. "They may escort Lincoln," he said, "but not in the direction of the White House."

Ben, assured that the man meant every word he said, warned him he was undertaking treason. The confident Southerner just grinned. "Oh, there'll be no trouble about it," he said.

On that note they went their separate ways, the Southerner to his nearby home, Ben to his hotel to pack for an immediate return to Massachusetts. From all that he had seen and learned, he was certain that his Massachusetts militia brigade would be needed for active service. General Butler proposed to make sure that his men would be fully outfitted and ready to march. He was eager to lead them.

13

Ben and Sarah Butler had little time for holiday celebration as the last few days of 1860 dwindled away. Butler's hasty return from Washington had been delayed by a heavy snowstorm. When he finally reached Boston on December 28, he was preoccupied with an urgent sense of mission. He proposed to see Gov. John A. Andrew right away, to warn him of dangers threatening the impending inauguration and to urge him to make the Massachusetts militia ready for immediate field duty.

The militiamen, in fact, were in sorry shape for anything more demanding than a holiday parade. Their uniforms, anything but uniform, reflected the individual tastes and whimsies of the various companies and, while decorative enough, were tailored of light materials scarcely suitable for serious campaigning. In all the militia there was not to be found a single knapsack suitable for carrying rations and other gear. Most important, in view of the season, these were summer soldiers without an overcoat among them.

Moreover there were political questions a Republican governor had to consider, with the inauguration of a Republican president pending. Butler thought Andrew ought to take serious note that his soldiery consisted in large part of young and fervent Democrats who might think long and hard about responding when the call to arms was sounded by a Republican.

"What can I do about that?" asked the bemused governor.

"Let each company be quietly called to its armory," said Butler, "and the question put to every soldier, 'Are you ready to march when called upon to defend the national capital?'"

Butler urged Governor Andrew to order this done immediately, without public announcement, but rather in great secrecy so as to minimize public alarm. He also suggested a secret session of the legislature to adopt an emergency appropriation for equipment.

The governor was by no means convinced that Butler's sense of urgency was justified, nor was he prepared to fly into action at the behest of an old political enemy—at least not until he had done a little checking

around. Butler persisted, however, and in several subsequent meetings recommended the same course of action. Finally, on January 16, Andrew
issued a general order that called in effect for a purge of the militia.

The general order required all company commanders to screen their
companies and determine whether there were men in the ranks who "from
age, physical defect, or business or family causes, may be unable or indis-
posed to respond at once to the orders of the commander in chief made in
response to the call of the President. . . "

Andrew ordered company commanders to discharge all unfit or unwilling soldiers, then to fill their places with men prepared to serve whenever
called upon. When this was done, the officers were to prepare a fully
detailed muster roll to be submitted to the state adjutant general. How
Butler or anybody imagined all this could be accomplished in secrecy bog-
gles the mind, but the process was duly carried out as ordered, and all
Massachusetts militiamen of infirm body or dubious zeal were plucked out
of the ranks and dismissed.

In his own brigade Butler was especially proud of Lowell's hometown
regiment, the Massachusetts 6th, and of its energetic commander, Col.
Edward F. Jones. Butler hovered about as Colonel Jones supervised the
examination of each man in the outfit. When all healthy men in the proper
age brackets signed on without exception to serve if called, Ben was properly gratified.

Butler was also pleased to hand Governor Andrew a formal resolution,
voted by the field officers and company commanders, tendering the services of the regiment whenever it should be called upon. The 6th was the
only Massachusetts regiment to do this and, though the resolution was only
a formality, it still provided enough Butlerian drama to impress the legislators when Governor Andrew presented it to them. The legislature, after all,
still faced the problem of that emergency appropriation for equipment and
supplies. With the 6th Regiment showing such zeal, could legislators balk at
a small matter of money?

While all this was going on, New England's polar opposite, South Carolina, was enthusiastically carrying on the business of armed insurrection.
Secessionist propaganda there cast Carolinians in the role of proud gentry
refusing to be bullied by baseborn, bigoted, detestable clods of the North.
The hottest words in the rebel lexicon were reserved for New Englanders,
and *Damn Yankee* became a single word in the litany of rebellion. More
practically, rhetoric aside, at this time the South Carolinians were following
up their ordinance of secession by seizing all federal property in their
reach, especially cash, arms, and munitions. Only the harbor fortifications
at Charleston, notably the new and nearly completed Fort Sumter,
remained untouched for the moment.

Even as Butler was conferring with Governor Andrew, additional

Southern states were following South Carolina's lead. By the end of January, Mississippi, Florida, Alabama, Georgia, and Louisiana had voted ordinances of secession. Texas was to follow this course on February 1.

In Washington, as Buchanan dithered, outright treason was being committed in the president's own cabinet. His corrupt secretary of war, the Virginian John Floyd, had used his office to profit from padded bills and larcenous dealings in government property. Now Floyd was bending every effort to ship federal arms, munitions, and other supplies to Southern forts and Army posts—not to strengthen those installations, but to provide the rebel South with the means to make war. Buchanan knew of the corruption and knew of the arms shipments, but he did nothing until Floyd resigned on December 28 and openly joined the secessionists. Then the president merely concurred in countermanding Floyd's final treachery, his order consigning a shipment of 125 cannon from the Federal arsenal at Pittsburgh to posts in the deep South.

Trying to stiffen Buchanan's spine was a hopeless undertaking. Nevertheless, the Massachusetts legislature forwarded a resolution whose "whereas" clauses cited acts of Southern rebellion and whose resolve broadly offered the president "such aid in men and money as he may require, to maintain the authority of the national government." With Butler attending both as advocate and expert witness, the legislature in secret session then voted an appropriation of $100,000 to arm and equip the militia.

Butler, for the moment working closely with the Republican governor, moved immediately to see to it that the Massachusetts 6th got first crack at the funds. Colonel Jones prepared a shopping list in writing for Governor Andrew to peruse. Four companies had serviceable rifles, but not enough of them. Another four had outmoded and useless muskets which, moreover, used nonstandard cartridges. Two companies had no uniforms at all, their old ones having worn out. Six companies had uniforms of varying hues, all of light materials unsuitable for field service.

Colonel Jones first asked for proper arms and ammunition. With that attended to, he said, each man should be supplied with a uniform cap, pants, jacket, boots, overcoat, knapsack, and blanket, all of heavy material. He added that it would take at least ten to fourteen days to put his command in marching order.

In response, the commonwealth moved promptly to fill the order. Among other purchases, cloth for two thousand overcoats was bought from a Lowell textile corporation, the Middlesex Company, of which Butler was a prominent stockholder. This was by no means done as a concession from the Republican administration to an opposition Democrat. The Middlesex mill was among others invited to submit bids, it had the woolens, and it could deliver the cloth at once at a competitive price. However, Butler's editorial enemies were prepared to make capital of the circumstance if an occasion arose, and, in a false lull that followed, the occasion did arise.

Led by Virginia, the northerly states of what was to become the Confederacy called for a peace convention to be held in Washington. The Massachusetts legislature readily joined the effort, sending seven commissioners to take part in the proceedings. Butler, in dissent, saw the conference as a mere ploy on the part of the slave states to gain time for their war preparations.

The peace convention wound up its proceedings late in March without any useful conclusions. In the meantime Abraham Lincoln, having smuggled himself into Washington on a secret train that rushed through hostile Baltimore in dark predawn hours, had been inaugurated without untoward incident. The crisis persisted, but optimists could note that it had not yet deteriorated, after all, into a clash of arms. The Massachusetts legislature, rather buoyed up at events, proceeded to repeal that $100,000 emergency funding measure, excepting only such moneys as had been already spent.

Repeal of the appropriation brought prompt and happy comment in the press. One newspaper jibed that Ben Butler had just wanted to feed the moths with woolen overcoats. Another sarcastically congratulated him on his cleverness in landing a fat contract for the mill in which he held stock.

The members of the legislature, with a feeling of great relief, adjourned on April 11 and went home, deciding there was no urgency after all in preparing the Massachusetts militia for service. Their timing proved to be quite remarkable. In the predawn hours of April 12, the rebels of South Carolina opened fire on Fort Sumter.

14

Ben Butler was not the only one warning Governor Andrew of impending disaster as Buchanan wavered through the last months of his presidency. Edwin M. Stanton, the newly appointed attorney general, had set up a curious private network, and the Massachusetts governor was included in this intelligence loop. Stanton had quickly lost all confidence in Old Buck, if he had ever had such confidence in the first place. Promptly enough, Stanton took the extraordinary step of leaking details of cabinet sessions to a network of key Republican politicians, most notably William H. Seward. Stanton's inside information was passed along also to John H. Clifford, a former Massachusetts governor, and to Massachusetts Sen. Charles Sumner, who kept Andrew informed. Buchanan, occupied in an endless waltz with South Carolina's secessionist "ambassadors," had no idea that Stanton was reporting his every move, as well as directing a constant flow of additional data and opinion, to his Republican associates.

Stanton had assumed his cabinet post on December 27, to be greeted at once with the news that Maj. Robert Anderson, the night before, had evacuated Charleston's Fort Moultrie as indefensible and moved his small garrison to the island stronghold of Fort Sumter. It was Major Anderson's view that the move was in accordance with the last vague orders he had received from Washington. These directed him, loosely enough, to use "sound military discretion."

South Carolinian secessionists, eager for a showdown, chose to regard Anderson's secret midnight redeployment as insult and provocation. So did their allies within Buchanan's cabinet, much to Stanton's anger and disgust. The newly elected governor of South Carolina, Francis Wilkinson Pickens, responded immediately to Anderson's maneuver by ordering the seizure of Fort Moultrie, the arsenal, the post office, and the customhouse.

Fort Sumter, still unfinished, was a formidable structure of dark brick, built on an artificial island made of heavy stone blocks. It was designed to mount three full tiers of guns, but only fourteen cannon were in place: three on the uppermost level, none on the second level, eleven on the bottom level. Anderson's entire command consisted of sixty-one enlisted men, seven officers, and thirteen musicians.

As cabinet debate continued, Buchanan nervously permitted Gen. Winfield Scott to dispatch an unarmed, unescorted merchant vessel, *Star of the West*, to Anderson's relief. Laden with supplies, arms, ammunition, and two hundred men, the steamer nosed into range of rebel shore batteries, came briefly under fire, sustained two inconsequential hits, then turned about and fled back to New York.

Still, the Sumter impasse remained unresolved. No outright attack was made on the fort. Just as Butler and others believed, the South appeared to be playing for time, bullying Buchanan for whatever concessions were to be gained and meanwhile arming and training for the war ahead. Sumter's garrison, on short rations, went unmolested. In those uneasy circumstances Buchanan succeeded in riding out his term without precipitating the big crisis. That was left for Lincoln.

The new administration, after some hot internal debate, finally decided to send a respectable force to relieve Sumter, this time including warships. But every move in Washington was promptly telegraphed southward. As the diarist Gideon Welles, Lincoln's secretary of the navy, described it, "the atmosphere was thick with treason." Through a complicated plot conceived in outright conspiracy between Secretary of State Seward and Navy Comdr. David D. Porter, the most powerful warship assigned to the expedition (the *Powhatan*) was diverted elsewhere and failed to make rendezvous with the other ships.

Pierre Gustave Toutant Beauregard, who began 1861 by serving five days as superintendent of West Point, was now a Confederate brigadier assigned to Charleston. Fully alerted to Lincoln's plans, General Beauregard waited until the last possible moment, then demanded the fort's surrender. When that was refused he ordered a heavy bombardment to begin as of 4:30 A.M. on April 12.

While the weakened Union fleet stood by without entering the fracas or firing a shot, Sumter was pounded by Confederate guns. The garrison, during thirty-four hours under continuous fire, returned round after round until there were but four barrels of powder left and the wooden structures within the fort were in ruins. Then Sumter surrendered. Notably, if the Union force was ever seriously charged with an all-out defense of the fort—something Seward was at considerable pains to avoid, whatever Lincoln intended—those structures would have been pulled down as standard procedure before the Confederate guns ever opened.

There was no easy or honorable explanation for Seward's note to a secessionist contact when the *Powhatan* conspiracy succeeded: "Faith as to Sumter fully kept. Wait and see." But whatever Seward had in mind, and presumably it was compromise and peace, the outcome instead was intransigence and war.

When Sumter fell, Beauregard became the South's hero of the hour. As Douglas Southall Freeman, that chronicler of Southern glories was to phrase it: "From the hour of his arrival there, March 6, 1861, the patriots of Charleston had welcomed him. After he had forced the surrender of Fort Sumter on April 14 without the loss of a man, they had acclaimed him and adopted him." For that matter, Beauregard's heavy guns got the job done without even the loss of a civilian, although the whole town had turned out to watch the show. Idolatry came cheap at that stage of hostilities.

Now, at any rate, the Lincoln administration had a full-scale war emergency to meet. On the day after Sumter's surrender, Secretary of War Cameron telegraphed Governor Andrew, asking him to dispatch two regiments of Massachusetts militia to Washington as soon as possible. Since the Massachusetts 6th was the best prepared, Andrew called it into service first.

Butler was trying a case before a court in Boston when he received hand-carried orders to muster his 6th Regiment the following morning at Boston's historic Faneuil Hall. Lawyer Butler promptly rose from the counsel table, explained that he had been called to arms, and asked the judge for a continuance of the case. That done, General Butler marched out of the courtroom. The case he was trying may still be buried somewhere in the archives, since to the best of Butler's knowledge it was never brought to a conclusion.

Butler now not only had military business to attend to, but also some quick political maneuvering to plan. If Washington wanted a brigade, he meant to see that the brigadier at the head of it would be Benjamin Franklin Butler. And given the fact that a hostile Republican governor was commander in chief of the militia, getting the assignment was going to take a bit of doing.

Butler's first step was to fire off a telegram containing a broad hint to an old friend and former Democrat, War Secretary Cameron: "You have called for a brigade of Massachusetts troops; why not call for a brigadier general and staff. I have some hope of being detailed."

Cameron got the message. Promptly, the same night, the secretary of war called upon the Commonwealth of Massachusetts to dispatch a brigadier general along with the brigade. The official telegram went to Governor Andrew. An unofficial telegram went at the same time to Butler, informing him that the request had been made.

Still plotting his moves, Butler remembered, as nobody else had, that moving troops around costs money and that Massachusetts had no appropriated funds for the purpose. He also noted that the legislature had adjourned and was not available to vote any funds.

Butler was mulling this angle the next morning on the train from Lowell to Boston. When he spotted another old friend in the same car, an idea glimmered. There sat James G. Carney, president of the Bank of Mutual Redemption, one of the major Boston banks. Carney, who also lived in Lowell, was a regular commuter.

As a plan took shape in his mind, Butler moved to sit beside Carney. He told Carney the word he had got from War Secretary Cameron. In his most persuasive style, Butler outlined the state's compound military and financial problem and suggested how it might be solved. If Carney's bank were to make its considerable funds available in a quick loan to the state, the troops could move at once. All that was needed was a letter to that effect from Carney, which Ben volunteered to carry in person to Governor Andrew. At the same time, Ben added ingenuously, Carney might recommend that Andrew select Butler as the brigadier detailed to command.

The banker quickly agreed to all of this and added that he would get a similar commitment from all the other Boston banks. Following through, Butler and Carney went together to Carney's bank, where the letter was promptly drafted and signed. The other banks fell in with the plan, making something over $3 million immediately available to the state.

Armed with the banker's letter, Butler trotted over to the governor's office. As it happened, Governor Andrew and Treasurer Henry K. Oliver had been pondering the same financial problem without a notion as to how it could be solved without much delay. Waiting in the anteroom was a brigadier senior to Butler, who expected to draw the coveted command assignment.

Ben, however, got in to see the governor first. He tersely outlined his plan, presented Carney's letter, and called pointed attention to the banker's endorsement of Butler as the general who ought to be given command.

Treasurer Oliver was sold. "Well, Governor," he commented, "since Butler has found the means to go, I think he ought to go."

"I will take it under consideration," replied Andrew coldly.

But later in the day the governor put aside his partisan reservations, named Butler to the command, and put an office in the State House at his disposal. Now General Butler was in full charge of organizing the Massachusetts troops and putting them on the move. Within the next few days not two, but four, militia regiments were on their way south. One of them, Butler's favorite, the 6th, was destined for a wild encounter with a secessionist mob in Baltimore and its first blood sacrifice in the war that had begun.

The War Department, anticipating rebel attack on Fortress Monroe at the mouth of the James River, asked that two regiments be sent there to reinforce that key post. Butler dispatched the 3d and 4th regiments to Fortress Monroe by sea. They reached their destination on April 20.

Meanwhile the 6th, under command of Colonel Jones, left by train on the first leg of its move to Washington. The regiment arrived in New York on the morning of April 18, where the troops paused for an elaborate breakfast furnished by the Astor House. Then, at 11:00 A.M., they boarded the train for Philadelphia and camped in that city for the night.

While the 6th was progressing southward, the 8th, under Col. Timothy Munroe, was making its final preparations, some of them very hasty. On the afternoon of April 18, the regiment paraded before the State House and heard speeches by Governor Andrew and General Butler. While they harangued the troops, busy tailors in the rear of the regiment were sewing the last buttons on the men's new overcoats. Finally, at 6:00 P.M., the 8th, along with Butler himself, was aboard a train and on its way to New York.

In New York the Astor House gave a repeat performance of the elaborate breakfast it had earlier provided for the 6th. Butler and his staff were treated to breakfast at the Fifth Avenue Hotel, followed by an informal review of sorts as Butler, standing on a balcony of the hotel, was cheered to the echo while his troops marched past.

Sen. Edward D. Baker of Oregon, a veteran of the Mexican war, was standing with Butler on the balcony. He took dour note of the ovation. "All very well, General, for them to cheer you when they go out, but take care of them so that they will cheer you on their return," he said.

At Jersey City there was a slight hitch when the railroad official in charge said he couldn't put a train together for the troops without interrupting service for the road's regular civilian passengers. Butler made short work of that argument, and at 11:00 A.M. the 8th was on its way to Philadelphia, arriving there somewhat before 5:00 P.M.

Butler and his staff headed for their hotel, to be greeted by frantic extras of the Philadelphia *Press* carrying an account of a riotous attack on the 6th at Baltimore. Those first reports, based on sketchy telegrams from Baltimore, said that a part of the regiment, and maybe all of it, had been captured by Maryland secessionists. Butler later got more accurate reports and forwarded them to Governor Andrew. By the time it was all sorted out, the battered 6th was on the last leg of its journey to Washington and Butler was considering how best now to move the 8th.

Butler's orders called for a move by rail through Baltimore, but that was now impossible. Officials of the Philadelphia, Wilmington & Baltimore Railroad had promised the mayor of Baltimore that no more troops would be carried through that city on their trains. Moreover, to make the matter moot, secessionists had burned the long railroad trestle bridge on the route out of Baltimore, so no trains could pass anyway. In view of these reports, Ben sat down to study the maps.

15

During the national expansion of the previous decades, railroads had spread across the countryside like creeper vines. For financiers, they were a sure source of wealth; for job-hungry immigrants, a ready means of employment. The various lines had not yet evolved into an entirely efficient network, however, and it was this circumstance that brought the Massachusetts 6th to grief at Baltimore. A primitive procedure in effect in that city required the cars carrying the troops to be hitched, one by one, to horses and thus drawn across town to another railroad station, there to be linked together again behind an engine for the trip to Washington.

While still in Philadelphia, Colonel Jones had received warnings of trouble ahead if he took his regiment through Baltimore. But that diligent officer insisted that the urgency of his orders left him no option but to proceed. Jones took up the matter of transportation with officials of the Philadelphia, Wilmington & Baltimore Railroad. Wary, they proposed to take the 6th only to their station in Baltimore, leaving the soldiers to find their own way on foot across town to the other terminal.

Colonel Jones agreed to these arrangements. But he stipulated that the railroad must see to it that bridges on the route were guarded and that a lone engine was run ahead of the troop train to ensure that the track was clear. With this understood, a train of ten cars was made up and the regiment boarded shortly after midnight.

En route, Jones advised his men that they might well run into trouble in Baltimore. He instructed the troops that, if a hostile mob stoned them or fired on them, they were not to return fire except on direct order of their officers. In any case they were not to fire indiscriminately, but rather to take aim only at the persons firing at them. Since the contingency involved a civilian mob riot, not a battle, these orders may have been somewhat less than realistic, but at least they served as a caution.

While the train was under way, the railroad telegraph chattered busily. The road's officials got late word from Baltimore that there was no sign of a gathering mob. This led them to alter their plan, so that instead of evicting the regiment from their cars they would, as usual, hitch up the horses and haul the loaded cars across town. Orders to that effect were telegraphed to Baltimore, but Colonel Jones was left in ignorance about the change in procedure.

When the train reached Baltimore, Colonel Jones stepped off the first car, prepared to form up his regiment for the expected march. But the railroad people quickly hitched horses to that first car and started it off briskly. They had got three cars moving before anybody told Jones about the revised orders the railroad men were now putting into effect. Jones leaped aboard the next car, expecting that the rest of the regiment would make the crosstown passage without incident after all.

Seven cars were shuttled to the other station without difficulty, but by this time the secessionist mob had formed. As the three remaining cars got part of the way along, rocks and bricks began to fly, shattering windows and causing injuries to the men. Soon the way was blocked entirely, so the trapped militiamen abandoned the cars and formed up to force their way through on foot. They marched steadily under a hail of rocks until pistol shots began to ring out. A man in the leading platoon was killed. The troops then returned fire. By the time they reached the crosstown station and joined the rest of the regiment, the disputed passage had cost them dearly. Four Massachusetts men had been killed and seventeen seriously wounded. The Baltimore mob counted twelve killed in this first spilling of blood in the Civil War.

That the bloodshed occurred on April 19 had special significance for Massachusetts men, for that was a date proudly observed in their home state, the day on which those embattled farmers at Concord Bridge had defied King George's redcoats and "fired the shot heard 'round the world."

Advised by railroad officials that the mob was regrouping to tear up the tracks ahead, Colonel Jones got his regiment aboard the waiting train and started off for Washington. Those were his orders, and he proposed to carry them out to the letter. The 6th arrived in the capital in the morning to be greeted warmly by President Lincoln. Later the president visited the wounded, and in talking with them made no secret of his despair at the isolation of the capital. He was heard to wonder aloud if there really was a North and whether the New York 7th Regiment truly existed other than on paper.

Back in Philadelphia with the 8th Regiment and now fully informed about the stormy passage of the 6th, General Butler pondered his orders to proceed to Washington by way of Baltimore. He wasted little time, however, before deciding to ignore them.

Huddling over the maps with Capt. Samuel F. Du Pont of the Philadelphia Navy Yard, Butler noted a branch railroad line with a terminus at Annapolis, but he reckoned that Maryland secessionists would surely block

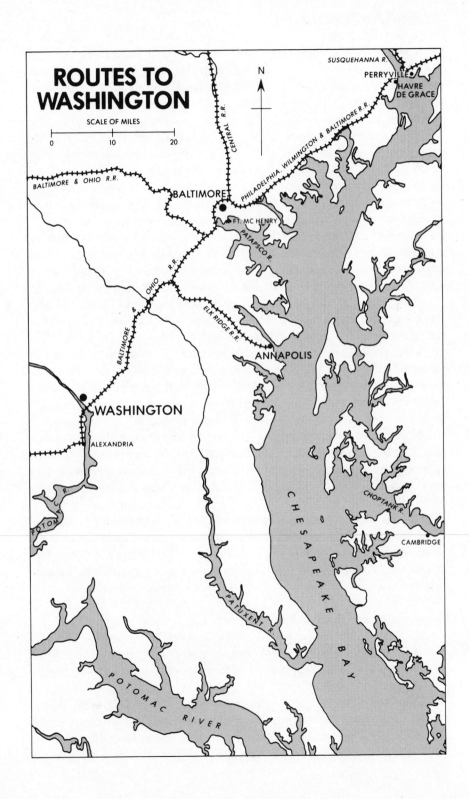

ROUTES TO
WASHINGTON

SCALE OF MILES

0   10   20

N

SUSQUEHANNA R.

PERRYVILLE

HAVRE
DE GRACE

CENTRAL R.R.

PHILADELPHIA, WILMINGTON & BALTIMORE R.R.

BALTIMORE & OHIO R.R.

BALTIMORE

FT. MC HENRY

PATAPSCO R.

OHIO R.R.

BALTIMORE &

ELK RIDGE R.R.

ANNAPOLIS

WASHINGTON

ALEXANDRIA

POTOMAC R.

CHOPTANK R.

CAMBRIDGE

C H E S A P E A K E   B A Y

PATUXENT R.

P O T O M A C   R I V E R

that route. However, there was another rail line that could carry the regiment to the town of Perryville, on the north side of the Susquehanna River, and at Perryville the railroad maintained a large steamboat, the *Maryland*, for ferry service to Havre de Grace at the mouth of the river where it emptied into Chesapeake Bay.

Now the New York dandies of that state's high-society regiment, the 7th, entered into Butler's calculations. That regiment was expected momentarily in Philadelphia. If Butler could persuade its commander, Col. Marshall Lefferts, to cooperate with the plebeian Massachusetts 8th, their united force could seize the ferryboat, cross to Havre de Grace, then march in strength to Washington against any opposition the secessionists might muster. However, Lefferts declined to join Butler, proposing instead to put his regiment aboard ship, sail south, and reach Washington by way of the Potomac. Left to his own resources, Butler then decided on a bold amphibious operation. He resolved to grab the *Maryland*, ferry his regiment down Chesapeake Bay all the way to Annapolis, land his troops there, and capture the town. He planned then to hold Annapolis as a bridgehead for troop reinforcements coming down from the North by sea.

S. M. Felton, president of the Philadelphia, Wilmington & Baltimore Railroad, gave Butler full cooperation. Felton tried to alert the skipper of the *Maryland* by telegraph, but the wires had been cut. Meanwhile he gave Butler full written authority to use the ferryboat any way he saw fit, even if he had to burn and sink the vessel in whatever emergency might arise.

At this point it was not known whether the *Maryland* had already been seized by rampaging secessionists, in which case Butler's men would have to board and capture it, pirate-style. Butler indeed was rather under the impression that the ship was in hostile hands and that a sharp fight would be required.

Butler's older brother, rough-and-ready Andrew, was along on the expedition as a kind of civilian aide. Andrew, packing a muscular 180 pounds on a six-foot frame, was a taciturn Yankee who rather enjoyed a fracas and was looking forward to this one. As Ben was completing his plans, he sent Andrew to purchase a supply of pickaxes, wood axes, and shovels to be used as entrenching tools, and also to buy some cooking and camping equipment in case the regiment had to bivouac.

By 3:00 A.M. Butler had worked out all the details and forwarded a full report to Governor Andrew. In passing he noted that he had no field artillery, and asked that the Boston Light Battery be sent forward by ship to join him as soon as possible.

Eight hours later the 8th Regiment was on a train heading south. Butler went through the cars, briefing the troops personally on what lay ahead and advising them that they might have to take the steamer *Maryland* by force. He and his officers also inspected the men and their equipment, requiring each soldier to run through the proper procedure for loading and firing a rifle. All this done and after instructing the conductor to run his train at the highest speed the engine could manage, Ben settled down for a nap.

Not long after closing his eyes, Butler was startled awake by somebody yelling, "Man overboard!" The train had come to a grinding stop.

Looking out the window, Ben observed one of his sergeants, stripped of all equipment but his pants and boots, running like a rabbit across the fields, with several soldiers in full pursuit. Contemplating the skirmish ahead, the jittery sergeant had panicked and jumped from the moving train, a feat he managed somehow without breaking his neck.

Irked at the incident and the delay, Butler ordered a bugler to sound an urgent recall, leaving the fugitive to his own devices. As the train lurched into motion again, Butler shouted to a couple of track workers at the scene that he'd pay a $30 reward to anyone delivering the deserter to him at Annapolis.

Butler halted the train when it reached a point somewhat short of the Perryville landing, where the *Maryland* was moored. He formed the regiment in marching order. Riflemen of one company were detailed as flankers covering the woods on either side of the dusty country road. The rest of the regiment marched on the road in a column of platoons, with the general leading the way. As they approached the steamboat landing, Ben was joined by brother Andrew, who was ambling along carrying an ax handle.

"What are you going to do with that?" Ben asked.

"Well, you expect a fight, don't you?" replied Andrew, jauntily swinging his weapon of choice.

When they reached the landing, the Butler brothers stepped on board the *Maryland* together. They found no belligerent secessionists awaiting them. In fact, there was nobody aboard except a few deckhands. The rest of the crew, including the captain, had skedaddled.

Spared a skirmish, Ben put the regiment to work preparing the vessel for its unusual voyage. The men shoveled coal, filling several cars and pushing them aboard on the deck tracks the railroad normally used in ferrying trains across the river. Rations were scarce, the green troops having gobbled most of the provisions issued them in Philadelphia, and there was no drinking water aboard. But Ben solved the latter problem, at least, by filling a number of empty whiskey barrels found at the landing with clean, fresh water, and stowing them aboard. The firebox was then stoked and, with smoke billowing from her stacks, the *Maryland* was on her way down the river, heading for Chesapeake Bay.

Butler's improvised expedition arrived at Annapolis Harbor in the deep dark of night, with the *Maryland* chugging slowly toward the wharf of the

Andrew Jackson
Butler
Butler's Book

Gov. John A. Andrew
Battles and Leaders of the Civil War

United States Naval Academy. Ben had expected to achieve total surprise, but it was evident at once that the academy was on full alert—no sooner had the ferryboat come into view than drums were beating assembly and lights were beginning to glimmer everywhere. Butler, assessing the situation, ordered his flagship to heave to and drop anchor while he considered what to do next.

After some careful thought Ben decided to send ashore a staff officer, Capt. Peter Haggerty, with a note to whoever was in command. Andrew Butler, standing close by while Haggerty got his instructions, was not to be left out of an adventure. Andrew decided he would go along with Captain Haggerty. He didn't ask for anybody's permission; he just announced he was going. As Andrew stepped into the boat, he handed his pistol to the nearest officer. "Here, take this," said Andrew in his quiet Yankee drawl. "I ain't likely to capture Annapolis with it, and if they take me I don't want them to get a good revolver." So saying, Andrew disappeared into the darkness with Captain Haggerty.

About an hour later those on board the *Maryland* heard the sound of muffled oars as a boat approached. Soon Butler could discern the figures of four men rowing and a fifth man, who was apparently in charge. Ben hailed the boat, demanding identification. A smart answer came back, likewise demanding to know what steamer was this.

"None of your business," yelled Butler. "Come alongside or I'll fire into you."

The boat approached, and a young man in navy uniform came aboard. As soon as he was on deck a couple of militiamen nabbed him. In their tight grasp the officer quickly identified himself in formal fashion: "I am Lieutenant Matthews, sent by Commodore Blake, commandant of the Naval Academy, to learn what steamer this is."

Butler was cautious in replying, since it was common knowledge that the naval service was well riddled with officers choosing to align themselves with the rebels.

"Very well," said Ben. "I can tell *you* that easily enough, but whether I'll allow you to tell Commodore Blake is another question."

Butler then informed the young officer that the ship was the ferryboat *Maryland*; that he himself was Gen. Benjamin F. Butler, commanding Massachusetts militia aboard; and that he proposed landing his troops shortly.

"Glad to hear it," said Lieutenant Matthews, "and Commodore Blake will be glad to hear it, too."

He explained that the commodore had feared that he faced a shipload of Baltimore secessionists come to capture the naval station. Still cautious, Butler told the young man he'd have to stay on board the *Maryland* until word came from the men he had sent to assess the situation ashore.

Dawn was breaking when Captain Haggerty and Andrew Butler

returned to the ship, bringing Commodore Blake with them. The latter turned out to be an elderly officer all but weeping with relief. Brokenly, he kept insisting that Butler had to save the *Constitution*, a plea that puzzled Lawyer Butler for a moment, since his mind slipped a gear and he assumed the old man meant the historic document. But Blake soon made it clear that he meant the historic ship, Old Ironsides, which lay nearby.

"Can you stop and help me?" Blake asked.

"I don't have much choice but to stop," Butler replied. "This is about as far as I can go at the moment."

The commodore, under questioning, briefed Butler on the military situation. The 8th Regiment would have no opposition ashore. As for defense, while Annapolis was open to assault from the sea, a small detachment of Butler's militia could easily hold the narrow neck of land connecting the Annapolis peninsula to the mainland.

Word of Ben's steamboat expedition had become widespread as soon as the *Maryland* had cast off at Perryville. When Butler arrived at Annapolis, he found a message waiting for him from Thomas Hicks, the desperately neutralist governor of Maryland. It said: "I would most earnestly advise that you do not land your men at Annapolis. The excitement here is very great, and I think it prudent that you should take your men elsewhere. I have telegraphed to the Secretary of War against your landing your men here."

Butler, having already told Commodore Blake the 8th Regiment had gone about as far as it could go, broke the same news to Hicks, although in more formal terms. He reminded the governor that mobs in his state had already torn up rails and burned railroad bridges, although he didn't add, as he might have, that this had been done largely with the governor's own quivering consent. Butler did not propose to budge, and that in sum was what he told Hicks.

After breakfast with Commodore Blake, who had the *Constitution* on his mind almost to the exclusion of everything else, Butler assigned a Salem company to go on board Old Ironsides as a guard. He gave a Marblehead company, fishermen almost to a man, the job of towing the ship out of its dock and into deep bay water. After some exertions, including moving all the warship's upper-deck armament to the workhorse *Maryland*, the ferryboat hauled the *Constitution* out into the bay.

With Old Ironsides safe and the Commodore's mind eased, Butler could relax for an hour or two. He proposed to hold Annapolis, which was to remain an important Union base for the rest of the war. As Lincoln's revered biographer, Carl Sandburg, was to note, without crediting Butler one whit for the accomplishment: "A troop route to the North had been found. In a few days Washington had 10,000 defense troops. Now, for a time, Lincoln knew the capital would still be at Washington."

16

Ashore at Annapolis, Butler held his first face-to-face conference with the aggrieved Governor Hicks, who arrived at the Naval Academy in the company of the mayor of the town. Hicks was agitated, and the mayor more so. They described an enraged population barely restrained from wiping out the Yankee regiment. They said the railroad link to Washington had been torn up and that the route was now guarded by hordes of secessionists. They urged Butler to turn his steamboat around and flee with his troops while he still could.

Ben listened impassively to their anxious tirade. Then, ignoring the blood-and-thunder scenario of the two Maryland politicians, he calmly inquired where he might buy provisions for the regiment.

"You can't buy an ounce of provisions in Annapolis," sputtered the mayor. "No patriot here will sell provisions for Yankee troops so they can march to Washington."

After quite some more discussion along the same lines, Butler finally began to get a little hot under the collar. "If the people won't sell us provisions," he growled, "a thousand hungry armed men have other means of getting what they need to eat."

On that note the meeting ended. In the meantime old Commodore Blake had come through with emergency rations from naval stores at the academy: salted beef and hardtack. Then General Butler discovered, much to his chagrin, that he and the other Massachusetts militia officers had neglected one important element of training over the years. His troops didn't know how to cook. In all those prewar exercises and encampments, food preparation had been left to caterers hired for the job. Now the Massachusetts soldiers, eyeing their field rations, were totally perplexed. All over the academy parade ground, where they were encamped, the men were managing to get fires going with the firewood they had been issued. But after that they milled around, more or less baffled.

"Ludicrous!" said the disgusted general as he observed the performance.

However, in a few days the tradesmen of Annapolis changed their minds about refusing to deal with Yankees, and the supply problem eased. As a minor bonus, the runaway sergeant who had jumped from the train on the way to Perryville showed up at Annapolis, contrite. Ben decided not to have him shot for desertion. Instead he made him a cook.

Ben took time to write Sarah a brief report:

> Dear Sarah—I have worked like a horse, slept not two hours a night, have saved the "Old Ironsides" Frigate from the secessionists, and have landed in the capital of Maryland against the protest of her Government. . . . I think no man has won more in ten days than I have. We will see, however. Goodbye—kiss the children for me. —Butler.

Meanwhile there was another arrival. The steamer *Boston* put in at Annapolis, with the New York 7th aboard. Colonel Lefferts, it turned out, had taken his regiment all the way from Philadelphia to the mouth of the Potomac, pausing there to take stock of the situation. Rumors were current that there might be rebel guns posted to keep Union ships from going up the river to Washington. In something of an excess of caution, Lefferts accordingly ordered the *Boston* turned around, and headed back north for Annapolis after all, somewhat to Ben's sardonic delight.

Butler, as senior officer present, immediately assumed command of both regiments, "assumed" being the operative word, since Lefferts hotly resisted the assumption. In the same loose manner in which Ben's brother Andrew was along for the ride, Lefferts too had a civilian friend accompanying him. Lefferts's chum professed to have once attended West Point, but he held no commission and had no status except as a kind of gentleman tourist. In any case, whatever his true qualifications, the man turned out to be a source of enormous irritation to Butler, since Lefferts never met with the general without having his "military adviser" along.

Butler's initial order as commanding general was a wordy one, which in essence did little more than call for rousing the troops at 5:00 A.M. for close-order drill by companies. It also expressed the intention, without giving details, of marching both regiments to Washington. Then there began a series of conferences between Butler and Lefferts, with Butler trying to persuade Lefferts to march and Lefferts insisting he preferred to wait for reinforcements. The last such council was a stormy one, as Butler, exasperated beyond all patience, finally gave up on persuasion.

"All right," said Ben. "By the Articles of War, I am in command, and I now take the responsibility of giving you an order to march, and I expect it to be obeyed."

Lefferts's civilian adviser immediately spoke up, protesting that a militia general had no right to command New York State troops.

Turning to Lefferts, Ben demanded, "What rank does this man hold in your command?"

"None at all," said Lefferts.

"Well, then," Butler said, "I have nothing to do with him. And now I ask you again, will you march?"

While Lefferts pondered, the civilian adviser spoke up again. "What will you do," he asked Butler, "if the colonel refuses to march?"

"Well, sir," replied Butler, with the 7th's society background much in mind. "If he refuses to march, I will denounce him and his regiment as fit only to march down Broadway in gala dress to be grinned at by milliners' apprentices."

With this, the general summoned Lt. Col. Edward Hinks of the Massachusetts 8th.

"Colonel Hinks, take two companies of the 8th Regiment and march out two miles on the Elkton Railroad toward Washington," said Butler. "Hold it against all comers until I reinforce you, if necessary. Colonel Lefferts with his whole regiment is afraid to go, but you will obey orders."

The civilian adviser spoke up again. "Such language as that, General, requires reparation among officers and gentlemen."

"As far as Colonel Lefferts is concerned," Butler replied, "I shall be entirely satisfied with him if he shows a disposition to fight anywhere at all. But as for you, if you don't leave this room instantly, I'll direct my orderly to throw you out."

Lefferts and his friend left together, after which Butler, still simmering, joined Colonel Hinks and his two companies on their march. They paused at the railroad depot, securing all the buildings there. In one of them they found a small, rusty, dismantled locomotive engine, its parts strewn about so as to render it unusable. Turning to the Massachusetts men who were standing in line in front of the depot, Butler called out, "Do any of you know anything about a machine like this?"

Pvt. Charles Homans of Company E stepped forward and examined the locomotive. "That engine was made right in our shop back home," he said. "I guess I can fix her up and run her, all right."

Homans, assisted by a detail of skilled helpers, did exactly that. They found all the parts, cleaned them up, reassembled them, made a few adjustments, and soon the little engine was in running order. Meanwhile Colonel Hinks and the rest of the men, as ordered, moved two miles out on the track.

At sunrise Hinks was in position, the repaired engine had been fired up and run out on the tracks, and the New York 7th had concluded after all to join in the march, along with men of the Massachusetts 8th. Whatever the friction at the top, the men in the ranks were getting along just fine. The progress of the two regiments was not strictly a march, but rather a sustained work detail, since they had miles of railroad track to repair and replace as they made their way toward Washington. That the manicured gentlemen of the 7th were willing and able to raise blisters working alongside the commoners of the 8th, and, moreover, to accept instruction in basic track-laying, surprised and pleased the New Englanders. At the same time the New Yorkers gained new respect for the skills and determination of the men from the factories and fisheries of Massachusetts.

When the two regiments reached Washington at last, with additional troops following close behind them, it was the handsomely uniformed 7th, with its splendid band, that got the most public attention. The 7th, whose first rations for the journey from New York had been prepared at Delmonico's, continued to eat well. The companies marched for meals to the best Washington hotels, and they marched in style.

Their Massachusetts comrades were left to josh them, half admiringly, about the loss of their one thousand velvet-covered camp stools, part of the 7th's fancy field equipment that had to be left behind at Annapolis. General Butler, also amused, somehow never could find spare cargo space to forward those elegant stools to the capital. The 7th asked, but Ben just chuckled.

The 7th's service as a regiment was brief and bloodless. After a short stay in Washington, the regiment returned to New York. However, a large proportion of the 7th's gentleman rankers quickly won commissions and served with distinction in many of the new volunteer regiments that were forming in answer to Lincoln's call. Two of the rankers, as a matter of fact, joined Butler's staff. Pvts. Theodore Winthrop and Schuyler Hamilton, in their new assignments, became Major Winthrop and Colonel Hamilton, and Butler prized them highly. Lieutenant Colonel Hinks, who led those first two companies to begin the march from Annapolis, was destined to become a major general.

Butler had no sooner got rid of Colonel Lefferts than he was required to deal with another challenge to his authority as general in command. A Lieutenant Colonel Keyes showed up at Annapolis on his way back to Washington from New York. Keyes introduced himself as a member of Gen. Winfield Scott's staff and announced that, since he was a Regular-army man, he would assume command. At this point the 7th and 8th regiments were about a day's journey from Washington and Butler had not yet established communication with General Scott, so he determined to be patient.

Keyes at once set about issuing formal orders, labeling them "General Order No. 1," and so forth. He had reached General Order No. 4 by the time Butler was ready to deal with him. As soon as he got word that the rail link to Washington was open, Butler sent Colonel Hamilton to Washington to report to General Scott the whereabouts of his staff officer, Keyes, and to show him copies of those bombastic general orders. In the meantime Keyes continued to boss Butler around, while wily Ben bided his time and contained his anger.

Scott's written response, when it finally came, was a furious summons to Keyes to report to him in Washington at once and a promise to Butler that he'd take care of the upstart. "Keyes must be under the delusion he's a field marshal," Scott said.

Ben relished the scene that ensued.

Massachusetts Senator Henry Wilson was in Butler's office, talking with the general. Keyes arrived and rudely broke into the conversation, lecturing Ben on the qualifications of a good officer. Keyes, of course, was putting on a performance for the senator's benefit. He had taken to doing this kind of thing whenever there were others around as an audience.

Ben deliberately led him on, asking many questions in a great show of humility. Finally he dropped the hammer.

"Can you think of any other qualification to make a good officer, besides those you have described to me and the senator here?" he asked with a sweet, humble smile.

"No," replied Keyes, "I can't think of anything I need to add."

Butler's facial expression hardened, and his best courtroom voice cut like cold steel. "Well, Colonel, there *is* one thing more that's necessary."

Butler paused just one beat for effect, then he growled, "Brains, Colonel Keyes, brains! You don't have any, and you've bothered me here long enough. Here's your order from General Scott to report to him forthwith. If you're not on the next train I'll send you there under guard."

Shortly afterward, Scott issued an order formally creating a new military department, the Department of Annapolis, and placing Brig. Gen. B. F. Butler, Massachusetts Volunteers, in command. Butler continued sending troops and supplies forward on the vital line of communication he had opened to the capital.

Secure in Annapolis, Ben wired Sarah, "All well. How would you like to come on here and live with me?" To which Sarah wrote, "I would gladly go to you if you would not find me an incumbrance. Always yours, Sarah."

"I have a very excellent house here," Ben replied in a following note, "well furnished, a good corps of servants, and am keeping house. . . ."

In short order Sarah was presiding over Ben's well-furnished house, which soon became a hospitable stopping place for various members of the Butler and Hildreth families, as well as for political associates and Washington officials who flowed in and out of Annapolis on one errand and another.

Meanwhile he had to deal with political problems involving the vastly worried Governor Hicks, who was still trying to maintain an attitude of neutrality.

17

Governor Hicks was a Unionist at heart, and also a pacifist, and also a politician. Whatever occurred in other states, he proposed to keep Maryland in the Federal Union. As to those other states, the "wayward sisters," however they chose to go was their own concern, not Maryland's. The governor's problem was how to keep Maryland secessionists in check while refusing to take part in Lincoln's military preparations.

Hicks won general popular support for his policy of neutrality. If neutrality could have been achieved by vote, Marylanders probably would have voted it. But the governor's high-wire act failed to please the activists of either side. In fact, some of the more wild-eyed secessionists, centered mostly in Baltimore, soon took to threatening his life.

The pressures increased. After the Baltimore riot that bloodied the Massachusetts 6th, Hicks had bent to the storm. He approved decrees barring Federal troops from passing through Baltimore and backed those paper barriers with certain physical measures, including demolition of railroad bridges on lines linking the city to Philadelphia and Harrisburg. Nor did he balk at destruction of telegraph lines which Washington needed for communication with the Northern cities.

During all of this time Hicks had maneuvered to delay convening the state legislature, fearing with good reason that it might run wild and pass an ordinance of secession. Now, pressed hard, he finally summoned it to convene. But even with Ben Butler holding Annapolis and secessionists active in Baltimore, Hicks still managed to steer a middle course by choosing Frederick as the meeting place, a city where pro-Union sentiment, while quiet, nevertheless prevailed. The legislature there would be under no heady stimulus of the kind generated by Baltimore mobs.

The way Hicks maneuvered this showed how Butler and Hicks had come to understand each other. As a pair of practicing politicians, they both knew the delicate art of going through the motions. Thus Hicks wrote a letter to Butler, and Butler wrote a letter to Hicks. In his letter, Hicks formally protested Butler's seizure of the Annapolis & Elk Ridge Railroad, contending (for the record) that this would prevent Maryland lawmakers from reaching Annapolis for their session. Butler's letter, in smooth reply, suggested that the general would be absolutely delighted to vacate Annapolis one of these days, but in the meantime he needed that railroad to move his troops. This little epistolary minuet gave Hicks a most plausible excuse for calling the legislature to the compromise city of Frederick, and he quickly did so.

Meanwhile Butler's cooperation with Hicks, along with his dedication to law and order, got him in trouble back home, somewhat to his surprise. Upon landing at Annapolis he had been approached by the tremulous Hicks with information that inhabitants there were fleeing the city in fear of a slave insurrection, that nightmare which forever haunted the white populations of slave states. Butler at once announced that, if any such uprising should be attempted, he would instantly use his Massachusetts troops to suppress it.

When word of Butler's pledge reached Governor Andrew back in Boston, it created an uproar. Andrew promptly sent a cold reprimand. The Massachusetts governor declared that slave uprisings were simply to be considered as one of the enemy's military weaknesses "from the disastrous operations of which we are under no obligation to guard them." Abolitionist orators and editors roundly cheered Andrew for proclaiming this view and had scalding words for Butler.

Nevertheless Ben's reassuring response to Hicks had not only eased relations between the Yankee general and the Maryland governor, but had also calmed the populace. Panic at Annapolis was checked. Commerce resumed. And Butler's troops gained access to local sources of provisioning.

Butler cited all of these benefits in warm and wordy response to Andrew's reprimand. But he did not neglect to capture the high moral ground while he was about it. He told Governor Andrew in the loftiest terms that no troops under his command were ever going to wage war on women and children and that, moreover, they would never allow any other force—specifically, slaves in insurrection—to do so either.

While fending off high-level criticism from home, Butler was not diverted from energetic consideration of more immediate military measures. From long experience Butler knew railroads, and he also knew how to read a map. The major railroad junction at Manassas, Virginia, attracted his eye. It was clear from the map that Manassas Junction was an obvious marshaling point for rebel troops in any attack on Washington.

Manassas Junction had also caught the attention of Salmon P. Chase, Lincoln's treasury secretary. After conferring together, Butler and Chase took up the matter with General-in-Chief Scott. Butler urged Scott to dispatch six regiments to hold Manassas Junction, but the old Virginian refused to consider it. Chase pressed the matter with President Lincoln and the cabinet, but to no avail. Later, when the first big clash of the war occurred at Manassas, Confederates held that junction and Gen. Joseph E. Johnston's force of eleven thousand men was able to use one of those key connecting rail lines to reinforce General Beauregard. As a direct result of this mobility, the first Battle of Manassas, better known as Bull Run, became a Union disaster.

Though Butler had nothing to do with the Bull Run debacle, other than to urge measures that might well have prevented it, he had better luck with another maneuver that was also concerned with strategic control of rail traffic. The Washington branch of the Baltimore & Ohio Railroad joined the main line to Harpers Ferry at a point known as the Relay House, about eight miles from Baltimore. If this point were left undefended, rebel forces concentrating at Harpers Ferry would have quick and free railroad passage in any attack on Washington from that direction.

In conference with Scott, Butler said he could hold the Relay House with two regiments and a battery of field artillery. If a major threat to Washington occurred along that line of advance, he said, the position could easily be held while reinforcements were dispatched by rail from Washington. In this case the Union forces, not the rebels, would be in possession of the key rail routes.

Scott was unsure whether two regiments would provide sufficient strength, but he approved the plan and Butler carried it out immediately. Within twenty-four hours he had his artillery in place on a fortified height commanding the long railroad bridge that crossed the Patapsco River just below the Relay House, and he had his infantry encamped in support. The strong point was never relinquished.

While his military affairs prospered, Butler's political gavotte with Governor Hicks was proceeding nicely. At the Frederick session of the Maryland legislature, fire-breathing secessionists stopped well short of drastic action. The legislators contented themselves with castigating the Federal government for forcing war on the Confederacy. But they went on to proclaim loudly that Maryland would take no part in it. As a practical matter, cooler heads in Maryland's political and business leadership well knew that the state's economic welfare was totally dependent on commerce with the North. Their counsel prevailed.

For eight days Butler undertook personal direction of affairs at the Relay House strong point. He spent part of his time overseeing a program of drill and instruction, since he found his troops less than sharp in such basic matters as guard and picket duty. The rest of his time was spent trying to gather intelligence about conditions in Baltimore. Ben had some plans in mind for that city, remembering what had happened there to his favorite hometown regiment.

Informants straggled in every day with reports, none of which he trusted. He was told of large numbers of secessionists organizing in Baltimore and of huge stores of arms, ammunition, and supplies cached there. After several days of this, Butler decided to send in an undercover operative of his own; he detailed Capt. Peter Haggerty, one of his staff officers, to the mission. Haggerty, in plain clothes, snooped around in Baltimore for three days. When he returned he gave Butler a precise accounting of the military situation in the city. It confirmed Ben's suspicion that, however much noise the secessionists were making, Baltimore was his for the taking whenever he was ready to move. And he did intend to move.

Butler knew there was no chance that Washington would issue simple orders for him to capture Baltimore. He had in hand a letter in which General Scott outlined his own ponderous plan for a full-scale Baltimore expedition, to be undertaken someday when all the troops involved could be mustered, readied, and coordinated. Scott envisioned no fewer than four columns of three thousand men each, all converging on Baltimore from north, south, east, and west. As a map exercise it looked beautiful, but Ben privately thought that Scott's plan was ridiculous and he fully intended to ignore it.

Now General Ben turned to Lawyer Ben for counsel: how could he capture Baltimore within the authority he already had? Suspecting that Scott's reaction to a successful march might well be one of humiliation and rage, Butler thought it would be prudent if he were prepared to give a sound defense for his action. The vain and pompous old general in chief had scant tolerance for independent action on the part of subordinates, particularly those outside the close-knit family of the old Regular Army.

Butler did have in hand a few random and ambiguous communications from General Scott about seizing reported rebel supply caches in Baltimore. These even included information about a bakery said to be supplying bread to rebels at Harpers Ferry. But none of Scott's letters offered any suggestion as to how Butler was to seize supplies in Baltimore without actually going there to do it, nor did they even intimate that he should go there.

In the end Butler decided to undertake the mission on his own and, if necessary, argue the legalities with General Scott later. After all, Ben reasoned, Baltimore was within the military department he commanded, so action there should be clearly within the scope of his authority. To avoid being whistled off, however, he went about organizing his expedition in highest secrecy.

Butler assembled a train, with flatcars for the artillery. Knowing he was under constant observation by secessionist spies, he took care to make it look as though he was preparing to attack Harpers Ferry to the south. He and his staff particularly noticed that two young civilians riding light wagons behind fast trotting horses were watching every move. Butler left

Winfield Scott
The Great Rebellion

Gov. Thomas Hicks
Collection of the Maryland
Historical Society

them unmolested. He was counting on them to carry disinformation to Baltimore.

Since the rail line to Harpers Ferry climbed a steep grade, Butler even placed an extra locomotive as a pusher in the rear of his train so that all details would look right. Toward evening he started the train in the direction of Harpers Ferry, both engines chuffing away. The young men with the trotting horses promptly sped off toward Baltimore.

"Let 'em go," said Ben. "Their business is to report at Baltimore. They'll report that we have gone to Harpers Ferry, and that may cause their troops, if they have any, to go there too."

Two miles along the rail line Ben halted his train. He had a special detail for a company of men from the 6th Regiment. They were to go to Frederick and there arrest Ross Winans, an eccentric multimillionaire whose activities in behalf of the Confederacy were a scandal, so far as Butler was concerned. They were to take Winans to Butler's headquarters at Annapolis and hold him under guard.

Carrying the rest of the troops, the train then backtracked to the Relay House and proceeded north on the main line to Baltimore. Butler had planned the move so as to arrive in the city at sunset, at which time other rail traffic there would have ceased. At Baltimore he issued the men their first orders; both their destination and mission had been kept secret up to that time.

Butler meant to occupy Baltimore. Under darkening clouds his troops detrained at the station and formed up to march, the objective being the commanding heights of Federal Hill. No sooner had the march got under way when an especially violent thunderstorm broke. The troops were drenched. Heavy gusts all but blew them off their feet as they staggered forward in a blackness that was pierced only by the brilliant flashes of lightning that glimmered off their fixed bayonets. At the head of the column rode Butler, bent to the storm, his long cavalry boots slowly filling with water. The storm completely concealed the marching men. Nobody was about. Not even the Baltimore police had any inkling that a military force had landed in Baltimore and was proceeding to occupy Federal Hill.

When the column reached the base of the hill, Butler noticed a large wood yard and set troops to work gathering a supply of firewood. This served well on such a night—once in position on the hill, the men were able to get fires going against the wet and the chill and to brew up some coffee.

Butler quickly took possession of a German beer garden and tavern at the top of the hill and made himself comfortable in a room there, warmed by a roaring fire. Then he sat down to write a dispatch to the Federal commander at nearby Fort McHenry: "I have taken possession of Baltimore. My troops are on Federal Hill. If I am attacked tonight please open upon Monument Square with your mortars. I will keep the hill fully lighted with fires during the night so that you may know where we are and not hit us."

However, the night passed without alarm, except for a report that the hill had been mined with the intention of blowing Butler and his troops sky-high. Ben investigated personally and found that there was a mine under the hill, to be sure, but that it had been excavated peacefully at some time past, simply as a source of sand.

Butler returned to his room in the tavern. There the general, always a hearty trencherman, summoned up a supper of bacon and eggs, along with some very powerful Limburger cheese. He then busied himself preparing a proclamation of occupation, setting forth the rules and regulations he proposed to enforce. This he sent to be published in the Baltimore newspapers the following morning. Ben expected no trouble whatever from the citizens of Baltimore. But he was reasonably sure that he'd catch hell from Washington.

Butler felt great satisfaction at the outcome of his careful planning, including the efficient arrest of the rich secessionist, Winans. The prisoner, a rare old bird in his seventies, had made his millions as an inventor. Among other things he had perfected a patented axle bearing for railroad wheels, and he had also pioneered the use of eight wheels on railway cars. He had built the Baltimore & Ohio Railroad's first engine and operated, in Baltimore, the nation's largest railroad machine shop.

In his more recent activities, Winans had undertaken to manufacture some four thousand steel pikes with which he proposed to arm the rebels. He had also invented a kind of remote ancestor of the tank, a steam-propelled monster armed with a cannon of his own contriving, designed to fire one-ounce balls at the rate of five hundred per minute. He had hoped to put his steam cannon to the service of the Confederacy.

Butler's reaction to all this was simple: Ben proposed to hang him. However, what the happy general did not know was that Winans's millions bought him friends in high places. Arresting Winans was the easy part. Holding him, much less hanging him, was to prove impossible, no matter how flagrant his treason.

18

People in the North greeted word of Butler's march on Baltimore with fireworks and jubilation. For the moment at least, in the absence of any other decisive action to look to or any other hero to applaud, Butler was their man. In GHQ Washington, however, news of the coup brought mixed reviews. It sent Gen. Winfield Scott into a towering rage. But from the White House came signs of approval, if not enthusiasm. Thus at Baltimore there arrived for Butler a wild series of top-level orders which, in rapid sequence, reprimanded him, promoted him to major general, and relieved him of command. This more than suggested the confusion that existed as Lincoln, in his learning stage, tried to cope with intermingled political and military problems, not the least of which involved possible replacement of his weary old general in chief.

General Scott, at age seventy-five, was rather justified in viewing the war not only as a national tragedy but also as a damned personal annoyance. Up until the crisis Scott had been enjoying his highly ceremonial position as top general of a small and widely scattered army. There they were, all of Scott's unseen soldiers, most of them manning insignificant posts, garrisons, and forts, occasionally engaging in scattered skirmishes with hostile Indians, all happily far away.

When the break came it was suddenly evident that Scott's most significant accomplishment in office, ironically enough, had been the advancement of his fellow Southerners in their army careers. Available promotions and plum posts went to Southerners simply because he liked them better than Northerners. Young Northern officers had the choice of sticking around anchored in grade or else resigning their commissions, as many of them did. When war loomed, Scott tried to designate the very best of his good old boys to top command of the Union armies, but Col. Robert Edward Lee turned him down. Other Southern careerists Scott had favored likewise turned in their commissions and opted for Confederate gray. Scott soon found he had spent a couple of decades unwittingly providing the new Confederacy with a trained cadre of field-grade and general officers.

Scott had moved his headquarters to New York after losing his run for the presidency against Franklin Pierce in the election of 1852. New York, with its fine hotels and restaurants, was the most pleasant place this side of Paris for a man who found gourmet dining the greatest pleasure in life. Then came the great national imbroglio, ending his happy nonretirement and forcing his return to Washington, a city mostly under construction and practically under siege. There Scott took up his post, painfully hauling his huge three-hundred–pound bulk around, loyally shoring up the capital's defenses. Caution was his watchword. Anxiety was his constant state of mind. And now came this amateur, unauthorized, hare-brained adventure at Baltimore. It was enough to upset a man's digestion.

Scott fired off a hot message to Butler:

> Sir: Your hazardous occupation of Baltimore was made without my knowledge, and of course without my approbation. It is a godsend that it is without conflict of arms. It is also reported that you have sent a detachment to Frederick; but this is impossible. Not a word have I received from you as to either movement. Let me hear from you.

Butler, on his own high horse, refused to answer any communication addressed to him rudely as "Sir." He ignored the message and busied himself throughout the day happily raiding every hoard of rebel arms and supplies he could uncover. The booty included three thousand muskets found in one secret cache.

Next he got word from Washington that President Lincoln and the cabinet had decided to promote him to major general. Then, almost simultaneously, Baltimore now being secure for the passage of troops, Gen. George Cadwalader showed up at the head of three thousand Pennsylvanians. He carried an order from Scott relieving Butler of command and ordering him to get himself hence to Fortress Monroe in Virginia and assume command there.

Ben promptly left Baltimore, but not for the Virginia fortress. His commission as major general had been signed as of May 16, and he meant to pick it up in person at Washington, but only after he had a talk with Scott. The confrontation was stormy. When he reported to the general, he found the old man bristling with anger.

Ben marched in, tossed off a formal salute, and then found himself standing at attention like a recruit while Scott delivered an expert chewing-out that would have done credit to an old-line drill sergeant. Among other things, Scott deplored the risk Butler had taken and complained that his own safe and sane plans for the occupation of Baltimore had been upset by Ben's rash actions.

"You can be trusted with nothing in this army again," said Scott by way of summation.

But at this point Butler's own temper had reached the boiling point, and he was more than ready to tell Scott what he could do with his army. Never the soul of patience, Ben wound up and let fly an angry counterblast.

"I had orders from you to go and get arms which had been sent from rebel Virginia to arm the rebels of Baltimore," said Butler. "How did you think I was going to get them unless I went where they were?"

After a point-by-point defense of his actions, Ben burned all his bridges with his concluding farewell: "What was the use of my reporting to you? I have been before you several times before, and I doubt whether you would have kept awake long enough to listen to me. As you have no further command over me, good morning, General!"

Butler turned on his heel and marched out of Scott's office, back straight and head high. He made his way back to his quarters in the National Hotel, and in privacy there he finally gave in to nervous exhaustion, so thoroughly overwrought that he threw himself on a couch and wept. He had expected perhaps some form of reproof from pompous General Scott, but to be raked over the coals in such a fashion was a totally new experience. From hero to villain in a matter of hours was too much of a transition for fiery Ben.

When he had time to compose himself, he reported to Secretary of War Cameron. He told Cameron he had had enough of the army under General Scott and now proposed to go home and resume his law practice. Cameron, probably as Ben fully expected, was sympathetic and conciliatory. The secretary of war reminded his fellow Democrat that Scott had reached such a point of decrepitude that he could not remain in command much longer. Perhaps this was a hint intended to raise a glimmer of future glory in prospect for Butler, but Cameron offered nothing in concrete terms. He merely went on to argue strongly that a united North required a positive showing that prominent Democrats were in support of the Lincoln administration.

Later, Treasury Secretary Chase also urged Butler to calm down and accept his brand-new commission as major general. What the administration had in mind, said Chase, was to put him in command of an entire military department—the Department of Virginia and North Carolina—and not just the Fortress Monroe outpost.

After these reassurances Butler had no sooner simmered down than he got another peremptory "Sir" communication from Scott. It ordered him to Fortress Monroe "to assume command of the post." The old general added:

> Boldness in execution is always necessary, but in planning or fitting out expeditions or detachments, great circumspection is a virtue. In important cases, when time clearly permits, be sure to submit your

plans and ask instructions from higher authority. Communicate with me often and fully on all matters important to the service.

Butler blew up again. He wrote Cameron a hot letter once more threatening to quit and demanding that his quarrel with Scott be put before President Lincoln. "To be relieved of the command of a department and sent to command a fort, without a word of comment, is something unusual at least," Butler wrote. "And I am not so poor a soldier as not to understand it otherwise than in the light of a reproof."

Nevertheless, Butler reported for command at Fortress Monroe and there waited for clarification of his orders. After a couple of weeks of chafing, he finally wrote Scott, suggesting that perhaps through some clerical oversight orders creating the Department of Virginia and the Carolinas had not been published. He signed the letter, "Benj. F. Butler, Major-General Commanding," just in case Scott missed the point.

The entire matter was finally resolved in a face-to-face talk with President Lincoln, who proposed to present him personally with that commission as major general and urged him to accept it.

Butler still played hard to get.

"The withdrawal of myself and troops from Baltimore is a reproach upon me for what I have done," said Ben. "I came here in the hope of doing some good for the country, I have tried my best and have been successful, and yet I am brought to see that the Army is no place for me."

"Certainly, General, the administration has done everything to remove every thought of reproach upon you," said Lincoln. "I wish very much that you accept this commission."

Butler then said he'd like to talk it over first with Sarah before deciding what to do.

"Certainly," said Lincoln. "You cannot do a better thing."

Ben returned to his hotel, where Sarah was waiting to hear what had happened. After listening to Ben's account, she told him that, if he went home to Lowell, he'd probably fret at being sidelined and would be discontented. "Take the commission," she advised.

Thus heartened, Ben returned to Lincoln's office.

"I shall loyally support your administration as long as I hold your commission," he said. "And when I find any act that I cannot support, I shall bring the commission back at once and return it to you."

"That is frank, that is fair," said Lincoln. "But I want to add one thing. When you see me doing anything that for the good of the country ought not be done, come and tell me so, and why you think so, and then perhaps you will not have any chance to resign your commission."

On that note Benjamin F. Butler became the ranking major general in the army. Two days later General Scott issued clarifying orders creating the

Department of Virginia and North Carolina, Butler commanding. When Scott in conciliatory fashion handed over the envelope containing the revised orders he seized upon his favorite topic, food.

"General, you are very fortunate to be assigned to duty at Fortress Monroe," said Scott almost wistfully. "It is just the season for soft-shelled crabs, and hogfish have come in, and they are the most delicious pan fish you ever ate."

Butler went off reasonably content to Fortress Monroe, where Sarah was to join him. Only one thing still rankled, and that was his total defeat in the matter of the millionaire secessionist Ross Winans. Butler had proposed to make a spectacular example of Winans, but that wily old rebel had resources and influence far beyond Butler's power to negate. For one thing, he knew what buttons to push in Washington.

When Butler's men placed him under arrest, Winans promptly called on the services of the renowned Baltimore attorney Reverdy Johnson. He did not propose to have Johnson represent him in any treason trial, because he did not intend that there should ever be a trial, for treason or anything else. Reverdy Johnson was one of those lawyers possessing that saleable asset known as access. He had access, notably enough, to Abe Lincoln, among many others in powerful places, and Winans expected him to use it.

Johnson himself was at best a Maryland neutralist, but Butler considered him an outright secessionist, the worse for being a secret one. Some justification for Butler's view was to be found in an earlier incident involving Johnson and Lincoln. Johnson had gone directly to the president and asked him for personal assurance that he did not intend aggressive action against the South. Lincoln put it in writing: "I do say the sole purpose of bringing troops here [to Washington] is to defend the capital. I do say I have no purpose to invade Virginia with them or any other troops." Lincoln's letter added, in effect, that it was up to Virginia whether there would be a clash of arms.

The letter was given to Johnson under his solemn promise that it would be held completely confidential. Yet in a matter of days the critically important substance of Lincoln's letter was in the hands of Jefferson Davis. If the South needed time to arm, here was reliable promise of all the time the South required, direct from Lincoln, in the form of a written pledge to Reverdy Johnson.

In the Winans matter Johnson went directly to Lincoln and asked that Winans be released at once. Lincoln promptly referred the matter to Secretary of State Seward, the jack-of-all-trades in the cabinet, who immediately issued an order turning Winans loose. It was all done smoothly, with a minimum of fuss other than a few hot telegrams from Butler protesting the action. Unofficially, Butler fumed that Winans's $15 million fortune was speaking louder than words.

Reverdy Johnson
Collection of the Maryland
Historical Society

Ross Winans
Collection of the Maryland
Historical Society

As matters turned out, neither Winans's factory-made pikes nor his rapid-firing steam cannon ever did the Confederacy any good. Butler shipped the Winans cannon north for tests by Yankee ordnance experts, who found it totally useless. The time for an armored, self-propelled, cannon-firing vehicle had not yet arrived. As for Winans's other contribution to Confederate arms, the time for the military use of pikes was long past.

In a conversation recorded by Navy Secretary Gideon Welles in his remarkably detailed diary, Butler told Welles he had fully intended to hang Winans in Monument Square, on the theory that public execution of a multimillionaire would make it particularly clear that treason would not be tolerated. If he had remained in command at Baltimore, Butler said, he would simply have ignored Seward's release order, considering the secretary of state to be out of the chain of command.

Curiously enough, after Butler's hasty recall and reassignment, his concept of search, seizure, and summary arrest immediately became national policy. Seward's stroke of the pen quickly released the rich Mr. Winans, but arrests of less affluent secessionists in Baltimore were carried out at once by Butler's successor, General Cadwalader. And this time they had the full approval of President Lincoln, who suspended the right of habeas corpus provided in the Constitution.

Thereafter access of the sort enjoyed by Lawyer Johnson would prove to be much more powerful than mere court rulings, even if the judge making those rulings was the chief justice of the Supreme Court of the United States.

The arrest of John Merryman, a Maryland landowner and secessionist, provided the test case in the matter of habeas corpus. Merryman had taken part in burning railroad bridges and destroying telegraph lines. Cadwalader sent a squad of soldiers who plucked Merryman from his bed at 2:00 in the morning of May 25 and lodged him in the guardhouse at Fort McHenry. Butler himself could not have staged the arrest more dramatically.

At that time justices of the Supreme Court also presided over federal district courts, and in this case the justice presiding was no less a figure than Roger B. Taney, he of the famous Dred Scott decision. Lawyers for Merryman promptly appeared before Taney and asked that he issue a writ of habeas corpus to spring their client from the military jail. Taney issued the writ. General Cadwalader ignored it. Taney issued another writ, which held the general in contempt of court. The general declined to receive it. Taney then issued a formal opinion that the president could not suspend the writ of habeas corpus nor authorize any military officer to do so. But he added that as a practical matter issuing writs was all he could do, since the court was up against unyielding superior force.

President Lincoln didn't get around to rejecting Taney's opinion until the following Fourth of July, when in a message to Congress he formalized suspension of habeas corpus as a war measure. Meanwhile, much as Butler would have done, the military proceeded to round up many Baltimore secessionists, including the mayor and the chief of police. However, Cadwalader did stop short of hanging any of them.

Butler, probably with some satisfaction, viewed all this from his new post at Fortress Monroe, where he found much to do and very little to do it with.

19

The geographical scope of Butler's command at Fortress Monroe was impressive, at least on paper. In official fantasy, his military department included both Virginia and North Carolina. In reality, he commanded no more than the fine old waterfront fort southeast of Richmond, plus a lot of acreage around it. Though Ben's subsequent orders from Washington more than suggested that he just hold fast in his castle and not go adventuring, he went to his new command in earnest expectation of commanding major operations.

Butler's new post was an important one. Fortress Monroe was designed to dominate the entrance to Hampton Roads, thus also controlling access to the James River, whose winding but navigable course led to the Confederate capital. As a game piece on the war board, therefore, Fortress Monroe was of special value. So long as this stronghold was in Union hands, Richmond could never be secure. From Monroe as a base, an army could advance directly on Richmond, only eighty-five miles away. If combined army-navy operations were to clear the James, the river could provide a parallel line of advance, as could the York, just north.

Strategic importance of the point of land occupied by Fortress Monroe had been recognized since Colonial times. Its military history dated as far back as 1609, when the English first fortified the site. Also, by curious coincidence, it was to this point that the English in 1619 brought the first black slaves to America. From that far, faint beginning, the North-South conflict would come full circle to this same place when, at the war's end, Fortress Monroe would become a prison for Jefferson Davis, leader of the Lost Cause.

Before taking command at Monroe, Butler thought to wind up his business affairs back in Massachusetts. He wrote a somewhat moody letter to his law partner, William P. Webster:

> You will see that I have accepted a Major Gen'l. position for the war. I am to go to Virginia to prosecute the war vigorously into the heart of the enemy. God only knows what will be the result. I am in His hands. I speak with reverence.

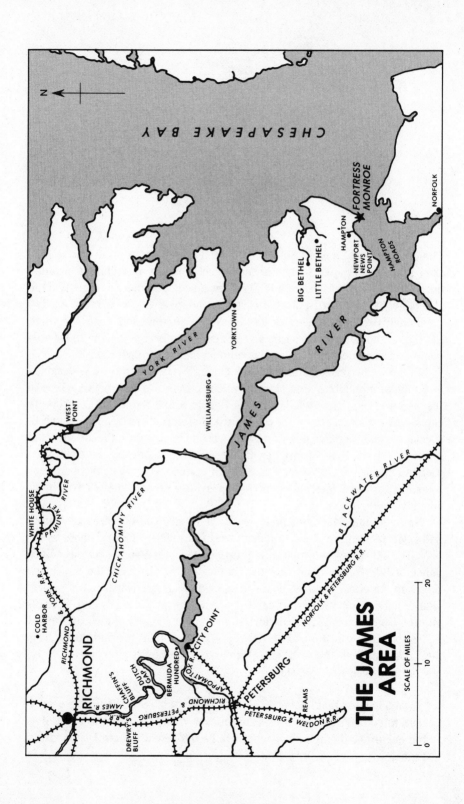

THE JAMES AREA

SCALE OF MILES

0   10   20

CHESAPEAKE BAY

NORFOLK

FORTRESS MONROE

HAMPTON ROADS

HAMPTON

NEWPORT NEWS POINT

LITTLE BETHEL

BIG BETHEL

YORKTOWN

YORK RIVER

JAMES RIVER

WILLIAMSBURG

WEST POINT

PAMUNKEY RIVER

WHITE HOUSE

CHICKAHOMINY RIVER

COLD HARBOR

RICHMOND & YORK R.R.

RICHMOND

DREWRY'S BLUFF

CHAFFIN'S BLUFF

DUTCH GAP

BERMUDA HUNDRED

JAMES R.

YORK R.R.

CITY POINT

APPOMATTOX RIVER

RICHMOND & PETERSBURG R.R.

REAMS

PETERSBURG

PETERSBURG & WELDON R.R.

BLACKWATER RIVER

NORFOLK & PETERSBURG R.R.

N

Meantime there is an end to all professional business on my part. Wind up, therefore, our affairs. Save for me what you can. I shall be ruined, I know, but that can't be helped. You will, I know, do this with that scrupulous regard to right and fair dealing that has always characterized your dealings with me. Get as large amounts of money as you can and put to credit for me. I shall need it all. I have, however, a great relief in knowing that you are at home to take care of my interests. . . .

In regard to the papers of my property, they will substantially be found in two paper boxes at the house if you need them. All in those boxes are open for examination. *None* others of my private papers . . .

Love to all, and God bless you! If anything happens, you and Fisher [Hildreth] will take care of those I leave.

When Butler arrived at the sixty-five–acre fort, he found it to be a comfortable Regular Army post only somewhat gone to seed. One of its better features was the commanding general's handsome headquarters building, with its high ceilings and broad verandas. But there were many problems to be solved, some of them serious. Most immediately, the fort had no water supply to speak of. In easy peacetime a four-hundred–man garrison had depended on rainwater captured in cisterns, and in dry seasons even that had been known to fail. Now Butler had to provide for artillerymen of the old Regular Army, the better part of two Massachusetts regiments, plus a complete Vermont regiment, with nine more regiments from New York on their way.

Although obviously a great deal of hauling would have to be done just to move supplies, the post had no transport animals other than one small, lonesome mule. Monroe's mule, as Butler reported it, "was the only four-footed animal I found there besides the cats." As senior quadruped, the mule was assigned to sanitary duty, hauling night soil for disposal in the sea. The cats, presumably, were delegated to varmint patrol.

Structurally the fort was sound, but the wide saltwater moat that surrounded it needed attention for a rather curious reason. Delicious oysters were plentiful in the area and had been a welcome supplement to army rations. Men assigned there over the years had been in the habit of tossing the shells into the moat. Many of the discards contained live oysters, and those survivors had set up housekeeping in the hospitable moat, where they had multiplied to such an extent that oyster beds actually blocked the free flow of water.

Another weak spot in the defensive works was the siting of the magazines. These had been designed only to withstand bombardment from the sea, since the possibility of heavy assault from the land seemed remote. As a result, the magazines were open to plunging fire from rebel mortars, should the enemy approach near enough to close the range. So Butler, noticing the flaw, at once set about sandbagging the magazine entrances. Whatever else may have been lacking at Fortress Monroe, there was no shortage of sand.

Since there was obviously no room inside the walls to house the regiments Scott was assigning to Butler's command, campsites had to be found for them. The encampments required dry ground; a water source; and provision for regular supply from the fort, which in turn had to be supplied from the sea. The task ahead was one for a man with a genius for organization, and Ben Butler was just such a man.

Butler established two camps, each with adequate groundwater for wells. For the fort itself it was later found necessary to bring water by ship all the way from Baltimore. In addition, Ben constructed a coal-fired distillation plant to render seawater drinkable.

Finding that supplies brought by water to the wharves had to be muscled by hand nearly a mile across sand to reach the fort, Butler decided he would build a railroad, using ties, rails, and rolling stock Federal troops had captured at Alexandria. He was particularly inspired to this decision by a task Washington had set out for him. The high command had decided to ship him the largest cannon yet made, for testing and experimentation. The monster weighed some twenty-six tons, and getting it from the beach to the ramparts over shifting sand was clearly no job for muscle alone.

The post engineer, an elderly colonel, washed his hands of Butler's railroad project, contending flatly that it couldn't be done—not over sand. But Ben enlisted the help of an expert from the Pennsylvania Railroad, and in a matter of days the rails were in place, providing a main line to the fort, with branches to the magazines and ramparts. The big gun was readily hauled along the rails, as were all subsequent supplies and equipment arriving by sea.

Meanwhile Butler occupied himself with two other important matters— one purely military, the other involving politics and the law and high national policy. In his military move, Butler dispatched a force of two thousand to seize and occupy the commanding bluff at Newport News, ensuring safe anchorage in the James for United States naval vessels. This was viewed with some satisfaction in Washington.

But it was the legal coup that brought him new fame throughout the North. Lawyer Ben, as it turned out, was the first to promulgate a workable basis for dealing humanely with the problem of runaway slaves, even though the notorious Fugitive Slave Act was still in effect. Later it would be seen that Butler had both anticipated and inspired Lincoln's Emancipation Proclamation, but at this time the president was still holding to his opinion that simple emancipation would be financially unfair to slave owners. Lincoln's view, often expressed, was that somehow the blacks must be bought and deported, and he constantly explored one colonization scheme and another. One such plan would have extended the period for gradual emancipation and colonization all the way into the twentieth century.

Much more immediately, the legal problem posed for Butler arose when three fugitive slaves belonging to a Confederate colonel, C. K. Mallory, made their way by boat to Fortress Monroe. They told Butler they had been laboring on earthworks where the Confederates were emplacing a battery. They had heard that Mallory intended to take all of his slaves to Florida and, not wanting any part of that move, they had decided to escape into Federal lines. After listening to their story Butler ordered up a meal for the three and put them to work around the fort.

Next day Confederate Major M. B. Carey appeared at the Federal picket line, carrying a flag of truce and asking permission to see Butler at the fort. Butler, for security reasons, refused to let Carey into the fort but agreed to meet him at the picket line. As it happened, Carey and Butler had met before, in the Charleston convention of dissident Democrats. Now their parley was conducted on horseback, in a leisurely ride along the sandy trails.

Carey began the discussion by asking whether Virginia families wishing to go north out of the war zone would be allowed to pass through the sea blockade. Butler replied that this would be impractical, since outgoing vessels would have to be searched, causing no end of time wasting. However, families traveling north by land routes could do so freely, Butler said.

At this point Carey got to the real reason for his visit. The night before, Colonel Mallory had come to Carey's headquarters and asked him to recover the Mallory slaves. Now Carey broached that subject and Lawyer Ben addressed himself to the case.

"I am informed that three Negroes belonging to Colonel Mallory have escaped within your lines," Carey said. "What do you mean to do with them?"

"I intend to hold them," said Butler.

"Do you mean to set aside your constitutional obligation to return them?" demanded Carey, citing the Fugitive Slave Act and the Dred Scott decision.

"I mean to take Virginia at her word, as declared in the ordinance of secession passed yesterday," Butler replied. "I am under no constitutional obligations to a foreign country, which Virginia now claims to be."

"But you say we cannot secede," argued Carey, "and so you cannot consistently detain those Negroes."

"But you say you have seceded, so you cannot consistently claim them," said Ben. "I shall hold these Negroes as contraband of war, since they were engaged in the construction of your battery and are claimed as your property."

And sardonic Ben added, "If Colonel Mallory will come into the fort and take the oath of allegiance to the United States he shall have his Negroes, and I will try to hire them from him."

That closed the parley. Butler had invented the stratagem and coined the phrase that was effectively to free many thousands of slaves: *contraband of war.* The words echoed North and South. In the North heretofore frustrated abolitionists seized on the phrase with enthusiasm as a device that cleanly cut through all the tangled legalities. In the South, to the rage of slave owners, Butler's words showed slaves a path to freedom. Thereafter, escaped slaves were slaves no longer. They were "contrabands," and many eagerly identified themselves as such whenever they succeeded in reaching Federal territory. It was only a step toward full emancipation, but at that time—when other Northern generals were still routinely returning fugitive slaves to their masters—it was a long one.

As word of Butler's "contraband" edict spread, hundreds of runaways made their way to Federal lines at Fortress Monroe. Within a couple of months Butler was sheltering nearly one thousand fugitives—men, women, and children. The influx was such that Ben appointed a Commissioner of Negro Affairs to deal with it. It was the commissioner's job to sort out the newcomers, enter their names in a kind of census record, classify them for suitable employment, and generally look after their needs.

Meanwhile, probably recalling how General Scott had reacted to his last independent decision, Butler pressed GHQ for a clear directive covering the matter of the contrabands. But the response he got from War Secretary Cameron was anything but definitive. It did not instruct him to do anything differently in regard to sheltering the fugitives; it merely directed that Butler keep accurate records.

Still pressing the point, Butler wrote Cameron asking for an official clarification of the legal status of his contrabands.

"Are these men, women, and children slaves?" Butler asked. "Are they free?"

If these people were to be considered property, Ben continued, and as property had been confiscated by the Federal government, what now was their status? "We do not need and will not hold such property," said Butler. "Have not, therefore, all proprietary relations ceased?"

Lawyer Ben was putting the clear proposition to the Lincoln administration: If the Federal government did not want to become an owner of slaves, then it must consider all these fugitives to be slaves no longer, but free.

Lincoln continued to temporize. In the absence of any action by the administration, a restless but cautious Congress approached the matter only slightly less gingerly. A vaguely worded bill was passed authorizing confiscation of any slaves who had been directly employed in the service of the Confederate army. But whether such "confiscated" slaves were then free, Congress did not say; the proposition posed by Butler was left unanswered.

And while it remained unanswered, Ben kept to his own course, guided by his own counsel, secure in the knowledge that in this matter, at least, nobody at GHQ was likely to interfere.

During all the flap over contrabands, Butler continued to press General Scott for supplies, equipment, artillery, and horses. He needed tents and camp equipment. He needed wagons. Most especially he needed horses. Impatient with delays, Ben finally sent his brother Andrew to Washington to stir things up. He also sent home to Lowell for nine of his own horses.

Andrew got permission from the authorities to buy some horses in Baltimore, where he rounded up 125 sound animals and purchased them for shipment to Fortress Monroe. However, Andrew had not counted on the taking ways of the burgeoning bureaucracy. Somebody somewhere signed some papers, and Andrew's horses wound up in Washington, never to be seen at Butler's post. The nine horses sent from Butler's home in Massachusetts were the only ones that did arrive safely.

Life at headquarters, military problems aside, took on a homey touch, thanks to the presence of Sarah. Writing to her sister Harriet, who was minding things at home in Lowell for the Butlers, Sarah reported:

> The house here is full of company all the time. Fourteen at table every meal, and, often more than that number. To-day the Secretary of War was expected, but did not come. Several people from Boston are here, Mr. Odeon, Green, Kinsman, and a Unitarian minister by the name of Hepworth. No place to escape but to our own rooms.
>
> The beach here is one of the finest I ever saw. It is very long, very smooth, and the surf rolls in splendidly. We have not had time yet to bathe. We have a horse and carryall, but cannot drive to any great distance. The most agreeable thing is to drive to the Beach, and look at the green and foamy waves as they roll in and break to pieces. Just now there is a little thunder storm. It is very welcome. The ground is as dry as ashes . . .

General Butler continued, in growing despair, to press General Scott for supplies and equipment, and especially for horses. The lack of horses for cavalry reconnaissance and for hauling field artillery was to have some bearing on a defeat suffered by Butler's troops in a minor skirmish that took place shortly afterward at a place called Big Bethel.

20

It fell to General Ben Butler to preside over the Union's first combat setback of the Civil War. The clash occurred at a Virginia crossroads named for Big Bethel, the larger of two churches in the vicinity. Big Bethel, thirteen miles from Yorktown, served a white congregation; close by was Little Bethel, a church attended by blacks. Nothing of any real importance had ever happened at Big Bethel until Confederate and Federal forces met there in a confused and amateurish brawl on the morning of June 10, 1861. But since serious land warfare had not yet begun, the skirmish at Big Bethel was a clash great enough to become headline news North and South, make a Confederate hero of Col. John Bankhead Magruder, and nearly cost Butler his Senate confirmation as major general.

For all its tragedy—men died there, after all—the "battle" of Big Bethel was not without its elements of the bizarre. Seen less solemnly, the Federal attack might be viewed as the stuff of slapstick. And on the opposing side the Confederate commander, widely known as Prince John Magruder, provided his own comic touch. Magruder was an unbridled romantic whose sheer flamboyance was an ongoing exercise in self-caricature. His play-by-play dispatches to Richmond, sent by relays of riders, would have done justice to combat on the scale of Waterloo.

Prince John, despite a remarkable lisp, was an avid amateur thespian, and indeed his theatrical talents were to serve him well in the opening stages of the war. The diarist Mary Chesnut would record a sly little teatime social note: "Dr. Berrien shows us how Magruder lisps and swears at the same time. And the combination leads to comical results. 'Chawge—and chawge fuwiously.' "

In the peacetime army, West Pointer Magruder had been commanding officer at Fort Adams in Newport, Rhode Island, where he was famous for the pomp and glitter of the dress reviews he loved to stage, the lavish dinners at which he presided, and the heavy ham content of his amateur theatricals. Eccentricities aside, Magruder had served well in the Mexican war and afterward achieved reputation as an artillery expert. At the break

John B. Magruder
Battles and Leaders of the Civil War

Gustavus V. Fox
Battles and Leaders of the Civil War

between North and South, he was in command of a battery defending Washington. Until the very last moment, as Prince John assessed his options, it was uncertain to which cause he would lend his talents.

When he finally joined the Confederate forces, the flamboyant Magruder remained in character. "Give me five thousand men," he demanded of the Confederate cabinet, "and if I don't take Washington you may take not only my sword but my life!" But just earlier than this he had made an equally melodramatic speech to none other than President Abraham Lincoln.

When he was told of Magruder's defection, Lincoln was taken aback. "Why, only three days ago Magruder came voluntarily to me in this room," said the astonished president, "and with his own lips and in my presence repeated over and over again his asseverations and protestations of loyalty and fidelity."

Now, in the spring of 1861, Magruder was a freshly minted Confederate colonel with a new costume and a new role to play. He had in hand the defense of Yorktown, which was subject to attack from Butler's position at Fortress Monroe, should Washington ever supply Ben with the means. Since the Federals already commanded the mouth of the James, similar control over access to the York River would further threaten the Confederate capital at Richmond—as Butler continued to remind General Scott, but to no effect whatever. Butler was on the old courtier's hate list; after Baltimore, Scott meant to see that the New Englander never again achieved such an upsetting success. In effect, the posturing Magruder had a strong ally in Washington.

Installed at Yorktown, Magruder at once began an incessant demand for reinforcements, to the point where his long daily reports to Richmond GHQ came to be met there with a chorus of satirical groans. But he did get help. Troops sent to him notably included the newly arrived 1st North Carolina Volunteers, eleven hundred well-trained men commanded by the West Pointer Daniel Harvey Hill. Magruder promptly stationed Hill's regiment and some supporting troops, along with a battery of artillery, in rough field fortifications at Big Bethel.

It was this fortified position that Butler proposed to attack, after first having ordered a careful reconnaissance of the terrain. In making his preparations Butler had the dubious benefit of intelligence supplied by incoming contrabands, which, after discounting exaggerated numbers by 60 to 70 percent, gave him a rough estimate of rebel strength.

Butler's written order for the attack was scarcely a model of military precision, but generally it called for the converging of two regiments, one from Newport News, the other from Hampton. The regiments were to wipe out any outpost at Little Bethel and then go on to overwhelm the Big Bethel field fortifications, capture the guns there, and bag as many of the defenders as possible. The troops were to advance by night and attack either before first light or in early dawn. Both the Bethels were to be destroyed, after which the Federal troops were to withdraw. It was to be more of a raid than a serious advance.

The ranking officer under Butler—Brig. Gen. Ebenezer W. Pierce, one of Governor Andrew's appointees—was assigned to command the attack. He decided to take four regiments rather than two, although Butler's order had suggested that perhaps even two regiments were more than enough and that maybe a lesser force would be easier to handle.

Things began to unravel before the troops even reached their first objective, Little Bethel. As two converging regiments neared each other, one of the regimental commanders mistook mounted officers of the other regiment for rebel cavalry and opened fire. Before order was restored one man had been killed and twenty-seven wounded in the regiment that was fired upon. All chance of surprise was lost in the uproar.

After this mess was straightened out, Little Bethel fell without incident, since the Confederate picket detachment there had abandoned it and fallen back to the main line of resistance at Big Bethel as soon as the firing began. Pushing forward, one Federal artillery officer got his guns in action against the Confederate battery, but he remained unsupported by the infantry, whose officers had decided to hold a council of war before proceeding further.

The council flinched at the notion of a direct attack and decided to try an enveloping maneuver, left and right around the Confederate position. However, one wing of the attacking force fell into confusion, its commander mistaking some of his own troops up ahead for Confederates and ordering an immediate retreat. Meanwhile Maj. Theodore Winthrop, one of Butler's staff officers, was trying vainly to untangle the muddle. When he stood up on a fallen log to get a better view, Winthrop was shot by a Confederate rifleman and instantly killed. All the Federal troops by this time had fallen back without waiting for orders.

At this point General Pierce called for another council of war, whose decision was to give up the whole enterprise and head back to camp. A few volunteers stayed behind long enough to pick up the wounded and load them in wagons, which they then dragged some nine miles back to safety. The attacking Federals had sustained a total of seventy-six casualties, many of which they had inflicted on each other. About fourteen hundred entrenched rebels had driven off a Union force of forty-four hundred at a cost to themselves of eleven casualties. The full weight of the Union numbers, of course, had never been employed, since troops had either been fed piecemeal into the fray or not advanced at all.

Richmond editors called upon their most dramatic and pious superlatives to describe the victory at Big Bethel, seeing in it clearly the workings of the hand of God. So did the commanders, Magruder and Hill. Within a week, Magruder was a brigadier general on the strength of his new fame. Within a month, Hill was also promoted to brigadier.

The Northern press called upon equally poetic powers of hyperbole, mostly to castigate Ben Butler as the author of disaster. The rebel position at Big Bethel was pictured in terms ordinarily reserved to describe an impregnable fort. One newspaper editor declared that Butler had been mad to send troops against "a rampart thirty feet high." In point of fact the rude fieldworks at Big Bethel were so low that cannon wheels had to be dug in to sink the Confederate guns to parapet level. But editors, far from the fray, had to imagine details their scant information lacked.

Butler's popularity as author of the slave-freeing contrabands order suddenly evaporated. In the Senate, where his appointment as major general was up for confirmation, Butler narrowly escaped the wrath of the lawmakers. His political friends managed to rally just enough support to save him his commission.

The ill-concealed feud between General Scott and General Butler meanwhile continued. Butler peppered Scott's headquarters with formally worded but urgent pleas for men and equipment; Scott, with equal formality, saw to it that Butler got neither. It had become clear that Butler would be allowed to accomplish nothing so long as Scott remained as general-in-chief, so Ben did not hesitate to call on his friends to apply pressure for Scott's retirement.

Postmaster-General Blair, for one, used every opportunity to demand of Lincoln that Scott be replaced, and he urged his fellow cabinet members to join him in pressing Lincoln to act. In a typical memo to War Secretary Cameron, Blair wrote:

> I cannot understand why Butler is kept with such reduced forces. I had hoped ere this that he would have twenty thousand men under his command, supplied with Artillery, transportation and Cavalry to make a march upon Richmond. Instead of which, from the latest information I have been able to obtain, he has not one half of that force, no means of transportation, is totally without Cavalry forces, and has very little artillery.
>
> With such means, of course, so far from being able to effect anything, he must, I think, within a short time, be pent up within the walls of the Fort, unless the Secretary of War takes the matter within his own hands and gives him the means of effective service. My want of confidence in the enterprise of the General-in-Chief is no secret to you; and this is not the first time I have counselled you to take these matters into your own charge, seeing that you had the responsibility.

This blast from an old West Pointer like Blair was not to be taken lightly. But Scott continued to rely on Lincoln's support, and stubbornly remained in his post. As best Blair could explain it, Lincoln, as a former Whig, was naturally supportive of Scott, who had been the Whig candidate for president when Lincoln was a relatively obscure politician.

Soon enough, in any case, the defeat of Butler's troops at Big Bethel was all but forgotten. Editors and lawmakers had a genuine disaster to contemplate when on July 21 the first Battle of Manassas, or Bull Run, ended in a total rout of thirty-five thousand Federals.

On the very day of the Bull Run disaster, Butler finally received some of the horses and artillery for which he had been begging ever since taking command at Fortress Monroe. However, it was still quite clear that General Scott intended to see that they didn't do Butler much good. In fairly rapid sequence Scott stripped Butler's command of troops to reinforce Baltimore, which didn't need reinforcing, and then assigned the aged and infirm Brig. Gen. John Ellis Wool to supersede Butler as department commander in Virginia.

Wool, seventy-seven, had begun his army career by serving with distinction in the War of 1812. Like Scott, Wool was a Regular, hence Scott considered him a good choice to keep a tight rein on Butler, the troublesome amateur. Also, some of the more vocal Northern newspapers had been pressing the administration to find useful employment for Wool, whose reputation was of high order at a time when talent in the Union army seemed scarce. Scott's instructions let Butler retain command of five infantry regiments and certain other troops, but the implication was clear that Wool was not to permit him to do much of anything with them.

Butler's influential friends in Washington were quick to point out the slight implicit in Wool's appointment, but Ben professed to be unperturbed.

"Wool doesn't like Scott any more than Scott likes me," he reassured them.

As Butler summed up the situation, all that the elderly and easygoing Wool really wanted was a comfortable berth at Fortress Monroe, with somebody else to do all the work. Conversely, Ben said, for his part he wanted to do all the work and have Wool take the responsibility. The arrangement, he protested perhaps a bit too strongly, was perfect.

Ben, as it happened, was indeed considering an adventure. He had been gathering information about the Confederate forts guarding Hatteras Inlet, the only deep-water channel through the barrier islands along the North Carolina coast. With Hampton Roads barred by Fortress Monroe and the blockading fleet, Hatteras Inlet was Richmond's remaining passage to the sea. Blockade-runners were making free use of it, carrying supplies in to the Confederates and rich cargoes outward bound. The U.S. Navy, Butler had been quietly informed, was planning an amphibious operation against the forts and was more than eager to provide both troop transport and heavy firepower. Butler meant to command the troops.

To reassure Wool that all was quiet on the Peninsula, Ben sent up an observation balloon to reconnoiter Magruder's activities. Butler's enthusiasm for innovation had led him earlier to hire the noted balloonist John La Mountain, who then set up his equipment at Fortress Monroe. La Mountain had even suggested that his huge balloons might well be used for bombing raids over enemy lines, but when Ben forwarded the proposal to General Scott it was met with profound silence. Nevertheless, La Mountain continued to provide Butler with regular reports on rebel activity. On this occasion Butler's aerial observer found the rebels in a defensive posture at Bethel and Yorktown. Butler was able to assure Wool that he would not be disturbed by any rebel attack and therefore could easily spare the few men needed for the Hatteras expedition.

Wool, who seemed to have taken a liking to Butler, readily approved the plan. In a soldierly order he detailed 860 infantry troops to the enterprise, along with an artillery company, and set forth the details of their provisioning with rations, water, and ammunition. Major General Butler was assigned to command. The order was issued on August 25 and was to be executed by 10:00 A.M. on the following day.

The naval force, consisting of seven warships and two transports, was under the command of Commodore Silas Stringham of the Atlantic Squadron. In the plan of attack, the heavy guns of the task force were to bombard the forts while Butler's troops landed and mounted an assault from the rear.

The flotilla got off promptly, arriving at Hatteras in the midafternoon of August 26. Butler, aboard the *Harriet Lane*, directed the first landing and succeeded in getting 345 men ashore before high winds and a heavy surf swamped the boats. But the troops were scarcely needed, since the navy's big guns accomplished just about all that was necessary to quell resistance. The ships' rifled armament outranged the smooth-bore cannon of the forts, so the fleet had only to stand off and fire away. After very little of this, resistance wavered.

When a white flag appeared over the ramparts, Butler sent a lieutenant ashore to meet with the commander of Fort Hatteras. The lieutenant returned to Butler with a formally written message: "Flag-Officer Samuel Barron, C.S. Navy, offers to surrender Fort Hatteras, with all arms and munitions of war; the officers to be allowed to go out with side arms and the men without arms to retire."

As an interesting sidelight to this affair, Flag-Officer Barron, as a United States officer a short time before, was the very man Seward and Commander Porter, at the time of their Fort Sumter conspiracy, had attempted to install as the de facto head of the United States Navy.

Butler rejected Barron's proposal out of hand, demanding unconditional surrender, with both officers and men to become prisoners of war. The Confederate commander took nearly an hour to consider this, and it was an anxious hour for Butler because in the meantime one of his transports and the *Harriet Lane* had both gone aground and were under the guns of the fort. To Butler's great relief, the Confederates finally decided to surrender without further hostilities.

Ben's report cataloged the results in some detail. The expedition had captured the forts, which with supporting sea power could be held by small Federal garrisons indefinitely. Some seven hundred prisoners had been taken, along with 1,000 rifles, thirty cannon, a brig loaded with cotton, a sloop loaded with provisions and supplies, two light boats, an unladen schooner—and 150 bags of coffee. Now sea-lane communications from Norfolk to Beaufort, South Carolina, were in Federal control. It was a bleak day for blockade-runners and for the defenders of Richmond.

Under what Butler termed "the wonderful stupidity of Washington," he had been given orders to sink two sand-laden vessels in Hatteras Inlet, thus blocking the channel. Ben chose to disobey those orders. He had a notion that an open channel, properly guarded, would be a priceless asset to Federal forces in the future. He took this action with some apprehension, however, and decided he had better make haste to Washington to explain it personally and rally support, lest he land in more trouble with Scott. While Commodore Stringham remained behind to consolidate the victory, Butler took off on a mad dash to the capital.

Ben borrowed the transport steamer *Adelaide*, loaded the wounded aboard, and headed for Fortress Monroe, where he delivered a quick formal report to General Wool. Then he proceeded to Annapolis, where he saw to putting the casualties ashore. After that he requisitioned a train for himself and his staff and set off on a midnight run to Washington.

The train had reached a junction nineteen miles from Washington when railroad officials halted it, explaining that if Butler tried going any farther his train might well collide with a freight train coming east from Washington on the single-track line.

Butler was not to be stopped. He talked the engineer into making the run with the engine alone, on the theory that if they did meet anything coming the other way they could put the unburdened engine into a quick reverse and back out of trouble. Abandoning his staff, Ben swung aboard the cab.

"Shall we go slow?" asked the engineer. "That way when we see a train is coming we'll have time to back out."

"With just the engine you should be able to back out very quickly," said Ben.

"Well, I want your directions," said the engineer.

"Let her go as fast as she can go," said Ben.

"Then hold on to your cap, General," replied the engineer. And they were off.

They covered the nineteen miles in what was high speed for those days, averaging about thirty-three miles an hour and reaching Washington in forty minutes—just five minutes before the first freight train headed out of the city in the opposite direction. Ben slipped the engineer a $20 gold piece and leaped off to find a carriage.

Minutes later he was at the home of Postmaster-General Montgomery Blair, opposite the White House, Blair being one of Butler's closest Washington contacts. There he joined Blair and Gustavus V. Fox, assistant secretary of the navy and Ben's old classmate at Lowell High School. When Butler related the details of the Hatteras expedition, they insisted that President Lincoln ought to be awakened at once and told about it. A few minutes later they were in the White House, encountering only a minor delay because the lone watchman there was asleep and had to be roused.

The scene that followed had little of high protocol about it. Lincoln came down to the Cabinet Room in his nightshirt. When Fox told him of the victory, the tall, spindle-shanked president grabbed the little navy secretary and they danced around the room in delight. As Butler described it: "Fox put his arms around Lincoln about as high as his hips, and Lincoln reached down over him so that his arms were pretty near the floor, and thus holding one another they flew around the room a couple of times and the night shirt was considerably agitated." Butler threw himself on a sofa, he said, and "roared with merriment."

Lincoln was overdue for some good news, after the gloom of the Bull Run disaster. "You have done all right," he told Butler. "You have done all right!"

At a cabinet meeting the following morning, Ben delivered his report more formally and on this occasion met Gen. George B. McClellan for the first time. McClellan had assumed command of all Federal forces in Washington and Virginia, and it was clear that Scott's reign as general in chief was nearing an end. Butler's decision to keep Hatteras Inlet open and hold the forts was unanimously approved.

Now Ben felt he was owed some leave, which the president immediately approved. "You have a right to go home for a little rest, General," said Lincoln. "But study out another job for yourself."

The nation, like Lincoln, had also hungered for some good news. Back in Lowell, Butler was to find himself coping with the not entirely unwelcome vexations that go with status as a celebrity. Not the least of his satisfactions was that the setback at Big Bethel was now forgotten.

21

Almost from the beginning of his military career, even back to his prewar struggles with a hostile Know-Nothing governor, Ben Butler had been required to play the power game deftly and hard. A less prideful man might well have given up the struggle as not worth the grief, but Ben's self-esteem was such that surrender was not in his nature. Antagonists were quick to recognize and resent this quality in Butler; it sometimes inspired them to take the most extraordinary measures to bring him down. Often enough he was not merely opposed, but hated and feared. However, his complex temperament also attracted staunch friends, and Butler's friendships were usually of the kind that endured for a lifetime.

Two such allies were Postmaster-General Montgomery Blair and Assistant Navy Secretary Fox, who was Blair's brother-in-law and Butler's old school chum. Both were beneficiaries of the Blair paterfamilias, Francis Preston Blair, widely known as Old Man Blair, whose powerful political support had been crucial to Lincoln's nomination. A grateful and pragmatic Lincoln numbered the Old Man among his chief advisers. From his position of influence, the elder Blair had all but dictated the selection of Gideon Welles as navy secretary, as well as those appointments that went to Blair's family connections. Montgomery Blair was not in the cabinet to oversee the U.S. Mail; he was eyes and ears for Old Man Blair.

Thus it was no happenstance that Ben Butler made haste to Montgomery Blair's house to report on the Hatteras expedition, nor that Fox was there waiting to greet him. The Hatteras show had been a navy affair, and the handful of troops involved scarcely needed a major general to command them. The implication is clear that Butler's friends had alerted him to an opportunity to erase the Big Bethel defeat from his record, and to put himself in position for something more active than garrison duties under General Wool.

Butler's biggest immediate problem, of course, was the cold enmity of Winfield Scott, which the old general had taken no pains to conceal ever since Ben had marched on Baltimore with economy of force and made

Scott's own grandiose plans for capturing the city look ridiculous. When Scott capped everything by removing him from command at Fortress Monroe, Butler lost no time in planning alternatives.

Success of the Hatteras expedition sparked a bigger concept along the same lines. Butler would raise a fresh division of his own in New England. Relying on Blair and Fox for Lincoln's approval and navy participation, he would lead that division in yet another amphibious operation somewhere on the east or south coast of the Confederacy.

During all of these troubled months Sarah, who had left Fortress Monroe with the change of command there, had written many passionate letters to Ben urging him to return home, at least for a short period of leave. Ben's replies, equally ardent, promised that he would. The letters reveal a side of Butler's character that might well have astonished his enemies.

"Dear, Dear, Dearest Wife," Ben wrote. "I got your note this morning, and oh! so welcome! I shall be home in ten days or a fortnight. I won't go away without you, certain. . . . Love me, Dearest. I love you more and more every day. . . ."

Finally home in Lowell, on leave as he had promised, Butler found himself the object of public adulation. Wherever he went hometowners gathered around him. Men came up to shake his hand or clap him on the back. Women stared admiringly. At first he thought it was his uniform, with all its brass and braid, that was attracting so much attention. But when he shucked it for drab courtroom attire, his newfound celebrity diminished not a whit. Crowds still gathered, and people continued to point and wave or just stand and stare. Very little of this was soon more than enough for the general. He fretted at inactivity and was anxious to get on with his plans.

It could be argued, he thought, that Lincoln's war was becoming a Republican enterprise. Republican governors were holding tight control over regiments raised in their states. They distributed colonelcies among the Republican faithful, who in turn pinned bars and oak leaves on their Republican friends, who thereupon recruited their Republican neighbors into the ranks. Democrats, therefore, were scarcely to be blamed if they showed a growing indifference to the struggle.

To correct this situation, at least in New England, Butler devised a stratagem to apply heavy pressure upon the governors, foremost among them his bitterest foe, Governor Andrew of Massachusetts. All Ben needed was the president's signature. If Lincoln would authorize the effort, Butler himself would choose the colonels, who would then raise entire regiments of Democrats.

With this line of reasoning in mind, Ben headed for Washington to talk with the president. In his conference with Lincoln, he did not neglect to remind him that there was an upcoming congressional election to be considered. If so many Republicans were away on service while Democratic voters in large numbers were left at home, Butler argued, this would work against Lincoln's party. Trying to counter this by setting up complex machinery for getting out a soldier vote, said Ben, would simply entail far too much trouble and delay.

"Your aim should rather be to get every Democrat possible in the war," said Butler.

"There is meat in that," said Lincoln. "What would you advise me to do?"

Butler was quick to tell him. And Lincoln shortly afterward signed a special order drawn by Ben himself: "Maj.-Gen. B. F. Butler is hereby authorized to raise, organize, arm, uniform and equip a volunteer force for the war, in the New England States, not exceeding six (6) regiments of the maximum standard. . . . "

Service and supply elements of the army were ordered to honor Butler's requisitions, with the proviso that Butler's recruits were not to cost the government any more per man than it had cost to recruit those already in the service.

Lincoln was not eager to analyze or argue the minimal effect that six thousand Democrats might have, one way or the other, in the upcoming election. Butler wanted a job; Lincoln wanted troops; and Ben's argument, meat in it or not, was less important than the consideration of keeping Butler usefully busy, and his powerful friends in the cabinet reassured.

Armed with his high-level credentials, Butler promptly made the rounds of the New England statehouses, where he found Lincoln's signature entirely effective in producing cooperation from all but one of those Republican governors. Governor Andrew, as he expected, was the exception. Only Andrew refused to accept Ben's handpicked nominees for commissions in new regiments.

The Massachusetts governor had already authorized Ben's old subordinate, Colonel Jones of the 6th Militia Regiment, to raise a new command, the 26th Massachusetts. Andrew said Ben could have that regiment and also a skeleton regiment consisting so far only of officers Andrew himself had named. Butler was happy to accept Jones, whom he regarded highly, but refused to take any other nominees of the governor.

Regardless of Governor Andrew's vehement opposition (war or no war, the governor fought Butler tooth and nail), Ben was not to be stopped. He dashed off to Washington again, and this time obtained the president's signature on an order creating a new military department. The order read: "The six New England States will temporarily constitute a separate military department, to be called the Department of New England; headquarters, Boston. Maj.-Gen. B. F. Butler, United States Volunteer Service, while engaged in recruiting his division, will command."

Governor Andrew struck back by announcing that no soldier who enlisted under Butler's new command would get the financial aid ordinarily extended to families of volunteers. "Andrew," Butler commented, "cultivates malignity as he would a parlor plant."

Butler countered by publishing an open letter in which he personally guaranteed to make the family-aid payments out of his own pocket should the state withhold them. In any case, Ben had anticipated that he would have to deal with Andrew's purse-string powers, so he had got yet another War Department order, and that one granted all troops enlisted under his command a month's pay in advance as a bonus. (Troops enlisted by Governor Andrew's appointees did not qualify.) But Andrew remained firmly vindictive in regard to those state aid payments. When the legislature passed a special measure requiring the payments to be made to families of Butler's troops, Andrew promptly vetoed it.

Undaunted by the governor's continuous and bitter opposition, Butler carried on, but recruitment remained slow until a dramatic development on the international scene lent new impetus to his drive. Suddenly there was a serious threat of war with England, a prospect Butler welcomed warmly, his childhood dreams of fighting the redcoats still vivid in his mind. More practically, fantasies aside, the crisis brought into his ranks a flood of Irish immigrant volunteers indifferent to the Confederacy but eager at the prospect of a brush with the British—a speculation Butler did nothing to discourage.

22

International uproar and war emergency began on November 7, 1861, when Capt. Charles Wilkes, commanding the cruiser *San Jacinto*, halted the British mail steamer *Trent*, boarded her, and arrested the Confederate commissioners James Mason and John Slidell, who were on their way to England. Wilkes caught them outbound from Havana, where they had paused after running the blockade. The two commissioners and their secretaries were removed from the *Trent* and taken as prisoners to Fortress Monroe, and when the news was flashed from there, Wilkes at once became a national hero. The navy—chagrined at having failed to intercept the blockade-runner *Theodora*, which had carried the diplomats to Cuba—cheered Wilkes's exploit with the special satisfaction of honor redeemed.

Mason, a former United States senator, was especially despised by Northern abolitionists because of his part in drafting the infamous Fugitive Slave Act. Conversely, Mason's unyielding proslavery stance made him a popular figure in the South, although certain of the more genteel regarded his diplomatic appointment with alarm, since he was given to uncouth tobacco chewing and notoriously careless as to where he spat. Proper Southerners wondered aloud how that kind of behavior would be viewed in the Court of Saint James.

Slidell, on the other hand, was a rich and famous attorney, suitably suave. As it happened, Slidell was an old political ally of Butler's. He had worked closely with Ben as a prominent activist in the "stop Douglas" movement at the Charleston convention of 1860. But old political ties did not deter Butler from proclaiming that Slidell should be locked up as a prisoner of war, and damn the British, and damn the consequences.

Butler's hope that the Mason-Slidell affair would bring war with England was not entirely without basis, although Butler himself, however reluctantly, doubted that the British would go that far. Nor did that hope for war go unshared in the public mind. There was much for Americans to resent, since the British had been making calculated preparations for war with the United States almost from the outset of the North-South conflict.

The British Admiralty had strengthened the West Indian and North American fleets. The British War Office had sent significant troop reinforcements to Canada.

Perhaps more annoying, Britain's ruling politicians lost no opportunity to display their pro-Confederacy bias. Many—including Lord John Russell, the secretary of state—were openly pleased to entertain a hope that they might see two lesser republics on the North American continent rather than one potential giant. As a practical matter they assessed the sudden growth of American land and naval power as something that might have to be reckoned with one day. Should the American civil war turn out to be a short one, those powerful armed forces could be used to invade Canada or to seize some of England's strategic island possessions. Although these were only slim possibilities, they furnished an excuse for giving none too subtle aid to the Confederacy, the better to keep the war going. The ultimate and quite remote strategy, in keeping with Britain's talent for useful coalitions, envisioned British sea power acting in conjunction with French land forces, the French having great ambitions for imperial expansion in Mexico. In fact, Napoleon III was all for outright and immediate aid to the Confederacy. The British knew they could count on him; he chafed to be turned loose.

Against this background, British propaganda put forth the pro-Confederate official line. The *Times* of London, along with lesser newspapers, castigated the North and praised the South. The Reuters news agency, with a monopoly in Europe, systematically slanted its bulletins and dispatches to favor the South. The British cabinet took deliberate measures to embarrass the United States, stopping just short of rendering full, formal recognition of the Confederacy, that measure held dangling as a useful threat. In England only the common folk tended to sympathize with the North because, quite simply, they despised slavery.

When the *Trent* affair erupted, Butler was all for holding firm and letting the British do their worst. In fact, for as long as he lived, Butler held to the belief that war with England at this time would have galvanized the nation into patriotic fervor and that, as a result, the Civil War would have been shortened by at least two years. Curiously enough, Secretary of State Seward, early on, had dallied with a similar notion. If he could foment a foreign war—preferably with Spain or France—he thought it would unify the country and prevent the fatal break between North and South. By the time of the *Trent* incident, however, the malleable Seward had become far more circumspect. War with England was not to be considered. As Lincoln put it to his cabinet members, "one war at a time" was enough.

There was also one potent force in England that quieted the *Trent* uproar before it got out of hand. Prince Albert, dying of typhoid, drafted a note for Queen Victoria's signature, although his hand was scarcely strong enough to hold the pen. Wearing an old padded dressing gown against the winter chill, Albert tottered to his unheated study at 7:00 A.M., lighted his desk lamp, took a sheaf of paper, and began writing. The draft was his final service to his queen and his adopted country. It eliminated the deliberately brutal and provocative language that had been included by Lord John Russell in an ultimatum to be handed to the government of the United States.

The much modified communication was duly delivered to Seward. It still demanded the release of Mason and Slidell and an apology for the incident, but it was presented in a form that could be accepted without humiliation. With Lincoln and the cabinet concurring, the terms were approved. Mason and Slidell, who had been held in a Boston fort for safe-keeping, were transported on a rented tugboat to the tip of Cape Cod, where a British vessel took them aboard. The U.S. Navy, still miffed, refused to have any part in the proceedings.

Britain, meanwhile, continued to build up strength in Canada. Ironically enough, the logistics of moving troops to British North America had to take into account that they would arrive in rigorous winter, when the shipping route up the Saint Lawrence River would be icebound and impassable. This meant that the British government had to ask the American government for permission to land troops at Portland, Maine, and march them through that state and across the border. Butler thought this was a ridiculous favor to grant to potential enemy forces, but Seward approved the movement without a moment's hesitation.

Canada remained a backwater, although Confederate terrorists found ready hospitality there for incursions into the Northern states. One such band undertook to spread conflagration in New York by means of incendiary devices. Another group dashed down from Canada, burned the Vermont town of Saint Albans, robbed the bank there, and fled back into Canada for refuge after the raid. Butler's comments on these results of cautious American diplomacy were sulphurous. If Lincoln and his cabinet had stood firm, Butler growled, he could have raised not two regiments of Irishmen, but ten, and the conquest of Canada would have been a triumph.

Butler, anyway, now had his fresh regiments, which he had installed in several training camps, and in the midst of much Washington intrigue was waiting for word as to where they should be employed. He had planned to move them south to Fortress Monroe, which would be a staging area for some aggressive move or other, the objective and details still uncertain. But the *Trent* affair, which for a time did raise the possibility of a move north rather than south, kept Butler's troops in place even after Seward had settled the matter. The secretary of state had issued his formal apology and turned Mason and Slidell loose on December 23, but the New England regiments were ordered to stay in place for nearly another month.

Long before they were free to move, Butler knew something that was supposed to be secret: the navy meant to capture New Orleans, and now he had his objective. And now there was another good reason for cultivating his Washington connections, because Lincoln had named a new secretary of war, Edwin M. Stanton.

Stanton, a remarkably devious man, had been a legal adviser to his predecessor—the Pennsylvania Republican boss, Simon Cameron—and as such had led him into a political ambush. This came about when Cameron asked Stanton's help in drafting the annual War Department report. Stanton dictated a paragraph that called for arming slaves who had been seized as property and putting them into the field to fight for the Union. Cameron adopted the suggestion and published the report containing that flagrant paragraph before Lincoln had even seen it.

The president, whose conservative views on the subject of slavery were well known to his cabinet, immediately ordered the withdrawal of all copies of the Cameron report. But the key paragraph had already been circulated in the press, and the damage to Lincoln's position was done. Radical abolitionists praised Cameron while raising yet another storm of criticism regarding Lincoln's reluctance to take a firm stand against slavery. Now Lincoln decided that the time had come to let Cameron go, and Stanton's friends, as though on cue, began at once to lobby for his appointment in Cameron's place. However, few believed that Cameron's indiscretion really was the reason for firing him. Obviously there was less of logic than of rationalization in the move, since Cameron, who signed the offending paragraph, was to be replaced by Stanton, who wrote it.

In fact there were other considerations in the removal of Cameron, and these were more important. Under Cameron a slovenly War Department had quickly become the focal point of enormous and far-reaching graft and corruption. Contractors bought up condemned army muskets for next to nothing, then promptly sold them back to the army at huge profits. Owners of steamers chartered them for transport service at rates that, in a matter of a few months, netted them more money than it had cost to buy the vessels in the first place. The army bought shoddy blankets at triple the going price, fatigue uniforms that disintegrated, shoes that fell apart, defective ammunition, rotten tentage, and substandard rations. Spavined and windbroken horses were bought for the cavalry and artillery at prices that would have been exorbitant for the finest mounts. And so it went, every opportunist with political connections finding in the war emergency a quick way to make fabulous profits.

Even so, there was nothing rude in Lincoln's firing of Cameron. He was eased out rather than kicked out, and no public connection was made between the war secretary and the thievery that flourished under his jurisdiction. Since he remained, after all, a powerful political figure in the key state of Pennsylvania, Lincoln had no wish to alienate him or his followers. So

William H. Seward
Battles and Leaders of the Civil War

Edwin M. Stanton
The Great Rebellion

Cameron was discreetly hustled off about as far as Lincoln could politely send him; the president named him minister to Russia. And it was a mark of Stanton's smoothness that, well before Cameron left for the remote court of the czar, even the deposed war secretary had joined those who were urging Stanton's appointment in his place.

Stanton—like Butler, a war Democrat—entered an undisciplined cabinet that was seething with internal strife and intrigue, all of which Butler for his own purposes watched closely as he shuttled back and forth between Boston and Washington. Little that went on in the high councils escaped Ben's attention. It was a tense and lonely time for both the general and his wife.

From Washington Ben wrote Sarah a belated letter, apologizing for not having written sooner.

> My poor, dear little Heigh-Ho! I have treated you very shamefully, wretchedly. Will you ever forgive me? I have not written yet, but I have been each day in expectancy of getting home. But the change of secretaries and change of plans of the campaign have detained me from day to day. Every morning I have packed my carpet bag in expectation of going home, but each day have had to wait. I am determined not to leave until everything is fixed in my mind. I am on most intimate terms with the new Secretary [Stanton] who is an old political and personal friend of mine. I breakfasted at his house by special invitation on Sunday and spent the whole morning with him. . . .

The "campaign" was the proposed expedition to capture New Orleans which, remarkably enough, Navy Secretary Gideon Welles had been keeping secret from the War Department for months. Welles, who didn't even trust all his own navy officers, trusted everybody outside his jurisdiction even less. He was certain, in particular, that anything made known to the army was sure to be passed along one way or another to Richmond.

A rueful note in Welles's meticulous diary recorded the New Orleans leak. "Shortly after Mr. Stanton's appointment," Welles wrote, "Mr. Fox, the Assistant Secretary of the Navy, inadvertently and incautiously made known to General Butler and necessarily to Mr. Stanton, the great object in view, which had occupied the attention of the Navy for several months."

Given Butler's connection with Fox, it is a matter of some doubt just how inadvertent that inside tip about New Orleans was. In fact, it was the prospect of the New Orleans expedition that had sparked Butler's New England recruiting drive. Sarah, always Ben's closest and most acute counselor, had advised him not to accept status as a "mere recruiting officer." But raising troops for a major campaign that he would lead was something quite different from merely raising troops. The secret New Orleans command provided him with both present purpose and certainty of future prestige. Butler in time let it be known that he was bent on an important mission. He masked the true objective, however, hinting broadly that his troops were intended to occupy Mobile, a cover story that Welles had previously found useful in explaining movements of the fleet.

Governor Andrew continued his furious and fruitless campaign to discredit Butler, in both official Washington and calculated stories planted in the press. Andrew's feuding zeal caused even Sen. Charles Sumner, no great friend of Butler's, to look askance at Andrew's nearly maniacal efforts. Butler was privately informed that Andrew had sent Sumner a box containing some eighty pages of denunciation, which he asked the senator to read to President Lincoln personally. The dignified Sumner of course refused to be used as an errand boy, particularly on such a demeaning errand.

While coping with Governor Andrew's ceaseless harassments, Butler had a maze of details to handle in addition to maintaining close contact with the powers in Washington. There were ships to be chartered; supplies to be arranged; troops to be uniformed, trained, armed, and equipped. He had a line of supply to establish and maintain that would stretch from Portland, Maine, to Ship Island in the Gulf of Mexico. And now he also had a new commanding general to cope with, since his old nemesis, General Scott, had at last given way to that young and imperious drillmaster, George B. McClellan. Little Mac was an improvement over Scott, but in the months ahead McClellan's near-paranoid personality would create problems Butler would have to solve if the New Orleans expedition was ever to go forward under his command.

23

Throughout a bleak fall and dreary winter, Butler held to his course. While fending off Governor Andrew's unceasing attacks and shuttling between Boston and Washington to shore up political defenses, he still managed to deal efficiently with a thousand logistical details. By December he had dispatched an advance force aboard the chartered steamer *Constitution* to Ship Island, which was to be the staging area for the New Orleans operation.

Butler issued comprehensive orders for the forward echelon. It was to establish communication with navy forces already in the area, take possession of the unfinished fortifications on the island and look to its defense, warehouse all supplies, and return the *Constitution* to Boston as quickly as possible. All these things were done with dispatch, and the island was made ready to receive the next shipment of troops and supplies. At this point Butler was confronted with the obstacle he had been dreading: opposition from General-in-Chief McClellan, who had been developing what President Lincoln called "the slows."

On January 1 Butler wired McClellan, "Am ready with 2200 men. Shall we embark?"

By return telegram Butler got the terse message: "The General-in-Chief says 'Remain where you are.' "

Butler headed for Washington once again, where he found himself dangerously close to an open clash with McClellan. With his nerves stretched taut after coping with all the other barriers that had been placed in his way, Ben found McClellan's reluctance to clear the New Orleans expedition almost more than he could stand. In a letter to Sarah he wrote:

> Two weeks now have I been waiting for a decision that should have been made in an hour by any person fit to be trusted with the affair at all. The Secretary, Mr. Stanton, has done all and more than all I could ask of him. Intrigue, petty malice, and a jealousy, have all had their share. . . . The state of things here cannot continue. Either McClellan has got to advance or he will be superseded. . . .

While Butler fretted, McClellan continued to dither, frozen in the belief that his Army of the Potomac faced a Confederate force of overwhelming strength. Not even the strongest pressure from the president, including a direct order, could get Little Mac to put his well-trained and fully equipped army into harm's way. These circumstances led to a strange conversation between Butler and Lincoln.

In response to a request from the Committee on the Conduct of the War, Butler on February 12 had provided the lawmakers with his own estimate of the Confederate strength facing Washington. He had given the matter elaborate study, compiling long columns of statistics upon which to base a conclusion. First, he told the committee, it was absurd to imagine that Confederate forces could have more than doubled since the Battle of Bull Run. Citing his listings of rebel forces unit by unit, Butler testified that the number of effective enemy troops certainly could not exceed sixty-five thousand. Butler's testimony was pointedly at variance with McClellan's wild estimate, which credited the Confederate force with a strength of some two hundred thousand effectives. Butler said he could find no conceivable way that the South could have found, armed, and equipped anything like that number.

The cautious McClellan, for his part, merely asked Butler to repeat to him what he had told the committee, and Ben did so in thorough detail. After examining the analysis McClellan had only one comment. Butler, he said, simply had to be wrong.

Later, on February 21, Lincoln asked Butler to recap his testimony before the War Committee. Upon hearing Butler's summary, Lincoln put a question to him: "Assuming you had one hundred thousand effective men in Washington, and were permitted to move over the river to attack, would you do it?"

"Certainly I would," said Butler. But he quickly added that all he wanted to do was to get under way with his comparative handful of troops to move on New Orleans. Ben was shrewd enough to see that McClellan's head was quite possibly on the block, but he was not at all eager to enter into that looming power struggle.

"I won't say, General, whether I will let you go or not," replied Lincoln, who appeared to be in one of his dark moods.

McClellan had ordered some of Butler's troops held and disembarked at Fortress Monroe, with the intention of sending them back north to Baltimore. Butler had protested this weakening of his forces, and this was one of the matters he now placed before the president for a decision. Lincoln said, cryptically enough, that he was not holding Butler in Washington to resolve the matter of those few more troops for the New Orleans expedition. Still he refused to say just why he did want Butler to remain in the capital. And he abruptly ended the interview with a hint that heavy decisions were in the making. "Well, General Butler," said Lincoln, "I think you had better call on me the day after tomorrow, and we will see what will come out of this."

"Tomorrow" was February 22, on this occasion more than a mere national holiday. Lincoln had issued an unprecedented General Order No. 1. It called upon all Union commanders to move to the attack on February 22, Washington's birthday. It was an order particularly directed at McClellan, whose "slows" had finally driven the president to demand action. Quite obviously, in specifying "the day after tomorrow" for further talk with Butler, Lincoln was waiting to see how—or whether—McClellan complied with General Order No. 1. The significance of this was not lost on the astute Yankee general.

Immediately after his talk with Lincoln, Butler called on McClellan to ask once again that he revoke the order recalling his expeditionary troops to Baltimore. But Little Mac's mind was on his own problem, the matter of his continuing tenure as general in chief. McClellan shrugged off Butler's comparatively trivial request and abruptly changed the subject by demanding a full recounting of all that had gone on in Butler's conference with the president. Butler gave this account in detail, but he was as persistent in his own topic of interest as McClellan was overbearing in his. While pointedly citing Lincoln's Delphic utterances, Butler continued to demand that McClellan issue clear orders for the New Orleans expedition to proceed with its force intact.

Fixing General McClellan with his one good eye, Butler demanded, "Shall I call on you before or after I see the president?"

"Better come before," said McClellan.

Butler knew he had carried the point. Quickly he issued orders to his staff officers to be ready to move at once. The next morning, as he had expected, he got written orders from McClellan authorizing the move on New Orleans. Obviously the last thing McClellan wanted to cope with right then was the presence of yet another general whom Lincoln might consider as a candidate to replace him.

Jubilant at getting final clearance for his long-planned expedition, Butler reported at once to War Secretary Stanton with the news. He found Stanton conferring with Lincoln. Stanton's reaction was one of jubilation, but Lincoln seemed somber, as though his thoughts were elsewhere. He shook hands with Butler. As Ben later described it, the president wore "a far-off, pensive look."

Butler was to reminisce: "I stayed in Washington long enough to have a little bird sing to me that General McClellan's father-in-law and chief of staff, R.B. Marcy, had said, 'I guess we have found a hole to bury this Yankee elephant in.' "

On February 24, finally, Butler was on his way to Baltimore to take ship for Fortress Monroe. At 9:00 P.M. the next day, with Sarah beside him, he was aboard the steamer *Mississippi* and issuing the order, "Up anchor for Ship Island." The *Mississippi* was carrying sixteen hundred of Butler's troops on the start of what was to be an adventurous and perilous voyage. At that moment all Ben had by way of funds to finance his expedition was $75 in gold that he happened to be carrying in his pocket. The Union war effort, then and later, was to lean heavily on just such improvisation.

24

The steamer *Mississippi* was a hard-luck ship. Butler, calling on sailor lore acquired on many a youthful fishing voyage, even came to believe that there just had to be a Jonah aboard. As sequential disasters developed, he even identified the Jonah and, for defensible military reasons, shipped the culprit back home in disgrace. Long before those glum speculations and developments, however, he found that the *Mississippi* had an incompetent skipper and that the first mate was something of a moron.

At Fortress Monroe a tugboat transferred Ben and Sarah to the *Mississippi* from the ship that had brought them from Baltimore. In a letter to her sister Harriet, Sarah described the boarding: "I found a way to the top of the tug, from that they threw a plank to the 'Mississippi,' and led by the captain came safely on board. The others came up the side of the ship, by ladders and ropes."

Sarah described the confusion amid which Butler's sixteen hundred troops milled about, finally finding space aboard for themselves. She added tartly: "It is expected we shall be off tonight. In the meantime I should be glad of a place to warm my feet."

Butler stayed on deck as the ship sailed south. He was seaman enough to be worried about the passage around Cape Hatteras, where currents flowed strongly shoreward and where dangerous shoals extended far out to sea. These were additionally hazardous waters in that the Confederates had extinguished all the lights in the coastal lighthouses. Under these circumstances Ben was not a little annoyed to find that the captain of the *Mississippi* was not at his post, but had gone below to sleep.

Toward morning the first heavy winds of a gale began to blow, and breakers were sighted. Ben had the captain roused immediately. The *Mississippi* was brought hard over, heading east, and was kept on that course for some time through gale winds and heavy seas, putting distance between the ship and that dangerous shore. The *Mississippi* buried her nose in the troughs, taking on green water as mountainous waves broke over her deck. Fearing the ship would founder, the captain finally pointed her north to run with the wind. Meanwhile Butler's troops had been formed into long bucket brigades extending from hold to deck and were bailing furiously.

By late morning the storm had worn itself out. The ship was put about, heading south once more, this time with the considerable help of canvas, three sails adding their thrust to that provided by the hard-pressed engine. At noon the captain took an observation, plotted his position on the chart, and set his course. No land was in sight. Butler was assured that the *Mississippi* was now far out to sea and would pass well clear of the dreaded Frying Pan Shoals, the graveyard of ships that extended some twenty miles off Cape Fear. The night passed quietly, and Ben caught up on his sleep.

At breakfast next day a jovial captain confessed he had made a little mistake in his calculations. The true position, he said, was actually twenty miles farther east, so the ship was that much safer from the sandbars of Frying Pan Shoals. But no sooner had he said this than there was an ominous grating sound and the ship trembled. The engine stopped, then started again. The ship lurched, timbers groaning, and then the engine stopped once more. The captain rushed up on deck, Butler close on his heels. What they saw was land, scarcely five miles away. The *Mississippi* was hard aground on a sandbar in Frying Pan Shoals.

"Let go port anchor," ordered the captain.

As the anchor dropped a few feet and plunked into sand, Butler decided it was high time for a conference. He led the way into the captain's cabin.

"Now, then, where are we?" he asked.

The captain placed a broad thumb on the small chart. "We are here."

Since the captain's thumb covered a lot of shoal and ocean, Butler demanded a more precise answer. "*Exactly* where?"

"I don't know," the captain confessed, adding that he not only didn't know where he was, he had no idea how he had got there.

Soundings disclosed that the *Mississippi*, which drew eighteen feet, was in fourteen feet of water, its bottom resting on a large round sandbank. Meanwhile Lt. Edward A. Fiske (one day to be General Fiske) brought more bad news. When the captain ordered the anchor dropped, it had punched a hole in the forward compartment where Fiske's troops were quartered. Water in the compartment was rising fast.

Ben turned to the captain again. "Do you know whether the valves that close the watertight compartments are in order?"

"No," was the reply. "I've never tested them."

At this point Butler had had enough. Brusquely he ordered the captain confined to his cabin. To make sure he stayed there, Ben posted a guard at the door. Then he directed the mate to go forward and see what could be done about coping with the water that was pouring in through the hole in the hull. He didn't expect much of the mate, however. In questioning the man earlier, he had already written him off as a dolt.

Now, for a bleak moment, even Butler's indomitable spirit sagged as he assessed the situation. Here he was on a damaged ship with water filling the forward hold, the vessel hard aground awaiting a rising tide in which it would surely break up, and the lives of sixteen hundred of his soldiers depending on whatever action he might take. As he sat slumped, with his hand covering his face, he felt a light touch on his shoulder. For the moment he had actually forgotten that Sarah was aboard.

"Cheer up," she said. "Do the best you can, and perhaps all will be well."

That was enough to restore his spirit. First he sent a sailor aloft to sight any vessel that might be passing. Then he bent his telescope on the shore, where Confederate horsemen were galloping about in obvious excitement and artillery was being shifted around. The rebels appeared to be either expecting an attack or planning to launch one against the stranded ship. To discourage the latter notion, Ben ran up the flag and fired a round from one of the long-range rifled cannon he had on board.

Next he gave orders to lighten the ship by tossing much of its cargo overboard, including the contents of the many barrels of salt pork that were being shipped as rations. Ben had a use for the empty barrels. After seeing that they were made watertight, he had his men improvise some anchors, using six-inch artillery shells as weights and attaching these weights to the ends of cords. Then Butler sent out boats to find and mark a channel, using the barrels as improvised marker buoys anchored in place by the weighted lines. If he did get the ship free of the sandbar, he would need to know where that channel was. All this time he had the engineer turn the engine over at intervals, so the ship's propeller would clear as much sand as possible from the rear of the vessel.

Then came an alarm. The lookout aloft had spotted a ship and reported it to be an approaching steamer flying what looked like the Confederate flag. Ben detailed an officer to go in one of the boats toward the oncoming ship and hail it.

"But, General, suppose she is a reb?" the officer protested.

"Then God help you, Major," said Ben.

The ship, to Butler's relief, turned out to be the U.S. Navy steamer *Mount Vernon*, on blockade duty. Her commander, Capt. O. C. Glisson, shortly set out in the ship's gig and came aboard the *Mississippi*. Glisson agreed to try to haul the stranded vessel off the sandbank, but in several attempts to do so he only succeeded in breaking the towing cables, and almost ran his own ship aground.

The wind rose again, and heavy waves began battering the *Mississippi*. Glisson agreed to take some of the troops aboard his ship but said the most he could safely accommodate would be three hundred. Butler cut the heads off some matches and had the officers of Massachusetts and Maine companies draw straws to see which companies would go. As this turned out, the winning five companies were all from Maine. At Butler's insistence and over her protests, Sarah was also taken aboard Glisson's ship.

"I would rather remain here," said Sarah.

"Are you mad," replied Ben, "that you would risk to the children the loss of us both?"

When Sarah wrote Harriet at the conclusion of the adventure, she reported the details.

> Mr. Butler went away to the pilot house. The ship was beating heavily on the surf, and men's hearts beat heavier still, and the night swept toward us. The deck was crowded with men. Major Bell gave me his arm. There was a move, a "make way for Mrs. Butler." I was helped over the railing, Captain Glisson preceded me down the side of the ship, and aided as much as possible. The boat was tossing like a nut shell far below us, and down the unsteady ladder we slipped. When nearly at the bottom the Capt. said, "Jump, madam, we'll catch you," and down I went into the boat.

It was during this episode that Ben identified the Jonah. The chaplain of a Maine regiment came rushing up to him, eagerly volunteering to accompany Mrs. Butler to safety.

"Oh, no, Chaplain," said Butler.

"General, I prefer to go."

"The devil you do!" growled Ben, and turned to his more important duties. He was determined on a last-ditch effort. Night was coming. The tide was rising fast.

Ben ordered every stitch of canvas raised on the tall masts of the *Mississippi*, and at the same time ordered the engineer to pour on all the steam his engine could handle. Finally, with a slow lurch, the ship broke loose from the sandbank and moved into deep water. With her forward compartment flooded, she was down by the bow by three feet, but she was free and she was moving forward.

With his ship safe, Ben rowed over to the *Mount Vernon*, thinking to bring Sarah back with him. "As I approached the quarterdeck," Ben reported later, "whom should I see on her deck but my chaplain of the long flowing curls and Byronic collar."

All but ignoring Captain Glisson, the furious Butler sprang toward the chaplain, demanding to know how he had got aboard the navy ship.

"I came over last night," said the chaplain.

"What? In the last boat with Mrs. Butler?" roared Ben. "After I ordered you not to?"

Butler ordered the red-faced chaplain to go below at once and write out his resignation. "I'll accept it," Ben grated, "but don't let me ever hear of your trying to get in the Army again."

Turning to the bemused navy officer, who had been observing all this, Butler added, "Now, Captain Glisson, you can keep this fellow or throw him overboard, just as you choose. I haven't any use for him, although he may be the Jonah that went overboard and saved the ship."

Even the least superstitious sailor might well have been tempted to agree with Butler's assessment. It was undeniable that no sooner had the nervous chaplain left the *Mississippi* than the stranded vessel broke free, all efforts up to that time having been unavailing.

Accompanied by the *Mount Vernon*, Butler's battered troopship made her ungainly way toward the Sea Island of Port Royal, one hundred sixty miles away, where Butler hoped the navy might have the skilled workers needed to effect repairs. The *Mississippi* rode uneasily in rough seas, bow down, stern high. To add to the tense drama, an unusually severe electrical storm raged. Thunder crashed and rolled, brilliant lightning flashed all about, and glittering displays of Saint Elmo's fire danced on all the masts and yards. Butler, exhausted, slept through it all.

Safe, finally, at the navy base, the *Mississippi* was towed to moorage at the wharf of an abandoned Sea Island cotton plantation. The troops, encamped ashore, were set to work emptying the hold of everything aboard, including some thirteen hundred tons of coal.

Efforts to pump water out of the damaged forward compartment, however, met with total failure, and navy carpenters pronounced the repair job hopeless. At this point Butler decided to draw on his early shirtsleeves experience in the railroad machine shops back home. Since nobody else could repair the damage, Ben was determined to do it himself, trusting to Yankee ingenuity.

First Butler sent a diver down to determine the position of the hole that had been punched in the hull by the anchor. The diver was also directed to measure the size of the hole and determine its outline. When Ben had these dimensions, he took an iron plate of the proper size and shape and bored some holes in the corners. Then he contrived a cushion of heavy canvas stuffed with oakum, and he secured this to one side of the plate. Attaching lines through the holes that had been drilled, Butler passed two of these lines under the ship while holding the other two above deck. Finally, with the diver guiding it into place, the padded plate was drawn tightly against the hole and held there by the cords. After that, the pumps cleared the flooded compartment without difficulty.

The navy carpenters were now free to make repairs inside the hull, so they set to work on a patch they thought would hold. But as soon as Ben's cobbled plate was removed, their work crumbled and water once again filled the compartment.

Perhaps as much fascinated as exasperated, Butler fashioned a second plate much like the first one he had contrived. After reattaching the outer plate and again pumping the compartment dry, Butler installed his second plate inside the hull, holding it in place with jackscrews and timbers. Then he sealed the whole clumsy patch with melted rosin which, after it hardened, closed off the leak entirely.

Blacksmith Ben was as proud of this handiwork as of anything he had accomplished thus far. He reported later that the *Mississippi* sailed from Port Royal to Ship Island, from Ship Island to New Orleans, and from New Orleans all the way back to Boston before any more permanent repairs were required.

In the meantime, however, the reputation of the *Mississippi* as a jinxed ship was working on the morale of the troops. As Sarah reported in a letter to sister Harriet: "They have a superstitious dread [of the ship] from the repeated disasters that have befallen her. They say she was launched on a Friday, sailed on a Friday, and call her a doomed vessel."

Butler's hard-worked troops restowed all the equipment and supplies they had removed from the ship. Their fears were eased somewhat when it became known that the commanding general and his wife had refused passage on another vessel and meant to stay with them aboard the *Mississippi*.

Butler placed the less than competent captain under arrest, awaiting a court of inquiry to be conducted at Ship Island. He then borrowed a skipper from the navy and set sail. His principal fear, shared by the more eager of his officers, was that he would not get to the Gulf before the navy had launched the New Orleans assault. As it turned out, however, the navy was encountering its own difficulties, and Butler's force would have ample time to assemble on Ship Island and make final preparations for the campaign.

25

Ship Island is a low-lying sand patch in the Gulf, ten miles south of Biloxi and about seventy-five miles northeast of New Orleans. There, true to her reputation, the *Mississippi* arrived in the midst of a furious thunderstorm, battered by winds and waves of such proportions that the ship's captain had to turn her away and run for deep water. Next morning he steamed back again and this time made anchorage. But no sooner did it seem safe to maneuver the ship to the wharf than high winds again began to blow, at which point the *Mississippi* staged another tantrum. Sarah wrote pensively to her sister Harriet, "It is rather funny the trouble we have with this ship. . . ."

The pilot undertook to take the ship in, but by the time the *Mississippi* drew alongside the wharf a furious wind was whipping up huge waves. The ship's captain decided not to tie up at the wharf after all, fearing that the rogue steamer would demolish it. Instead he tried to hold the ship in place by use of his engine. This worked for a very short time only, after which the *Mississippi* reared backwards and collided with a brig, damaging that ship's bow and getting entangled in her rigging. Held fast by the wreckage, the steamer at last came to rest. Next morning, when the crews tried to separate the two vessels, the wind was still blowing strong. Sarah wrote:

> As the brig tried to draw off, it gave a lurch, came in endwise, and ran her bow clear up on to our deck. There it hung, broken and dangling, like an elephant's trunk, hoisted into our rigging. Everybody on deck was in danger, with this great thing striking in all directions, yet nobody could help laughing, and besides we expected anything now.
>
> At last, with pulling and cutting, they tore it away, and we started again on our adventures. This time we rushed madly at the *Black Prince*, which was anchored a little farther on, knocked her out of her moorings and tore at her rigging. Then we plunged at another ship, the *Wild Gazelle*, caught and grazed her, scattered a few splinters,

then stood out into the harbor, and anchored apart from the other vessels. Their extended arms told their terror of encountering again this new monster of the deep. . . .

Once she finally set foot on land, Sarah set up housekeeping in a rude shack whose floor consisted of a stretch of canvas sprinkled with sand.

The general, who had managed to get ashore earlier, was already coping with dozens of details, large and small, as he prepared his command for the New Orleans assault. Not the least of his problems was the matter of supply. Back home in Massachusetts the implacable Governor Andrew was busy as ever in prosecuting his private war with Butler, using his office and his influence to dismantle Ben's supply echelon in the Bay State, while still endeavoring, with occasional success, to replace Butler's regimental officers with appointees of his own. At one point Andrew Jackson Butler, the general's tireless brother, had managed to keep the Ship Island force in rations and other basics only by organizing an emergency shipment on his own authority and with his own resources. Not for nothing did Ben equate the Massachusetts governor with the governors of states in rebellion.

There were other troubles. The physician Butler had brought along from Massachusetts suffered a mental and physical collapse ("from the perils of the voyage," Sarah wrote). The unfortunate doctor died before he could be sent north for treatment, and now there was no time to recruit a substitute. There was the erstwhile captain of the *Mississippi* to be dealt with. (Butler had him replaced.) There was a mountain of official and private correspondence for Butler to answer or act upon. In one of these communications he was informed that McClellan was no longer general of the armies, and that Butler was to report henceforth to War Secretary Stanton.

The navy ran short of coal, and it fell to Butler to make up some of the deficit from his own supplies. There was even the matter of a punitive expedition that Butler felt he had to launch against a rebel force at Biloxi, which had infuriated him by firing on a flag of truce.

The latter curious incident occurred when Butler undertook to return a shipwrecked child to her family. The child, a little girl about seven years old, had been aboard a vessel bound from Havana to New Orleans when the ship was sighted and pursued by a navy blockader. One of those sudden Gulf storms put an end to the pursuit, but the ship the child was aboard foundered and those on board had to take to the boats. In the confusion the child was separated from her parents. Later, a navy ship picked up the boat she was in and carried her in safety to Ship Island.

Butler promptly assigned his chief of staff, Maj. George C. Strong, to take the little girl to Confederate-held Biloxi aboard the *Cox*, a small schooner, trusting that authorities there would send her on to New Orleans. The rebel troops at Biloxi honored the schooner's flag of truce and held their fire until the child had been turned over to the town officials. But when the *Cox* went aground on the outbound leg the Confederate force opened fire.

With the schooner in peril, Strong decided that all those aboard except himself and two others should row in a ship's boat all the way back to Ship Island for help. Shortly afterward two boats carrying Confederate riflemen cautiously approached the stranded vessel. The rebels called out, demanding surrender. But Strong, loudly shouting fake orders to non existent crewmen, bluffed the nervous rebels into backing off without a fight.

A rising tide freed the *Cox* eventually, and the schooner made its way back home, a navy vessel accompanying. Butler was not content to let the matter rest at that, however. He promptly dispatched a regiment, backed by artillery, to deliver a message and demand an apology. His message was terse: "The repetition of such or similar outrageous action will be the signal for the destruction of your town."

The troops Butler sent were the wild Irishmen of the Connecticut 9th, a regiment that had been so totally undisciplined that the governor of Connecticut had begged Butler to take it off his hands. Afterward, learning soldierly ways under Ben's firm tutelage, the unit had become one of his favorites, so in his report to Stanton, Butler was happy to praise the Biloxi expedition as "gallantly performed." The regiment had taken Biloxi without firing a shot. The 9th then had driven an equal force of Confederates from their nearby camp and burned it down, secured that formal apology, and retired with just two casualties, both lightly wounded. Butler was proudest of the fact that his men had left all civilians and their goods unharmed. In his official report Ben wrote:

> These well disciplined soldiers, although for many hours in full possession of two rebel villages, filled with what to them were most desirable luxuries, abstained from the least unauthorized interference with private property, and all molestation of private citizens. This behavior is worthy of all praise.

As a postscript to the incident, Butler later received a letter from a pro-Unionist planter, G.F.W. Claiborne, who told him he was arranging to reunite the lost little girl with friends of her family in New Orleans.

The novelist John William De Forest, (praised by William Dean Howells for the "inexorable veracity" of his writings) drew an interesting word portrait of Butler at this time. De Forest, then an infantry captain on Ship Island, wrote long letters to his wife during all of his service in the war. The bulk of these were subsequently collected and printed as a volume of memoirs. In his letter of April 6, 1862, he wrote:

You would perhaps like a sketch of General Butler. Three of us Twelfth officers called on him apropos of rations, and in my character of novelist I made a study of him. He is not the grossly fat and altogether ugly man who is presented in the illustrated weeklies. He is stoutish but not clumsily so; he squints badly, but his eyes are very clear and bright; his complexion is fair, smooth and delicately flushed; his teeth are white and his smile is ingratiating. You need not understand that he is pretty; only that he is better looking than his published portraits.

He treated us very courteously and entered into the merits of our affair at length, stating the *pros* and *cons* from the army regulations like a judge delivering a charge, and smiling from time to time after the mechanical fashion of Edward Everett, as if he meant to make things pleasant for us and also to show his handsome teeth. On the whole he seemed less like a major general than like a politician who was coaxing for votes. The result of the interview was that we got the desired order and departed with a sense of having been flattered.

It was typical of Butler that he was both able and willing to take the time for a lengthy conference with a few company officers. No general on either side of the conflict made better use of all the hours in a day. During this period of hectic preparation for a major military operation, Ben was even able to satisfy his curiosity about the white sand on Ship Island and why it did not irritate the eyes. He decided, after making a study of some grains under a microscope he happened to have packed with him, that unlike sharp-edged desert sand, the sand of Ship Island was worn round and smooth by the action of wind and waves; hence it was nonabrasive.

By March 30 Butler was able to report to Flag Officer David G. Farragut that he was ready to embark six regiments for New Orleans. But Farragut, who was having his own troubles, was not in that much of a hurry. So far he had not yet been able to get all his ships over the bar and into the Mississippi channel. The response from Farragut to Butler added up to a friendly "stand by."

Butler's cordial relationship with Farragut was to last a lifetime. But still ahead for Ben was one of the great feuds of his life, that with Farragut's associate in the New Orleans expedition, Comdr. David D. Porter.

26

The New Orleans expedition was not without that murky element of intrigue that pervaded the Lincoln administration. From the beginning of his presidency, Lincoln was surrounded by power players, all of whom believed him to be in need of guidance at the very least and of outright manipulation when he could not be led. Lincoln was remarkably tolerant of this, so perhaps it is less than curious that one of the planners of the New Orleans operation was David D. Porter—he whom Lincoln himself characterized as "a busy schemer," and who, at the very outset of hostilities, had conspired to cripple Lincoln's attempt to relieve Fort Sumter.

The Sumter chicanery occurred at a time when Navy Secretary Gideon Welles was harboring strong doubts about Porter's loyalty to the Union. During the critical winter of 1861, Porter had moved conspicuously in the company of active secessionists and afterward had applied for coast-survey duty in the Pacific. Welles, a shrewd Connecticut Yankee, had noticed that navy officers who asked for Pacific assignments tended to be rebel sympathizers at heart but not quite ready to give up their navy commissions until they had figured all the angles.

While Welles was organizing the Sumter relief effort, Porter and Secretary of State Seward conspired to hand Lincoln a certain sheaf of papers for his signature, trusting that he would not find it necessary to read them closely. The dodge was successful. What Lincoln unknowingly signed authorized Porter to seize command of the warship *Powhatan* and remove it from the Sumter fleet. To Welles's great anger, Porter sailed the *Powhatan* out of New York Harbor on a fool's mission to Florida so that its heavy firepower would be absent when the showdown came at Charleston. To compound Porter's mischief, his underhanded action occurred when, under orders from Welles, he was supposed to be on duty in the Pacific.

When Welles made Lincoln realize what he had done in signing those papers, the president was chagrined but by then the matter was beyond repair. Welles's order restoring the *Powhatan* to her proper commander was ignored by Porter, who purported to be answering to higher authority—that previous order signed unwittingly by Lincoln himself.

Seward's motivation in all this may have sprung from hazy peace schemes he was independently pursuing at the time. Seward was in close contact with South Carolina secessionists, whom he hoped to pacify even if it required recasting the Federal Constitution in a form more to their liking. He also thought that a convenient foreign war, possibly with Spain or France, just might unite the country. Therefore he was moved to undertake any measure, including sly sabotage, to keep the relief expedition from upsetting his private negotiations with the South Carolinians, to whom he had given certain secret assurances regarding Sumter. Whether it was he or Porter who originated the plan to divert the *Powhatan*, it suited Seward's notion of grand strategy, and the two of them did collaborate in thus deceiving Lincoln and subverting the authority of Secretary Welles.

However forgiving Lincoln may have been, Welles cultivated a long memory. Even much later, when Porter had settled down to faithful service in the United States Navy, the secretary retained his reservations about the man. In his diary Welles noted:

> I did not always consider David to be depended upon if he had an end to attain, and he had no hesitation in trampling down a brother officer if it would benefit himself. . . . He has great energy, excessive and sometimes unscrupulous ambition, is impressed with and boastful of his own powers, given to exaggeration. . . [and] is not generous to older and superior officers, whom he is always ready to traduce . . .

In sum, Porter was a glory hunter of dubious veracity and limited scruples, but possessed nevertheless of intelligence, energy, professional ability, and personal courage. At a time when warrior talent was scarce, he was not a man to be overlooked. Thus it was that Porter, at age forty-eight a mere navy commander, came to have access to the highest wartime councils and to the White House itself. By the time the New Orleans expedition was under study, he was working closely with Gustavus Fox, the assistant secretary of the navy, who approved the operation with enthusiasm and supported it with great energy.

It was Porter who, grudgingly enough, recommended Capt. David Glasgow Farragut as adequate—but no more than adequate—for overall command of the naval force. Porter had another assignment in mind for himself, foreshadowing in a way the enthusiasms of air power advocates of a later age. Porter was fascinated by the plunging fire of heavy mortars, whose bombshells, with their high trajectory and sharp angle of descent, produced an effect not unlike bombing from the air. Porter sought and was given command of a supporting fleet of mortar ships.

Key positions of the New Orleans defense system were the two strong forts that, from opposite sides of the Mississippi, commanded the upriver approach. Fort Jackson, typical of the military architecture of the times, was solidly constructed of stone, its walls within walls forming a vast, many-pointed star enclosing a large citadel. Fort Saint Philip was of similar heavy construction, with walls of brick and stone. Between them they mounted 126 guns. Porter believed he could knock out those forts with his bombshells, thus clearing the way for Farragut's conventional warships to take the city under their guns.

Porter's command of the mortar fleet led eventually to the feud that ensued between him and General Butler. In the aftermath of the battle, Porter claimed enormous success for his mortar attack. Butler said this wasn't so, and he produced heavy evidence to prove that it wasn't. For two such strong personalities, the dispute was more than enough to fuel an enmity that was to last a lifetime.

To Captain Farragut, command of a fleet represented the ambition of a lifetime in the naval service, which he had entered as a boy midshipman in 1810. Farragut received word of his assignment as a kind of Christmas present from Porter on December 21, 1861, and got formal orders from Welles a month later. Still another month was to pass before Farragut arrived at Ship Island in his flagship, the twenty-four–gun *Hartford*, and began to gather there the rest of his fleet. Besides the *Hartford* the heavies included the *Pensacola*, *Brooklyn*, and *Richmond*, all equally armed, and all like the *Hartford* wooden vessels of the old design. In addition, Farragut commanded three corvettes and a sidewheel steamer, each mounting seven to ten guns. Nine lightly armed gunboats made up the rest of his force.

For his own flotilla Porter gathered nineteen schooners, and got them equipped with one thirteen-inch mortar and two long guns each. He assembled seven armed steamboats, which would be needed for supply and support and for maneuvering the schooners about in the close waters of the Mississippi. Ammunition supplies included no fewer than thirty thousand bombshells for the mortars.

During nearly all of the naval preparations, Porter produced an unceasing flow of letters to Gustavus Fox in which he criticized nearly everyone in the expedition from Farragut on down to a hapless "fool of a lieutenant" who had incurred Porter's anger. In spite of having recommended Farragut for the command, Porter now suggested the fleet commander was too old for the job. Porter kept up a continuing tirade against "old fogyism" in the navy's higher echelons. "I never thought Farragut a Nelson, or a Collingwood," Porter wrote. "I only consider him the best of his rank and so consider him still; but men of his age in a seafaring life are not fit for the command of important enterprises. . . ."

Butler, meantime, against stubborn and unceasing resistance on the part of Governor Andrew, had succeeded in raising his regiments, equipping and training them, transporting them to Ship Island, and establishing his long and tenuous supply lines—also against constant interference on Andrew's part. Whatever the wariness between Butler and Porter, relations between Butler and Farragut were more than cordial and remained so. Butler's genius for organization even enabled him to supply Farragut's fleet with coal when the navy's ships ran short. Porter's odd action in sending fuel-laden ships back to Pensacola had not helped supply matters any.

The matter of fuel for the warships was critical. The fleet could not move from Ship Island to the mouth of the Mississippi for lack of anthracite, hard coal that produced the clean, high heat necessary for the ships' boilers. The Navy Department had dispatched cargo schooners carrying coal for the fleet, but between Porter's interference and administrative lash-up, the schooners had failed to reach Ship Island. At this point nobody in the Navy Department seemed to know just where they were.

Butler, however, with his usual foresight, had directed his people back in Boston to ballast his supply ships with anthracite instead of the usual ballast of stones. Thus, when Farragut told him of his fuel problem, Butler was able to offer him some three thousand tons. Farragut, the regulation-minded Regular, was uneasy that Butler might be breaking army regulations by diverting army supplies to the navy, but Ben dismissed the thought with a wave of his hand.

"I never read army regulations," said Butler.

In a council of war attended by Farragut, Butler, and their top staff officers—Porter not being present—the plan of attack was agreed upon.

Porter was to lead the advance upriver with his mortar fleet and engage Fort Saint Philip and Fort Jackson. Porter was to bombard the forts until either they were reduced or his mortar ammunition was nearly expended. Farragut's main fleet was to remain below the mortar vessels, out of range of the forts, awaiting the outcome of Porter's effort. Butler's troopships were to stand by at the mouth of the river. If Porter silenced the forts, the army was then to move up and occupy them. If Porter failed to reduce the forts, Farragut would attempt to fight his way past them. If he succeeded in this, Farragut would engage and destroy rebel warships and cut off all supplies to the forts. Once Farragut had passed the forts, Butler was to take his troops through the swamps in the rear of Fort Saint Philip and carry it by direct assault.

In preparing these plans Butler had excellent technical advice from Lt. Godfrey Weitzel, his staff engineer. In the peacetime army Weitzel had been assigned for two years to Fort Saint Philip while it was under construction. Weitzel had been an enthusiastic duck hunter and, during his service in the region, had become entirely familiar with its swamps and bayous. Another peacetime professional, none other than Gen. George McClellan, knew of

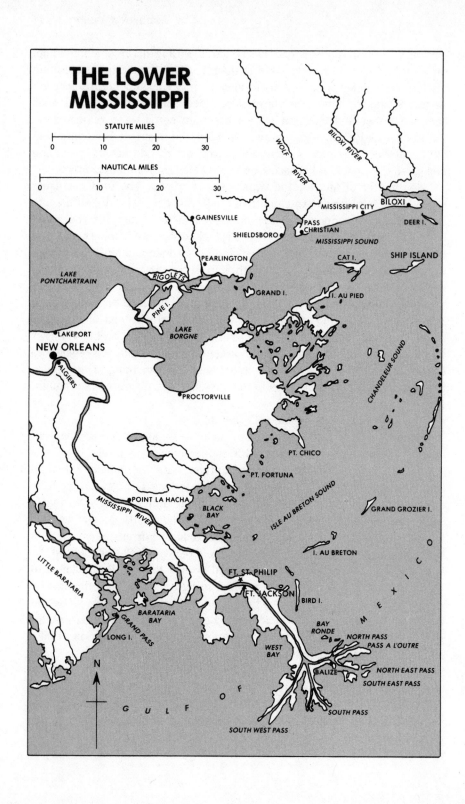

THE LOWER MISSISSIPPI

STATUTE MILES

0   10   20   30

NAUTICAL MILES

0   10   20   30

WOLF RIVER

BILOXI RIVER

GAINESVILLE

MISSISSIPPI CITY   BILOXI

PASS CHRISTIAN

SHIELDSBORO   DEER I.

MISSISSIPPI SOUND

PEARLINGTON

CAT I.   SHIP ISLAND

LAKE PONTCHARTRAIN

RIGOLETS

PINE I.

GRAND I.   I. AU PIED

LAKEPORT   LAKE BORGNE

NEW ORLEANS

ALGIERS

CHANDELEUR SOUND

PROCTORVILLE

PT. CHICO

PT. FORTUNA

POINT LA HACHA

MISSISSIPPI RIVER

BLACK BAY

ISLE AU BRETON SOUND   GRAND GROZIER I.

I. AU BRETON

LITTLE BARATARIA

FT. ST. PHILIP

FT. JACKSON

BIRD I.

M E X I C O

BARATARIA BAY

GRAND PASS

LONG I.

BAY RONDE

NORTH PASS

PASS A L'OUTRE

WEST BAY

BALIZE   NORTH EAST PASS

SOUTH EAST PASS

N

SOUTH PASS

G U L F   O F

SOUTH WEST PASS

Weitzel's special qualifications. McClellan's contribution to the New Orleans expedition, to which he was otherwise indifferent, was that he insisted on Weitzel's being posted to Butler's command. As for Butler, he grew to prize Weitzel's military skills beyond those of any subordinate who served with him in the war.

What with one difficulty and another, including the problem of maneuvering the larger ships across the bar and into the mainstream of the Mississippi, it was not until April 16 that Farragut had his fleet in place and ready for the assault. Porter had carefully staked out well-concealed positions for his bomb vessels, placing most of them where they would be shielded from enemy view by the heavy foliage of trees along the riverbank. Butler was standing by with eight regiments of infantry and three artillery batteries aboard the transports downriver.

It was two days later by the time Porter completed a mathematically precise placement of his mortar schooners, calculating ranges to the yard. On the morning of April 18, he ordered the bombardment begun, each vessel to fire a mortar round every ten minutes. In quick reaction, both Confederate forts began replying heavily and to some effect as they found the range. Finally the more exposed bomb schooners were taking so much punishment that Porter decided to move them back under the trees with the others. By 5:00 in the afternoon, wooden structures in Fort Jackson were ablaze.

At sundown the Confederate gunners ceased firing, but Porter's mortar crews for a time doubled their rate of fire. Later during the night the Union gunners contented themselves with firing at half-hour intervals. Next day the mortar vessels resumed their rapid-fire bombardment, continuing it day and night.

After two days of standing by and observing Porter's furious bombardment, Farragut's patience wore thin. He called a council of his ranking officers, noting that Porter was using up ammunition at an enormous rate. It was decided that the fleet should wait no longer for the mortar schooners to silence the Confederate guns. Farragut, who never had put much confidence in the effectiveness of the mortars, now proposed to force his way past the forts in a night action, all guns of the fleet blazing away. In sum, this was the alternative Butler and Farragut had agreed upon before the expedition got under way.

Farragut's council took note of the odds. The Confederates had mustered a motley flotilla of defense vessels, which lay beyond the forts. These included a pair of large ironclad rams, the *Mississippi* and the *Louisiana*, and they worried Farragut's officers more than a little, since the Federal fleet consisted of wooden ships vulnerable to ramming attack. What they did not know was that the *Mississippi* was uncompleted, and that the *Louisiana*'s engines had not yet been installed. The commanders were also concerned about the huge fire rafts they knew the defenders had been preparing and about the massive chain, secured to a series of hulks, that barred the way upriver. Against these considerations, the firepower of Fort Saint Philip and Fort Jackson seemed almost of lesser importance.

Farragut had been content to leave the chain barrier unmolested, since it locked Confederate vessels in as much as it held Federal ships out. Now, however, he detailed the gunboats *Pinola* and *Itasca* to dispose of the chain barrier in a quick night raid. Men from the *Pinola* were to place a charge aboard one of the hulks and explode it by means of an electrical detonator. Men from the *Itasca*, meanwhile, were to board another hulk, cut it loose, and let the force of the river current swing it around, carrying the broken chain barrier with it.

In the execution of this plan, strong currents swept the *Pinola* away from the target hulk so quickly that the electrical connection was broken before the detonator could be activated, so the charge failed to explode. Meanwhile men from the *Itasca* boarded their targeted hulk and succeeded in severing the chain by use of cold chisel and sledgehammers. When the chain parted, however, both the hulk and the gunboat were swung around by the current, and the *Itasca* was driven aground. In the midst of these activities, Confederates ashore had spotted the gunboats. Both forts now directed a heavy but inaccurate fire on the vessels, while the forts themselves came under redoubled attack from Porter's mortars.

While all this uproar was going on, the *Pinola* moved quickly to rescue her companion gunboat and, after an effort that lasted a full hour, finally hauled the *Itasca* into deep water. Both vessels returned to the fleet unharmed and with mission accomplished. Now the way was clear for Farragut's fleet to run upriver past the forts.

The way was also clear for an immediate response by the Confederates. As soon as the chain barrier was broken, they set a blazing fire raft afloat downriver. This raft was a monster, prepared by packing a two-hundred–foot coal barge with resinous wood and turpentine-soaked cotton. With a strong wind fanning the flames, it passed within scorching distance of the *Hartford*, grazed the gunboat *Scioto*, and then passed the rest of the fleet without causing any damage.

The next three days were spent preparing the fleet for the final assault. All too aware of the vulnerable wooden hulls of his warships, Farragut draped them with as many heavy chains as were available, with particular attention to protecting engines and boilers as much as possible. In addition to this work, some of the ships required certain minor repairs. Finally, at 1:58 A.M. on April 24, Farragut hoisted two red lights at the peak of his flagship, signaling the fleet to set forth on what was to be the most remarkable naval exploit of the war.

Butler, aboard his headquarters steamer, the *Saxon*, followed Farragut's heavies to within eight hundred yards of the forts, and from that vantage point observed the battle. Porter's mortar boats stepped up their rate of fire to such an extent that at one point Butler was able to count no fewer than eleven mortar shells, their bright fuses burning, all in the air at one time. The light haze that hung over the river was soon thickened by the smoke from Farragut's guns, and visibility became limited to less than one hundred yards. Not until dawn did it become clear that the Federal fleet had successfully passed the forts and destroyed the Confederates' scratch force of warships, river steamers, and tugboats. The forts, however, remained defiant.

In the melee Butler's vessel *Saxon* was partially disabled, so he borrowed the *Miami*, which before the war had been a New York ferryboat, and proceeded downriver to organize an envelopment of the forts from the land side. After setting up a staging area at Sable Island in the Gulf, Butler landed troops of the Massachusetts 26th and 4th Wisconsin regiments. With these troops Butler proceeded inland, reaching the quarantine station above the forts after an advance begun in small boats and concluded by wading through the swamps, Butler himself sloshing along with the rest of his men for two miles in water up to his hips.

At the quarantine station, where Farragut had left the Federal ship *Mississippi* to cover Butler's troops, Captain Smith of that vessel ferried a detachment of infantry across the river. As a result of these maneuvers, Butler now had his troops firmly positioned in the rear of both forts, cutting them off from all hope either of escape or supply. On April 27, finally, the garrison soldiers of Fort Jackson mutinied, abandoned the fort, and surrendered themselves to Butler's pickets. The following day the Confederate officers of both forts sent a flag of truce downriver to Porter, who had withdrawn some distance. Porter accepted their surrender.

It remained for Butler's men to tidy up and occupy the forts, and for Porter and Butler to begin their quarrel over who had done what at Forts Jackson and Saint Philip. Meanwhile, in New Orleans, Farragut was dispatching a detachment of marines to raise the American flag over the United States Mint, signifying that the city was now once again part of the Federal Union.

27

Now between two prideful men there began that dispute which was to mature into a lifetime of enmity, fueled by the contempt each held for the other. At New Orleans Farragut was clearly the hero of the day; what was left for Butler and Porter amounted only to that shred of celebrity generated by the fall of the guardian forts, Saint Philip and Jackson. Porter said his mortar shells deserved the credit. Butler claimed the victory for his infantry.

On April 29, in a report datelined Forts Jackson and Saint Philip, Butler sent Secretary Stanton his account of the New Orleans battle. He paid full homage to Farragut and his men for the "gallantry, courage, and conduct of this heroic action, unprecedented in naval warfare." And he did not fail to note that Farragut's whole fleet had fought its way past the forts "except that part thereof under the immediate command of Capt. Porter." Porter's mortar flotilla, he reported, had withdrawn some miles downriver, fearing the Confederate ironclad *Louisiana*, which, lying moored off Fort Jackson, had been bypassed by Farragut's fleet.

The truth of this was that Porter, prudently enough, wanted some sea room for his ships, should they have to contend with the ironclad. What he did not know at the time was that the *Louisiana*, lacking proper engines, was nothing more than a floating battery, incapable of maneuvering. As this turned out, the hapless *Louisiana* was not destined for a fighting finish. In a desperate finale, the derelict was packed with ammunition, set afire, and turned loose to drift downstream against Porter's mortar boats. But before she could do any damage, the *Louisiana* blew up and sank. Her violent end was the last defiant effort of the Confederate river defense.

Officers of the forts were negotiating terms of surrender with Porter at the very moment the *Louisiana* exploded. The Confederate navy people had taken the view that they were not bound by the Confederate army's decision to quit.

All this occurred on April 28, a day after the garrison troops at Fort Jackson had mutinied and surrendered to Butler's men. "No shot had been fired at them for three days," Butler wrote. "Nor had they fired a shot."

As to the effect of Porter's mortar bombs, Butler was unimpressed. "I have taken possession of the forts," he reported to Stanton, "and find them substantially as defensible as before the bombardment, Saint Philip precisely so—it is quite uninjured. They are fully provisioned, well supplied with ammunition, and the ravages of the shells have been defensibly repaired by the labor of the rebels."

Porter, naturally enough, preferred to see the outcome of the mortar bombardment in a more favorable light. He dispatched an enthusiastic report to Navy Secretary Welles: "Fort Jackson is a perfect wreck. Everything in the shape of a building in and about it was burned by the mortar shells, and over 1,800 shells fell in the work proper, to say nothing of those which burst over and around it."

Porter's various reports on his mortar bombardment tend to raise some doubts both as to the marksmanship of his crews and the accuracy of his arithmetic. In a much later account, Porter wrote of the preliminary firing by his mortar fleet: "We had kept up a heavy fire night and day for nearly five days—about 2,800 shells every 24 hours; in all about 16,800 shells." Yet Fort Saint Philip was virtually unharmed, and as for Fort Jackson, only eighteen hundred bombshells—by Porter's own accounting—had found that large target. Even an observer less biased than Butler would have been justified in wondering where all those thousands of shells had struck. Add in the results of heavy direct gunfire from Farragut's warships, and there is additional cause to wonder.

As to the effect of the bombardment on the soldiers manning the forts, who had suffered fewer than fifty casualties, it was left for Confederate Brig. Gen. J. H. Duncan, in command, to report about the mutiny and the surrender to Butler's troops:

> So far, throughout the entire bombardment and final action, the spirit of the troops was cheerful, confident, and courageous. . . . A reaction set in among them during the lull of the 25th, 26th, and 27th, when there was no other excitement to arouse them than the fatigue duty of repairing our damages. . . .

General Duncan was at a loss to explain why, after the bombardment had ceased, the men decided to mutiny. All he noticed before his troops rebelled was that they were "still obedient, but not buoyant and cheerful" until, at midnight of April 27, they staged their revolt and marched out to surrender.

A terse report by Lt. John C. Palfrey, U.S. Engineers, summed up the condition of Fort Saint Philip: "The fort is as efficient as before the attack.

Its armament is as follows, viz. On Face 8, running from 7, are two 8-inch columbiads, one columbiad platform without rails, one 8-inch columbiad, one columbiad, one columbiad platform complete."

Lieutenant Weitzel, Butler's trusted engineer, made a similar report as to the relatively undamaged condition of the forts. At Fort Jackson, the more heavily hit, damage was most evident only in wooden structures that had been burned.

Immediately after the surrender, Butler issued his orders to Colonel Jones, whose Massachusetts 26th was assigned to garrison duty in the forts. Jones was instructed to remove all frame buildings and everything combustible to the outside of the walls and to put the forts "in a proper state of police and defense." This was something that the Confederate force, if directed with any intelligence, should have done before they came under attack. It was standard procedure.

Still another kind of cleanup was suggested in a separate report by the army engineers. This report concluded in so many words that the worst damage inside the forts had been due to the "extreme slovenliness" of the Confederate soldiery.

Capt. John W. De Forest, the novelist whose memoirs were preserved in the letters he wrote home during his service, got a look at the forts as his regiment was being transported for duty in New Orleans. De Forest wrote:

> Some days later, the forts being abandoned, we were towed up to them, and I got a chance to go ashore. The long, green, moundlike earthworks of Fort Saint Philip were quite uninjured. The mouldy old brickwork of Fort Jackson showed no damage besides some broad scales knocked off the facings, and a few enormous holes bored in the summits of the ramparts by the eleven-inch bombs. The barracks, however, were a curiosity of ruin, shattered into miscellaneous tatters and splinters. If the garrison had remained in them it would have been made mincemeat of; but it had the casemates for shelter, and it suffered but moderate damage.

Porter's report to the Navy Department did not catch Butler's attention for several days, but when it did he reacted sharply. Writing to Secretary Stanton on June 1, Butler gave ample vent to his indignation:

> I have read Commander Porter's official report of the surrender of the Forts, and here permit me, for the sake of my brave and enduring soldiers of the 26th Mass. and 4th Wisconsin Regiments, who waded in the swamps in the rear of Fort Saint Philip up to their armpits in water, in order to cut off its garrison and get ready to assault the enemy's works, to put the truth of history right before the War

Department and the country, by the simple enumeration of the fact that it was due to their efforts and that of their comrades, and to these alone, that Forts Jackson and Saint Philip surrendered when they did.

After again recounting events at the forts, Butler declared, "I will not permit too great greed of praise on the part of anyone to take away the merit fairly due my brave soldiers."

For "anyone" it was easy to read *Porter* in the context of Butler's hot summation. But nobody in Washington was even slightly interested in who did what at Forts Saint Philip and Jackson. Farragut was the hero, and New Orleans the prize. Farragut had captured the largest city in the Confederacy and its most important port. Ships that had been assigned to blockading New Orleans were freed for other duties. In New Orleans the Federal army and navy now had a base from which to advance up the Mississippi to meet Union forces driving down from the north. However prematurely, it was Porter who summed up the results of the campaign in his jubilant report to Welles: "Truly the backbone of the Rebellion is broken."

For Butler, the prospects ahead left little time for nurturing his private quarrel, hereditary and dedicated feudist though he was. As usual, he had much to do and very little to do it with. There were other Gulf towns to be taken, an advance upriver to be executed, and a rebel city to be pacified and held—all operations to be conducted at the business end of a very long and complicated line of supply, and all subject to the shifts and eddies of the political currents that constantly swirled around Mr. Lincoln. Butler set to work with furious energy.

28

Butler formed his troops at dusk on May 1 and led them to the massive granite custom house, which he had decided would serve as his citadel. He took his post at the head of the column, as he had when he staged his surprise occupation of Baltimore; but this time there was no Wagnerian thunder and lightning to accompany the march, nor was there a horse for the commanding general to ride. Butler strode along with his men, keeping step to the brisk cadence of a regimental drum corps.

Up to this time, although New Orleans was under the guns of the fleet, there still was no Federal detachment ashore adequate to control the territory contained within the boundaries of the city and its outer defenses. Municipal government had gone into hiding. Mobs ruled the streets.

Gen. Mansfield Lovell, heading a ragtag force of Confederates, had prudently withdrawn to the hinterland. Until Farragut's startling victory the Confederacy had considered New Orleans impregnable to attack. No Union force existed that could be considered a threat from the land side, and the river, guarded by its two massive forts, seemed entirely secure. Thus Lovell's command was scarcely taken seriously as a fighting unit. Not even Lovell himself knew for sure how many men he led. Estimates ranged from three thousand to eight thousand, depending on whether Confederates or Unionists were doing the guessing.

In any case Lovell's command was highly fluid in its composition, since large numbers of his foot soldiers were lukewarm rebels now eyeing their chances to slip away and become civilians again. Many of them did melt into the civilian population even as Lovell took to the swamps. Others in large numbers were to flood back into the city once Butler had established law and order there.

In the brief interval of anarchy between Lovell's departure and Butler's arrival, the city's minority of rebel hard-liners seized the opportunity to wreak as much destruction as they thought prudent. They destroyed nearly all the commercial shipping left in the port. They burned cotton, sugar, pine tar, tobacco, timber, and coal, valued altogether in the millions. They also applied the torch to crops and cotton in storage on some of the plantations outside the city. But the rebels stopped short of destroying the city by fire, as some of the wilder spirits among them demanded. Above all else, New Orleans was a commercial center, and the commercial interests that ruled it put commerce far above sentiment, even when their sentiment favored the Confederacy.

Against this background Butler planned the timing of his march carefully. He knew, of course, that he was entering a hostile city. Although it contained a great many Unionists, these were discreet and cautious Unionists for the most part, principally concerned with staying out of harm's way. There were a few rash exceptions, like the one encountered by Capt. John W. De Forest, the literary man turned soldier. De Forest described the reception accorded his Connecticut regiment as it debarked:

> Down the ladder we crept and fell into line fronting the city, surrounded by male and female roughs and ragged urchins, who hooted and sneered and swore. . . . A red-nosed man addresses me personally, declares with many oaths, "We don't want you here, damn it! You haven't come among friends, not by a damn sight. We don't want you, d'ye understand? We wouldn't give you a cup of water."
>
> I don't want a cup of water, and I make no reply. But a ragged Irishman emerges from the crowd with a shillelah four feet long, which he holds by the middle and whirls around his wolfish head, meanwhile damning and God-damning and God-damning-to-hell the red-nosed man, who hastily departs around the nearest corner. Then the Irishman salutes me in military style, takes off his shabby hat to the colors and makes them a low bow.

Butler, counting on no help from sympathizers, Irish or otherwise, moved on the custom house as night fell. He judged that it would be less likely for a rebel mob to gather in darkness than in daylight. He calculated further that, if his troops were fired upon from any of the houses, the flash would reveal the source, which could then be dealt with all the more easily. In any case, whether from good planning or good fortune, the march was completed without incident. Butler posted his troops; selected a company of the Massachusetts 31st Regiment as a headquarters guard; and proceeded to the Saint Charles Hotel, which was to be his command post.

After his staff took over the hotel, Ben returned to the steamer *Mississippi*, where Sarah was waiting on board. She had made the trip from Ship Island in the *Saxon*, which Butler had detached from the expedition and sent back to pick up tentage for his troops. Sarah had transferred to the more commodious steamer when she arrived.

Next day the Butlers were installed in their new quarters at the Saint

Charles. Sarah was exultant at having had a part in the adventure, but she had had enough of campaigning, although she was reluctant to say so. As always, consideration of Ben's needs and wishes was uppermost in her mind. She wrote to her sister promptly on May 2:

> I am very desirous to see home again but cannot say exactly when I may leave. . . . I do not know how I can leave Mr. Butler here with the summer before him, and this load of care and work on his shoulders. . . . If I go he will miss me terribly, and if I stay and get very sick it will be ten times worse for him. . . .

What Sarah feared most, weariness aside, was the reputation of New Orleans as a plague spot for yellow fever, which regularly swept that city when the steamy summer heat arrived. Ben, whose adventurous father had died of the fever on that faraway Caribbean island, was more than casually aware of its menace and had already planned stringent measures to keep the city fever-free.

Lawyerlike, Butler had prepared rules and regulations to go into effect in the conquered city as soon as he assumed control. One set was contained in a brief general order to his troops. The other, much lengthier, was a proclamation addressed to the municipal government and citizens of New Orleans.

Butler's troops were bluntly told to behave themselves: no plundering, no running wild in their new urban surroundings. They were instructed never to go about unarmed and never to go anywhere alone. Butler promised that punishment for infractions would be swift and severe, and that officers would be held responsible for enforcing these orders to the letter.

The second document was far more detailed (see Appendix 1). It placed New Orleans under martial law and called upon all rebels remaining in the city to surrender themselves, their arms, and their equipment. Union loyalists were directed to come forward and renew their oath of allegiance to the United States. It provided that erstwhile rebels who returned to their peaceful occupations would be left undisturbed. The municipal government would be permitted to continue collecting taxes and providing certain services, notably those of the police and fire departments. Churches, shops, and places of amusement were to remain open, as were saloons, provided the latter applied for and received licenses from the occupying authority.

Butler knew he would have an immediate problem with currency reform. But in the meantime he authorized the circulation of Confederate bills and locally issued notes, since the people of New Orleans had no other ready means of exchange. Press and telegraph offices were placed under military censorship. And Butler warned that killing an American soldier would be regarded not as an act of war, but as murder, and would be judged and punished as such.

Editors of the newspaper *True Delta*, testing for limits, refused to print the general's proclamation. Whereupon Butler immediately ordered publication of the newspaper suspended, seized the printing plant, sent in some skilled printers from one of his versatile Massachusetts regiments, and in that way got his proclamation reproduced in volume and distributed on May 2. The editors, properly chastened, made suitable apology and promises of good behavior, after which (the very next day) Butler gave them back their paper.

In his order restoring the *True Delta*, Butler did not neglect to include a sharp paragraph:

> The commanding General having demonstrated the ability of his officers and soldiers to do everything necessary for the success of his plans without aid from any citizen of New Orleans, and shown the uselessness of aimless and unavailing opposition by the people, desires to interfere no further with that press.

While Butler's official dispatch to Secretary Stanton summed up the military situation in terse detail, it remained for Sarah to fill in some of the color in her letter home to Harriet. The Butlers found the Saint Charles Hotel closed, she reported, and the proprietor refusing to open it.

> Mr. Butler gave him his choice, to open and receive us as guests for liberal pay, or to have it taken for barracks. They concluded to take us, and the Gen'l. and staff have ample room, nobody else in the house. The people [of New Orleans] were at the point of starvation. Speculators held what flour there was at twenty-five dollars a barrel. Butter a dollar a pound, eggs a dollar a dozen, and so on. Mr. Butler ordered flour to be sold at New York prices. . . .
>
> And what do you think of my being among the first to enter New Orleans! Our vessel drew up at the wharf, the troops were disembarked that night, and in silence marched through the black and sullen town to the Custom House. The next day Mr. Butler ordered the opening of the St. Charles, compelled a hackman at the point of the bayonet to drive us to the hotel. We had no guard but an armed soldier on the box and another behind the carriage. A regiment was drawn up around the hotel and four howitzers on the corners. If we were to encounter a mob, it was decided to give them an opportunity. The band was stationed on the piazza, and they played with fiery energy all the national airs from Yankee Doodle to the Star Spangled Banner. . . .
>
> There was some disturbance in one of the streets but it was quelled. A crowd collected, listened to the music, and dispersed

without any demonstration. Every day there will be greater security, for the poor will be relieved, and confidence increased. . . .

Indeed relief of the poor was Butler's first priority, and he took immediate measures to provide food supplies from every source available. He expended his own funds to purchase flour, tapped the slender stores of army rations, opened rail and water traffic to bring supplies into the city, and diverted to the relief effort one thousand barrels of captured stores intended for the rebel forces in the area.

In an angry general order, Butler castigated the city officials for neglecting their own citizens of the working classes.

This hunger does not pinch the wealthy and influential, the leaders of the rebellion, who have gotten up this war, and are now endeavoring to prosecute it without regard to the starving poor, the working man, his wife and child. . . .

The United States have sent land and naval forces here to fight and subdue rebellious armies in array against authority. We find, substantially, only fugitive masses, runaway property burners, a whiskey-drinking mob, and starving citizens with their wives and children. It is our duty to call back the first, to punish the second, root out the third, feed and protect the last.

Ready only for war, we had not prepared ourselves to feed the hungry and relieve the distressed with provisions. But to the extent possible, within the power of the commanding general, it shall be done.

In this frame of mind, Butler arrested Pierre Soulé, sheriff of New Orleans and a former U.S. congressman, and shipped him off to Washington with a recommendation that he be tried for "flagrant treason." If Soulé had been caught while armed, Butler said in his covering letter to Stanton, he would have tried the man himself and executed the sentence. Soulé was active in a secret secessionist society, the Southern Independence Association, sworn to resist reestablishment of the Federal Union whatever the outcome of the war.

Soulé's treason was perhaps the least of the difficulties Butler was to face in his dealings with the New Orleans commercial establishment. In company with nearly all the foreign consuls in the city, the establishment had been making a very good thing financially out of the war and the blockade, shipping cotton and other cargoes out, bringing munitions and medical supplies in.

Butler was to lose this contest eventually, thanks to the pliable nature of Secretary of State Seward in his soft and yielding relationship with the

European powers, and also to the strange tangle of political interests in which the Lincoln administration was perpetually snarled. In the meantime, however, working eighteen hours a day, the general fed the poor, put the city in order, and carried out successful military operations with the limited manpower allotted him by GHQ.

29

Flag Officer Farragut's conquest of New Orleans stopped at the water's edge. The guns of the Yankee fleet covered the city, but Farragut had no force sufficient to occupy and police it; that had to await the arrival of Ben Butler's troops. Lacking any reasonable alternative, Farragut resorted to symbolism. He sent a detachment of marines ashore to plant the American flag on the roof of the United States Mint. But this solution was not reached immediately or without a great deal of uproar and tension.

Farragut first sent Capt. Theodorus Bailey, his second in command, to demand the formal surrender of the city. Captain Bailey, accompanied by an aide, Lt. George H. Perkins, made his way to the city hall through the howling New Orleans mob. There he met with Mayor Monroe and Confederate General Lovell. The mayor said he couldn't surrender the city, and the general said he wouldn't. This left Bailey with little choice but to return to the flagship and report the impasse. Farragut then gave up the attempt for the night, ordering every man in the fleet to arm with pistols and cutlasses against the possibility of an attempt by the rebels to board the ships in darkness.

Next day he sent Capt. Albert Kautz, accompanied by a midshipman and twenty marines, to renew the demand for a formal surrender. Now the mob, encouraged by yesterday's absence of a display of force, was wilder than ever. Farragut had told Kautz that, if his party was fired upon, he intended to open with the guns of the fleet and level the town. Kautz, however, solved the dangerous situation with diplomacy. He called upon a city policeman to escort him to city hall, and sent his marine guard back to the ship.

While Kautz was talking to little effect with Mayor Monroe, a mob approached carrying an American flag, which they tore to tatters, throwing the shreds through the windows of city hall at Kautz and Monroe. This was the first inkling Kautz had that Farragut had hoisted the Stars and Stripes over the Mint. The flag had been promptly seized and paraded through the streets with fife and drum. Kautz, totally unsuccessful in his mission, was persuaded to leave city hall by a rear entrance, where a carriage awaited to spirit him back to his ship.

Two more days passed in negotiations that led nowhere. Finally, on April 29, Farragut dispatched a full battalion of the fleet marines, backed by howitzers, to march in strength to the Custom House. Mayor Monroe was invited to haul down the state flag, which was flying over the building, but he refused to do so. Kautz cut the halyard with his sword, and the flag that fluttered down was delivered as a trophy to Farragut. The national banner was hoisted aloft, and there it flew, guarded by the marines until Butler and his troops arrived on May 1 to take over the occupation of the city.

When Farragut told Butler of the incident at the Mint, and how a particularly vociferous ringleader had led three others in cutting down the American flag, Butler's response was quick.

"I will make an example of that fellow by hanging him," said Butler.

Farragut smiled. "You know, General, you will have to catch him before you can hang him."

"I'll catch him," said Butler.

It was at this point that an unlikely character, William B. Mumford, entered history. Mumford was a New Orleans gambler somewhat given to high living and hard liquor. He found the excitement of the rioting city exhilarating and the opportunity to play hero irresistible. Perhaps, with a gambler's eye for the odds, he calculated his personal risk in hauling down the flag to be slight. He relished the notoriety of the moment. What he did not count on, however, was the price of true fame.

More than any other player on the New Orleans scene, Mumford was to realize the wry truth contained in the adage, "God protect me from my friends; I can protect myself from my enemies." The rebel press did him the disservice not only of identifying him as the leader of the flag desecrators, but of praising him to the skies as a true Confederate hero. The rioters took him to their hearts. He was cheered and idolized as he went about wearing a spattered shred of the flag in his buttonhole.

As a rambunctious drunk, Mumford might have got off with a prison sentence when Ben Butler finally caught up with him. But as a symbol of Confederate resistance, he wound up on the gallows. The New Orleans mob did not petition clemency for Mumford. It simply defied Butler to hang him, and in the end it became a matter of whether Butler or the mob would rule. To the strong-willed Yankee general, there was but one answer to that proposition.

Mumford was also an unlucky gambler in that his arrest and trial followed close on another capital case in which Butler had indeed granted clemency. Six Confederate soldiers captured at the river forts had given their parole and been set free in New Orleans. There Butler's alert secret service found them organizing a volunteer company which, according to their plans, was to break through Butler's lines and join the rebel forces of General Beauregard, operating to the north.

Taken and tried by court-martial, the six were condemned to be shot to death by a firing squad for violating their parole, a sentence routinely established in the military code of the times. However, after examining the evidence and the proceedings of the court, Butler was not at all sure that the six soldiers really understood what was meant by the giving of their parole. Butler noticed that one of them, in fact, had said he thought parole was something that applied only to officers.

Fortunately for the six prisoners, neither the mob nor the rebel press took up their cause with the fervor that came to be lavished on Mumford. Several staunch Unionists of New Orleans pleaded for the six and presented a petition signed by many other Unionists, all asking for clemency. Butler, already convinced in his own mind that leniency was indicated, commuted the death sentences. The six were given prison terms and assigned to hard labor at Ship Island. Encouraged by this show of softness on Butler's part, the New Orleans rebels stepped up their campaign in behalf of Mumford. The boast now being made was that Butler would not dare to hang the gambler, as he had not "dared" to hang the six parolees.

At the court-martial of Mumford, the prisoner pleaded not guilty. His main defense was based on the theme that he really was not, after all, the leader of the group that had torn down the flag, and that "other parties" were more culpable than he, no matter what the rebel editorialists had been writing. But Thomas A. Dryden, a former policeman, testified that he witnessed the incident, and that he heard Mumford say that he was the first man who put a hand to the flag to tear it down.

The outcome had scarcely been in doubt from the time Mumford had been taken up as a rebel hero, so it was no surprise when the court found him guilty and sentenced him to hang "at or near the Mint," where his crime had taken place. At this point the case was referred to Butler for review and final action.

The pressure on Butler was enormous. One of Butler's secret-service operatives attended a meeting in which the assembled hard-liners vowed to assassinate the general if Mumford was hanged. Butler's operative himself prudently joined the clamor, delivering a hot speech in which he urged that Butler be shot.

Later that same night the shaken spy reported to the general. He said the assemblage had first voted to name a committee to deliver a death threat to Butler, but soon found that nobody was eager to serve on such a committee. So instead they voted that everybody at the meeting should send Butler an anonymous letter telling him that, if Mumford died, Butler would die. Next morning Ben did indeed receive forty or more death-threat letters, each crudely adorned with such devices as crossed pistols, coffins, and skulls-and-crossbones.

Butler's operative was convinced, if the general was not. "Do one thing for me," said Butler's man. "If you really mean to hang Mumford, give me what money I ought to have, and give me an order so that I may go away at once before the execution. If it should be found out that I had been in your service, whether you were alive or dead my life would not be safe a minute. I want to go north."

Butler paid him off and dispatched him northward by ship in a manner suggesting he had been put under arrest as a rebel.

"I frankly admit that I was frightened myself," Butler recalled later. "I gave more attention that night to Mumford's execution than I did to sleep." But the Yankee general had decided, whatever the pressures, that Mumford had to hang.

Next day Butler agreed to see Mumford's wife, although this added to the stress he was under. She arrived at headquarters with her small children to plead for her husband's life. She and the children wept bitterly, while the children threw themselves to the floor and clutched the general's knees. Butler was shaken, but the best he could do, in view of his decision of the night before, was to send Mrs. Mumford and the children in his carriage to the prison where Mumford was held, there to make their farewell visit. The general expressed his sorrow for their enormous misfortune. He assured Mrs. Mumford that, if she called upon him in the future for any favor that would alleviate the harm that was being done to her and the children, she would find him willing to help. Butler said he had heard that Mumford did not really believe he would be executed.

"I wish you to convince him that he is mistaken," said the general. "Whether I live or die, he will die. Let him in the few hours he has to live look to his God for pardon."

The gallows for the execution had been erected at the Mint, with the American flag flying over it. Mumford was allowed to make as long a speech from the scaffold as he wished. As he did so he kept looking down the street to catch sight of the staff officer he expected to come galloping up with a reprieve.

Around the gallows the roughs had gathered, waving pistols and swigging from whiskey bottles. To the last, Mumford's admirers continued to encourage the condemned man with shouts to the effect that there would be no hanging because Ben Butler wouldn't dare to go through with it.

At headquarters, meanwhile, the eighty-year-old president of the Bank of Louisiana, Dr. William N. Mercer, rushed into Butler's office to make a last-minute plea. With tears running down his cheeks, the old man begged for Mumford's life. But the general was not to be moved.

Mumford at last fell silent. The trap dropped, and the gambler went to his death. A hush fell over the unruly crowd, which then slowly and quietly dispersed.

With this one painful act, Butler had effectively tamed the New Orleans mob for once and for all, but the South now had a martyr and the Confederacy's adroit propagandists knew just how to make use of him. Ben Butler now became the South's most hated figure. From Jefferson Davis on down, Confederate politicians heaped abuse on Butler, the Yankee Savage. Southern editorialists all but frothed at the mouth as they penned their elaborate diatribes.

"The miserable hireling Butler is playing the tyrant with a high hand," raged the Hannibal, Missouri, *Herald*. "His savage instincts are far ahead of the most ferocious native of Dahomey or Patagonia. . . ."

Gov. Thomas O. Moore of Louisiana issued a bitter eulogy. "The noble heroism of the patriot Mumford has placed his name high on the list of our martyr sons," said the governor. "He met his fate courageously, and has transmitted to his countrymen a fresh example of what men will do and dare when under the inspiration of fervid patriotism. I shall not forget the outrage of his murder, nor shall it pass unnoticed."

The postscript to the Mumford affair was not to come to light for many years. After the execution of her husband, the Mumford family was declared a public trust of the Confederacy, and large sums were subscribed for their support. But, as it happened, the sums were in Confederate money, which in fairly short order became worthless.

The widow turned to Butler for help in 1869, addressing the general through a friend of hers in Malden, Massachusetts. Butler promptly gave her an appointment to see him at his Washington office. She told him she had used the last of her funds to build a house in Wytheville, Virginia; had gone broke; and was about to lose the house because of a mechanic's lien held by the builder.

Butler promptly got in touch with an attorney-friend in the area, a former Confederate officer as it happened. He instructed his friend to settle the matter and charge all costs to Butler's account. Then he got Mrs. Mumford a clerical post in the internal revenue office. Still later, when the Hayes administration purged many employees to make way for Hayes patronage appointees, Mrs. Mumford was among those who lost their jobs. She called on the general for help once more, and Butler at once made the rounds of several federal offices until finally he got her another clerical job in the Postoffice Department.

"There she remained as long as she chose to stay in office, as far as I know," Butler recalled in his memoirs. "I saw the boys from time to time. They called on me with their mother, and seemed very gentlemanly and bright."

30

From his efficient intelligence sources, Butler learned that the Confederate high command was rather counting on yellow fever as the secret weapon that would decimate the unacclimated Northern troops in New Orleans when the summer fever season arrived. This infuriated him. It also heightened his resolve to deal with the menace by every means at his command. Butler knew nothing about yellow fever except that when it took hold in a population it spread rapidly, and that the best defense against it was a rigid quarantine of ships that might be carrying the infection to New Orleans from the notorious fever ports of the Caribbean. As an immediate measure, therefore, he imposed such a quarantine.

All incoming vessels, arriving from whatever port, were required to undergo a strict medical inspection at a quarantine station he established at Fort Saint Philip. The guns of the fort were manned and ready to enforce Butler's order, should any skipper be rash enough to try bypassing the compulsory stop. If a ship was found to have fever of any kind among passengers or crew, it was required to stay downriver for forty days, then undergo a second inspection. Only if then found free of disease would it be permitted to proceed. Restrictions were even tighter for any ship arriving from a port where yellow fever was known to be present. All such vessels were required to undergo the forty-day quarantine period even if inspection found crew and passengers fever-free.

Butler appointed a qualified quarantine officer and paid him double the usual salary for such service. That was the carrot. For the stick, Butler gave the man to understand that if he slipped up in any way whatever he might very likely be shot.

For overall supervision of the health of the city and of his command, Butler secured the services of Dr. Charles McCormick, reputed to be the nation's foremost authority on yellow fever. Dr. McCormick had been one of those hard-pressed physicians who had to cope with the dreadful fever outbreak of 1853, when more than seven thousand residents of New Orleans had died of the disease, and when those inhabitants who were strong enough to do so had fled the city in terror. McCormick was named Medical Director, Department of the Gulf.

Neither Butler nor any medical authority of the time had any inkling that the disease was caused by a virus transmitted from person to person by the bite of the *Aedes* mosquito. That was not to be firmly established until 1901, through the brilliant work of Dr. Walter Reed and his associates in the Panama Canal Zone. But, though ignorant of the true nature of the fever, Butler had a tidy New England notion that prevailing filth might have something to do with it, and he had found New Orleans to be a desperately filthy city.

Four days after landing in New Orleans, Ben and Sarah, accompanied only by a staff officer and an orderly, went for a drive in a light carriage to look around the city. Their drive took them along a canal connecting a large pond with Lake Pontchartrain. As they approached the area, the stench was nearly asphyxiating. Both pond and canal were covered with a green scum amid which floated the bodies of dead cats and dogs. Remains of dead mules lay along the banks. Very little of this was inspection enough: the driver quickly turned the carriage away and found a different route back to headquarters.

Butler sent at once for the city official whose duty it was to supervise maintenance of streets and canals. What, he demanded to know, was the problem with that canal?

"Nothing that I know of, General," the man replied.

"Have you been up there lately?"

"Yes. There yesterday."

"Didn't you observe anything special when you were there?"

"No, General."

"Not an enormous stink?"

"No more than usual, General."

"Do you mean to tell me that the canal always looks and stinks like that?"

"In hot weather, General."

"When was it cleaned out last?"

"Never, to my knowledge, General."

Butler, who could scarcely believe what he was hearing, managed to keep his patience.

"Well, it must be cleaned out at once," said the general.

"Can't do it," the man replied.

"Why not?"

"I don't know how."

That was enough for Butler. He fired the man on the spot, hired a replacement, and set the cleanup in motion immediately. Given Butler's reputation for quick and stern justice, it is possible to consider that the Superintendent of Streets and Canals got off lightly.

Meanwhile fear of yellow fever was creating a serious morale problem in Butler's command. Inhabitants of the city spared none of the gruesome details as they told Butler's men about the horrors of the 1853 epidemic. Very soon both officers and enlisted men talked of little else but the fever, and the more ingenious among them plotted ways to get honorable reassignment to the north, where there was nothing but rebel shot and shell to worry about. The regular surgeons in Butler's regiments were of no help, since they knew no more about yellow fever than the men did.

Butler determined to clean up the city. Studying a map showing the areas where the fever usually struck hardest, he was strengthened in his hunch that total lack of sanitation had something to do with the generation and spread of the disease. He particularly noted the area around the old French Market as a hot spot, and when he inspected the market he was convinced his hunch was right.

Butler observed that the women operating food stalls at the market simply tossed the refuse of their trade on the floor. Since they dealt in poultry, fish, and various meats, among other things, the accumulated debris was noisome in the extreme—and it had been accumulating for more than a hundred years. The stone floor originally installed by the Spaniards was now buried to a depth of eighteen inches or more by decayed and decaying matter that had been trodden into a massive crust. Butler ordered it cleaned right to the foundation, and dispatched a body of troops to enforce the order.

To accomplish a general cleanup of the city's streets, Butler put two thousand of the city's unemployed men to work, married men getting preference in the hiring. The New Orleans city treasury was ordered to pay each man fifty cents a day; for his part the general undertook to supply every man in the work force with a soldier's full ration of more than fifty ounces of food per day. This was enough, he noted, to support not only the laborer but the man's wife as well.

Butler issued orders that all houses in the city and all the land around them should be put in order and kept that way, and he set up an inspection force to see to it that householders obeyed instructions. Houses that were not painted were to be whitewashed. No refuse of any kind was to be deposited on the ground, but rather had to be placed in a proper receptacle. He established a collection service, using mule teams and carts, to empty and cleanse the receptacles and haul away their contents. Violation of any of the new cleanliness rules meant jail time in the city prison.

One defiant businessman, scoffing at Butler's new regulations, took it upon himself to test the rule that forbade throwing anything into the street. Taking a piece of paper from his desk, the man called a city policeman over to witness his action, then threw the crumpled paper into the street. The puzzled policeman, not knowing whether *anything* covered such minor debris as a sheet of paper, simply reported the matter to the general. Butler's response was prompt, and his definition of *anything* was made clear. He ordered the offender to report to headquarters at once, and there sentenced him to three months in the city prison. The example worked. Thereafter the streets were kept clean. Rebel sympathizers found that cooperating with the despised Yankee general might be irksome, but they reckoned the alternative would be worse.

Butler had one final measure to undertake in order to complete his cleanup of slovenly New Orleans. He had to do something about the reeking surface drains that served the city in place of a sewer system.

With his insatiable curiosity Butler had found out something interesting about Lake Pontchartrain, the ultimate terminus for whatever flowed through the drains, ditches, and canals. Freshwater streams entered the lake at several places. It was also a receptacle for salt water entering from the Gulf. Strong surface winds had an effect on the interchange of fresh and salt water. When wind blew strongly from the north, it lowered the level of the lake by driving water toward the Gulf; fresh water would enter more rapidly. Conversely, a strong wind from the south would drive salt water into the lake, and the inflow of fresh water would be slowed. This behavior of the lake suggested to Butler a way in which those pestilential drains could be thoroughly cleaned.

Butler waited for a strong norther, then put his plan into motion. The city's water-supply plant was ordered to put all its pumps to work to flush the city's streets, one after another. Butler's two thousand-man sanitation crew—with hoes, rakes, and brushes—loosened all the debris. The main drainage canal was cleared so that water flowed freely into the lake, carrying all the refuse before it. The lake itself, its level lowered by the norther, readily received all the inflow and as readily purged itself.

The general even got providential assistance: heavy rain fell, the runoff raced down the drains, and the scouring of the drains was completed. In all of its colorful history, New Orleans had never been so clean.

There was but one scare. Dr. McCormick came into Butler's office one day looking worried. In spite of all the heroic measures that had been taken, two cases of yellow fever had been reported in the Frenchtown sector of the city. The two fever victims had been passengers on a small tug that had arrived in New Orleans from Nassau, where the fever was prevalent.

The tug had been passed through quarantine on the captain's sworn statement that his ship, bound for New Orleans from New York with a cargo of provisions, had stopped at Nassau only to take on coal, and that he had not picked up any passengers there.

Butler at once posted an armed guard around the square where the fever had been found. Using a medical technique thought efficacious in those days, Butler ordered blazing tar barrels placed at the corners of the square, and had them kept burning day and night. This medieval method of disease control was designed to create a constant updraft that would carry away and disperse the "miasmal vapors" believed to be the source of the disease. No one was allowed to approach the patients except those who had been acclimated to the area and were considered insusceptible to the fever.

Little hope was held out for the patients themselves, although they were given whatever comfort and treatment Butler's medical staff could provide. When after six days both fever victims died, their bodies were cremated. Everything they could possibly have come in contact with was then taken out and burned in a huge bonfire.

If Confederate strategists counted on disease as an ally, they were doomed to disappointment. In the end the two unfortunate passengers smuggled past Butler's quarantine were the only yellow-fever victims in New Orleans that year. As a result of the general's heroic measures, the city was kept clean and fever-free.

31

In faraway Washington that sharp and testy observer Gideon Welles would note in his diary, with an all but audible sniff, "Butler has shown ability as a police magistrate both at Baltimore and New Orleans."

Police administration in New Orleans, as a matter of generally unacknowledged fact, was only one of the innumerable details receiving Butler's sharp supervision. But indeed it was true that he was policing the city with extraordinary efficiency. During his tenure New Orleans was freer of crime than it had ever been or than it would be once he had left. As he had cleansed the city of filth and disease through extraordinary measures, Butler took equally diligent steps to collar and punish criminals of all kinds, most notably any rogues uncovered in his own command. He was also vigilant against all hints of rebellion on the part of the more virulent Yankee-haters who, in their protestations at least, found his presence in the city an insult and humiliation difficult to bear.

Butler's attention to detail—proverbially the essence of genius—had been evident from the start in his preparations for the New Orleans campaign. Nor did he overlook police matters in those preparations. Far back in Massachusetts, long before staging began at Ship Island, Butler had thought to include in his budget a special $10,000 appropriation that went toward hiring a secret agent and sending him ahead to New Orleans to gather intelligence. On this slender base, after the conquest of the city, Butler built a compact and effective network of operatives. Also, in a less organized way, the general never hesitated to receive informants and tipsters, to whom he dispensed $5 gold pieces from a capacious pocket.

Butler's agents more than supplemented the work of the city police force, which Butler trimmed, sharpened, and kept in action. In addition, there were the efficient patrols of the military provost guard, all under the close scrutiny of the general himself. When occasion required, Butler was not above filling the dual roles of police chief and chief of detectives, as he did in a criminal case that led to the only other hangings that took place, after the Mumford affair, during Butler's administration of New Orleans.

The case involved a particularly nagging series of nighttime burglaries that had aroused Butler's angry attention. He leaned hard on police, provost guard, and secret service alike to find the perpetrators, but their efforts were without result. The break did not come until a householder at 93 Toulouse Street appeared at headquarters to complain personally to the general. His house had been entered the night before by a Federal officer and four men, ostensibly there to search for weapons. He said that, in fact, the search party had ransacked his house, taking all the jewelry they could find as well as about $2,000 in cash.

The householder produced an official-looking paper labeled "certificate of search," which he said the officer had given him. The bogus certificate was signed "J. William Henry, Lieut., Eighteenth Mass. Volunteers," and this Butler recognized at once as a fake, since there was no 18th Regiment in his command. The complainant could not describe the men who had raided his house. All he could remember was that they had arrived and left in a cab.

"Can you at least remember the number of the cab?" asked Butler.

"Yes," the man replied. "It was cab number 50."

Butler immediately dispatched a provost lieutenant to find the driver of cab number 50 and bring him to headquarters. Under Butler's interrogation the driver recalled that he had taken his passengers from 93 Toulouse Street to a coffeehouse, which he identified. That was enough for the general.

"Lieutenant," he ordered, "take a party of the provost guard and go to this coffeehouse, and bring to me every living thing in it, including the cat, and don't let one speak to the other until they have seen me."

Butler's widely cast net produced a random catch. When the provost guard returned with the prisoners, Butler had them paraded before him. As he studied their faces, he recognized one of the men as an old acquaintance from police court days in Massachusetts, a man who had been convicted there of burglary.

Butler pounced. Dismissing the others, who were still held under guard, he confronted the erstwhile burglar with his Massachusetts prison record. There would be no mere prison sentence this time, Butler told the man.

"You have been caught once again robbing houses," Butler said. "And this time you are going to hang for it."

Thoroughly terrified as Butler glowered at him, the prize catch of the coffeehouse raid begged for a deal. All but blubbering under the general's sharp questioning, he offered to provide the whole story of the New Orleans burglaries and to testify against his companions.

"You had better tell the truth," Butler growled, "because lying is a sin I never pardon."

The wretched burglar told it all. He and six others had formed a secret gang. Using the search for arms as a pretext, they had plundered eighteen different houses. The man named names and provided addresses, whereupon Butler dispatched the provost guard to round them all up. Among them, much to the general's chagrin, was William M. Clary, second officer of the *Saxon*, his personal command vessel.

It developed that the gang had not yet distributed their loot, although they had spent about $400 of the cash they had stolen. Butler saw to it that it was all restored to the householders who had been robbed. Then he turned to the matter of summary trial and conviction. His decision was swift: the offense was a hanging matter.

When news got around that Butler had readied the gallows for five of the seven gang members, including the second mate of the *Saxon*, New Orleans secessionists immediately seized on a propaganda line. They put out the word that, unlike the patriot Mumford, none of these rascals would actually hang. Most certainly of all, they said, Butler would never hang an officer of his own steam launch.

The two gang members who escaped the death sentence were the informer, who was sentenced to serve five years' hard labor at Ship Island, and Theodore Lieb, an eighteen-year-old New Orleans youth whose mother pleaded with the general for her son's life. In the latter case Butler professed to take judicial note of the fact that the young man had been only a kind of messenger for the gang and that (as his mother said), until led astray, he had always been a good boy. Young Lieb was sent to Ship Island to serve an indeterminate sentence at hard labor.

Though Butler was always careful to preserve his public image as the hard-minded magistrate, in private he found the responsibility difficult to bear. The night before the fatal day was a sleepless one for the general, as it had been before the Mumford execution. All night long he paced the floor of his quarters, sorely tempted to issue a reprieve, but fearful that a show of weakness and favoritism would be used by the secessionists to undermine Federal authority in the thinly held city. In the end the five executions took place as ordered.

After the hangings there was little to occupy the provost court while Butler was in command other than petty larcenies and assaults. The burglary rate in New Orleans dropped to zero, and the city remained calm. New Orleans, Ben noted, had become one of the safest cities in America by day or by night—far safer, certainly, than either Washington or New York.

Although responsibilities like the Mumford affair and the burglars' execution weighed heavily on him, there was a lighter side to Butler's duties as a police administrator. He rather enjoyed fostering his reputation as the iron-fisted autocrat who knew absolutely everything that went on in New Orleans. He also had a practical reason for reinforcing the belief—almost a superstition—that nothing, however trivial, ever escaped his attention. The more widely this conviction was held, he felt, the fewer would be the conspiracies. In the meantime it provided him with a certain wry amusement.

Besides his regular and very active secret service, which ranged far and wide into rebel-held territory to obtain useful military intelligence, Butler had the unofficial help of many of the black servants and waiters in New Orleans, who eagerly provided him in private with bits and pieces of information gleaned in the finer homes, clubs, and restaurants of the city.

The latter kind of intelligence Butler sometimes used in Puckish fashion to further his all-knowing image. The case of the society sewing circle, formed in secret to fabricate a handsome Confederate battle flag for General Beauregard, gave him special delight.

Word of the sewing circle and its activities was brought to the general by a servant in the fine house of its organizer, one of the fashionable rebel ladies of New Orleans. Butler, highly amused, kept the sewing bee under surveillance until the flag had been completed, along with a beautifully embroidered canvas case to contain it. As soon as he got word that the work was finished, he very formally sent his fine carriage to the lady's door, along with an aide bearing an invitation to visit the general at once. When the flustered woman arrived at headquarters, she found the general gravely perusing what appeared to be a lengthy report.

After a time Butler raised his eyes from the paper. "Madam," he said, "my information is that you have been having a series of sewing bees at your house, making a flag to be sent to Beauregard's army."

The woman sputtered an indignant denial, but the general ignored this and went on to say that he thought that Confederate flag would be just the thing to send to some schoolchildren back in Lowell, since they had never seen one. They were planning a Fourth of July celebration, he said, and would certainly enjoy having the flag as a centerpiece of the observance.

"Now then," he continued, "won't you please go with my orderly and get that flag and bring it here?"

After some further unavailing denials and protests, the rebel Betsy Ross, still gasping, went with the officer and shortly afterward returned with the flag. Butler took it out of its case and examined it long and admiringly. It was made of the finest silk, with a splendid gold fringe.

"If I happen to want another, I will certainly send to you," he said, "for this is very beautiful."

Butler then dismissed the lady, after fending off all her questions as to where he could possibly have got his information about her sewing bee. She left in the firm belief that one of her fellow needleworkers had provided Butler with the word. She was utterly certain of one thing, she told the general: it could not have been one of her servants. But, as an element of pathos underlying the incident, it was in fact her most trusted servant who had been Butler's informant—the black woman who was her foster-sister, suckled at the same breast when the two women were new-born babes.

There was warm talk among the sewing-bee ladies and their friends for weeks afterward. Thus the flag incident, along with many others of the same trivial nature, added to the legend of Butler's omniscience.

More flagrant expressions of rebel zeal brought quick and heavy punishment. A bookseller, Fidel Keller, had the rash bad taste to display in his show window a human skeleton labeled "Chickahominy," intending the gruesome exhibit to be taken for the remains of a fallen Union soldier. By special order Butler sent Keller to Ship Island for two years of hard labor and solitary confinement. Another fire-eater, Judge John W. Andrews, was indiscreet enough to exhibit among his club members a cross said to have been fabricated from a bone of a fallen Yankee. Andrews was also sentenced to Ship Island for two years at hard labor.

Along with his duties as "police magistrate," all else that Butler accomplished required a brilliant mind, a stout constitution, and the energy to maintain eighteen-hour workdays seven days a week. Gideon Welles didn't know the half of it.

32

Butler had no sooner landed in New Orleans than he was faced with the task of feeding a hungry and helpless civilian population. The municipal authorities had given first priority to Confederate military needs, and so far as they were able they continued to do so. General Lovell's rebels in arms, when they fled the city, had taken with them whatever foodstuffs they were capable of carrying away. Afterward they tried to see to it that owners of outlying plantations shipped none of their produce into the city. Drovers who had supplied Texas beef to New Orleans were likewise interdicted.

What stocks of staple foods remained in New Orleans were priced sky-high by the local profiteers, and became unavailable except to the rich. It rather suited the wealthy and the civilian authorities that the food shortage affected working folk and the poor, since it was mainly among those people that Unionist sympathies lay. City officials were also quick to appreciate that the food crisis, from which they stood aside, would be yet another heavy problem for the Yankees to deal with—a problem, and a harassment, and a potential source of great unrest.

Butler, however, moved with characteristic vigor. The 21st Indiana Regiment was assigned to take control of the Opelousas Railroad, literally a feeder line to the city from planter communities along the west bank of the Mississippi. The Indiana troops seized all the road's rolling stock and cleared its eighty miles of track for full operation. Butler ordered the railroad's civilian owners to run trains all along its route to bring foodstuffs into New Orleans.

"No passengers other than those having the care of such supplies, as owners or keepers, are to be permitted to come into the city," Butler directed. "All other supplies are prohibited transportation over the road either way, except cotton and sugar."

Butler intended that cotton and sugar, the two big money crops, should be available to restore commerce through the port. Famine aside, he wanted to revive the seagoing trade of New Orleans while, at the same time, reassuring the planters that Union occupation meant a return to something like prewar normality.

Learning that the City of New Orleans had bought a considerable stock of flour in rebel-held Mobile and that it was being held there, Butler negotiated a limited truce. He offered safe conduct for a steamboat to carry the flour from Mobile to New Orleans. The boat would be allowed to return to rebel-held territory after discharging its cargo. It was to carry no passengers, however.

Informed that there was a supply of livestock, along with flour and other provisions, lying somewhere upstream near the mouth of the Red River, Butler sent word that he would provide safe conduct for two steamboats daily for the purpose of carrying food to the city for sale. While free passage was given to rebel steamers engaged solely in bringing food to New Orleans, vessels not thus engaged were considered prizes of war.

In the waterlogged country around New Orleans, light draft steamboats were the most practical means of heavy transportation, so Butler needed all the boats he could get. Thus Butler's rangers and the outlying rebels began a serious game of hide-and-seek, with rebel steamboats as prizes. Confederate authorities ordered the boats hidden in creeks and byways to keep them out of Federal hands, with instructions that they were to be burned or blown up if Federal troops found them. But those orders were not always carried out, and Butler's fleet expanded accordingly.

Money was an immediate problem. With the army quartermaster completely out of funds, Butler placed all of his own private resources at that officer's disposal, permitting him to draw against the general's considerable credit while counting on Washington to unscramble the accounts whenever the bureaucracy finally got around to it. In addition, he donated $1,000 outright in cash and food supplies for immediate relief of the poor.

Andrew Jackson Butler, the general's older and considerably more cynical brother, took a different tack. Andrew, ever the adventurer, decided to range far upriver on his own to see if he could make deals with Texas cattle drovers for beef on the hoof. Somehow or other he succeeded in this. New Orleans got some beef, and Andrew, no ideologue and certainly no altruist, made a profit in his risky enterprise.

Butler's diligent provost guards helped the relief effort considerably when they raided a warehouse and seized a thousand barrels of beef intended for General Lovell's troops, who were now encamped to the northeast. Butler ordered the food released to the city's poor and, with an eye to useful propaganda, saw to it that they knew where it had come from. In General Order No. 25, Butler castigated the Confederate authorities for their failure to feed the people of New Orleans and announced that the confiscated food would be distributed "among the deserving poor of this city, from whom the rebels had plundered it. . . ."

General Butler in New Orleans
Sophia Smith Collection

Stung by General Order No. 25, Louisiana Gov. Thomas Overton Moore responded with a furious outpouring of rhetoric. He was particularly sore about the confiscated beef but, besides that, seemed to be obsessed with the notion that a wickedly clever Butler had somehow schemed his way into New Orleans.

Moore addressed his remarks "To the Loyal People and True of the City of New Orleans."

> He [Butler] appeals to your selfishness, and attempts to arouse the baser passions of your nature as though he was addressing Yankees. Unfortunately for him he knows not the character of the people with whom he has to deal. He seems wholly to forget that Southerners are a high-toned, chivalrous people, who entertain a holy abhorrence and hatred for traitors, cowards, and petty tyrants. . . .
>
> General Butler no doubt congratulates himself on the cleverness of the trick he played in seizing a large lot of Confederate beef, and distributing it among those who have been unable to procure meat during the great scarcity caused by the cutting off of trade with the Red River and Texas.
>
> In this he has made a great mistake. The large majority of those who received this beef well know that he would never have given it to them had he required it for his own troops, and not been afraid to use it. Had our city authorities been aware that this beef was on store, General Butler would not have had the trouble of setting his spies to work to hunt it up. His having done so shows more conclusively that he gained access to this city through treachery and cowardice—that his victory was bought, not gained by honorable conflict.

Nevertheless, the captured stores were eagerly received, as were the U.S. Army rations and other foods Butler made available to stave off the city's hunger.

Arrival of the first Federal supply vessels from New York took the edge off the crisis. Butler no longer had the considerable worry of how to feed his own troops, civilian relief aside. He authorized his commissary to sell army food stores in small amounts to needy civilians at fixed low prices: ten cents a pound for beef, ham, pork, and bacon; seven and a half cents a pound for flour. Payment had to be made in bank notes, United States notes, or coin—no local shinplasters or Confederate bills. Butler's improvised public works program—employing hundreds of workers, including many paroled and jobless Confederate soldiers—provided much of the cash poor families needed for the purchase of food.

Still, Butler continued to be hard-pressed for funds to maintain his relief effort. He had hoped for a quick revival of the city's trade in cotton and sugar through his assurance to the planters that they were free to bring their shipments to port, without fear of Federal confiscation. But Confederate authorities preached fear and urged destruction, and many crops were burned. As he cast about for revenues, Butler decided on a special tax, which he invented in a moment of inspiration.

In his search for enemy assets, Butler discovered that, when Farragut's fleet entered the lower Mississippi, $1,250,000 had been contributed by the city's wealthiest businessmen as a defense fund. Along with records of the fund itself, Butler found a list containing the names of all contributors and the amount each had subscribed.

Butler decided to issue General Order No. 55, which began:

> It appears that the need of relief to the destitute poor of the city requires more extended measures and greater outlay than have yet been made.
>
> It becomes a question in justice upon whom this burden should fall. Clearly upon those who have brought this great calamity upon their fellow citizens.

Butler then cited the manner in which the defense fund had been raised: "The subscribers to this fund, by this very act, betray their treasonable designs and their ability to pay at least a much smaller tax for the relief of their destitute and starving neighbors." Butler went on to levy that smaller tax against the same contributors, assessing each of them 25 percent of their original "treasonable" contribution.

In addition he published a list of cotton brokers who had publicly urged planters not to bring their cotton to the city. These were assessed $100 to $500 each for their sins. The two special assessments raised nearly $350,000 for the relief program.

The wealthy New Orleans geese were not plucked without a great deal of hissing, and this was the subject of satirical comment in the *Delta*, a soldier publication which Butler had placed under the editorship of Capt. John Clark, a former newspaperman on the staff of the Boston *Courier*. Clark noted in print the sad gatherings of "aldermanic looking gentry with white vests and stiffened shirt collars," assembled to mourn the special assessment. "Weep though you might," the soldier-editor commented, "the poor must be employed and fed, and you must disgorge."

In a report to Secretary of War Stanton, Butler summed up the results of his relief program. In regard to General Order No. 55, Butler wrote: "Not a dollar has gone in any way to the use of the United States."

Butler reported that he was employing 1,000 poor laborers on the streets and wharves and distributing food to 9,707 families—32,450 persons. For these purposes he was spending $70,000 a month. Another $2,000 a month was going to the support of five asylums for widows and orphans. The Charity Hospital was being maintained at a cost of $5,000 a month.

In addition, Butler was providing substantial help out of his own pocket to various Catholic charitable institutions, although he did not make note of this in his formal report to Stanton.

Butler's activities as a relief administrator won him the support and gratitude of the ordinary folk of New Orleans, a majority of whom came to declare their allegiance to the Union. But he earned the bitter enmity of the merchant class and became the prime target of Confederate propaganda, even to the extent of being declared an outlaw by his old pre-war associate, Jefferson Davis, who ordered that Butler, if captured, was to be hanged on the spot.

33

Each in the steady stream of general orders issued from Butler's New Orleans headquarters had predictable effects—except for General Order No. 28, dated May 15, 1862. That one, which speedily became known as the Woman Order, took spins, bounces, and ricochets that astonished its author.

In its entirety it read as follows:

As the officers and soldiers of the United States have been subject to repeated insults from the women (calling themselves ladies) of New Orleans, in return for the most scrupulous non-interference and courtesy on our part, it is ordered that hereafter when any female shall, by word, gesture, or movement, insult or show contempt for any officer or soldier of the United States, she shall be regarded and held liable to be treated as a woman of the town plying her avocation.

By command of Major General Butler
George C. Strong, A.A.G. Chief of Staff

Under New Orleans city ordinance, a "woman of the town" plying her trade was subject to an automatic overnight stay in the city jail, followed by a $5 fine. But it was never Butler's intention to enforce the letter of the ordinance. He had enough problems on his hands without inciting a general riot. What he did intend was to remind the fiery rebel ladies of New Orleans that their conduct was, or ought to be, beneath their dignity, and at the same time to remind his officers and men that, when ladies behaved like streetwalkers, they should be pointedly ignored as persons beneath notice.

The wording of General Order No. 28 was drawn deliberately from an ancient London ordinance that Butler culled from his extraordinary memory. But its language seemed inflammatory enough to cause his chief of staff much concern. Strong's opinion was that, while Butler's extremely well-behaved troops—most of them fresh-scrubbed New England and Western farm boys—would never misinterpret the general's intention, still . . .

"It would be a great scandal," said Major Strong, "if only *one* man should act upon it in the wrong way."

Butler, however, had complete confidence in the discipline of his troops, who were at all times under their own strict orders as to how they must comport themselves in the captured city. When he issued General Order No. 28, it was as a measure of psychological warfare against a rebellious segment of the New Orleans population toward whom he could not, as a soldier and a gentleman, direct any other weapon. And, as events finally proved, it worked.

The rebel ladies had found an effective way to harass Union troops precisely because those troops were held to an uncompromising standard of behavior. When a gentlewoman of New Orleans ostentatiously drew her skirts aside lest they be contaminated by contact with a Yankee uniform, or made a great show of leaving if a Yankee entered a streetcar, or held her dainty handkerchief to her nose when passing a Union officer, there was little the soldier could do but redden under the ridicule. One or two such incidents meant little, but as time went on the soldiers, young Federal officers in particular, began to feel increasingly chafed by this unaccustomed humiliation.

A sense of humor helped. Butler himself, when a group of gentlewomen made a great show of turning their backs on him and his staff officers, was heard to remark, "Well, these ladies certainly know which end of them looks the best."

The *Delta*, Butler's soldier-edited newspaper, was a touch more bitter. Remarking on some of the ladies who made a show of retching in disgust when a Union soldier passed, the *Delta*'s editorialist commented that some of those upset stomachs would surely be empty if it were not for Butler's relief program.

At first, when the ladies began their haughty campaign, Butler's troops did find it funny. Incidents of the kind were stored up as material for humorous anecdotes, as was the case of one stout old lady who, in a whirl of skirts, turned her back so vigorously on a pair of young Union officers that she fell over backward and landed in the dusty street. When the officers went to help her, she waved them off, struggled to her feet, and proceeded on her way—hat askew, raiment in disarray, but still a proud figure of defiance.

With troubles enough to occupy him, Butler was inclined at first to ignore the petticoat campaigners, trusting to the good sense and sound discipline of his troops to contain the problem. What finally stirred him to act was an incident in which a New Orleans lady confronted a young lieutenant and spat in his face. Butler decided that enough was enough. What had started out as a minor annoyance had now become a nagging problem seriously affecting morale. Moreover, it contained the potential to spark a serious incident.

General Order No. 28 succeeded at once in curbing the aggressiveness of the spirited ladies of New Orleans, who became more genteel in expressing their contempt for the invaders. They still drew their skirts aside, they still turned their backs, they still hammered out the melody of "The Bonny Blue Flag" on their parlor pianos whenever a Union officer passed by their open windows. But spitting and ranting—as common women might be seen to do—ceased, and in time even the lesser insults became rarer. No woman was ever arrested under Order 28. As a legal measure it served only to set understandable limits, and those limits were understood.

As propaganda for the Confederacy, however, Order 28 was fuel to the fire. Orators and editorialists in unison cried, "Rape!" Some of them might even have believed it.

It furnished a delicious item for the gossipy diary of Mary Chesnut. "There is said to be an order from Butler, turning over the women of New Orleans to his soldiers," she wrote. "Then is the measure of his iniquities filled. We thought that generals always restrained by shot or sword, if need be, the brutal soldiery."

Governor Moore of Louisiana took up the cry:

It was reserved for a federal general to invite his soldiers to the perpetration of outrages, at the mention of which the blood recoils in horror, to quicken the impulse of their sensual instincts by the suggestion of transparent excuses for their gratification, and to add to an infamy already well merited those crowning titles of a panderer to lust and a desecrator of virtue.

In New Orleans the more immediate "bounce" effect of Order 28 had little to do with the conduct of the ladies or the behavior of the troops. The result, in short, was the dismissal of the civilian government and its replacement by an entirely military administration. This followed a waltz of words between the mayor and the general.

Mayor John Monroe was a cautious Confederate who felt himself trapped between fire-breathing colleagues of his own political persuasion on one side and the imperious, implacable General Butler on the other. So far as government in New Orleans was concerned, this led him to a course of nervous inaction and passive resistance. When Order 28 was published, however, Monroe's rebel advisers pushed him to sign a letter of protest. To make sure it contained at least a muted cry of "Rape!" they helped him to draft it.

The letter said Order 28 was so "extraordinary and astonishing" that as chief magistrate of the city Monroe had to object "to the threat it contains." Monroe's letter continued:

> Your officers and soldiers are permitted, by the terms of this order, to place any construction they may please upon the conduct of our wives and daughters, and, upon such construction, to offer them atrocious insults.
>
> To give a license to the officers and soldiers of your command to commit outrages, such as are indicated in your order, upon defenseless women is, in my judgment, a reproach to the civilization, not to say the Christianity, of the age, in whose name I make this protest.

Butler's reply was prompt. It was delivered by the military police. It read tersely: "John T. Monroe, late mayor of the city of New Orleans, is relieved from all responsibility for the peace of the city, and is suspended from the exercise of official functions, and committed to Fort Jackson until further orders."

Monroe, shaken, asked if he could talk with Butler before being packed off to prison, and the interview was granted. The granite general told him that, if as mayor he felt he could not ensure the tranquility of the city, then he'd be better off in a place of safety, like Fort Jackson. Monroe protested that he had never meant to insult the general, and in the end signed an endorsement disavowing his original letter. It read: "General Butler: This communication having been sent under a mistake of fact, and being improper in language, I desire to apologize for the same, and to withdraw it."

Mayor Monroe, upon signing his apology, was freed of arrest and went on his way. However, his more hot-blooded advisers promptly spun him around again, and only hours later he dispatched another letter to Butler withdrawing his apology. This led to a further meeting with the general.

Once again Monroe wavered. He said he would withdraw his original letter if the general assured him that Order 28 did not apply to *all* the ladies of New Orleans. Butler agreed, and promptly put it in writing: "You may say that this order refers to those women who have shown contempt for and insulted my soldiers, by words, gestures, and movements, in their presence."

Monroe hovered over the paragraph and asked if Butler would add the word *only* after the word "women." Butler did so, and the mayor departed. But that was not to be the end of this verbal gavotte.

When Monroe next appeared at headquarters, he was accompanied by his lawyer, his secretary, his chief of police, and several other associates. It may have been his misfortune that over the weekend Butler had scotched a conspiracy among paroled Confederate soldiers to form a unit called The Monroe Guard, intending to break through Union lines and join rebel forces in the field. The captured parolees had confessed that they had named their unit in honor of Monroe because the mayor was giving them secret assistance.

In any case Butler was short of temper. One by one, the members of Monroe's entourage were asked to state, yes or no, whether they supported the mayor's statement regarding Order 28. The police chief said yes. The lawyer waffled. The secretary said he had helped to draft Monroe's letter. Others said they had not even seen the letter.

Butler then consigned Monroe, his lawyer, his police chief, and his secretary to Fort Jackson and dismissed the rest. Then, with a feeling of some relief, the general set up a new municipal administration headed by Gen. George F. Shepley, whom he named military commandant, assigning him the duties of the mayor. Shepley, a prominent Maine attorney before the war, promptly set about reorganizing the city government along efficient Yankee lines, issuing his first set of rules and regulations the very next day.

But the Monroe affair, however happily it ended from Butler's point of view, was by no means the end of the furor stirred by the Woman Order. Hostile European statesmen, British and French in the forefront, seized on Order 28 as a means of further harassing the Federal Union. Confederate propagandists abroad rolled out their heaviest orotundities to describe the horrors awaiting the helpless female population of New Orleans.

The order precipitated a sharp clash between Lord Palmerston, the prime minister, and Charles Francis Adams, the United States minister to Britain. For a few days at least it appeared to officials at the United States Legation that diplomatic relations might be severed, so warm was the exchange.

Lord Palmerston began the uproar by appearing in the House of Commons to denounce General Butler and all his works. Puffed Palmerston:

> Sir, an Englishman must blush to think that such an act has been committed by one belonging to the Anglo-Saxon race. If it had come from some barbarous race that was not within the pale of civilization, one might have regretted it, but that such an order should have been promulgated by a soldier, by one who has raised himself to the rank of general, is a subject undoubtedly of not less astonishment than pain.

The prime minister followed up on this by sending a letter of protest to Adams. The letter took up the cry of "Rape!" somewhat more graphically than had his speech in the House. Palmerston wrote that he could not adequately express the disgust "which must be excited in the mind of every honorable man" by General Order No. 28. Palmerston castigated Butler as "a general guilty of so infamous an act as to deliberately hand over the female inhabitants of a conquered city to the unbridled licence of an unrestrained soldiery."

Adams, considerably angered by the tone of the letter, responded by demanding to know whether Palmerston's letter was an official communication, and if so why it had not been forwarded, as protocol required, through Lord John Russell, the British foreign secretary. Palmerston replied that his note was indeed official.

Adams then took the matter up with Russell. He told the foreign secretary that Palmerston's letter was both offensive and irregular. And to put an end to the exchange he then informed Palmerston that he would accept no further such communications from him.

Benjamin Moran, secretary of the legation and another indefatigable diarist of the times, recorded his comment on the affair:

A more impudent proceeding than that of Palmerston in this case cannot be discovered in the whole range of political life. Knowing the brutality of his own officers and soldiers, he readily imagined ours of the same stamp, and insolently presumed to lecture Mr. Adams on a thing which was not his business. His ill-manners were properly rebuked.

Palmerston, of course, had been at no pains ever to conceal his bias in favor of the Confederacy. Fortunately for relations between Britain and the United States, Palmerston was held in check by two potent forces for peace: the British royal family and British public opinion.

In Washington, Secretary of State Seward lightly turned aside Britain's alleged concern over the Woman Order, assuring the legation that whatever British sexual mores might be, those of America were such that no New Orleans lady would ever be molested under Order 28 or any other order. "*Honi soit qui mal y pense*," quipped Seward, reminding the British of the motto of their royal Order of the Garter: "Shamed be the one who thinks evil of it."

And there the flap ended, except in constant and remarkably enduring Confederate propaganda.

34

While Butler was dealing successfully with pestilence, hunger, crime, and overt rebellion—not to mention the many problems involved in supplying and commanding an army—he also found himself heavily engaged in a struggle he would not be allowed to win: a battle against the entrenched wealthy and their ally of convenience, slippery William H. Seward, the secretary of state. Ranged against Butler were New Orleans bankers, foreign consuls, and directors of the bigger business firms. All had profited heavily from the war. Many had made a very good thing out of blockade-running and supplying arms to the Confederacy. Few were at any great pains to conceal their support of the South and their enmity toward the hard-hitting Union general who now threatened their gains. In Seward, pursuing his own convoluted agenda, the rich rebels of New Orleans found a remarkably pliable friend.

Cosmopolitan New Orleans, over which so many flags had flown, was home to numerous foreign-born entrepreneurs, great and small, to whom allegiance seemed a matter of convenience. These foreigners had been Americans one day; loyal Confederates the next; and now, under Butler's hostile flag, they were suddenly alien nationals once again, claiming the protection of any one of a dozen convenient foreign countries. The consular corps, composed of men with their own financial interests to advance, was more than happy to play the protective role. Complaints from the consuls were incessant. Nothing was too trivial to be considered as basis for a sharp diplomatic note. One such even invoked international law in disputing the ownership of a horse. Another concerned itself with allegedly pilfered oranges.

The one notable victory Butler was able to claim in his war against enemy wealth lay in his special taxation of those chameleon rebels, who, whether they liked it or not, were made to provide relief funds for the poor. Through the various consulates they protested fervently to Washington. Butler, however, stood firm, and in this instance even succeeded in stiffening the resolve of the War Department—however much hand-wringing went on in Seward's Department of State.

In a lengthy and hotly worded report to Secretary of War Stanton, Butler put the case:

> Before their excellencies, the French and Prussian ministers, complain of my exactions upon foreigners at New Orleans, I desire that they would look at the documents, and consider for a few moments the facts and figures. . . .
>
> They will find that out of ten thousand four hundred and ninety families who have been fed from the fund, with the raising of which they find fault, less than one tenth (one thousand and ten) are Americans; nine thousand four hundred and eighty are foreigners. Of the thirty-two thousand souls, but three thousand are natives.

Out of some $80,000 a month spent to feed the starving poor, Butler said, about $72,000 was going to the relief of the very same foreigners whose consular officials were complaining so insistently through all available diplomatic channels.

> Almost all property . . . useful to the United States which has not been burned or carried off will be found to be held here by persons who have lived in Louisiana all their lives, and now claim to be foreigners. Every schooner and fishing smack that cannot venture out of the river raises a foreign flag. All wood for steamers for miles up the river has been burnt except isolate yards covered by such flag.

In one typical instance, Butler wrote, the owner of a wood yard had refused to sell any fuel to the captain of a Yankee steamboat. When the exasperated captain moved in to take the wood anyway, the owner quickly hoisted a French flag over it. In this instance, flag or no flag, the captain was not to be deterred.

"The steamer wooded up," said Butler.

Although Butler found no skirmish of this kind too trivial for his attention, and for warfare with the foreign consuls as required, his main effort concerned far heavier sums. For one thing, he wanted to search out and recover as much as he could of the Federal treasure that had been looted from the United States Mint, much of it in coins and bullion and most of it diverted long since to the chronically impoverished Confederate treasury. He proposed to examine all deposits and accounts of the New Orleans banks with the sharp eye of an unfriendly auditor.

He soon found, somewhat to his sardonic amusement, that, when the Union fleet threatened New Orleans, some of the bankers had packed off

$6 million of their hard cash and bullion for safekeeping. In the upshot this gold wound up in Richmond, never to be returned, even though the bankers tried to reclaim it.

In the first days of the occupation, Butler's immediate fiscal problem was what to do about the circulation of Confederate notes, paper money that, in Butler's view, was worthless, and even among devoted secessionists was rapidly depreciating toward zero value. Confederate $5 and $10 bills were supplemented in local use by shinplaster scrip issued by local merchants. Citizens of New Orleans were even using streetcar tickets in place of small change.

As it happened, canny New Orleans bankers in the early days of secession tended to hold aloof from Confederate currency. But when pressured they had agreed to deal in the new Southern bills, which then took over the marketplace. By the time Butler arrived on the scene, ordinary folk had no other money. So, reluctantly enough, he at first permitted it to circulate, provided (as he said) there were still folk about who were trusting enough to accept it.

The bankers were not of that trusting breed. Though they had accepted Confederate currency on deposit and made loans based on that currency, once under Butler's regime they became more circumspect. They now preferred a kind of traffic control when they could get away with it: hard money taken in, Confederate money paid out.

That issue came to a head when, after a short period of tolerance, Butler published on May 16 an order setting May 27 as a deadline date, after which all circulation of Confederate currency was to cease. The banks hastily met this by publishing notices that all who had made deposits of Confederate notes had to withdraw them before the twenty-seventh, after which date the banks would not be responsible.

Butler responded promptly on May 19 by publishing his General Order No. 30, whose opening paragraphs were worded like an indictment. After first citing the banks for flooding the city with Confederate paper, Butler continued:

> The banks and bankers now endeavor to take advantage of the reestablishment of the authority of the United States here to throw the depreciation and loss from this worthless stuff of their own creation . . . upon their creditors, depositors, and bill-holders.
>
> They refuse to receive these bills while they pay them over their counters.
>
> They require their depositors to take them.
>
> They change the obligation of contracts by stamping their bills, "Redeemable in Confederate Notes."

They have invested the savings of labor and the pittance of the widows in this paper.

They sent away or hid their specie, so that the people could have nothing but these notes—which they now depreciate—with which to buy bread.

With this preamble, the general went on to order the banks henceforth to pay out no more Confederate notes to depositors or creditors, but to meet those obligations in bank notes, United States Treasury notes, gold, or silver.

Likewise, all the shinplaster currency was required to be redeemed in solid money by those who had issued the scrip. Penalty for noncompliance with the shinplaster order was to be confiscation of property to meet the redemption costs or a prison term at hard labor.

Butler followed his monetary reform measure by issuing a further order that the bankers found painful. It required the banks to turn over to the Federal government all sums that had been deposited to the credit of the Confederacy. This brought the usual desperate objection that those deposits had been made in Confederate notes and that, therefore, they should be paid out in the Confederate notes. But the general was not having any of this. In the end Butler collected the money to the last sound dime and was able to send Treasury Secretary Chase exactly $245,760.10 in hard cash, the confiscated assets of the Confederate government. This transaction was entirely in keeping with Chase's previously expressed opinion that Butler was "the cheapest general we have"—meaning, of course, that he was the general who made fewest demands on the hard-pressed resources of the United States Treasury.

Order was restored to the currency in everyday mercantile use in New Orleans. Sound money replaced Confederate paper. Shinplaster scrip, transit tickets, and the like disappeared from circulation when the military government completed the reform by issuing official "small change" notes backed by the funds of the city treasury. It was said that Butler's banking reforms did more to solidify Union sentiment among ordinary citizens of New Orleans than anything accomplished by Union armies in the field.

The wealthy traders, however, huddling under their various flags of convenience, had been hard-cash dealers from the first. They remained so, and were now motivated to protect their gains and add to them wherever and however possible. But their first conflict with Butler, as it happened, was only indirectly concerned with money.

In the few days between Farragut's conquest of the river and Butler's arrival in force, a motley quasi-military force made up of foreign nationals had assisted the city government to maintain some semblance of order—

their principal concern, of course, being the prevention of looting and the protection of business interests. Butler welcomed their effort very briefly, after which he directed them to disband. At this the British contingent, some sixty Englishmen making up a unit known as the British Guard, thought to strike one final blow for the Confederacy, which was where their sympathy lay. In a midnight meeting they voted to send their uniforms, rifles, and other equipment to General Beauregard before Butler would have time to solidify his lines about the city, and this they did.

Butler learned about this at once, and his response was quick. He ordered all members of the British Guard to report to him immediately with their uniforms and rifles. Any man unable to produce his arms and uniform, Butler ruled, would be given twenty-four hours to get out of town or go to jail. If they thought Beauregard could use sixty good rifles, Butler commented, then they had to believe he could use sixty more men to go along with them.

The British consul, George Coppell, entered an immediate protest. He admitted that he had heard that "some" members of the Guard had sent their accoutrements out of the city. "Their own private property, I believe," Coppell commented suavely. "I feel convinced that they, when they took such action, were ignorant of the importance that might be attached to it, and did it with no idea of wrong or harm." Coppell continued: "It may not, Sir, be irrelevant for me to mention that I much regret to hear that the position of British subjects in this city, as neutrals, should have been questioned or doubted."

Coppell concluded his response quite loftily:

It will not be possible for some of the British Subjects who were members of the British Guard to obey the verbal order . . . that they report to you as soldiers, and it would become my duty to solemnly protest, in the name of Her Majesty's Government, against the alternative stated by you, the enforcement of which would infringe the rights of British Subjects residing in the United States.

Coppell mistook his man if he thought Ben Butler, New Hampshire Yankee, was likely to cringe before the awful threat of Her Majesty's royal wrath. All but the captain of the British Guard and one member of it were summarily expelled from the city when they could not produce their arms and uniforms. The two who did not leave were arrested and sent to Fort Jackson.

"I am content for the present to suffer open enemies to remain in the city of their nativity,"Butler told Coppell. "But law-defying and treacherous alien enemies shall not." The members of the British Guard, Butler added, knew exactly what they were doing when they sent arms and equipment to Beauregard.

It was a foreshadowing of events to come, however, when Coppell complained to the British minister, Lord Lyons, who complained to Seward, who then wrote a memorandum to Stanton, who then sent the memorandum to Butler with a covering letter. The net import of all these diplomatic dance steps was that Butler had better turn the two imprisoned Britishers loose.

The language of these communications was almost quaint. Lord Lyons, the memorandum said, had received complaints from his consul in New Orleans of harsh proceedings by General Butler. Lyons had "called to see if the Secretary of State would not think it worthwhile to have the military authorities of New Orleans cautioned against exercising any doubtful severities. . ." The capture of New Orleans, instead of relieving tensions between Britain and the United States, was creating "new causes of uneasiness."

The memorandum continued:

> Mr. Seward replied that he cordially appreciated the value of Lord Lyons' suggestions, and that he would submit to the Secretary of War the expediency of giving instructions to General Butler of the character suggested, *and he felt authorized to say at once that they would be adopted.*

Thus did Seward's memorandum conclude with the steel that had been concealed in all the soft talk that had gone before.

Nor did Stanton's covering letter give Butler any comfort or any room to maneuver:

> General: I transmit herewith a copy of a memorandum of a conversation of this date between the Secretary of State and Lord Lyons . . . and will thank you to be guided by the spirit of the assurances given by the former to the latter in any proceedings for which there may be occasion in regard to British subjects.

Butler turned the prisoners loose. He then took a certain small satisfaction in challenging Coppell's lack of formal credentials, refusing to recognize him as British consul until Her Majesty's government forwarded the necessary documents. But, from Washington's faint and maidenly response in the British Guard affair, Butler was quite certain that he could count on little support when, in more serious matters, he tried to deal with the sharp activities of pro-Confederate New Orleans foreigners. Nevertheless he meant to persist.

Butler made a spectacular beginning when a Negro informant brought word that wagon loads of silver pesos had been spirited out of the Citizens' Bank in the darkness of night and deposited with Amedie Conturié, a liquor dealer who also functioned as Netherlands consul. Strongly suspecting that this might be silver looted from the United States Mint, Butler sent a squad of six men commanded by Captain Shipley of the 30th Massachusetts to find Conturié and the silver.

Conturié was not in his liquor store. The squad found him, finally, in the back room of an insurance company office which, it developed, he had rented for a special purpose. The main feature of the room was a large locked vault. Conturié, glowering over his vault, was defiant. This, he proclaimed, was the Dutch consulate, and Union soldiers had no right to be there.

Shipley, the soul of courtesy, was taken aback. Uncertain how he should proceed, the well-bred Yankee officer simply left the consul under arrest and hurried back to headquarters for further instructions. Butler, more than a little annoyed, promptly sent him back with emphatic orders to search that office and, most particularly, to search that vault.

Confronting Conturié once again, Shipley asked him to produce the key to the vault. The consul defiantly refused.

"Then I shall be obliged to force the door," said Shipley.

"Do as you please," shrugged Conturié.

Since he had not the least idea how to crack a safe, the baffled Shipley returned once again to headquarters for more instructions. This time Butler summoned Lt. J. B. Kinsman, a tough-minded Boston lawyer in civilian life, and sent him along to deal with the recalcitrant consul. On Butler's staff Kinsman had acquired a reputation for firmness second only to that of Butler himself.

Kinsman wasted little time on ceremony. "Sir," he said, "I wish to look into your vault. Give me the key."

Conturié rose to his feet and declaimed, "I, Amedie Conturié, Consul of the Netherlands, protest against any occupation or search of my office, and this I do in the name of my government."

Kinsman turned to the squad. "Search the office and find that key," he said. "If you have to, break open the doors of the vault."

Conturié stood silent for a short time as a rough and vigorous search got under way. Finally he said there would be no use turning the place upside down looking for the key, because he had it on his person.

Kinsman pounced. "Search this fellow thoroughly," he ordered. "Strip him. Take off his coat, his stockings. Search even the soles of his shoes."

"You call me *fellow*!" shrieked Conturié. "That word is *never* applied to a gentleman, far less to a foreign consul."

"I don't care if you're the consul of Jerusalem," said Kinsman. "I'm going to look into that vault."

Conturié, thoroughly out of countenance as the highly personal search began, indicated that the key was in his pocket.

Without further fuss, then, the vault was opened, revealing 160 kegs of coin. A count showed that each keg contained 5,000 Mexican silver dollars. In addition to the huge cache of silver, the searchers found $18,000 in bonds, some steel-engraved printing plates for the $5 and $10 notes of the Citizens' bank, plates for printing Confederate notes, and a supply of bank-note paper. It took three wagons to haul the treasure to the Mint, whereafter the diplomatic minuet commenced in full swing, with nearly the entire New Orleans consular corps joining in the protest. Only the Mexican consul remained aloof from the fray.

Back in Washington, Seward fell all over himself apologizing to the Dutch Minister Roest Van Limburg. Seward did say that Conturié might have saved himself a lot of trouble if he had merely explained at the outset to General Butler what all that silver was doing in his vault. But even so, he added:

> It appears beyond dispute that the person of the Consul was unnecessarily and unduly searched; that certain papers which incontestably were archives of the Consulate, were seized and removed, and that they are still withheld from him; and that he was not only denied the privilege of conferring with a friendly colleague, but was addressed in very discourteous and disrespectful language. . . .
>
> This Government disapproves of these proceedings, and also of the sanction which was given to them by Maj. Gen. Butler, and expresses its regret that the misconduct, thus censured, has occurred.

Fine words, as usual, were far from enough. Seward meant to see that what counted—the silver—was returned to whatever powerful interest claimed it. Van Limburg was informed that Washington had appointed a military governor for the State of Louisiana to take all matters of this kind out of Butler's reach and was appointing a special commissioner to go to New Orleans and resolve this and all other financial disputes between the general and the New Orleans money men.

That commissioner would be none other than Reverdy Johnson, the Baltimore power broker of decided Southern sympathies—the man who, by seeing the right people, had freed the millionaire secessionist Winans after Butler had clapped him in jail in Baltimore and charged him with treason.

Butler would have no objections to the new military governor. The appointment went to Brig. Gen. George Shepley, whom Butler had already installed as military governor of New Orleans at the time he dismissed the civilian mayor and council. Shepley was a loyal friend of Butler's, as Seward well knew, and the appointment was in the nature of a sly wink. But as to Johnson, Butler's enmity ran deep. He regarded Johnson not only as a Confederate sympathizer at heart but as a calculating hypocrite as well.

Baldly stated, the affair of the $800,000 in silver was part of an effort to transfer all the cash of the Citizens' Bank to safety in Europe. It developed that the directors of the bank had entered into a similar paper transaction, this one with French bankers, to remove yet another $716,000 in coin out of the bank's vaults and into French custody. This hoard wound up in the French consulate, where Butler found it and seized it.

In the end, however, it was Johnson's decision, as Butler expected it would be, that the bank had merely engaged in good, sound business practice. Even if the purpose of the bank was to put all its cash beyond the control of the United States, said Johnson, there was no state or federal law to prohibit it from doing so. And if it was intended to put the hard money in Europe for the benefit of the Confederacy, well, there was no proof of that. He ordered everything restored except the plates for printing notes. They went to Washington in the nature of souvenirs.

Still later, Reverdy Johnson was effective in releasing other hard cash held by the French consul, and that cash wound up paying a French firm for a huge shipment of cloth for Confederate uniforms. This transaction had been engineered by the New Orleans firm of Ed. Gautherie & Company, agents for Baron Viller, the main supplier of French Army uniforms. In July of 1861, Gautherie & Company had negotiated contracts between Viller and the Confederate government. In April of 1862, the cloth had reached Havana. From Havana it was shipped to Matamoros, Mexico, after which it was smuggled across the border to Brownsville, Texas, and there delivered to a Confederate quartermaster.

With Farragut at the city, haste was required in getting the cash for these goods. What ensued was another paper conspiracy: a fake loan of $405,000 in hard cash (at no interest) made to the Confederate government by the Bank of New Orleans. The money was put in the hands of the French consul, Count Mejan. At the same time the bank concocted another paper transaction, which had the effect of putting all its remaining hard money into Mejan's keeping.

Butler had uncovered the conspiracy and obtained Mejan's promise that he would not release any of the money without informing the general of his intention. But Reverdy Johnson promptly cleared these odd transactions in his report to Seward, and Washington ordered Butler to stand aloof. While the general did so, the cash was placed on board the Spanish warship *Blasco de Garay* and found its way to Europe for the uses of the Confederacy.

Butler supplied solid evidence that these transactions were not undertaken without personal profit to Mejan and his staff. Papers seized by Butler showed consular "expenses" in these deals totaling nearly $20,000, including such items as "present to Madame Mejan to close the affair well, $153"; "To Colonel Lamat, as a bribe for the affair to start well, $2,500"; and so on. In the upshot, the slightly embarrassed French government recalled Count Mejan.

Mejan's recall provided Butler with more than ordinary satisfaction, and not only because of the consul's financial conspiracies. In an earlier exercise in avarice, the French consul had infuriated Butler by attempting to deny the general's military hospital a badly needed supply of blankets. An intransigent French merchant had first demanded an exorbitant price for them and then had refused to sell them at all, whereupon Butler had ordered his medical chief simply to seize the blankets and issue a receipt for them. A warm exchange with Mejan had then ensued, the consul terming the seizure "an arbitrary act . . . a flagrant violation of a trust," and demanding return of the goods.

"The blankets are now covering sick and wounded soldiers," Butler replied, "whose interest I must care for before those of commerce, which of course lie more near the heart of a commercial agent." He advised Mejan never to address him again in such terms, and he added: "[The blankets] were of so poor a quality that had I any choice left me I would neither take them or purchase them."

As to the intercession of Seward's commissioner, Johnson, the case of the steamboat *Fox* was typical. Union troops captured the boat when they found it hidden in a bayou. It had on board a cargo of arms, munitions, and medical supplies, along with documents implicating the New Orleans firm of Kennedy & Company in running cotton to Cuba. Profit to the firm from this one enterprise was $8,641, according to the documents, and Butler fined it that amount. However, Reverdy Johnson promptly ordered the money returned to Kennedy & Company.

In all, of fourteen cases reviewed by Johnson, Butler's action was sustained in only two of them, and those for very minor amounts. Having completed this work, Johnson hastened out of the city before the start of the fever season, of which he wanted no part. As a Washington fixer, he had no equal. In view of his evident pro-Southern sympathies and actions, his influence in the Lincoln administration continued to be a source of chagrin and astonishment so far as Butler was concerned, and it was likely no small factor in the general's eventual recall from the New Orleans command.

35

As a prewar politician, Benjamin Butler had maintained a cool distance from the issue of slavery, holding that no matter how fervently the abolitionists preached, the Constitution left it up to individual states to decide whether the slave system should exist within their boundaries. As a Union general on active service, however, his outlook changed almost in direct proportion to his southward progress. The more he came in contact with blacks held in bondage, the more Butler used his intellect, training, and military authority to effect a kind of de facto liberation in the territories he controlled. By the time he had settled in to ruling New Orleans and a large part of Louisiana, Butler had become a totally committed abolitionist and, moreover, a practical one.

It was Butler, after all, who at Fortress Monroe contrived to effect liberation of slaves by declaring them contraband of war, a legal device that enabled him to feed, house, and employ black refugees who flocked into his lines once the word got out. Without reference to Washington, Butler provided for the needs of nearly one thousand men, women, and children as they made their way to his protection, eagerly claiming their new status as contrabands. In New Orleans he extended this policy, sheltering refugee slaves by the thousands, and in some cases literally striking the shackles from persons held in bondage.

Later, when Washington's power brokers refused his repeated pleas for troop reinforcements, Butler without formal authorization proceeded to raise three full Negro regiments on his own. These were made up of men recruited in theory among the prosperous "free colored" citizens, from whom Gen. Andrew Jackson had once drawn volunteers for defense of the city against the British. The first of Butler's new regiments, shrewdly enough, was reconstituted from an erstwhile Confederate auxiliary unit. Since the Confederacy itself had armed these men, the general reasoned, neither Richmond nor Washington could now complain that Butler was authorizing a slave insurrection. As he proceeded to recruit his Negro troops, Butler quietly welcomed all volunteers, ex-slaves or freemen. He simply professed to see no slaves among his new soldiers.

While President Lincoln was still vainly and vaguely pursuing some kind of plan that might buy blacks out of slavery for cash—with his expressed hope of perhaps deporting them to Haiti, or Liberia, or even to Central America—Butler was taking decisive and practical action. By now Butler was insisting, in both his private and official correspondence, that the institution of slavery must be abolished, rooted out, ended.

But as he pursued his own careful plans for the blacks, amid all the other problems and perplexities he was required to juggle, Butler suddenly found himself squeezed hard between the policies of the Lincoln administration and the fanaticism of one of his most valued subordinate generals. Without reference to Butler, Gen. J. W. Phelps, commanding the northeast defenses of New Orleans at Camp Parapet, undertook to raise and train several companies of fugitive slaves from among the many who had left the plantations for shelter within his lines.

A lanky, cranky, grizzled veteran, Phelps was not only a favorite of Butler's, but was regarded with warm affection by his men, who found in his shambling gait and high-pitched voice of command an endless source of material for humorous parody. His fierce loathing of slaveholders was all but psychotic in its intensity. It was said he could forgive their rebellion, but never their adherence to the institution of slavery.

Phelps had few equals as a drillmaster. He was to be seen (and heard) flawlessly maneuvering five regiments at once in the complicated evolutions that a brigadier of his time was expected to use in shifting and aligning his troops for battle. Under such an expert the Negro recruits responded quickly. Capt. John W. De Forest, the literary soldier in Phelps's command, commented on the adaptability of the rookie blacks in one of his letters home: "They take kindly to drilling; they learn to keep rank and step in a very short time, and those who have been tried at the heavy guns work them as well as our fellows."

From his voluminous correspondence on the subject, it is apparent that Phelps had grand visions for his enterprise. He had in mind dispatching the first of his graduates to South Carolina for active service, while in effect establishing at Camp Parapet a military training school for further Negro enlistees.

Operating in plantation country, Phelps found ample scope for his role as liberator, which he undertook with the kind of zeal that had motivated mad John Brown. In fact, the hysterical tone of his correspondence with headquarters strongly suggested that his nerves had been stretched taut and thin and that he was not quite rational anymore on the subject of slavery. Phelps found kindred spirits among his men, who undertook raids on plantation houses to carry off slaves to the shelter of the Federal camp. This led to many complaints from planters, demanding that Butler rein in his subordinate general and curb the activities of his troops.

In what both Butler and Phelps saw as a test case, a mass exodus of slaves from the plantation of Bobilliard LaBlanche was submitted to Washington for review. Phelps had sent a detachment to search the LaBlanche plantation. In the process it was found that LaBlanche's son was in the Confederate army, and this was enough for Phelps's zealots to declare the planter's slaves free. It was their contention that LaBlanche had then literally driven his slaves away, threatening them with the lash if they returned. Phelps, for his part, penned a lengthy report in which he used the LaBlanche incident as the springboard for an emotional appeal that a proclamation of general emancipation be issued at once. He insisted that the report be placed before Lincoln himself.

Butler duly submitted the Phelps manifesto to the War Department. In his covering letter to Stanton asking for guidance, Butler provided a less fevered précis of the affair. The slaves, encouraged by the Union troops, had crowded into a small boat to cross the river to freedom, but their numbers were such that it appeared the boat would be swamped. LaBlanche, thoroughly alarmed, offered to hire a large boat to carry them and suggested they take all their belongings with them while they were at it.

Butler said, "General Phelps, I believe, intends to make this a test case for the policy of the government. I wish it might be so, for the difference of our action on this subject is a source of trouble. I respect his honest sincerity of opinion, but I am a soldier bound to carry out the wishes of my government. . . ."

If the government's policy remained unchanged, Butler said, he would be in duty bound to continue to observe it, in which case "the services of General Phelps are worse than useless here." On the other hand, he added, if Washington were to adopt Phelps's position "then he is invaluable, for his whole soul is in it, and he is a good soldier of wide experience, and no braver man lives."

Washington dithered. When no response was received after more than a month had passed, Phelps decided that this official silence gave consent to his policy. He proceeded to request arms, ammunition, uniforms, and camp equipment for his Negro troops. Butler had received unofficial reports of Phelps's recruiting activities and had kept aloof. But now it became a matter of official record, and Butler was compelled to take official notice. He refused to equip Phelps's black units, reminding his subordinate that he had no authority to do so.

However much Butler agreed with Phelps in principle, if not in practice, he was strongly inhibited by such direction as he was able to perceive in the signals sent him from Washington. The most emphatic of these had come in the form of a rebuke administered by President Lincoln to Gen. David Hunter, commanding the Department of the South. Hunter had combined arming of Negro troops with a proclamation freeing all the slaves of South Carolina. Lincoln promptly nullified Hunter's action, issuing a proc- lamation in which he sharply reminded everyone that decisions of this kind were reserved to the president alone. In a note to Treasury Secretary Chase, who rather favored Hunter's procedure, Lincoln was emphatic: "No commanding general shall do such a thing . . . without consulting me." Meantime Lincoln meant to pursue his own vague dream of some day buying up slaves and shipping them out of the country.

Butler found dealing with Phelps increasingly difficult. Phelps balked at sending a party of black laborers to work under two planters who had taken charge of repairing a dangerous break in the levee above Carrollton. Butler said the problem was critical, since inundation threatened, and that it was reasonable to dispatch laborers who knew this kind of work, so that they might repair the break under the direction of overseers who were likewise familiar with the procedures for dealing with it.

Phelps was adamant. Patiently enough, Butler issued an order assigning 100 laborers to the levee work party, with a military guard commanded by a captain. Phelps was given a direct order to send every able-bodied contra- band in his camp to assist in the work. For his part, Phelps was now content to do so, since the work crew was to be commanded by a Union officer and not by civilian planters. That the planters would still provide the necessary expert supervision Phelps this time was willing to overlook.

A more serious clash between Butler and Phelps was not to be avoided when Phelps pressed the issue of arming his newly formed and partially trained ex-slaves. Butler again explained that he had to refuse this request because, under law passed by Congress, only the president himself could authorize enrolling ex-slaves into the military. But to put Phelps's unauthorized force to some practical use while in effect recognizing the quasi-liberation of its members, Butler tactfully enough directed Phelps to put them all to work clearing trees and brush away from the area in front of his defense line. He reminded Phelps that Lieutenant Weitzel, Butler's tireless engineer officer, had recommended this after an inspection tour of the defenses.

Phelps's reply was no less than explosive: "I must state that while I am willing to prepare African regiments for the defense of the government against its assailants, I am not willing to become the mere slave-driver which you propose, having no qualifications in that way. I am therefore under the necessity of tendering the resignation of my commission. . . ."

Butler did his best to calm the agitated general. He reminded Phelps that when Weitzel noted the need for clearing away the trees in front of Phelps's entrenchments, Phelps had agreed. At that time the swampy water was too high for the work to be carried out, and Phelps lacked the men to do it.

"But now both water and men concur," wrote Butler. "You have five hundred Africans organized into companies, you write me. This work they are fitted to do. It must either be done by them or my soldiers, now drilled and disciplined."

Butler said it was a military necessity to clear away trees and brush, to provide an unobstructed field of fire for the supporting Federal gunboats on Lake Pontchartrain and also to deny cover to attacking rebels.

"The soldiers of the Army of the Potomac did this very thing last summer in front of Arlington Heights," said Butler. "Are the Negroes any better than they?"

Warming a little, Butler commented that resigning in the face of enemy forces was not particularly seemly for a soldier. He concluded by refusing to accept Phelps's resignation and directly ordering him to proceed with the work, detailing a troop detachment to guard the workers against any guerrillas who might be operating in the area.

Along with the official letter, Butler sent a private note to Phelps, commending his ability, his patriotism, and his warm human sympathies. He all but begged Phelps not to persist in promoting a personal feud with his commanding general. But Phelps's reply was nearly hysterical. He could not obey Butler's orders "without becoming a slave myself," wrote Phelps.

"It can be of but little consequence to me as to what kind of slavery I am to be subjected to," Phelps ranted, "whether to African slavery or to that which you thus offensively propose for me. . . . I cannot submit to either kind of slavery, and cannot . . . comply with your order; in complying with which I should submit to both kinds—both to African slavery and to that to which you resort in its defense."

In a despairing note to Sarah, Butler sighed, "Phelps has gone crazy."

Stanton was of little help. He wrote Butler that the whole matter was being referred to the president and that in the meantime he hoped General Butler would avoid any embarrassment to the government and any difficulty with General Phelps. Butler dispatched General Shepley to Washington to seek firmer guidance, but Shepley's mission resulted in nothing more decisive than all that had gone before.

In the end of the Camp Parapet crisis, Phelps succeeded in shucking his uniform and returning to his farm in Vermont. Not even Lincoln's sharply limited Emancipation Proclamation, when it eventually was forthcoming, was of much help in the Louisiana command, since it proclaimed freedom only in those states still in rebellion. Universal liberation was still a long way off.

Butler, meantime, employing the full use of his shrewd eye for loopholes, continued to make practical improvements in the lot of the Negro population in his command area. In Butler's civil administration Negro supplicants were given full rights in the courts; prewar abominations such as the whipping stations in the jails were eliminated; black soldiers were trained and equipped without any clash on this point with touchy Washington; and the black population was fed and housed and, as far as possible, gainfully employed. Butler's regulations even established full access, black and white, to the formerly segregated public transit system. And by one legal order and another, carefully crafted, many slaves were given full freedom from their erstwhile masters, all without reference to Washington.

George S. Denison, special agent of Treasury Secretary Chase, and Chase's very private source of information, provided his own confidential summary report on the Negro enlistment controversy:

"I believe Gen. Butler's opposition to the enlistment of Negroes by Gen. Phelps was not a matter of principle," he wrote. "Gen. Phelps had the start of him, while Gen. B. wanted the credit of doing the thing himself, and in his own way. And he is doing it, shrewdly and completely, as he does everything."

36

It is perhaps the great irony of Butler's career that, of all the problems he solved while administering New Orleans, the one he solved most successfully did not enhance his reputation, but rather nearly destroyed it. That problem, in brief, was how to conduct an extensive and complex military operation without being given the funds required to sustain it.

When Butler was assigned command of the Department of the Gulf, Washington ordered him to hold New Orleans, open the port to commerce, and cooperate with Farragut in clearing the Mississippi. Having given him these directives, the Lincoln administration then left him to fend for himself. At the outset his cash reserve for the enterprise consisted of $75 in gold which he carried in his pocket, and even that was his own money.

More amused than troubled by the condition of his campaign treasury, Butler proceeded to put his knowledge of commerce and banking to use, and by one device or another met all the heavy demands implicit in running an enormous military and civil administration on a shoestring. He accomplished this with such success that in a short time he was the one Union general who was actually putting money into the Federal treasury rather than draining it out.

Given the number and influence of his enemies in New Orleans, Washington, Richmond, Boston, and abroad, it is perhaps not at all strange that his sagacity in solving the financial problems of his department was seized upon as a stick with which to beat him. Rebel propagandists, Tory politicians in Britain, inimical and nervous Northern politicians, all joined in this chastisement with a will, aided by shrill and hostile segments of the American and British press. Even Butler's old antagonist, Governor Andrew, seized the opportunity and joined the posse.

The mythology surrounding Butler's financial dealings in New Orleans had a beginning in the ingenious way Butler met the overdue payroll of civilian laborers on Ship Island. This was enough in itself to cause lifted eyebrows at GHQ, but only somewhat later did the dark legends gather around him—in direct proportion to his popularity as it increased and as the eminences, both political and military, began to perceive him as a dangerous rival.

For the civilian payroll at Ship Island, as for other responsibilities, the government had provided no funds. What ensued, under Butler's deft direction, came to be known as the affair of the *Black Prince*, and before it was concluded the general had to engage in a long wrangle with uncomprehending administrators both in Boston and in Washington.

A small schooner attempting to run the blockade with a cargo of cotton had been captured by the navy. At the same time the Federal transport *Black Prince* was awaiting ballasting for the voyage home. Putting the two circumstances neatly together, Butler had the captured cotton put aboard the *Black Prince* in place of the sand which was the only available ballast in the region. The general dispatched the cargo north to Boston, where his agent, Richard S. Fay, Jr., was instructed to sell it. At the same time he borrowed $4,000 from the sutler at Ship Island in return for his personal draft, and with this money paid the laborers their wages. Fay was told to honor the $4,000 draft from the proceeds of the sale of cotton and to turn over the balance of those proceeds to the government.

All went well until a zealous Federal official in Boston seized the entire cargo of the *Black Prince*. Since Fay was prevented from selling the cotton, Butler's $4,000 draft to repay the Ship Island sutler was not honored, and Butler had to direct his Boston banker, James G. Carney, to meet that obligation out of the general's personal funds.

It took much patient correspondence on Butler's part before Q.M. Gen. Montgomery Meigs understood the transaction. Finally, however, the government reimbursed Butler and profited from the remaining proceeds of the sale of cotton. More than that, as Butler explained, the government had saved a great deal of time and expense by using the captured cotton as ballast, rather than the useless and inconvenient sand. Loading the ship with sand would have been a slow process, and for a vessel under charter, time is money. Unloading and carting away the sand at Boston would likewise have been a heavy expense to the government.

Official reaction to the *Black Prince* incident nearly frightened Fay and Carney from cooperating in any further exercises in innovative finance, as Butler continued to apply his mind to the money problems of his command. Their uneasiness was evidenced at once when Butler set another scheme in motion, this one involving larger sums.

This time Butler borrowed $60,000 from a New Orleans banker, Jacob Barker, the loan secured by drafts totaling that amount drawn on Carney. With this money Butler purchased a large quantity of naval stores, turpentine, tar, and pitch, and consigned the shipments to Fay. At the same time he wrote to Assistant Navy Secretary Fox advising him of the transaction. In his letter to Fox, Butler noted that the owners of these supplies had feared their goods might either be confiscated outright or destroyed, and that the merchants needed strong reassurance at a time when he was trying to restore New Orleans as a commercial port. He suggested that the Navy Department should take the shipment and reimburse him for the outlay only. If the government did not take these supplies, he added, Fay could undoubtedly sell them at a handsome profit.

In his instructions to Fay, Butler directed that the shipments be sold and the proceeds posted to his account. He told Fay he had informed Fox of the availability of these supplies, and that they were to be offered to the government at cost.

Fay responded in some dismay. He said he was going to Washington to clarify the matter. He was not going to risk a $60,000 transaction, Fay added, "without knowing how I stand with the War Department."

Banker Carney was also jittery. He complained, mildly enough, that if he was going to be called on to honor drafts totaling $60,000 then Butler might have considered consigning the goods to him, rather than to Fay. But in any case, he wrote, Butler was not to be surprised if the drafts were not honored if they were presented to him right away. Carney said he was afraid government red tape might tie things up so that he would be a long time getting his money, if he got it at all. He wanted strong reassurance on that point.

In the upshot the Navy Department stood aloof. The War Department instructed Fay to sell everything at auction, pay Butler's costs out of the receipts, and turn the profit over to the U.S. quartermaster at Boston.

"General Butler's action in this matter has been wise and patriotic," pronounced Quartermaster General Meigs. But he warned: "At the same time, as a public officer, he ought not to be involved in private trades and profits arising out of his official position and power." With this cautious note Meigs may have planted the seedling of an idea which, as Butler's enemies cultivated it, grew into the enduring legend of Butler as wheeler and dealer for personal gain.

Meanwhile Butler's friend and adviser, Paul R. George, wrote from Lowell to assure the general that the whole matter of the naval-stores shipment had been resolved, including Carney's reservations. George, a retired army captain of Mexican war vintage and now a successful merchant, had been Butler's choice as quartermaster for the New Orleans expedition, but the general's political enemies had blocked the appointment. George said he and other friends of Butler's had signed personal notes guaranteeing Carney full payment of the $60,000 indebtedness within thirty days, and had thus calmed that cautious banker's fears.

Secretary Stanton, observing all this with mild alarm, closed the chapter by writing Butler that the transaction was officially approved. But he added, echoing Meigs, "Such operations should not be engaged in without an absolute overruling necessity." Butler thereafter was careful not to appear as a personal participant in commercial deals. However, he did lend his ample credit to the uses of Andrew Jackson Butler, his free-wheeling brother, who energetically joined the swarm of traders shipping goods north for quick wartime profits.

Andrew's activities soon caused scandalous rumors to circulate, all pointing up the suspicion that General Butler was reaping millions in illicit profits from his management of affairs. But in truth there were larger considerations on Butler's mind, most importantly his mandate to open the port of New Orleans and restore its prosperity. The principal prewar exports, sugar and cotton, were mostly in rebel hands. Indeed, Governor Moore, in one and another of his frantic proclamations, had called upon all patriotic citizens of the Confederacy to burn their crops in the fields and to withhold at all costs the substantial hoards of sugar and cotton that had piled up in the warehouses. The Confederate propaganda line was that Butler meant to confiscate all such property anyway, provided he could get his hands on it.

As to cotton, at least, Butler soon found a possible way around both Federal restrictions and Moore's fiery exhortations. Many planters and businessmen in the region were lukewarm in such convictions as they held in regard to the war. Trade came first. Those holding the hard business view meant to see that their property was neither destroyed nor put in reach of confiscation. Although Butler had proclaimed a safe conduct for cotton and sugar brought within his lines, the cautious owners of these commodities remained aloof.

The opening Butler sought was provided by a British cotton trader, I. Maury, operating in Mobile. Maury persuaded the Confederate commander at Mobile to permit cotton to pass through his lines, provided the Union command at New Orleans would allow salt and other goods to be shipped back to Mobile in exchange. Still, however eager he was to make the deal, Butler was wary—not of the Confederates, but of his superiors. In view of past difficulties with Washington officials, he now wanted defensible prior approval, and he wanted it on the record.

For this purpose, in a neat stroke, he called upon none other than his old antagonist, Reverdy Johnson, who at the moment was in New Orleans as Seward's alter ego, pleasurably overturning nearly all of Butler's decisions in those money matters the foreign consuls had challenged. After discussing the cotton deal verbally with Seward's commissioner, Butler was careful to get his semiofficial approval in writing.

Johnson's response was prompt:

> The proposal of the English gentleman I think you should not hesitate to accept. The shipment of cotton, whether to Europe or to the loyal states, from the rebellious states, from such of their ports as

are in the possession of our forces, is, I know, much desired by our Government. It was one of the principal advantages they expected to be the immediate result of the capture of this city. So anxious are they to attain the object that I am satisfied they would readily sanction such an arrangement. . . .

As soon as he had Johnson's letter in hand, Butler sent a message to the Confederate commander at Mobile. It set forth the terms of the deal: salt for cotton, the value of the two commodities to be set by the trading parties in agreement between them. Butler promised there would be no seizure of either cotton or salt, and that the vessel carrying such cargoes would have safe conduct to return to Mobile. "Other goods, not contraband of war, may be sent to equalize the commercial values," Butler added.

Brother Andrew Butler, who had been active in one speculation and another from the first days of the occupation, was quick to enter the salt-for-cotton trade, somewhat to the dismay of George Denison, Secretary Chase's man in New Orleans. Denison had been eyeing Andrew with increasing suspicion and had concluded, mostly on the basis of rumor, that Andrew was fast becoming a millionaire through one shady deal and another.

In a confidential report to Chase, Denison wrote:

> Ever since the capture of this city a brisk trade has been carried on with the rebels by a few persons under military permits . . . Government officers, citizens, and rebels, generally believe [Andrew] to be the partner or agent of Gen'l. Butler. He does a heavy business, and by various practices has made between one and two million dollars. . . .

Denison relayed a story given him by an army surgeon, captured by the rebels and later paroled. At the rebel camp, Denison said, the doctor saw a large quantity of salt in sacks piled up by the railroad tracks. Denison continued:

> A rebel officer said to him, "We bought that salt from Col. Butler. We paid $5 per sack for the privilege of shipment from New Orleans. Today that salt goes to Richmond for the army. Tomorrow or the next day another cargo will arrive. The army gets their salt from New Orleans. The Yankees will do anything for money."

Denison was not the only one to complain of Andrew Butler's trading activities. Sarah, who had returned to Massachusetts before the onset of the fever season, was all but shrill in her letters to Ben, insisting that Andrew's enterprises were scandalous and would destroy the general's reputation and bring him down. She termed Andrew "blustering and overbearing." She even relayed a rumor she had heard that Andrew was a secret partner in two New Orleans gambling establishments.

"A more obnoxious person to invest with power could not be found," she wrote. "You think you control him and know his acts. On the contrary, though subservient to your face, he controls where he wishes, insults and overbears everywhere."

For his part Butler chose to ignore Sarah's complaints. His sole response was cold. "I will not speak of Andrew or what he may or may not do," he wrote his wife. "I know your wishes on this subject and will be guided by them so far as I may. Of other business matters I will take very good care of myself, but these are trivial to me."

Andrew, as it happened, had been very useful to his brother in arranging for various New Orleans merchants to ship large quantities of sugar to the North. As with his effort to stimulate a trade in cotton, this was in accordance with Butler's instructions to revive the commerce of the port. It was also an enterprise of quite some profit, not to Butler, but to the Federal government. As for Andrew, he did not neglect to collect a handling fee of $5 per hogshead for acting as shipping agent. As in the case of the *Black Prince*, it was a matter of providing ballast for ships returning from New Orleans to New York. In peacetime ballast for ships had never been a problem, since they invariably left New Orleans heavily laden. At New Orleans, as Butler had occasion to remark a little testily, the only alternative to useful cargo as ballast was mud.

Butler's expedient was eventually approved by Quartermaster General Meigs, but only after a snarl of red tape had been disentangled through Butler's patient explanation of the facts.

As for Denison, who continued to maintain a more or less constant admiration for Butler's drive and ability, the treasury man's wavering absolution of the general had an almost wistful note. "I have never been able to discover any good proof that Gen'l. Butler has improperly done, or permitted, anything for his own pecuniary advantage," Denison reported to Chase. "He is such a *smart* man that it would in any case be difficult to discover what he wanted to conceal."

As Butler's military operations consolidated his control of more large areas of agricultural land, the many abandoned sugar plantations caught his attention. He devised and put into operation yet another plan, this one not only to increase exports of sugar through the port, but also to provide an experiment looking toward emancipation of slaves. He turned abandoned plantations over to factors who worked as agents of the United States. They were to employ ex-slaves (Butler still called them "contrabands" from time to time) and pay them wages to tend, gather, and process the crops. As to loyal planters who still remained on their estates, Butler issued much the same decree. Blacks were to be paid for their labor. Noteworthy, in view of Butler's early political days among the mill workers of Massachusetts, the workday on the plantations was set at ten hours and the work month at twenty-six days.

The plantation enterprise caught Lincoln's sharp attention. He wrote asking for more information about it. Butler was happy to tell the president that the plantations worked by paid labor were far more productive than they had been under the slave system. Butler said a sample barrel of sugar produced under the new working conditions was being sent to Lincoln. "The fact that it will have no flavor of the degrading whip will not, I know, render it less sweet to your taste," Butler added.

Butler's tenure in New Orleans was winding down by the time he issued farseeing orders that the plantations under his jurisdiction make the necessary preparations for next year's planting. He had learned that planters of doubtful loyalty had conceived a plan to let their land lie fallow in the coming year, and he proposed to counter that measure. However hard he worked, though, his enemies continued to circulate the propaganda that he spent most of his time piling up a fortune for himself. Butler did not deign to reply.

As to the wild rumors that Andrew had become a millionaire in New Orleans, these were eventually to be dispelled, sadly enough, with Andrew's untimely death in New York on February 11, 1864. His estate contained a balance of $35,921.45, according to the probate report filed in the Surrogate's Court of New York by Ben as his brother's executor. Andrew's modest fortune had been made principally in prewar pioneering in the West, where among his close friends and neighbors in northern California was the notable Count Haraszthy, the Hungarian nobleman who established the first vineyards in the Sonoma-Napa wine region.

37

After New Orleans, the prize to the north was Vicksburg. With the capture of Vicksburg the entire Mississippi would be under Federal control. The Confederacy would lose access to its western territories and all their resources, not the least of which were the vast beef herds of Texas. Moreover, in addition to its importance as a source of supply and manpower, Texas had great strategic value as the Lincoln administration kept a wary eye on the imperial designs of Napoleon III in Mexico.

Butler was fully aware of Napoleon's eagerness to exploit American strife as a means of advancing French expansionism. With brisk efficiency he had taken immediate steps to prepare for whatever danger might arise from that quarter. His contingency plan assumed an attempt by a hostile French fleet based in Martinique to repeat Farragut's passage of the downriver forts. Accordingly, Butler issued quiet instructions. If the French were to make such a move in stealth, without a declaration of war, the forts were simply to enforce the quarantine regulations as a means of unmasking French intentions. Should hostile vessels ignore the order to stop at quarantine, Fort Saint Philip was to fire a warning shot. If French ships returned fire, or even if they simply continued upriver, the forts were to open up with all batteries. The other worst-case possibility, an open attack by the French, would of course be met with full resistance at the forts.

In preparing these drastic plans, Butler was fully aware that Washington, as usual, had taken care to leave him strictly on his own. He had no scrap of written authorization to take any action whatever to counter a threat from the French. But Seward, in his own devious way, had seen to it that a completely deniable verbal alert had been sent to Butler through an emissary. For his own part, Seward continued to foil persistent French efforts to gain British cooperation in a policy of open support of the Confederate States or, failing that, drastic joint Franco-British measures to defeat the Federal blockade of Southern ports.

While planning for contingencies, Butler took steps to strengthen the river defenses. As soon as he secured New Orleans, Butler ordered captured heavy ordnance hauled downriver and installed in new water batteries designed by his tireless engineer, Godfrey Weitzel. He also ordered large fire rafts prepared and emplaced, not so much as incendiary devices, but rather for the purpose of illuminating hostile vessels, thus exposing them to accurate fire from the water batteries and main armament of the forts in any nighttime attack. He recalled, from having witnessed the operation, that Farragut's principal advantage had been darkness.

Not long after Butler's river defenses had been put in order, the French Admiral Reynaud sailed into New Orleans to show the flag and convey by his demeanor an unmistakably hostile message. Admiral Reynaud (Butler privately called him The Fox) was the ranking officer of that command officially and rather grandly known as The Naval Division of the Gulf and North America.

Butler, himself a master of subtleties, accorded the admiral a full ceremonial welcome, after which he invited Reynaud to inspect the improved defenses of the forts. Ben, in a grand show of naiveté, guided him around personally and explained all the details.

"Now, Admiral, what do you say?" said Butler after the conducted tour. "With these means of resistance, properly handled with skilled gunners, do you believe that any fleet of the British Navy could live to make that passage?"

The French admiral got the message. He agreed that British warships would never get past those heavily strengthened defenses. And Butler, smiling all the while, was quite satisfied that Reynaud really was thinking to himself that French ships could never pass those defenses, either.

Later, to a French request to buy a large number of pack mules, Butler replied with every bland indication of deep regret that not a pack mule was to be found for sale in the entire region under his control. Butler, of course, knew quite well that the only use the French would have for mules would be in support of operations in Mexico.

While Butler was quite willing to accept nods and winks from Washington in lieu of hard orders regarding the French, he was somewhat uneasy about the general lack of direction accorded him. Official Washington, aside from Seward's sharp attention to the prosperity of the foreign merchants, appeared to consider that Butler was operating in a kind of limbo. Attempting to clarify this, Butler wrote Stanton in some perplexity, noting that he had been receiving no instructions whatever from the War Department, not even copies of the army's routine general orders. Stanton's answer was terse, smooth, and possibly even sincere, but in no way helpful. He simply replied that Butler was just so very capable that nobody needed to tell him anything.

Nor were lesser War Department officials much more communicative. Shortly after landing in New Orleans, Butler wrote Quartermaster General

Meigs that he was totally without money. He told Meigs he had already spent $5,000 out of his own pocket to meet the government's money needs, and that he had no more cash "either here or on draft at home." Receiving no useful response to this, Butler fell back on Stanton's broadly implied grant of power and set about exercising his ingenuity to raise badly needed funds, whereupon Meigs, among others, came suddenly awake with many inquiries and objections.

Administrative problems aside, Butler's purely military moves were quick and effective. The 9th and 12th Connecticut regiments were dispatched to occupy and hold the defensive works the Confederates had engineered on the north side of the city. These extended from the river to the marshes bordering Lake Pontchartrain. Fort Pike and Fort Wood, defenses of the lake itself, were manned by the 7th Vermont and 8th New Hampshire, backed by patrolling gunboats. Butler also took measures to control rail lines to the northeast and northwest.

But the longer-range assignment remained: to clear the river northward in cooperation with Farragut and the fleet. Curiously enough, Butler, with his small and necessarily dispersed force, was expected somehow to seize the major Confederate stronghold at Vicksburg, yet the huge army under the command of Maj. Gen. Henry W. Halleck, operating to the north of Vicksburg, was given no such assignment. Nor did Halleck himself show any interest in the Vicksburg objective. Halleck's subordinates at this time, Gens. Ulysses S. Grant and William T. Sherman, both considered Vicksburg of prime importance, but both were directed elsewhere as Halleck pursued his own notions of strategy.

Halleck, one of the strangest figures in the Union high command, had gained eminent reputation as a military strategist, although his only field experience had occurred in the Mexican war when he served briefly as a junior engineer officer. His prestige was based almost entirely on his translation of the manual of war compiled in 1838 by the Napoleonic expert, Baron Henri Jomini. Halleck's version, *Elements of Military Art and Science*, was published in 1846, prefaced with an accurate disclaimer that as translator he made no claim to originality in the work. Afterward, Halleck's high command duties during the Civil War somehow left him the leisure to complete a translation of Jomini's massive *Life of Napoleon*, the Halleck translation, published in 1864, running to four fat volumes.

Halleck's *Elements* handbook was studied avidly by nearly all officers, Union and Confederate. It was even the foundation of Lincoln's scanty smattering of military education. Jomini's maxims, which placed high value on massed infantry in close formation, were many years out of date, but that was something neither Lincoln nor most of his generals came to realize until many thousands of dead foot soldiers had paid the price for their commanders' erudition. Jomini's tactics were mainly useful in filling military cemeteries.

Backed by old General Scott, who was properly awed by Halleck's scholarship, the owlish literary soldier was commissioned a major general. At this point in the war—the spring of 1862, as Butler and Farragut looked northward to Vicksburg—troops under Halleck's command had met near disaster and suffered ten thousand casualties at Shiloh. Halleck's troops had later concentrated at the important rail junction of Corinth, Mississippi, after a cautious march that took the entire month of May, and from that point were soon to be distributed in several directions, none of them toward the key Confederate position on the Mississippi.

In his memoirs Sherman was to comment:

> It was a fatal mistake . . . that halted General Halleck at Corinth, and led him to disperse and scatter the best materials for a fighting army that, up to that date, had been assembled in the West. . . Had he held his force as a unit, he could have gone to Mobile or Vicksburg, or anywhere in that region, which would by one move have solved the whole Mississippi problem.

In any case it was left to the shoestring force at New Orleans to deal with Vicksburg. Butler's northward move, hampered by a lack of troops and supplies, was also short of light draft steamboats. Although he had urgently advised Washington of the need for river craft, the high command ignored all his requests, and he was left to improvise as best he could. The retreating Confederates had burned or disabled nearly all such boats and hidden the rest in the bayous. It was typical of Butler's orphan command that, far from being supplied with major needs like a riverboat fleet, Butler could not even get so much as a supply of mosquito nets from Washington, although he submitted repeated and urgent requests to Quartermaster Meigs for these items so basic to operations in swamp country.

Butler contrived to make do. He repaired as many of the sabotaged boats as were salvageable, and he dispatched search parties into the backcountry to retrieve whatever boats they could find. That energetic Bostonian, J. B. Kinsman (he who had all but turned the Dutch consul inside out to shake him loose from his hidden silver cache) led one such party. Kinsman conceived a plan of marching north from Lake Pontchartrain and then turning east to begin a circular sweep that would cross the shallow headwaters of those streams that emptied into the lake. And it was in this search that Kinsman's party found perhaps the best boat to be retrieved, a large and powerful steamer later renamed *Kinsman*, in his honor.

The hidden boat had been hastily sabotaged. Engine parts had been removed as had some of the bearing packing and, of course, the boiler was empty. But one of those ever present Yankee craftsmen stepped forward and briskly directed improvised repairs. After the machinery had been put in order, a bucket brigade recharged the boiler with water, wood was cut for fuel, and the boat was ready to sail. Kinsman brought his prize back down the winding stream in triumph, its whistle blaring as it entered Lake Pontchartrain.

Thus, by one device and another, Butler assembled enough vessels to carry two regiments and a light field-artillery unit upriver to Vicksburg to cooperate with Farragut in the projected assault. On the way the troops, under Gen. Thomas Williams, secured Baton Rouge, which surrendered at the approach of the Federal fleet. By May 16 Williams and the navy gunboats were proceeding toward Vicksburg, but Farragut's flagship had gone hard aground at Natchez, requiring Butler to send up a couple of small cargo boats to lighten the warship and get it back into deep water.

At Vicksburg the expedition went through the motions of demanding the city's surrender, and the Confederate authorities sent back a haughty defiance. Williams expected the rebels to refuse the surrender demand, but he was a little taken aback by their sarcasm, however justified it may have been, given the obvious weakness of the Federal force. A week later the gunboats were still chuffing around to no effect, and Williams was reporting to Butler that it would take at least ten thousand men to storm the stronghold with any hope of success.

Farragut, after catching up with his fleet and surveying the situation, reached the same conclusion Williams had. He advised Butler that he now proposed to leave just a couple of gunboats on station to harass the town and establish a blockade. Meanwhile, he said, he would wait to see how Halleck fared at Corinth. General Williams, for his part, said he would take his troops to scour the Red River country for targets of opportunity, such as Texas cattle drives.

By June 1, Williams and his command were back in Baton Rouge, awaiting reinforcements and preparing defensive positions for an expected rebel attack which, at that time, failed to materialize. Most of his men were sick and all of them were tired. Malaria, scurvy, dysentery, and sheer fatigue had left but eight hundred men fully fit for duty out of a force of thirty-two hundred. Hospital facilities were taxed to the limit.

Butler duly forwarded to Stanton the army-navy consensus that it would take at least ten thousand men to assail Vicksburg with any hope of success. Butler's entire effective force for all purposes at this time amounted to only twelve thousand.

"I am of the opinion that it is all-important that we take Vicksburg, hold it or not," Butler insisted. He added that he was prepared to offer Farragut half of his entire force for another try at the stubborn Confederate stronghold. Meantime he suggested that Porter's mortar fleet, idle at Ship Island, might prove useful in directing high-angle fire against Vicksburg's batteries.

Another week passed. Butler scraped up additional reinforcements for Williams. These consisted of two more regiments, the 31st Massachusetts and 7th Vermont; a few more pieces of light artillery; and a cavalry troop. Williams's orders directed him to capture and hold Vicksburg or, at least and more reasonably, to take the place and burn it down.

Fully realizing the inadequacy of the force assigned, Butler suggested that Vicksburg, situated by a sharp loop of the river, could be cut off and isolated if the river itself was redirected. He instructed Williams to put his men and a corps of "contrabands" to work digging a short canal across the narrow neck of land. The Mississippi's current, he thought, should widen the cut into a new riverbed to provide free passage for the Federal fleet, with Vicksburg no longer dominating the passage.

Stanton replied approving the project. "If your force is strong enough, or if General Halleck could cooperate with you, there could be no doubt of success," said Stanton. He agreed that opening the Mississippi was of vital importance. But beyond those cheering words, the secretary of war offered no help and certainly no direction to the bemused Halleck.

On July 3 a supply boat brought unofficial news of the initial attack. Some of the gunboats had passed the Vicksburg batteries and joined the fleet operating north of the city. Williams had made a lodgment on the opposite shore and was lobbing shells into the Confederate defenses.

A more discouraging report, official, came from Farragut. Work was proceeding on the cut-off canal, but the level of the river was falling faster than the workers could dig. The fleet was continuing to shell the town, Farragut said, but the land force was too small to accomplish anything worthwhile. He estimated Confederate strength at ten thousand men.

Reports from General Williams were also dismal. He estimated that Vicksburg was held by seven thousand to ten thousand confident rebels, backed by thirteen to twenty heavy guns. He termed his own force "wholly inadequate." Farragut, for his part, pleaded with Halleck for troop reinforcements. "My orders, General, are to clear the river," Farragut wrote Halleck. "This I find impossible without your assistance. . . . Can you aid me in this matter to carry out the peremptory order of the President?"

Unimpressed by the presidential mandate, Halleck replied from Corinth that, "because of the scattered and weakened condition" of his forces, he could offer Farragut no help. Two weeks later Halleck covered home base by writing to Stanton to the same effect.

On July 16, finally, Butler ordered Williams to withdraw. Now he was writing official communications for the record. He reported fully to Stanton the next day, saying he had recalled Williams from Vicksburg "in expectation of an immediate advance on that place by General Grant." His order to

Williams noted pointedly that Vicksburg was in Halleck's department, not the Department of the Gulf. He followed this with a direct communication to Halleck all but apologizing for having ordered an advance on Vicksburg, saying that "only the exigencies of the service" had justified the movement. He added, smoothly enough, "It is now quite different, as I am informed that a division at least of your army is moving on Vicksburg." And to nail it all down he sent Grant a copy of this letter, labeled "for information."

But neither Farragut's plea nor Butler's none-too-subtle hints stirred Halleck to take any part in the Vicksburg operation. Finally Farragut, having no choice, withdrew the fleet. Vicksburg was not to fall into Union hands until July 4, 1863, by which time the operation involved a Confederate force of thirty thousand and an entire army commanded by Gen. U. S. Grant, with heavy and proportionate casualties on both sides.

In one bitter paragraph of a letter to Sarah, Butler summed up the failure of the Vicksburg attack: "Farragut has come down the river and given up Vicksburg. So we go, perhaps, over to Mobile. I have so large a force I can go anywhere, of course. . . ."

38

After the failure of Farragut and Williams at Vicksburg, Confederate troops were freed to take the offensive against Butler's outpost at Baton Rouge. For this purpose a force of five thousand was assembled under the command of John C. Breckinridge, Butler's prewar political associate, now a Confederate major general. To add a decisive punch, the Confederates called upon the newly completed ironclad ram *Arkansas*, which had just added its heavy armament to the guns defending Vicksburg. Now *Arkansas* was ordered to sortie downriver to Baton Rouge, there to support Breckinridge's attack with a heavy bombardment of the Union defenses. It was expected that the combined operation would make quick work of Butler's outnumbered garrison, since of the three thousand Union soldiers at Baton Rouge more than half were sick or disabled, and accurate word of this had reached Confederate headquarters.

In early morning of August 5, under cover of a dense ground fog, the Confederates began their attack, which achieved some initial success that was soon to be offset by two sharp disappointments. Adhering to their battle plan, the rebels pushed hardest at the camp of the 7th Vermont and 21st Indiana regiments, acting on reports they had received that it was less a camp than a field hospital. But when the alarm was sounded the sick rolled out of their hospital tents, picked up their rifles, and joined at once in the battle. The second disappointment was furnished by the stuttering engines of the *Arkansas*, which failed to propel the giant ironclad to the battle scene in time to be of any use.

Although their plan had gone awry in these two important details, the Confederates attacked fiercely. Three times they massed and charged, three times they were stopped and driven back, in a struggle that went on for nearly six hours. Initially the Confederates overran and all but destroyed one camp, but a determined Federal counterattack drove them out again. Rebel efforts to envelop the Federal force by flanking attacks, left and right, also failed. When the attackers finally gave up the struggle they fell back in some disorder, leaving three hundred of their dead on the field and abandoning many of their wounded along their line of retreat. Confederate casualties included four brigadiers—two killed, two captured, one of the latter severely wounded. On the Federal side, General Williams was killed instantly, shot through the heart while rallying the remnants of a hard-hit regiment that had lost all its field officers in the battle. Col. Thomas Cahill of the 9th Connecticut then took command and directed the battle to its conclusion.

The very next day fate caught up with the laggard ram *Arkansas*. The vessel, underpowered even when her faulty engines were functioning, finally capped all her misfortunes by being run aground. To prevent her falling into Federal hands, the crew of the *Arkansas* set her afire and abandoned ship, after which the ammunition aboard went up in a violent explosion, completing her fiery destruction.

But the *Arkansas*, erratic engines and all, had been a doughty craft while she lasted, causing the Federal river fleet much anxiety and the Union naval command much chagrin. Initially, a force of three of Farragut's gunboats, steaming up the Yazoo River in search of the new Confederate ram, had the misfortune to meet the giant coming at them head on. The *Arkansas* chased all three gunboats back down the river again, passed majestically through the rest of Farragut's fleet, and took up station under the guns of Vicksburg. A subsequent night attack by Farragut's full force scored but one hit on the Confederate ram, causing no damage whatever.

In the Baton Rouge afterpiece, Comdr. William D. Porter, in the ironclad *Essex*, came upon the stranded *Arkansas*, which was accompanied by two small rebel gunboats. On Porter's approach the light gunboats fled. The *Essex* got off one long-range bow shot at the *Arkansas*, and it was at this point that the rebel crew torched their vessel and fled into the underbrush. These were the circumstances later attested to by Capt. D.M.W. Fairfax of the Federal gunboat *Cayuga*, who had witnessed the entire episode. As a matter of fact, Fairfax said, the distance between Porter's ship and the *Arkansas* was greater than the range of either vessel's guns.

The circumstances of the Confederate vessel's demise led to warm controversy between William D. Porter and General Butler. Porter, estranged brother of David D. Porter, fully shared David's quarrelsome tendencies and his remarkable gift for self-glorifying hyperbole. This latest Butler-Porter encounter began, innocently enough, when Butler included what he thought was a more-than-tactful paragraph in a general order commemorating the Baton Rouge battle. It read: "To complete the victory, the ironclad steamer *Arkansas*, the last naval hope of the rebellion, hardly awaited the gallant attack of the *Essex*, but followed the example of her sisters, the *Merrimac*, the *Manassas*, the *Mississippi*, and the *Louisiana*, by her own destruction."

Porter, aboard the *Essex*, was far from satisfied with faint praise. As

Simon Cameron
Battles and Leaders of the Civil War

John C. Breckinridge
Battles and Leaders of the Civil War

Salmon P. Chase
The Great Rebellion

Thomas Williams
Photographic History of the Civil War

soon as he had finished reading the well-meant paragraph he fired off a hot letter to Butler. The commander of the *Essex* did not blush at casting himself in a heroic role. Porter wrote:

> The facts, Sir, are as follows. On the 6th ins. A.M. I steamed up the river to attack the *Arkansas*. . . . She immediately opened fire on this Ship, at about the distance of one mile. I stood on until I considered myself near enough for my shot to penetrate her iron-clad sides, when I replied to her fire. We continued the action for nearly half an hour, when a shell from this ship penetrated her side and *set her on fire.* Your statement in your General Order No. 57 is therefore incorrect.

Porter, after demanding an instant retraction, went on to assert that not only had he destroyed the *Arkansas*, but that by directing accurate fire from the *Essex* he had driven off the Confederate infantry at Baton Rouge, thus saving Butler's army from defeat. He added a postscript: "The *Essex* was the only vessel present at the action, and on the *Arkansas* starboard side I counted fourteen shot holes through her new plating. . . I was within 300 yds. of her, and was on deck and traced every shot to her."

Porter's account of the affair was denounced as fiction by Captain Fairfax, of the *Cayuga*, and his lieutenant, E. H. Perkins. Both were astonished and angered by Porter's bald assertion that he had hotly engaged the rebel ironclad and, moreover, had done so alone.

"In the first place," reported Perkins, "there was no fight between the *Essex* and the ram, only a few shots exchanged at the distance of a mile and a half apart, when the ram was set on fire by her officers and burnt up."

Fairfax was incensed at Porter's suggestion that the accompanying Federal gunboats had deserted the scene and left the *Essex* to go it alone. His report said:

> It can be shown that the *Essex* did not engage the Ram *Arkansas* at all—unless laying beyond the range of either vessel's guns, and occasionally firing a shot, can be so designated. The *Arkansas* was destroyed by her own crew, and abandoned before our little fleet then on duty at Baton Rouge. . . . Commander Porter failed to bring his vessel into action as he assured me he would. . . . .

Satisfied that eyewitness testimony had given him the truth of the affair, Butler let the record stand as he had written it. But the aftermath of the *Arkansas* episode was strange, to say the least. In Washington, Navy Secretary Welles was a bit puzzled when Farragut seemed reluctant to give Porter full credit for the exploit. But Welles placed his own value on it, and in conference with Lincoln got permission to promote Porter to the rank of commodore anyway. William's envious brother, David, made no attempt to conceal his chagrin at his brother's stroke of fame and fortune.

Scarcely a month later the newly promoted commodore was brought up on charges filed by Farragut. Those charges were described by Welles as accusing William "of misrepresentation and worse." William was then reprimanded and summarily retired from the navy. Among other erratic indiscretions, William had sent the War Department a wildly abusive letter, which Stanton had referred to Welles for appropriate action.

It may or may not have been relevant that Farragut himself was foster brother to the wild Porter brood, having been adopted as a child by the paterfamilias of the clan, the elder Capt. David Porter, hero of the War of 1812. William had been disowned by his father for the disgrace of having got a servant girl pregnant, and thereafter Farragut sided with the family in William's permanent ostracism. At this time, in the midst of the Mississippi campaigning, Farragut notably refused to be drawn into any controversy involving David, but he showed no hesitancy, as noted, in bringing about William's downfall. As for William himself, that stormy soul sickened and died not long after being called before the naval retirement board.

Totally remote from the navy's curious intrigues, Butler had more important matters that demanded his attention. As the month of August wore on, Butler received increasing intelligence of a gathering of Confederate forces intended for another try at retaking Baton Rouge, and possibly an attempt to regain New Orleans as well.

"The withdrawal of the troops at Vicksburg, and the apparent inactivity or withdrawal of troops from Corinth," Butler reported to Stanton, "has allowed the concentration of all of their troops upon me."

Butler again asked for reinforcements, preferably troops from the New England states. "Not that they are any better than others, but I know them better," Butler added. He asked for cavalry reinforcements to counter troublesome guerrilla activity. And, as an indication of the kind of logistical support he was getting, he reminded Stanton that four months had gone by since his ordnance officer had asked for rifle ammunition and that all he had received so far were the invoices describing the absent shipments.

Two days after writing Stanton, Butler ordered the evacuation of Baton Rouge in order to concentrate his limited force for the defense of New Orleans. In his initial order he called for putting Baton Rouge to the torch. But he later countermanded this for both practical and humanitarian reasons, since large public buildings there sheltered the sick, the insane, the orphaned children, and the inmates of the state penitentiary, none of whom he was in any position to accommodate at New Orleans.

The withdrawal from Baton Rouge was not without its embarrassments. Butler's troops, in spite of all his repeated and emphatic orders against looting, pretty well stripped the town of its valuables, some of his men even carrying off clothing and furniture from private houses. For his own part, and quite officially, Butler himself sacked the state library and had its books relocated in the New Orleans library. He also took care to have the state's handsome statue of George Washington packed up and removed to New Orleans for safekeeping.

At New Orleans Butler prepared to defend the city against uprising within as well as attack from without. He set about confiscating all weapons in private hands, from rifles to hunting knives. To speed the work, he published an order offering rewards for information leading to recovery of weapons. The sliding scale for tips ranged from $10 for a rifle thus recovered to $3 for each "dirk, dagger, Bowie-knife or sword-cane." As the search went on, weapons by the thousands were surrendered or seized.

Reporting to Stanton, Butler said, "It seems to be the tactics of the enemy to attempt to drive us out of New Orleans at all hazards. They agree the town will be destroyed in so doing, but they reason that there is so large a foreign interest here that the destruction of the town will embroil us with foreign powers."

On a more optimistic note, at the same time, Butler suggested that if properly reinforced he could not only guarantee the safety of New Orleans, but could undertake a wide-ranging expedition into Texas which, he said, he was eager to lead.

While Washington sent him no troops, Butler did succeed at last in getting the recognition he had long sought for the hard-working Lieutenant Weitzel, who may well have been the only veteran West Point engineer to have served in the war so long without promotion. Weitzel, in one grand leap, became a brigadier general. In the meantime, fortunately, prospects of a Confederate attack on New Orleans melted away, as heavy operations to the north absorbed the Confederacy's full attention.

Reporting now to General Halleck, whom Lincoln had named general in chief, Butler outlined his plans for a modest expedition through western Louisiana to seek out and disperse Confederate forces assembling there. On this mission General Weitzel was to lead five regiments of infantry, two artillery batteries, and four troops of cavalry. Weitzel was to be supported by Butler's own home-made navy, consisting of shallow-draft steamers the general had scrounged, fitted out with plate iron to protect their boilers and engines, and armed with light artillery guns. Butler planned to assign the 8th Vermont to a supporting role, along with his newly formed and trained 1st Regiment Native Guards, known more familiarly to the troops as 1st Colored. Those two regiments would operate along the Opelousas Railroad, providing Weitzel with supplies and also protecting planters who wanted to send sugar and cotton to New Orleans for sale.

"I should be glad if General Weitzel should be able to move upon Texas," Butler wrote Halleck, "and would suggest that an appropriate base of operations would be through Galveston which, I have just learned, has surrendered to the Naval force of the Union."

Butler again asked for substantial troop reinforcements, saying he could easily hold the richest portion of Louisiana if he were given the means, and that he could also extend his conquest so as to prevent practically all Texas supplies from reaching the Confederacy. But, though Halleck had been studying his own plans for a western offensive directed toward Texas, he sent Butler no resources whatever. In the end another general, Nathaniel P. Banks, was to get the regiments and the assignment and, accompanied by David D. Porter and his gunboats, preside over a military disaster—the Red River campaign.

Butler told Halleck that he scarcely had a regiment he could spare to hold Galveston but that he proposed to send one anyway. He said Farragut's impatience to attack Mobile had his full moral support, but he reminded Halleck that he was spread too thin to undertake the military side of the mission.

In reply to Butler's encyclopedic report, Lincoln's new general in chief, who had made an art form of looking wise and saying nothing, looked wise and said nothing. Assuming that silence meant consent, and taking full responsibility, as usual, Butler got Weitzel's expedition under way on schedule. As directed, Weitzel moved his force upriver to Donaldsonville, and then, after securing that place, marched west and south. There was some brisk skirmishing with a Confederate force of about twenty-five hundred that itself had intended to take and fortify Donaldsonville. But, in a matter of days, Weitzel disposed of Confederate resistance in the area and seized control of all the rich plantation country to the west of New Orleans.

Butler followed up his earlier moves by dispatching the 2d Regiment of Native Guards to reinforce the troops restoring and holding the Opelousas Railroad. Bridges destroyed by the Confederates were reconstructed, tunnels and land cuts reopened, new track installed where necessary, and the line picketed and patrolled against incursions. As a sidelight to this operation, Butler was required once again to placate Seward, who forwarded a complaint that British-owned rail iron had been seized by Butler's supply people for the Opelousas project. Butler patiently restored the rail iron as ordered and managed, in one way and another, to repair the road without it.

More serious, from Butler's standpoint, was a sudden and unexpected request from Weitzel to be relieved of his assignment in command of the newly constituted Military District of Lafourche. Weitzel objected to the inclusion of black troops in his command because, he said, their presence was leading blacks on the plantations to rise up against their masters, who had become terrified at the prospect of a slave insurrection.

Butler's response was patient but inflexible. He was adamant in pointing out that Weitzel's troops were in the field to seek out and destroy the enemy, not to be diverted into the role of a police force. Let all the rebel formations in the region surrender, he said, and Union troops would then offer all inhabitants the same security against violence that was now being accorded the citizens of that part of Louisiana already in Federal possession. Butler recalled that he had once before offered citizens full protection against violence on exactly the same terms when he was in command at Annapolis. He wrote:

> The same principle initiated there will govern [my] and your actions now. And you will afford such protection as soon as the community through its organized rulers shall ask it. In the meantime, these colored regiments of free men . . . must be commanded by the officers of the Army of the United States, like any other regiments.

Weitzel, thus instructed, settled down to command the new military district with his usual efficiency. As for dealing with the ex-slave population of the region, both Butler and Weitzel were now empowered to enforce the confiscation act passed by Congress and signed by Lincoln. The act had finally given full legal force to the "contrabands" device that Butler had originated at Fortress Monroe, and carried it a step further. It stated simply enough that fugitive, captured, or abandoned slaves of rebels were declared free. Butler's policy, set forth in his own regulations, was to put the freed blacks to work for wages while guaranteeing them food, clothing, shelter, and humane treatment.

But all this time, while patiently begging for reinforcements to strike a really heavy blow at what he termed the Confederacy's "beef barrel" in Texas, Butler was aware that Seward was maneuvering to remove him from command at New Orleans. Rebel press reports, ironically enough, provided the first word that General Banks was to replace Butler. His agents in the city told him that, in the clubs frequented by wealthy Confederate sympathizers, gambling gentlemen were offering ten-to-one odds that he would be relieved of command. His friends in the North furnished further confirmation, although they believed that Banks was only to command an expedition out of New Orleans, an assessment Butler himself preferred to accept.

In reaction to these reports Butler, on November 29, wrote a long personal letter to Lincoln stating plainly enough that if Banks was to command in the field then Butler wanted no part of a purely administrative post in New Orleans. If Lincoln thought he was not qualified for full operational command, the general said, then let Lincoln say so in so many words.

"Pray do me the favor to reflect that I am not asking for the command of any other person," Butler wrote, "but simply . . . that my own, which I have a right to say has not been the least successful of the War, shall not be taken from me in such a manner as to leave me all the burden without any of the results."

In any case, an air of conspiracy laced with hypocrisy clung to the entire affair. Stanton, in fact, had already signed General Order No. 184 on November 9. It read, in its entirety: "By direction of the President of the United States, Major General N. P. Banks is assigned to the command of the Department of the Gulf, including the State of Texas."

Yet some three weeks later, on December 2, Sen. Henry Wilson was writing an encouraging letter to Butler. The senator said he had called on Stanton to impress upon him the importance of sending substantial reinforcements to Butler without delay, and that Stanton concurred. "He agreed with me," wrote Wilson, "and promised to do what he could to aid you. He expressed his confidence in you and his approval of your vigor and activity."

At this same time other Washington personages were also relaying to Butler similar reassurances they had received: that he was not to be superseded, that he had the full confidence of the administration, that he stood well with the high councils. The bald truth of the matter was not to be completely revealed until December 12, when Banks arrived in New Orleans and personally handed him Stanton's peremptory General Order No. 184. By that time Butler had full knowledge of the order and knew that, although it was signed by Stanton, Seward's fingerprints were all over it.

39

Butler, sardonic as ever, greeted his successor at New Orleans with a somewhat overdone display of pomp and ceremony. Banks was greeted by the crash of a full artillery salute as he passed the forts on the lower river, and he was welcomed at the wharf by an honor guard. A fine carriage was on hand to take him to the Saint Charles Hotel in style. After all that, Banks's formal presentation of orders superseding Butler could scarcely be seen otherwise than as an anticlimax.

Since he had no instructions to proceed elsewhere, Butler made a point of remaining in New Orleans more than long enough to brief Banks on everything he thought the new commanding general ought to know. He turned over all his records and accounts—making sure that he got signed receipts for everything. He summed up the military situation in detail and suggested that Port Hudson, a potential Confederate stronghold some twenty miles upriver from Baton Rouge, ought to be outflanked and captured before the rebels moved to strengthen that position in greater force.

Butler issued a formal farewell to the citizens of New Orleans summing up, tersely enough, the accomplishments of his civil administration:

> Commanding the Army of the Gulf, I found you captured, but not surrendered; conquered, but not orderly; relieved from the presence of an army, but incapable of taking care of yourselves. I restored order, punished crime, opened commerce, brought provisions to your starving people, reformed your currency, and gave you quiet protection, such as you had not enjoyed for many years.

In the crowded days of his tenure at New Orleans, Butler had allowed very little time for diversion, but now he proposed to do something unusual: he decided he would go to the theater. What he actually had in mind, however, had less to do with stage drama than with real-life theatrics. He simply proposed to demonstrate his contempt for the latest assassination threat, which he had just received. Since he was accustomed to moving freely about the city in his open carriage, attended only by the soldier-driver handling the reins, it was in this way that he and Sarah went to the theater. Quite possibly to his gratified surprise, the entire audience greeted their arrival with an uproarious standing ovation. If there was an assassin lurking anywhere, he failed to show himself.

Butler had time for some humanitarian gestures before taking his leave of New Orleans. In one instance he responded to pleas from the family of Pierre Soulé, the ardent rebel whom Butler had shipped north to be imprisoned at Boston. Butler asked Stanton to free Soulé to live in Boston on parole. Later, informed that the wife of General Beauregard was danger-ously ill at the Beauregard home in New Orleans and not expected to live, Butler wrote to Beauregard offering him his sympathy, and enclosed a pass guaranteeing him safe conduct to New Orleans and return.

In quite some contrast, Jefferson Davis marked the change of command in New Orleans by issuing his proclamation declaring Butler an outlaw and ordering that he was to be summarily hanged if he fell into Confederate hands. The proclamation cited in thunderous prose a long list of "crimes" attributed to Butler. In it Davis swore to God that it was not revenge he had in mind, but the exercise of solemn duty. As he warmed to composition, the Confederate president proclaimed that not only was Butler to be lynched, but that all commissioned officers in his command were to be considered "rob-bers and criminals deserving of death," and were likewise to be "reserved for execution" whenever captured. Privates and noncoms serving under Butler, however, were to be treated "with kindness and humanity."

Scarcely concealed in the Davis proclamation, however, was the Con-federate president's real source of angst and anger. Concluding his list of Butler's "crimes," Davis declared: "And, finally, the African slaves have not only been incited to insurrection by every license and encouragement, but numbers of them have actually been armed for a servile war—a war in its nature far exceeding the horrors and most merciless atrocities of savages."

Butler's well-trained, well-disciplined, and eager black troops had served all too competently thus far and had given promise of further good service in the future. The "horrors and atrocities" existed only in Davis's overheated mind. What Davis dreaded most was the sure evidence that Lincoln was following Butler's lead, at last, in authorizing the recruitment and training of free blacks as Union soldiers, something Lincoln had stub-bornly resisted for such a long time. In answer to this, Davis now ordered, in his "Butler" proclamation, that captured black soldiers and their officers, white or black, were to be dealt with as criminals, not as prisoners of war. They were to be turned over to state authorities for punishment, which, depending on the severity of the pertinent code and the temper of the judge, could include hanging. Perhaps, knowing Lincoln's tendency to tem-porize, Davis thought he could slow down recruitment of black regiments.

Pierre Gustave
Toutant Beauregard
Battles and Leaders of the Civil War

David Glasgow
Farragut
Battles and Leaders of the Civil War

At the very least he assumed his order would discourage white officers from serving with black troops.

Remote from all this inflamed rhetoric, Butler took his leave of New Orleans amid as much ceremony as had greeted Banks. Officers and leading citizens lined up to wish him well, and he shook hands for two full hours. The final hour before his departure he spent aboard the *Hartford* with his good friend Farragut, recalling the trials and triumphs they had shared. When the time came at last for Butler to board the unarmed steamer that would carry him home, Farragut ordered a full salute fired from his flagship, the roar of the navy's guns blending with that of the field artillery battery also saluting the general. From the assembled crowd there were sustained cheers for Butler as his ship moved slowly away from the pier.

40

Ben Butler's governing characteristic was a total inability to accept defeat. A more tractable man, dealt the sharp political rebuke he had just suffered, might have quit and retired to his home, either to find solace there or perhaps just to sulk. But that was not Butler's way. His unyielding stubbornness was the attribute that plagued his political opponents most, infuriating some and terrifying others.

Unlike other Northern commanders at this point in the war, Butler had brought about no bloodbaths, engineered no calamities. Working with meager forces, he had ended the dangerous isolation of Washington by seizing Annapolis and providing a secure route for troops called to defend the capital. He had then seized and secured Baltimore in one quick and smoothly executed move. At Fortress Monroe his "contrabands" edict had provided a practical first step toward emancipation of the slaves.

And now he had effected a remarkably efficient occupation of New Orleans, had conducted successful military operations with the limited resources allowed him, had freed thousands of slaves and provided for their needs, had recruited the first Negro regiments, and had managed all this and more while returning some $500,000 to the Federal treasury. Success on this scale was something to be regarded with mixed feelings by an administration that was becoming uneasy about Lincoln's political future.

Removing Butler served Seward's immediate purpose in that it appeased those foreign powers that had been annoyed by the general's sharp attention to the conduct of their nationals at New Orleans. But it is not to be imagined that the crafty secretary of state failed to consider practical aspects of domestic politics as he pressed for Butler's recall. Butler's record, gained at a time when the North had little else to cheer about, had not gone unnoticed by those kingmakers and would-be kingmakers who considered Lincoln a weak and incompetent president. Popular sentiment favoring a Butler presidency was large and growing. Ordinary voters had to consider that the only Northern general Jeff Davis wanted to hang must have been doing something right in this otherwise tedious, bloody, costly, and largely bungled war.

Lincoln himself, who had devoted a lifetime to politics and office seeking, was too canny a politician to overlook these manifestations or fail to assess them as a possible threat to his renomination. Pressed by McClellan Democrats on one side and impatient abolitionist Republicans on the other, Lincoln had a right to feel uneasy. Nor did it help his peace of mind that so many of his associates were also openly alarmed.

The irony contained in all this was that Butler, at this stage in his life, was not seeking the presidency or any other political office. True to a childhood dream of adventure and a youth spent in deliberate preparation, Butler had found his war. It was not the one he wanted (he always had Britain in mind), but it was the only war he had. His ambition now was to enter history as a great commander. Political eminence seemed paltry by comparison and was, in any case, something to be considered much later. Butler, at forty-five, saw himself as a young man with plenty of time.

But whatever the considerations that had brought it about, Butler's recall from New Orleans was a blunder both in concept and execution. Its immediate political effect was to enhance, rather than erode, Butler's popularity. From a military perspective it was indefensible, since Butler's replacement was the inept if well-meaning Banks, who had less administrative ability and no perceivable military talent whatever.

Though Lincoln might have benefited from sound counsel in this affair, he had deliberately avoided seeking it. The move had been kept secret even from the Lincoln cabinet—only Seward and Stanton had been privy to it. Crusty Gideon Welles, hearing of the change only after it had become a done deed, noted in his diary: "Information reaches us that General Butler has been superseded at New Orleans by General Banks. The wisdom of this change I question, and so told the President. . . . Outside the State and War Departments I apprehend no one was consulted."

Welles thought it would have been common courtesy, at the very least, to inform the Navy Department, since the navy and army were collaborating in operations at New Orleans. Praising but faintly, as he often did, Welles judged that Banks could probably administer the department all right, provided he was not called upon to conduct any military campaign.

And now, even as Butler headed north, Lincoln was having second thoughts. He had nervously followed the move by asking Sen. Charles Sumner to reassure Butler in these exact words: "The President says that you shall not be forgotten." Sumner did so in a letter to the general and added that Stanton and Halleck had said substantially the same thing. Still later Sumner talked again with Lincoln, who now said he hoped to return Butler to New Orleans "very soon."

As Butler's ship neared New York, he received an urgent message from the president himself, delivered by a fast revenue cutter. It said:

> I believe you have a family, and I dislike to deprive you of an
> early visit to them. But I really wish to see you at the earliest
> moment. I am contemplating a peculiar and important service for
> you, which I think, and hope you will think, is as honorable as it is
> important. I wish to confer with you on it. Please come immediately
> after your arrival at New York.

Obedient to orders, Butler went straightaway to Washington and called
on the president. Lincoln was cordial, Butler was not, and the interview
was both brief and strained. Butler, a formidable presence in any encounter,
challenged Lincoln to state plainly why he had been recalled from New
Orleans. Without explaining why or how a president of the United States
should be so restricted, Lincoln could only reply that he was "not at liberty"
to tell him and that Butler should direct the question to Stanton. As for the
"peculiar and important" new assignment Lincoln had in mind, the nature
of that job was not disclosed.

Butler then called on Stanton, as Lincoln had suggested, and found him
not a whit more communicative.

"The reason was one which does not imply on the part of the government any want of confidence in your honor as a man, or in your ability as a
commander," said Stanton.

"Well, you have told me what I was *not* recalled for," said Butler. "I now
ask you to tell me what I *was* recalled for."

Stanton, however, refused to be pressed.

Butler next interviewed Seward, but he received no more from that
functionary than a cordial invitation to dinner. Seward, glib as ever, professed not to know the answer. But he said that General Halleck did and
that Butler ought to ask Halleck why he had been recalled.

Grimly enough, Butler called on Halleck and found him somewhat
more candid than the others. Halleck also said he did not know why Butler
had been recalled. But he did volunteer that the order was issued solely at
the behest of Seward, and that Seward was the man who knew all there
was to know about it. This, of course, did little more than confirm Butler's
fully formed conviction. He now understood, further, that Seward would
never be brought to say in so many words that the Federal major general
commanding at New Orleans had been recalled "at the request of the
Emperor Napoleon."

That night Butler attended Seward's dinner party, which, like all of
Seward's many parties, was a convivial affair. Afterward, as Seward accompanied him to the door, Butler could not resist loosing a shaft. "What an

infernal liar your man Halleck is," said Butler. "Why, he told me that he didn't know anything about the reason why I was relieved, and that it was done solely upon *your* advice."

Seward was far too bright to imagine that Butler was still unaware of the truth of the matter. He knew that Butler's oblique remark was intended to convey that Seward was the liar, not Halleck. But Seward did not blink, and Butler abruptly departed.

Early next morning Butler called on the president again. He found Lincoln all set up and waiting for him with an array of charts, books, and maps, prepared now to discuss that new assignment. However, the general had decided to press the issue of his recall and the refusal of the administration to state a reason for it. Butler had no intention of being kept in the position into which he had been maneuvered, with no charge made and therefore no defense possible. If Seward wanted him out of New Orleans because France and Britain wanted him out of New Orleans, Butler held, then that should be plainly stated. If there were other reasons, then those should be made public. In this intolerable situation, he told Lincoln, he had brought his commission with him and was prepared to surrender it.

Lincoln, not at all eager to have Butler careering about the country unbound by military discipline, refused to hear any word about Butler's giving up his commission. He still refused to answer Butler's question, but he protested warmly that his high regard for the general had not changed.

As quickly as he could, Lincoln turned the discussion to that important new job. Stripped of Lincoln's hard sell, however, that assignment, as Butler saw immediately, was to make him a kind of recruiting agent in a nominal Mississippi Valley command, where his main task would be to raise and train Negro troops. Butler could even nominate the officers for his new regiments, Lincoln said, and they would be automatically approved. The president gestured toward his maps, which had black population areas blocked out to show Butler, as if he didn't know, just where willing Negroes were most heavily concentrated.

Butler rejected the proposal out of hand. He reminded the president that, if the administration had permitted him to do so, he could have raised many more thousands of black troops while he was at New Orleans. If Lincoln was now anxious to raise such regiments, he said, the method was simple: "Send me back to my old command."

Lincoln, after pacing the floor for a while in what appeared to be deep thought, finally replied, "But I cannot recall Banks." Obviously a commitment had been made and had to be kept. But Lincoln, neither then nor later, ever explained why or how Banks, of all people, had acceded to the important New Orleans command, nor why Banks was to be supplied the armed strength and resources that had been denied to Butler.

Lincoln's evasiveness convinced Butler that this interview was going nowhere. He again proffered his commission, and told the president he now intended to return home to Lowell.

"You shall go where you please, General," sighed Lincoln. "But keep your commission."

Butler's progress home was marked by a succession of testimonials. Leading New Yorkers proposed a civic dinner in his honor. At Boston his special train was greeted by the Massachusetts dignitaries, a guard of honor, and a military band, and he was conveyed to his hotel in a carriage drawn by four white horses. On Boston Common an artillery battery fired a full salute. Butler was presented with a joint House-Senate resolution of honor, duly signed by his old adversary, Governor Andrew. There were speeches, banners, cheers, and even praise in the press.

In the months ahead, however, Butler grew weary of fending off the one question for which he had no answer. No more than the man in the street did the Union's ranking major general have any idea where the Lincoln administration proposed to assign him or, indeed, if he was to be assigned anywhere at all.

Butler chafed at his unaccustomed leisure. He wrote a lot of letters, answered many more, made some speeches. His major addresses warmly endorsed emancipation and civil rights for blacks. At Fortress Monroe and later at New Orleans, Butler had seen slavery close up and had come to despise the brutality of an institution which, manifest evils aside, was a ridiculous anachronism in a society that long since should have abandoned it. The indifferent Democrat had become a fiery abolitionist.

Butler's correspondents sounded him out on any number of moves. Supporters in Congress suggested that he ought to replace Stanton as secretary of war and that a cabinet shake-up should also remove Seward as secretary of state. Missouri congressmen urged Lincoln to assign Butler to command in their strife-torn area in place of Gen. John M. Schofield. And there was much activity among restless Republicans seeking to organize a Butler-for-president movement. In the midst of all this, Butler held firm in his determination to secure nothing other than a proper military assignment, either reinstatement at New Orleans or a comparable command elsewhere. To that end he applied every pressure available to him through his connections in Washington.

Among the odd side issues that occupied Butler's attention during this unhappy period was his successful effort to ease the plight of Confederate Gen. Jeff Thompson, who had been taken prisoner and lodged at an internment camp on Johnson's Island near Sandusky, Ohio. The incident was another of those brotherly interchanges between Yank and Reb that occurred often enough in this most American of wars to distinguish it from other great conflicts.

During operations around Baton Rouge, one of Butler's officers, a Captain Thornton, was wounded and fell into General Thompson's hands. Thompson saw to it that the captain's wound was treated, and then he arranged to send him back to New Orleans on parole. Now Thompson recalled the incident in a courtly letter to Butler that was forwarded from the prison camp where the Confederate general was being held.

"I promised Capt. Thornton that if I was ever captured I would notify him of my whereabouts, that he might return the favors which he thought I extended to him," wrote Thompson.

> I do not think that Capt. Thornton is under any obligations to me, as I simply acted toward him as I have to all gentlemen who have been so unfortunate as to be captured by me, but in conformity with my promise I would like to let him know that I am here, and as I do not know his address, and understanding at the time that he was a personal friend of yours, I hope it will not be presuming to forward him this letter, let me know his address. . . .

Butler did somewhat better than that. He immediately got off a letter to the commanding officer at the prison camp:

> General Thompson showed great kindness to wounded officers and soldiers who fell into his hands. I beg leave to speak for him all the indulgence and liberty which can be shown him consistent with your discipline.
>
> Please inform me if Gen. Thompson is destitute, so that he cannot supply himself with any little comforts that would alleviate his situation.

He enclosed a separate note to Thompson:

> I retain a lively sense of the courtesy . . . with which you conducted operations when in command opposed to me in Louisiana, and desire as before to thank you for your kindness to Capt. Thornton in sending him home wounded, by which kindness I have no doubt his life was saved.

Butler promised to do what he could to ease Thompson's imprisonment and to have him released if he could manage that.

While getting those messages on their way, Butler addressed a third letter to Stanton, giving the secretary of war full particulars of Thompson's chivalrous conduct.

"If not inconsistent with public service, I most earnestly ask that Gen. Thompson may be released upon his parole," Butler wrote. "As I am not in the habit of asking leniency for rebels, I trust the War Department will take it as a guaranty that this is a proper case for the extension of every indulgence."

There were some long memories in Washington, however. It was recalled that Thompson, as a fire-eating rebel in strife-torn Missouri, had countered Gen. John C. Frémont's threat to hang captured "rangers" with a threat of his own—nothing less than to "hang, draw and quarter a minion of Abraham Lincoln" for every Reb executed by the Union general. In the end Thompson was given limited freedom but not paroled. And Butler, doing what he could, sent him some money through the prison-camp commander, under strict orders that Thompson was never to know who sent it.

Meanwhile poor Banks at New Orleans was having his troubles. In the city itself active rebels, sensing a looser rein, began agitating ever more openly against the Union. Confederate Gen. Richard Taylor, in a handsomely executed surprise attack, seized Banks's supply depot at Brashear City and sacked it, carrying off munitions, equipment, and supplies valued in the millions. At Port Hudson, second only to Vicksburg as an objective in clearing the Mississippi, Banks mounted two heavy assaults, both of which were repulsed with substantial Federal losses. Then he settled down to an inconclusive siege. Upriver, Grant finally concluded a bloody campaign with the capture of Vicksburg, after which Port Hudson, its garrison starving, surrendered.

The Banks administration, in fact, had begun with a disaster at Galveston, where army and navy forces were overwhelmed by a Confederate assault. The redoubtable Union gunboat *Harriet Lane* was captured after running aground, its crew slaughtered by Confederate riflemen. *Westerville*, flagship of the Federal naval force there, was abandoned and blown up by its commander, Commodore Renshaw, who perished in the explosion when the charge was fired prematurely. The rest of the Federal ships fled, and survivors among the army garrison were captured.

Secretary Chase's man in New Orleans, George Denison, had a glum report to make as of March 4, 1863. He wrote to the secretary: "Since General Banks arrived this is what has been accomplished, viz: With an army three times as large as Gen. Butler's, we hold the same territory held by him. We have lost the steam sloop-of-war *Mississippi*, the gunboat *Kinsman* (iron clad), the *Hatteras* and the *Harriet Lane*. Also Galveston."

Denison said a change in command was urgently required. "Gen. Benj. F. Butler is the man and the only one," wrote Denison. "In two weeks he could restore everything, but I do not suppose he will be sent here, for he is too earnest a man to suit Mr. Seward, and if placed in a high position he might possibly become dangerous as a candidate for the Presidency."

Shortly after the Galveston debacle, Lincoln wrote a formal memo to Stanton: "Sir: I think General Butler should go to New Orleans again. He is unwilling to go unless he is restored to the command of the department. He should start by the 1st of February, and should take some force with him."

The presidential order said Stanton should take care not to wound the feelings of General Banks. That general's wish to command an expedition to Texas ought to be granted, Lincoln continued, but not if it interfered with the basic objective of opening the Mississippi. "I think we cannot longer dispense with General Butler's services," Lincoln concluded.

In any well-ordered command structure, that note ought to have been sufficient to resolve the matter, but directives from Lincoln were all too often seen as little more than a starting point for dissent, debate, compromise, and modification. It seemed that Lincoln's top cabinet members did not take the president's views all that seriously. Seward and Stanton, especially, appeared to put a higher value on their own opinions and, for that matter, on their own powers of intellect.

In this case Stanton decided to modify Lincoln's clearly worded order by attaching certain conditions. Remarkably enough, Butler was directed to proceed to New Orleans by passing down the Mississippi from the north. Nobody, least of all Butler, understood this curious itinerary, unless it was seen as a kind of obstacle course, with the general somehow floating past the Confederate strongholds at Vicksburg and Port Hudson. Alternatively, it could have been interpreted as an enforced delay in assuming command, while Butler awaited the outcome of Federal siege operations at the two river citadels.

In any case what had been initiated as a clear presidential directive became, as usual, a matter for much further discussion. In the meantime, and on the record, Butler at least had official vindication of his conduct of affairs at New Orleans. At the president's order, he reported in person to Washington repeatedly over the next several months to join in the debate. But by the time Stanton had finished editing the New Orleans order, Butler no longer was willing to accept the assignment. Most important, nearly all the troops brought there for the Banks command were short-termers whose enlistments were now close to expiring. As Butler saw it, he would be reduced to serving as little more than a glorified transportation officer, with his main job that of getting those troops back home—no small task in itself, given the shortage of transports and money.

In the end, however, after all the long and frustrating months of palaver, Butler finally received a welcome telegram. Dated November 2, 1863, it read, "You have been assigned to command at Fort Monroe. The Secretary of War directs you to repair there immediately."

41

Butler greeted word of his new assignment with a flurry of activity, dispatching brisk telegrams in all directions to reassemble his staff. Sarah, on the other hand, had grown weary of the war and of the endless machinations of those she considered enemies of her beloved Ben. Nevertheless she decided to accompany him to Fortress Monroe, even though it was a place she had quickly come to hate when Butler last commanded there. Sarah planned to stop long enough in Washington on the way, to make some social calls and also to arrange for their daughter, Blanche, to accompany them to the new post. It would be a vacation for the vivacious Blanche, who was about to start a new term at the convent finishing school she had been attending in the capital.

In Washington, Sarah and Blanche called on Mrs. Lincoln, who was "out," but they did visit with the president, who was charming. Lincoln, meeting the lovely blonde Blanche for the first time, could not help remarking, in his best country-courtly way, that Ben and Sarah certainly had a very handsome daughter.

As was her custom, Sarah kept her sister Harriet up-to-date on all her activities. Perhaps because of her classical education, she was a much better writer than Ben. Her letters, many of them written in haste, often fairly crackled with her sharp observations and candid opinions. In her first letter to Harriet from Fortress Monroe, she did nothing to conceal a cranky attitude toward the general's new assignment.

We took the pleasure boat, "Carrie Martin" at Washington and came down the Potomac. This is a little steamer kept for the use of the President and Cabinet and loaned to us by the Secretary of War. We thought it would be delightful, but dear me, when we got into the Bay, it was tossed about like a nut-shell, and by no means a seaworthy craft. We were all sick.

When we arrived, the usual salute was given, the gentlemen went on shore. I thought we might have an invitation to Mrs. Gen. Foster's, as so many had claimed our hospitality when at the Fortress before, but no courtesy was offered.

Butler had proposed to buy the Fosters' furniture, which would have saved them the trouble of moving it and the Butlers the bother of refurnishing the commanding general's quarters. But they had ignored the offer, somewhat to Sarah's disgust. In the absence of any hospitable gesture whatever on the part of the Fosters, the Butlers spent the night in an uncomfortable hotel room where, as Sarah described it, the floor was softer than the bed. Next day, after a less than indifferent breakfast, Ben and Sarah made their way to a bleak welcome at headquarters.

When we came in the next morning we found the house quite bare. We stepped into a vacant room and ordered a fire (the morning was quite chilly), and waited until they had left. Dirt, dirt, dirt, and a house to furnish. These Army people have a way of scuffling in and out of houses peculiar to themselves. . . . Dirt before and behind them. I have a horror of it. . . . Mrs. Foster stepped in for a moment before she left, but not a word of apology or regret at the forlorn look of things.

On the brighter side, Sarah reported, "Yesterday we rode on the beach, Blanche and the Genl. on horseback, Capt. Clark and I in a buggy. The day was very fine, the drive delightful. We rode four miles up the beach, smooth and firm as a floor."

But toward the end of her letter Sarah's deep discontent was vehemently expressed. "I do not like this place, never did," she wrote. "I keep scratching on,—really I have nothing further to say, only this is a doleful place and home is better. . . . I have an idea we may not stay here long."

At New Orleans Sarah, high strung and emotional, had soon wilted under the stress and all but fled back to the relative calm of home in Lowell. But, even in the secure and healthful atmosphere of New England, she had fretted and worried over her beloved Ben, burned with indignation about the political plots that swirled around him, agonized over hostile editorials, and even tortured herself with phantom fears that Ben's love for her had cooled.

For his own part, Butler—wherever he happened to be—wrote to Sarah constantly, reassuring her as to his own health and security; providing her with bulletins and snippets of news; and, above all, addressing her with little endearments and more than a hint of passion. However well matched these two were in intellect, each respecting the high mental endowments of the other, theirs was an earthy relationship.

Sarah, given to sick headaches and other illnesses whenever she drove

Blanche Butler Ames

herself to exhaustion, was always fearful about Ben's health. In one letter written to Sarah during his New Orleans tenure, Butler (at her fretful insistence) gave an account of his typical workday:

> Get up at six, write an hour or more in my room, then breakfast, then calls for an hour, then go to the office and business till 4 o'clock, then dinner at 5, then opening mail and answering letters and calls till eight, then tea; sometimes a walk of half an hour in the evening, then a chat or writing till twelve, and then to bed. And sometimes not to sleep. There you have a day, as like another as two peas, save a review, inspection of a hospital or something of that sort—or telegrams of trouble or any little diversification.

Butler's nonchalant note, only one of many similar reassurances, was intended to calm Sarah's constant fear that his rugged constitution would give way under the strain of all his activities, responsibilities, and conflicts. Nothing that had happened since New Orleans lessened her anxieties in this respect. Now, at Fortress Monroe, Sarah suppressed her worries and misgivings, briskly organized a household staff, and set about doing her supportive best to help her hard-driving husband.

To break the housekeeping routine, Sarah and Blanche accompanied the general and some of his staff on a quick inspection survey of outposts in North Carolina. Sarah's subsequent report to Harriet gave little indication that her mood had lightened.

> We returned last Tuesday from a tour of North Carolina. You will be ready to exclaim that without any justifiable cause I should again dare Hatteras. I was weary of the sight of cleaning and furnishing. Blanche was teasing to go, the weather is settled and mild, so that I gave general orders to the servants what to do for a week, and started without more ado.
>
> This was Blanche's first voyage. I hoped she would take after her father, and would escape seasickness, but she seems to be her mother's own daughter, and droops at the first roll of the vessel. We landed at Beaufort, the same marshy, sunken, sandy look that most southern towns have. . . . In the morning we took the cars for New Bern, thirty miles distant.
>
> All the remainder of the week we were sailing up the Pamlico and Albermarle Sounds, touching at little towns we have taken and fortified at great labour and expense, that are of no earthly use but oblige us to feed and take care of the inhabitants. Little villages many miles asunder, they were taken merely to give éclat to Gen. Foster. The only place worth taking was Wilmington, and that we have not got.

Sarah's gloominess extended to her two-sentence review of the book just written by the biographer James Parton, who had assembled an extensive, friendly, and highly detailed account of Butler's administration in New Orleans. "We have Parton's book," wrote Sarah. "I fear it is a failure."

As time would prove, Sarah's quick assessment was quite wrong. The Parton book was well received by the Northern public, became something of a best-seller, and remained thereafter a valuable record of the New Orleans occupation. But at this time it seemed to Sarah little more than a bitter reminder of the slanders, injustices, and crippling interference her husband had been forced to endure in Louisiana and, possibly, a portent of similar troubles he could expect in his new command. Washington, after all, had not changed. The only difference in Butler's situation, as Sarah saw it, was that at Fortress Monroe he was that much closer to the knaves in the national capital.

In these fears Sarah was not wrong. Evidence of an unchanging Washington, as a matter of fact, came rather promptly and from a familiar source. Seward was at it again, this time demanding steps to be taken that would give free passage to a huge shipment of tobacco to France from the rebel capital of Richmond. For Seward's purposes this time, a legal fiction was devised, purporting to certify that the tobacco had been purchased before the outbreak of hostilities, and was therefore somehow exempt from the blockade.

Seward also busied himself interceding for one James A. Gray, captured aboard a blockade-runner and now, after fifteen years' residence in Georgia, claiming the protection of the British Foreign Office. In Gray's possession at the time of his arrest, among other things, was documentary evidence that he had been trading in Confederate bonds, recruiting sailors for Confederate vessels, and dealing in cotton smuggled through the blockade.

Gray was only one of many busy profiteers who had found opportunity in smuggling and trading amid the exigencies of war. The elaborate and sometimes ingenious activities of traders of all kinds was well exemplified in the case of another busy merchant who fell afoul of Butler's vigilant provosts. Isaiah Respress, a former mayor of Washington, North Carolina, had been buying up large quantities of captured Confederate notes from Union soldiers at five to ten cents on the dollar. He would then smuggle the Confederate bills into Richmond, where his attorneys would buy tobacco, cotton, and naval stores with them. The goods purchased with Confederate money would then be run through the blockade for sale in the West Indies, where payment would redound to Respress in sound gold doubloons.

Butler directed his military court judge, Major Bell, to hear the ex-mayor's case and deal with a ton of chewing tobacco Respress had not had time to smuggle before he was arrested. "Make process both against the man and the tobacco," Butler ordered tersely. "Punish the one and confiscate the other if found guilty."

In reorganizing what had been a rather dormant and easy-going Department of Virginia and North Carolina, Butler soon found himself dealing with a blizzard of paperwork. For efficiency's sake he ordered a scattered clerical staff concentrated in a single building, which he enlarged for the purpose. Somewhat to Butler's amusement, this brought a protest from the Regular Army engineer assigned to the fort. Like all old Regulars, the engineer knew the army regulations by heart. He was quick to cite a pertinent paragraph to back his assertion that Butler needed the approval of the secretary of war before he could alter any building within half a mile of the fort. Butler, who found this kind of peacetime fustiness ridiculous, wrote Stanton requesting an ex post facto okay.

> I respectfully make application for your approval of this act, and it becomes more necessary because of the celerity of my Quarter-Master Department. The building was up before the vigilance of the Engineer discovered it was about to be erected, and we must pull it down at nearly the expense of erecting it in order to preserve the regulation unbroken.

Butler, somewhat appalled that buildings at the fort still depended on candlelight, set in motion a modest project to install gas lighting throughout the post, including lampposts for the parade ground and a more efficient beacon for the lighthouse. While still mulling this undertaking, he also ordered the seizure of the gas works at Norfolk, whose owners had found one reason and another to keep it out of operation after the city came under Union control.

"The City of Norfolk has been in darkness long enough, waiting for the action of the enemies of the country," Butler wrote to Brig. Gen. James Barnes, commanding that outpost.

Butler held that failure of the civilian directors of the lighting system to cooperate with Union forces holding the city justified outright seizure of the gas works. Barnes was ordered to "use the most energetic measures to put the thing in operation forthwith."

Eyeing the curious traffic in nearly worthless Confederate currency, as in the case of the trader Respress, Butler noticed that the authorities at Richmond were profiting handsomely from relief funds sent to Union prisoners there. Friends and family members were sending good Federal greenbacks and gold coin to Fortress Monroe to be forwarded to the prisoners by way of the regular "flag of truce" boat that communicated across the lines. But when this good money got to Richmond, the authorities there were holding it for their own purposes and exchanging it for Confederate notes, which then were paid over to the prisoners. Butler thought this ought to stop, and he knew how to stop it.

He wrote Treasury Secretary Chase, reminding him that the United States Treasury now held millions in captured Confederate currency that was of no use whatever to the government. He suggested that Chase send some bundles of these Confederate notes to Fort Monroe, where Butler himself would make the exchange. In this way Confederate money, pegged at the exchange rate prevailing in Richmond and published daily in the newspapers there, would be forwarded to the prisoners. Butler would return the good money to the United States Treasury, which in this way would be getting some benefit from its otherwise worthless hoard of Confederate notes. At the same time, and this would be no small benefit, Richmond rebels would be deprived of their easy source of hard cash.

All these matters and many others like them were the smaller details that received Butler's attention as the Christmas season approached. Larger problems, of course, also occupied his mind and taxed his energies. There were field operations of a limited scope. There was the opening of long negotiations for the exchange of prisoners. And leading in this as he always had, Butler was maturing plans to recruit Negro troops and Negro labor on a much expanded scale.

As for Sarah and Blanche, they were busy making the general's quarters livable, and by way of holiday cheer, planning a Christmas party. Pretty sixteen-year-old Blanche was holding out, as she wrote to little brother Paul, for a "mask ball."

42

From the outset in the fall of 1863, it was clear that the War Department intended to supply Butler with no more than would be necessary for purely defensive purposes and local mop-up of guerrilla bands operating in his department. This was a situation that was not to be changed until the following spring, with the accession of Gen. Ulysses S. Grant to full command of all Federal armies. In the meantime Butler, as usual, busied himself with countless administrative details while, at the same time, undertaking such military operations as his resources permitted.

Butler's immediate superior in Washington was now that curious incompetent, General Halleck, whose bookish command of long-outdated tactics had so impressed a largely ignorant president. Old Brains, they called Halleck, either in sarcasm or in something like awe, depending on whether foot soldiers or the high brass were assessing him. In his one notable achievement in the field, Old Brains had thoughtfully taken four weeks on the march to move his overwhelming force twenty miles from Shiloh to Corinth, and once having occupied that rail center, knew not what to do next. He thereupon scattered his armies in several directions, totally neglected the prime objective of Vicksburg, and was rescued from his quandary by being summoned to Washington to become Lincoln's general in chief.

To Butler this was like an echo from the past. Old General Scott, who disliked him heartily, had stored him away at Fortress Monroe and systematically withheld troops and supplies to make sure he stayed shelved. Now Halleck, one of Scott's old favorites, had inherited Scott's old job and Scott's old prejudices, and here was Butler once again at Fortress Monroe, once again depending on a hostile general in chief for support.

The War Department responded to Butler's repeated request for troops by sending him instead a plethora of surplus brigadier generals, until Ben at last lost patience. On the arrival of yet another brigadier at Fort Monroe, Butler sent Stanton a testy note saying he already had far more generals than he needed and, if permitted to do so, he would like to get rid of some.

As Washington continued to ignore him as far as possible, Butler determined to solve his manpower problem by stepping up the recruitment and training of black troops, for whose capabilities and potentials he had come to have a great and growing respect.

Butler's most enthusiastic subordinate in this effort was Brig. Gen. Edward A. Wild, a Yankee abolitionist only slightly less zealous in this respect than old John Brown. Wild's feelings toward the rebel slaveholders were all the more embittered by his loss of an arm at the Battle of Gettysburg. Since two of Butler's best black regiments, under Wild's command, were now ready for action, Butler decided to send them on an extended sweep into the swampy northeastern counties of North Carolina, where bands of guerrillas —mostly stragglers and deserters from the Confederate army—were terrorizing the countryside.

Wild's soldiers carried out the assignment with enthusiasm and efficiency, tracking guerrillas to their hideouts in the swamps, routing them out, and freeing the little towns and villages the irregulars had been harassing. Most inhabitants of the five counties greeted the presence of Union troops with some relief. Citizens' committees in all the counties voted resolutions expressing their adherence to the Union.

As the abolitionist Wild passed through the countryside, he swept the farms and plantations for Negro families desiring to be free. His black troops did not hesitate to use enthusiastic force when they encountered the occasional planter who thought to keep his slaves locked up. Before he was finished, Wild found himself leading a long train of troops, supplies, and hundreds of newly freed black families.

Wild's conduct on the march brought about one particularly ugly incident, however, which created more than ordinary tension between Butler and the Confederate authorities in Richmond. In a small town in Pasquotank County that had been plundered by the guerrillas and deserted by its inhabitants, Wild's men captured one Daniel Bright, erstwhile private in a Georgia regiment, and now (according to the finding of Wild's on-the-spot court-martial) a common bandit and murderer. Bright was taken at bayonet point to an improvised gallows where he was hanged. General Wild added dramatic emphasis to the episode by personally acting as hangman.

Nor was that all. Wild took it upon himself to seize the wives of two men he considered to be guerrilla leaders, holding the women as hostages to ensure the safety of one of his Negro soldiers who had fallen into the rangers' hands. This, along with the hanging of Private Bright, took Butler more than somewhat aback. In his report to Stanton about the expedition he remarked that "General Wild . . . appears to have done his work with great thoroughness, but perhaps with too much stringency. . . ."

Repercussions were not long in coming. A group of citizens of Pasquotank County sent a letter reporting in obvious anxiety that they had found the body of a Union soldier still dangling at the end of a rope, and with a placard pinned to the back of his shirt. The letter, signed by all the members of the group, said: "We trust you will not attach any blame to any of the citizens of the neighborhood, as we were entirely ignorant of any of the circumstances until we found the body. From all we can learn he was brought across the Chowan River to this place, and as soon as the men who had him in charge had hung him, they went back."

The hanging was in reprisal for Wild's execution of Private Bright. The placard on the victim's back read: "Here hangs Private Samuel Jones, of Co. B, 5th Ohio Regiment, by order of Major General Pickett, in retaliation for Private Daniel Bright, of Co. L, 62nd Georgia Regiment (Col. Griffins), hung Dec. 18th, 1863, by order of Brig. General Wild."

At first it was believed that "Private Jones," a Negro soldier, had been randomly chosen for execution from among the black prisoners of war being held in Richmond. Butler, in his report to Washington on the incident, held that this made it an act not merely of General Pickett, but of the Confederate government. He noted that there were no Ohio troops in his department, and that this underlined the fact that it was an official act for Washington to deal with at the highest level. But enough, he suggested, was enough.

"This action may be as well met now as any time," Butler wrote. "Our Government has suffered its officers and men to be outlawed for doing their duty. It has suffered its prisoners to be starved without retaliation, and now hanging is superadded. I state the fact, I do not presume to offer advice."

Later, however, it developed that "Private Jones" was really Pvt. Samuel Jordan, one of General Wild's men, and not a prisoner randomly selected from those in a Richmond prison.

Wild, meanwhile, had sent an inflammatory letter to Capt. John Y. Ellcott, whom he addressed as "captain of guerrillas." It read:

> Sir: I still hold in custody Mrs. Manden and Mrs. Wicks as hostages for the colored soldier taken by you. As he is treated, so shall they be: even to hanging. By this time you know I am in earnest. Guerrillas are to be treated as pirates. You will never have rest until you remove your present course or rejoin the regular Confederate Army.

Wisely enough, Ellcott's commanding officer, Col. James W. Hinton, bypassed the fanatical General Wild and addressed himself to Butler. Hinton pointed out that his organization, the 66th North Carolina Regiment, was no guerrilla band, but had been organized under the authority of the governor of North Carolina. Hinton said his regiment had captured many Union soldiers and treated them uniformly as prisoners of war. He demanded to know whether Butler intended to endorse Wild's policy. And he also demanded to know whether Butler meant to hold as hostages the women Wild had arrested. The response, said Hinton, would dictate what future course his regiment would adopt toward Union prisoners.

Butler's response to the uncomfortable situation created by General Wild's untrammeled zeal attempted a judicial approach. The two captive women would be released at once, said Ben, provided their husbands would take their place as prisoners of war. This, he said, was necessary because the Confederates were still talking about reprisals. As for the general conduct of war against Hinton's regiment, Butler said he meant to observe all the rules of civilized warfare so long as Hinton did the same. He said the matter of the hanging of the unfortunate Private Jordan, finally, had been referred to Washington for whatever action the Federal government saw fit to take.

With these improvised solutions, the heat was removed from the discussion of reprisals, if only temporarily, since General Pickett was later to develop a certain enthusiasm for hanging Union soldiers he designated as hostages. In the meantime Washington, of course, did nothing.

As for General Wild, he was retained in his command, although Col. J. Wilson Shaffer, Butler's chief of staff, considered the brigadier a first-class liability. Shaffer, in peacetime a newspaperman, served not only as an administrative officer but also as a kind of liaison man between Butler and various political figures, including President Lincoln, a personal friend. Military duties aside, he also filled the role of political adviser, since he saw Butler as an inevitable candidate for president some day. In this instance he counseled Butler to tell Stanton bluntly that "if he will give us one good, substantial, common sense man, he can have Wild." Said Shaffer: "I wish Wild was elsewhere. He has no common sense."

Butler, meanwhile, was planning a military move somewhat more dramatic than Wild's march through the backcountry. What he now had in mind was a direct raid in force on Richmond, with the object of rescuing Union prisoners held there. For this operation he was depending on a somewhat more stable officer, Brig. Gen. Isaac Wistar, who had served with him in his earlier tenure in command at Fortress Monroe.

The truce boat that made its regular run between Richmond and Butler's stronghold figured large in the general's plans. Both sides used this curiously amiable arrangement to gather intelligence rather freely. The Richmond post office even accepted "truce letters" addressed to Northern recipients and saw routinely to their delivery aboard the steamer. Letters arriving on the truce boat for addresses in the Confederacy were also handled as a matter of course by the post office. Travelers bearing the proper credentials from either side were permitted to move more or less freely through the lines aboard the busy steamer.

One such outgoing passenger, a German physician bound for Europe, told Butler casually enough that a young woman in Richmond, Miss Elizabeth Van Lieu, was a fiercely loyal Unionist anxious to do anything she could to help the Federal cause. Her credentials could be checked, Butler learned, by writing in confidence to a Commander Boutelle in the U.S. Coast Survey Office in Washington. Enclosing a letter to Boutelle, which Miss Van Lieu had entrusted to the German doctor, Butler wrote to the commander:

> Now, I much want a correspondent in Richmond, one who will write me of course without name or description of the writer, and she need only incur the risk of dropping an ordinary letter by flag of truce in the postoffice at Richmond, directed to a name at the North. Her messenger thinks Miss Van Lieu will be glad to do it.
>
> I can place my first and only letter in her hands for her directions, but I also place the man's life in her hands who delivers the letter. Is it safe to do so? Will Miss Van Lieu be willing either to correspond herself or find me such a correspondent?

Boutelle by return mail vouched for the young woman's sincerity, and Butler proceeded to put his plan in motion. It involved creation of a fictional nephew for Miss Van Lieu—Butler himself—who would exchange innocent family letters with her. For reasons best known to himself, Butler adopted a Welsh name for Elizabeth's fictional nephew, James Ap. Jones. The device he proposed to use involved concealing the true message in invisible ink between the lines of the fake letter. The materials for conducting this clandestine correspondence, along with Butler's first letter to his "aunt," were forwarded to Miss Van Lieu through an agent, code-named Quaker, whom Butler already had operating in Richmond.

With a somewhat sardonic sense of humor, Butler's initial note began: "My Dear Aunt: I suppose you have been wondering why your nephew hasn't written before, but we have been uncertain whether we should be able to send a letter. The Yankees steal all the letters that have any money in them. . . ."

The real message, developed by the application of acid and heat, was simply a set of instructions. The woman's letters were to be addressed to James Ap. Jones, Norfolk. Butler also used the limited space to pay warm tribute to her patriotism.

Late in January Miss Van Lieu, possibly for reasons of more apparent plausibility, addressed her "nephew" as "Dear Uncle." When the secret message was developed, it warned Butler that the Confederates were preparing to move all Union prisoners out of Richmond to prison camps in Georgia. "Butchers and bakers to go at once," the message said. "They are already notified and selected. Quaker knows this is true."

Miss Van Lieu and Quaker were concerned that Butler might do something rash. The message warned, wildly enough, that no attempt on Richmond should be made with fewer than thirty thousand cavalry and some fifteen thousand infantry. The message concluded with a note that Gen. Robert E. Lee had disbanded three regiments of cavalry for lack of horses.

Butler discounted the manpower estimates of his spies, but the planned relocation of Federal prisoners attracted his sharp attention. He proposed, if he could, to rescue them while they were still in reach. Far from the numbers suggested in the secret message, the most Butler could muster for his raid was an infantry force of four thousand, supported by twenty-two hundred cavalry.

Everything depended on surprise. The situation was favorable in that General Pickett, under direct orders from President Jefferson Davis, was operating to the south in an effort to retake New Bern, North Carolina, while Lee's main force was in defensive positions to the north, facing off against Gen. George Meade's Army of the Potomac. Little, therefore, was left by way of first-class manpower in Richmond itself.

Butler proposed to gather his force at Williamsburg. Bottom's Bridge across the Chickahominy was to be seized in a surprise cavalry dash, and the telegraph lines there were to be cut. When this had been done, infantry and cavalry would march the remaining twelve miles into the heart of Richmond. Once they had broken into the Confederate capital, General Wistar's troops would have as their main objective the freeing of all Federal prisoners. To underline the urgency Butler noted in his operational order to Wistar that Lee's own troops were on half rations, which meant that the prisoners must be facing sheer starvation.

As secondary objectives, Wistar was to destroy public buildings, arsenals, and the famous Tredegar Iron Works, as well as all railroad depots and rolling stock he could reach. If possible, he was to capture and bring away as many of the rebel government's leaders as he could nab.

In preparation Wistar carefully scouted the area around Bottom's Bridge. He found the bridge passable and guarded by only a picket of twenty men, with a supporting force of about three hundred occupying a hill a mile away.

Meanwhile Butler telegraphed General Halleck, asking that Meade launch a diversionary attack on Lee's forces, to keep the rebels occupied while Wistar's men carried out their dash for Richmond. Halleck, as usual, was noncommittal. He responded that Meade was on sick leave, his army commanded now by Maj. Gen. John Sedgwick. He declined to order Sedgwick to do anything, and suggested that Butler telegraph Sedgwick directly to ask for his cooperation. Butler did so. Sedgwick balked. Finally, using as much political pressure as he could apply through his Washington contacts, Butler got Halleck to issue an order directing Sedgwick to cooperate.

While all these preparations and quarrels were taking place at the highest levels of the Union command, the decisive factor was taking shape at the lowest level imaginable: a guardhouse at General Wistar's base. Confined there was Pvt. William J. Boyle of the New York Mounted Rifles, the cavalry unit designated for the attack at Bottom's Bridge. Boyle was no petty offender. He was under sentence of death for having murdered his superior officer, a Lieutenant Disoway. Boyle's death sentence was being held in abeyance under a general order from President Lincoln himself, who had directed that all executions be suspended indefinitely.

The second humble actor in this ironic drama was Boyle's softhearted guard, a Private Abrams of the 139th New York Regiment. Abrams's gentle nature was such that Boyle was able to play on his sympathies. Finally Abrams was so moved that he agreed to let Boyle escape.

Once free, the wily Boyle took to his heels and made his way to enemy lines, where he ingratiated himself with his new captors by giving them full details of the attack in which his cavalry troop was to play such an important part. Boyle's information was quickly forwarded to Richmond, followed by the prisoner himself, still talking volubly. His escape was to cost the lives of nine soldiers of his unit, while defeating the entire rescue raid that had been so carefully planned.

While Boyle was carrying out his escape and his treason, the Richmond attack was going forward as planned. To the north, at last committed, Sedgwick moved. On the morning of February 6, he opened with an artillery barrage and followed with an infantry attack at Morton's Ford on the Rapidan. In the south, Butler's forces were soundly defeating General Pickett's attack on New Bern, and the absence of Pickett's troops from the area of Butler's raid continued to be assured.

Wistar's cavalry reached Bottom's Bridge at 3:00 A.M., ten minutes ahead of schedule. The five regiments, with a picked company of men of the First New York Mounted Rifles in the van, were expected to surprise and overwhelm the light picket at the bridge, advance rapidly along the Bottom's Bridge Road, surprise and take Richmond's Battery No. 2 near the capital, and then occupy Capitol Square in Richmond. Wistar's infantry, after a march of thirty-two miles, reached its support position at New Kent Courthouse at 2:00 A.M., prepared to follow up the cavalry penetration.

However, at Bottom's Bridge the cavalry found no mere corporal's guard, but a full complement of defenders backed by artillery. The planned quick rush was aborted, but at first light next morning a detachment of the New Yorkers mounted a desperate charge along the causeway leading to the bridge. The horsemen had no other approach, since the causeway was flanked on both sides by marshes. Rebel artillery, firing deadly canister at point-blank range, readily repulsed the charge. The cavalry then scouted the riverbank for several miles in each direction from the bridge, but found every ford heavily manned and covered by artillery.

Wistar now had no options. The quick surprise attack had failed. To undertake a slogging offensive, knowing that Confederate reserves would now reach the area from all directions, was out of the question. His only choice was to pack it all in and return to his base.

In the aftermath Wistar found cold comfort in having demonstrated, as he said in his official report, that a small force actively handled could at least hold a far superior Confederate force close in around Richmond, keeping that much rebel strength from activity elsewhere.

Butler, for his part, sent a warmly worded message to President Lincoln, enclosing Wistar's bitter report of the guardhouse incident. The report included Private Abrams's confession that he had allowed Private Boyle to escape and that they had discussed the Bottom's Bridge operation in great detail beforehand. Butler told Lincoln of the articles in the Richmond newspapers describing how "a Yankee deserter" had warned the Confederates of the planned attack.

"I send [General Wistar's dispatch] to you that you may see how your clemency has been misplaced," wrote Butler. "I desire that you will revoke your order suspending executions in this department."

To this Lincoln made no reply. Only much later was a tacit understanding reached that the president's suspension of the death penalty was to hold only in the case of deserters.

As for Sedgwick, he was still sputtering. He griped to Halleck that the Confederate position he had attacked was so lightly held that, if only he had been given time to concentrate his entire army, he could have achieved a complete breakthrough. Bad weather and difficult road conditions had so far prevented him from bringing his full force to bear in a proper operation. Butler's little campaign, he said, had spoiled his chances to effect—at some time in the future—a major surprise and an important victory. Now, Sedgwick complained, the Confederates knew their position at Morton's Ford was weak and were already taking steps to strengthen it.

As this new controversy boiled around him, Butler was enveloped in much deeper personal grief. His older brother, the strong companion of his childhood in many a schoolboy game or battle on the South Common in Lowell, and later the subject of his loyal and lifelong protection, was dead. Butler requested leave to arrange the funeral and close out Andrew Jackson Butler's tangled affairs.

43

From the outset warfare between the North and South had been waged under rules that, in some respects, might have seemed more appropriate to an athletic contest or a playground game. This was particularly so in the way the opposing sides dealt with prisoners of war. Often—as in Butler's occupation of the forts below New Orleans and later in the fall of Vicksburg, where Grant bagged a substantial army—captured men were simply turned loose on parole. Under the rules they gave their word not to fight anymore until the arithmetic had been balanced—that is, a man on parole stayed out of action until a man on the other side was paroled or turned loose from a prison camp.

But by the autumn of 1863, when Butler took command at Fortress Monroe, this sportsmanlike arrangement had broken down everywhere. The subject of prisoner exchange was now an ongoing wrangle between the formally appointed exchange commissioners. To act for the rebels, the Confederate government had named Judge Robert Ould, formerly a distinguished Washington attorney. Gen. Ethan A. Hitchcock served as exchange commissioner for the Union. These two dignitaries argued from Richmond and Washington respectively, to little effect and in growing hostility, with the result that many thousands of prisoners were now held under close confinement in both the North and South.

The way the Federal government saw it, the Confederates had received more freed rebels than they had returned in kind. As a result, the balance in Union prisoners owed by the Confederacy amounted to no fewer than eighteen thousand men. A large part of that deficit came about because the regiments paroled by Grant at Vicksburg and by Banks at Port Hudson had been returned to the fighting ranks of the Confederacy without the Confederates turning loose an equivalent number of Yanks.

At Fortress Monroe, General Butler was keenly aware that at Richmond, just up the river, some thirteen thousand Union soldiers were languishing at Belle Isle and Libby Prison, suffering from cold and starvation.

Eyeing the ineffectual efforts of Washington to deal with this, Butler determined to intervene.

His immediate plan was to set up a special prison camp in which three thousand Confederates would be lodged under precisely the same conditions as those being endured by the Union prisoners in Richmond. The rebel prisoners would be furnished with the same clothing, equivalent shelter, and the same scanty rations. Butler also proposed to see to it that they would be given plenty of pens and writing paper, so that their families, friends, and government officials would be made aware of their plight in detail and often. As and if conditions for Federal prisoners improved under this less than subtle pressure, Confederate prisoners in Butler's camp would benefit to an equal extent.

Secretary Stanton approved the plan and issued a formal directive to put it into effect. With this in hand Butler began setting up his demonstration camp. But at this point Stanton thought to consult with Halleck who, as usual, looked wise and counseled doing nothing, whereupon Stanton sent Butler an official telegram canceling the directive and ordering him to scrap the program.

As late fall hardened into winter, both Butler and the Richmond authorities felt an increasing urgency to break the impasse. Confederate armies simply needed the manpower, while Butler's concern was for the health of Union prisoners being held under wretched conditions.

Through certain of his unofficial sources, Butler learned that the Confederates were now willing to approve a total exchange, man for man, officer for officer. The proposition, as Butler saw it, was one of simple arithmetic. The Union was holding some twenty-six thousand prisoners, while the Confederacy held thirteen thousand Yanks. A one-for-one exchange would still leave half the number of Confederate prisoners in Union hands. This, Butler felt, would provide an ample supply of hostages for the safety of Negro soldiers held in Confederate prisons, should the rebel authorities continue to remain obdurate in refusing to exchange black prisoners on the same basis as whites. Since Butler consistently led the way in recruiting and training black regiments, the principle of fair and equal treatment of black prisoners of war was one upon which he refused to budge an inch.

Butler put his thoughts in writing for Stanton's perusal. The exchange commissioners, he suggested, had allowed their negotiations to bog down in a morass of arithmetic. "The government, for all that appears from the correspondence of the two commissioners," said Butler, "is now suffering our soldiers to be starved to death upon the proposition of inequality in the computation and value of paroles."

Butler's warmly worded letter brought results. He was named as a "special exchange officer" and, without waiting for further word either from

Washington or Richmond, he ordered five hundred Confederate prisoners moved at once to City Point, where he dangled them like bait, offering a full and immediate exchange, man for man. Butler was betting that the Richmond government would not be able to withstand the public pressure that was bound to result when families and friends saw these soldiers so close to freedom. Amid uproar in the Confederate cabinet about dealing with the outlaw Butler, a full exchange nevertheless took place, Butler actually receiving more than five hundred Union prisoners into the safety of his lines.

The exchange had no sooner been accomplished, however, than the Confederate government served haughty notice that it would not deal with Butler. This was ignored by the outlawed general, who calmly dangled another boatload of prisoners under the noses of the Richmond authorities. He secured a second exchange.

While these exchanges were being executed, a group of 111 Union prisoners in Richmond took their own route to freedom by tunneling their way out of prison and making a try for Butler's lines. First inkling of this reached Union headquarters when two of the escaped prisoners reached General Wistar's outposts. Wistar immediately sent out strong cavalry patrols to cover the escape of the rest, while Butler dispatched an army gunboat to patrol up the James and Chickahominy rivers and aid in the rescue.

Commissioner Ould, after all this, had begun to doubt the efficacy of continuing the fiction of Butler's outlawry. Ould told James A. Seddon, the Confederate secretary of war, that it was about time to recognize Butler as the exchange commissioner with whom the Confederacy had to deal. "Butler has evidently set his heart, for some reason or other, on securing the release of the Yankee prisoners," Ould said, as though the general's zeal was somehow inexplicable. He added that he thought he could obtain agreement for a general exchange of prisoners if only he were authorized to talk directly with Butler at Fort Monroe.

While the Confederate politicians sputtered and argued over Butler's status, the general continued to swap imprisoned rebels for imprisoned Yanks. Butler paid special attention in these exchanges to shipping sick, wounded, and disabled Confederate soldiers home, so that Union prisoners in like condition could be retrieved for proper care at Federal military hospitals. Learning of an outbreak of smallpox at Richmond, Butler on his own authority sent a large shipment of vaccine to the city.

The most distinguished Confederate prisoner to benefit from good medical treatment while in Federal hands, as well as from Butler's generosity, was Gen. Fitzhugh (Rooney) Lee, son of Robert E. Lee himself. Rooney Lee had been wounded and captured in a cavalry skirmish. Union army doctors treated his injured leg, and Butler in due time saw to his release. While the courtly Robert E. Lee never acknowledged the favor in any way, apparently Rooney himself made no secret of his gratitude. The diarist Mary Chesnut jotted a note: "Rooney Lee says Beast Butler was very kind to him while he was a prisoner. And the Beast has sent him back his war horse. The Lees are men enough to speak the truth of friend or enemy, unfearing consequences."

By early March, Butler was convinced he was about to achieve an agreement covering all Union prisoners still in Confederate hands. He asked Washington to ship him as many Confederate prisoners as possible so that they would be immediately available for exchange. His Point Lookout prison camp could accommodate twenty thousand or more, he said. Butler's enthusiasm for the project was heightened by a certain success he was having in recruiting Union soldiers from the ranks of erstwhile Confederates. Disgusted prisoners who remained true to the South came to call these converted rebels "galvanized Yankees," a term which gave Butler a great deal of amusement.

Lincoln, viewing the exchange negotiations somewhat distantly, had prescribed a procedure that Butler came to think of as The Four Questions. Each Confederate prisoner had to be asked the questions in a precise order, and all four questions had to be asked before the prisoner was required to answer any of them. The answers had to be recorded and certified, along with the prisoner's name:

> *First. Do you desire to be sent South as a prisoner of war for exchange?*
>
> *Second. Do you desire to take the oath of allegiance and parole, and enlist in the Army or Navy of the United States, and if so, in which?*
>
> *Third. Do you desire to take the oath and parole, and be sent North to work on public works, under penalty of death if found in the South before the end of the War?*
>
> *Fourth. Do you desire to take the oath of allegiance and go to your home within the lines of the United States?*

Butler's galvanized Yankees were sent far out west to reinforce the slender cavalry units patrolling hostile Indian country. As of March 11, Butler reported to Washington, he had recruited nearly a full regiment of these converted rebels. He said he was confident that, the more prisoners he received at Point Lookout to be administered Lincoln's Four Questions, the more galvanized Yankees would emerge. True to his prediction, before Butler was through he had raised three such regiments, outfitted and equipped them, and sent them on their way.

In due course, while Butler was galvanizing some captive rebels and

Thomas Nast's drawing of Butler at Fortress Monroe, 1863

Lowell Historical Society

shipping others home, Ould finally arrived off Federal headquarters in a white-flagged Confederate steamer, ready to get down to serious bargaining. Butler was blandly courteous. He invited Ould to come ashore, where he could officially negotiate in comfortable surroundings with Commissioner Butler, who would be happy to view this official visit as a formal renunciation of that Davis decree of outlawry.

Exchanges continued to proceed in much the same haphazard manner, however, since both Butler and Ould were answerable to authorities in their respective capitals. Moreover, both Butler and Ould were adamant in their opposing positions regarding the status of black Federal troops. Butler stated his position succinctly: "We have no slaves in our Army, and the question is whether we shall permit the belligerents opposed to us to make slaves of the free men they capture in our uniform, simply because of their color."

The answer to that question was "Obviously not," Butler continued, in his official report to the War Department. And the only present course, Butler said, was to tote up the arithmetic of exchanges already made, and to halt further release of Confederate prisoners until the Confederacy yielded the point. Once again he reminded Stanton that rebel prisoners must continue to be hostages for the safety of Negro soldiers held by the Confederates. The prescription required, said Butler, was "exact retaliation, in exact kind and measure upon their men, of the treatment received by ours."

Aside from Butler's formula for the safeguarding of black Union soldiers captured in battle, all else in the prisoner exchange episode shortly became moot. The Union now had a newly created lieutenant general in charge of all the armies. Ulysses S. Grant applied arithmetic to the prisoner matter in a different way, without any leavening of mercy. General Lee needed men far more than he did, Grant decided brusquely, so there was to be no exchange of prisoners whatever from here on out. Each Confederate captured was one less soldier for Lee, and that was that. To Butler fell the thankless task of seeing to it—adroitly, as only an excellent lawyer might—that all negotiations were broken off abruptly and that the onus for this fell upon the Confederate authorities—not upon Grant, not upon Lincoln.

In his very first conference with Butler, Grant put the proposition bluntly. He was preparing a campaign whose outcome would depend on attrition. Counter for counter would be removed from the board until Lee had no more counters to spend. The days of grand maneuvering according to the scholarly principles of Jomini were over. Aside from wearing Lee down, Grant was determined to see to it that the Confederate general would have neither strength nor opportunity to interfere with General Sherman's ravaging campaign in the deep South. Grant added, with a touch of hard cynicism, that if it became recognized that there were to be no more paroles and no more exchanges, bounty jumpers and other Union soldiers of doubtful allegiance would be far less likely to give themselves up.

Butler, somewhat taken aback, asked and received at least tentative permission to continue an exchange of sick and wounded prisoners. But even that was shortly afterward canceled by Grant in a brusque telegram: "To Major General B. F. Butler: Receive all the sick and wounded the Confederate authorities will send you, but send no more in exchange. U. S. Grant, Lieutenant General."

As best he was able, Butler persisted in evading Grant's adamant order and continuing to exchange sick and wounded Confederates. In mid-August, to pacify Grant, he telegraphed the commanding general a slightly equivocal report: "No exchange has been made by me which will give the enemy any advantage. . . . I have exchanged nobody but wounded men since the first of May except for surgeons, non-combatants, and a few cases of special exchange."

That "special exchange" device, from time to time, was used in complying with requests from persons of influence in Washington that Butler make special arrangements to free a friend, a son, or other relative from rebel captivity. These requests were forwarded by Stanton and others, and even Lincoln himself was sometimes the intervener. A typical telegram of this kind from Lincoln read: "Hon. W. R. Morrison says he has requested you by letter to effect a special exchange of Lieut. Col. A. F. Rogers, of Eighteenth Illinois Volunteers, now in Libby Prison, and I shall be glad if you effect it."

Butler's last major effort to relieve the sorry plight of Union soldiers in rebel prisons occurred in late autumn of 1864. He organized a small fleet of transports and hospital ships to take some three thousand sick and wounded Confederates from his Point Lookout camp to Savannah, Georgia, for exchange. Lt. Col. John E. Mulford, Butler's principal assistant in this matter, was placed in charge of the operation, which was carried out successfully. From Savannah on November 21, Mulford reported to Butler:

I have up to the present time received over three thousand of our men. Their physical condition is rather better than I expected, but their personal [condition] is worse than anything I have ever seen—filth and rags. It is a great labor to cleanse and clothe them, but I am fairly at work and will progress as rapidly as possible. . . . I have got off two vessels today, and will try to get off two tomorrow, and so on. . . .

In obedience to Grant's adamant position on the subject, no full and general exchange was ever approved. Butler's final position paper on the subject, delivered to Commissioner Ould, was devoted almost entirely to his insistence that the Confederate government must recognize the rights of black Union soldiers, and he was eloquent on the subject. It served, as Grant had intended, as an ultimatum to the Confederate authorities—one that both he and Butler knew would not be accepted.

While Butler was never able to bring the Confederate authorities to terms, he did succeed at a much later date in a demonstration of the retaliatory measures he always advocated. The Confederates had forced some Negro prisoners of war to work on their entrenchments at Petersburg. When Butler learned of this, he immediately rounded up a detail of captured Confederate officers and put them to the same kind of hard manual labor on Union works, with orders to their guards that if any prisoner tried to escape he was to be shot. In a matter of days, the black Union troops were restored to their rights as prisoners of war, whereupon Butler likewise sent the Confederate prisoners back to their quarters at Point Lookout.

As to the breakdown of prisoner exchange negotiations, Butler dutifully shielded Grant and Lincoln from any blame in the matter and stoically accepted the lashing he expected and got in the hostile sections of the Northern press.

44

When Grant took command of the armies, Butler for the first time had a military superior who treated him as a colleague rather than as an upstart, a rival, or a menace. To General Scott, who preferred West Pointers in all positions of any importance and narrowed his favoritism to Southern West Pointers at that, the Yankee Butler was the ultimate outsider. McClellan, eyeing Butler's Washington contacts, was happy to see him dispatched far away to New Orleans. Halleck, who burnished his own image by tarnishing the reputations of others, adopted Scott's stratagem of burying Butler in a backwater command and denying him, as far as possible, any of the means required for significant field service.

But Grant, unlike the earlier generals in chief, was less concerned with the stars on his shoulders than with getting the job done for once and all. With grim practicality he saw this stage of the war as one enormous mop-up campaign: Sherman sweeping through the heart of the Confederacy, Grant himself grinding down Lee's depleted armies, holding them at bay, giving them no rest and no opportunity to free any force to aid the losing struggle against Sherman's inexorable march. As for Butler's command, Grant viewed Fortress Monroe not as a passive supply base, but rather as a staging area for an offensive to the south of Richmond. Where there were troops, Grant proposed to use them actively and to a purpose, and everything he proposed to do he proposed to do quickly.

The Army of the Potomac was now under the command of Gen. George Meade whose forces, the previous summer, had shattered Lee's army at Gettysburg. Meade had come under much-deserved criticism for failing to attack Lee's depleted and disorganized divisions, which he instead permitted to retreat and regroup in safety across the Potomac. Now, under Grant's close supervision, that kind of passive decision would no longer be left to him.

Under a succession of commanders, the unfortunate Army of the Potomac had battled hard to little effect and much outpouring of blood. McClellan, at Antietam, fought a drawn battle with Lee that left over twenty-three thousand dead and wounded on the field, Confederate casualties being only slightly fewer than those suffered by Union troops. At Fredericksburg, three months later, Gen. Ambrose Burnside, in a particularly stubborn and stupid assault against entrenched Confederates, lost twelve thousand six hundred men killed, wounded, and missing. At Chancellorsville, the following May, Gen. Joseph Hooker led the Army of the Potomac to a stunning defeat that cost the Union seventeen thousand in killed and wounded.

Despite all that had gone before, the two generals who were now exchanging views at Fortress Monroe both reflected an air of confidence. Butler had devoted much time to a careful study of the topography to the south of Richmond. He had become convinced that the best route for the final advance was by way of the south bank of the James River, and that the ideal staging area lay within the loop that was formed where the James and the Appomattox approached each other only two and a half miles apart.

High bluffs protected the flanks of this land area, known as Bermuda Hundred. At the open end of the loop, inland, deep gullies reached out on either side, leaving less than a mile of traversable terrain. By extending field fortifications across this mile, anchored left and right on those flanking gullies, the peninsula could be made impregnable. The loop enclosed a full thirty square miles of land, an area large enough to accommodate an army of any conceivable size. That army could be moved and supplied amphibiously, Butler thought, eliminating long miles of marching and the endless complications of transporting equipment and supplies entirely overland. City Point, at the mouth of the Appomattox, was an ideal place for an easily defended supply depot.

Butler also noted that Confederate entrenchments and fortifications on the south side of Richmond were much weaker than those to the north. Besides all else, the terrain to the south was on firm, high ground, presenting far fewer natural obstacles than the area to the north. For all these reasons, which he cited in detail, Butler urged Grant to consider shifting the weight of the coming offensive to this more favorable ground, using Union sea power as a decisive factor in the rapid deployment of the large number of troops that would be committed in the spring campaign.

Grant studied Butler's maps carefully and conceded that his proposal had much merit. But mindful of the nervous Lincoln White House—which at all times had nightmares about some sudden, swift move by Lee that would menace Washington—Grant was reluctant to thin out the land forces then holding Lee in place. Butler contended that Grant could move covering forces by sea transport faster than Lee could move attacking forces by land, but Grant was not convinced. He decided to press Lee from the north while Butler moved troops of his own command to open a southern front.

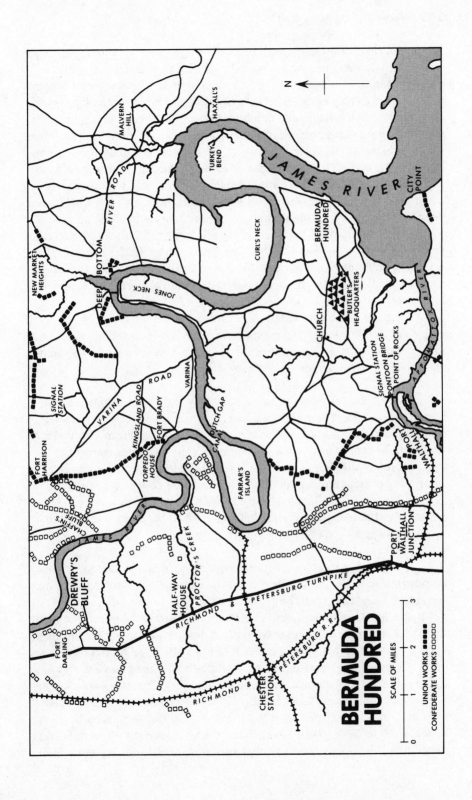

BERMUDA HUNDRED

JAMES RIVER

CITY POINT

MALVERN HILL

HAXALL'S

TURKEY BEND

CURL'S NECK

BERMUDA HUNDRED

RIVER ROAD

DEEP BOTTOM

JONES NECK

CHURCH

BUTLER'S HEADQUARTERS

NEW MARKET HEIGHTS

SIGNAL STATION
PONTOON BRIDGE
POINT OF ROCKS

APPOMATTOX RIVER

SIGNAL STATION

VARINA ROAD

VARINA

KINGSLAND ROAD

FORT BRADY

DUTCH GAP CANAL

PORT WALTHALL

FORT HARRISON

TORPEDO HOUSE

FARRAR'S ISLAND

CHAFFIN'S BLUFF

JAMES RIVER

PORT WALTHALL JUNCTION

DREWRY'S BLUFF

HALF-WAY HOUSE

PROCTOR'S CREEK

RICHMOND & PETERSBURG TURNPIKE

FORT DARLING

PETERSBURG R.R.

RICHMOND &

CHESTER STATION

SCALE OF MILES

0   1   2   3

UNION WORKS ■■■■■
CONFEDERATE WORKS □□□□□

More than that, Grant decided to reinforce Butler with ten thousand troops from South Carolina under the command of Maj. Gen. Quincy A. Gillmore.

In broad outline, Grant hoped to maneuver Lee backward to a point where Butler's army could unite with Grant's main force for the finale, with Lee besieged in the Richmond defenses and cut off from all his supply lines. Grant's plan was only somewhat flexible in that he proposed to drive hardest by whichever flank of Lee's army he thought could be most advantageously turned. Either way he hoped to reach the James, where he would then join up with Butler. As Grant saw it, the most desirable linkup would occur if Butler could establish a position in which his army's left would have been extended to reach the south bank of the James west of Richmond.

As the final point of their accord, Grant approved Butler's plan to concentrate troops at the head of the York River, where Butler believed their activity would convince Lee that his main effort was to take place there, some fifty miles away from Richmond, rather than at Bermuda Hundred to the south.

After their discussion, Grant issued formal orders covering the general pattern of Butler's part in the spring campaign. Grant's directive was vague as to details, but it emphasized repeatedly that Lee's army and Richmond were the objectives. In part the order read:

> When you are ready to move, take City Point with as much force as possible. Fortify or rather intrench at once, and concentrate all your troops for the field there as rapidly as you can. From City Point directions cannot be given at this time for your further movements.
>
> The fact that has already been stated, that is, that Richmond is to be your objective point, and that there is to be cooperation between your force and the Army of the Potomac, must be your guide. This indicates the necessity of your holding close to the south bank of the James River as you advance.

Grant added, almost as an afterthought, that if Butler thought it would be practicable to use his cavalry to cut the railroad lines to his south, that secondary operation would be of advantage.

Butler and Grant met in an atmosphere of guarded optimism, confident that the long string of Union disasters and defeats was at last behind them and that they were planning the details of the last campaign. But now, even as they conferred at Fortress Monroe, Butler's successor at New Orleans, General Banks, was stumbling around the Red River country with an army of thirty thousand men, beset and bewildered by a much smaller Confederate force, in a campaign that was to end in total disaster and a headlong retreat back to base. When Grant came to sum up the net effect of Banks's expedition, he was to complain that this effort, made on Halleck's direct order, had cost him the use of forty thousand veteran troops that had been diverted away from the spring offensive against his wishes and to no useful purpose. The Confederates could hardly have asked for anything more had they been directing both sides in the Halleck-Banks enterprise.

Butler had no time to fret over the problems in his old command in the Department of the Gulf, although his friends in Washington kept him informed as to a scandalous element in the affair, which concerned speculation in cotton. It developed that Porter and his gunboats were occupied to a large extent in seizing cotton bales from the plantations and carrying them off as "prizes of war," the profits to accrue to Porter and his men. The Red River expedition also accommodated the activities of civilian cotton speculators, and it was even charged that the campaign undertaken by Banks and Porter had no real purpose other than profit.

Concentrating on the business at hand, Grant and Butler agreed on May 4 as the date on which they would launch their coordinated drive. Now, with only four weeks to prepare his amphibious move, Butler had dozens of important details to arrange and many more smaller ones, all of which he handled with his usual energy.

Butler's combat force was organized under two field commanders. General Gillmore was assigned to command X Corps, made up of the ten thousand men he was to bring with him from South Carolina. Gen. William F. Smith was given XVIII Corps, formed from the various units already in Butler's department.

Lacking a cavalry division commander, Butler asked Grant to assign him one. Grant nominated Col. August V. Kautz as being highly qualified. Butler agreed that Kautz was an excellent choice, but he reminded Grant that cavalry colonels already present in Butler's command outranked Grant's nominee. The lieutenant general promptly solved that little problem by making Kautz a brigadier.

In the midst of his preparations, Butler was taken suddenly aback by an order from Washington to provide transportation for 2.5 million rations that were being dispatched to North Carolina. Assuming from this that Grant had changed his mind about the single thrust up the James River and now intended a major move from North Carolina, Butler wrote Grant expressing some disappointment and asking clarification, but offering full cooperation if that was what the lieutenant general had in mind. Grant replied that the order regarding those rations was some kind of commissary mixup and that he had not changed his plans. It would be a good thing anyway, Grant added, if word of this massive shipment of rations became general knowledge, since it would help mask their real intentions.

In the midst of Butler's preparations, the Confederates launched a drive to recapture some of the North Carolina towns they had lost, beginning with Plymouth. A strong rebel force under Gen. Robert Hoke took the

Union fort at Plymouth under siege, assisted by the newly completed ram *Albermarle*. The ram chased the defending U.S. Navy gunboats out of the Roanoke River, sinking one and driving another aground after a brisk encounter in which solid shot scarcely dented the Confederate vessel's heavy armor. Taken under fire from Hoke's artillery and the guns of the *Albermarle*, the Federal garrison surrendered. Hoke took twenty-eight hundred prisoners and a large quantity of supplies.

It appeared now that New Washington and New Bern were next on Hoke's list, causing Gen. John J. Peck, commanding the North Carolina district, to call upon Butler for help. "Unless we are immediately and heavily reinforced both by Army and Navy," he reported, "North Carolina is inevitably lost." Butler, however, stood firm in his conviction that the coming campaign against Richmond would draw Confederate troops to the defense of the capital. He told Peck he would have to defend his district with the resources he already had. Butler said he favored concentrating available forces at New Bern and withdrawing from other outposts, which he had considered valueless in the first place and a waste of manpower. He said a siege at New Bern would be just fine, and the longer the better, since it would hold rebel forces away from the decisive theater to the north.

Halleck, criticizing from Washington, took the opportunity to recount to Grant how he, Halleck, had once refused to permit abandonment of these same outposts even at a time when McClellan was pleading for reinforcements. Halleck told Grant he still felt the same way but that Grant could do as he pleased. And as a little jab Halleck added: "It is useless for me to consult with General Butler on this subject, for his opinions would not change my judgment."

That last remark Grant ignored. He agreed with Butler. "It is much better to hold New Bern strongly," said Grant, "than to have little posts picked up in detail."

All in all, Butler at this time was getting along well with Grant, whom he found refreshingly friendly. Even Sarah, who hated Fortress Monroe and was inclined to view official visitors there as a burden, liked both Grant and his wife. In a letter to the author Parton, Sarah expressed pleasure that a visit from the Grants had to be extended because bad weather prevented their departure. The extra stay gave the Butlers and Grants more time to enjoy each others' company, Sarah said.

While preparations for active campaigning occupied all of Butler's energies at Fortress Monroe, back in Washington the power figures were concentrating on little else but Lincoln's renomination. One of Butler's contacts reported that the capital's political circles were abuzz with a rumor that Butler, Chase, Frémont, and Banks had agreed to work together against Lincoln. When Butler's friend, J. K. Herbert, was able to reassure Lincoln authoritatively that the rumor was ridiculous, the president was delighted.

"Your stock with the President was never higher," Herbert wrote. This failed to move Butler very much, since he well knew that stock with Lincoln usually rose or fell in parallel with the president's political fortunes.

Those who sought to unseat Lincoln always tended to agree that this could not be done without Butler's help. Treasury Secretary Chase sent a confidential messenger to Butler to ask him directly if he would agree to a Chase-Butler ticket in opposition to Lincoln's renomination. Butler replied, as he had to all such invitations and speculations, that he had no wish to be vice president and that even if he were not now holding an important army command he would still have no wish to be vice president. This emphatic answer, he said, was not to be taken personally by Chase. To put it plainly he added, "I will not be a candidate for any elective office whatever until the war is over."

Chase's emissary had scarcely departed when Simon Cameron, back from Russia and politically active, showed up bearing a similar offer from Lincoln himself. In somewhat more jocular terms (Cameron was an old friend), Butler turned down the proposal. The joke was to seem grisly in retrospect, but in sum Butler said with a laugh that he wouldn't accept the job unless Lincoln would guarantee to die within three months of the inaugural. Asked for advice as to the vice-presidential choice, the general in an offhand way suggested Andrew Johnson of Tennessee. Subsequent proceedings among the Republican wheelers and dealers, including the wily Lincoln himself, managed Johnson's nomination in a manner designed to offend nobody. Other aspirants were left in permanent doubt as to whether or not Johnson was truly the president's choice.

However fascinated Washington was with the intrigues surrounding the 1864 election, at Fortress Monroe electoral politics was the last item on Butler's mind. Butler was thinking more about horses, for one thing. He had two thousand trained cavalrymen walking around without mounts. Months ago, he wrote Stanton, he had asked the Cavalry Bureau for two thousand horses and received what he thought was an approval—an order to send some inspectors to examine the mounts.

"I have not received a single horse," wrote Butler. "Will you not please make an extra effort to furnish me with at least 1,000 horses, and forthwith."

Stanton did Butler the dubious favor of referring his request to Halleck, who took his usual cold look at the buck and passed it on. There were not enough horses for both Butler's army and the Army of the Potomac, Halleck reported, and anyway it was up to Grant to decide which army got them.

Butler then promptly asked Grant for the horses, citing Halleck's dictum on the subject. At the same time he wrote Halleck, asking that two black regiments marking time in Maryland be sent to Fortress Monroe. A win-one–lose-one answer was combined in a terse wire from Halleck: "1,000 horses will be sent to you. The colored troops in Maryland are already assigned to Maj. Gen. Burnside." But weeks later Butler was still looking for horses and by this time had lowered his sights. "Would it be possible to send me at once five hundred cavalry horses?" he wired Halleck. To which Old Brains replied: "Not another cavalry horse can be sent to you at present."

In the midst of all other confusion, Butler still had to contend with the folly of Secretary of State Seward, who sometimes appeared oblivious to the fact that there was a war going on. Seward was still pressing the curious exercise that might have been titled, if it had been entirely a comedy, *Seward and the French Tobacco*.

Under the legal fiction that the French government had bought these many tons of tobacco before the outbreak of hostilities, Seward had entered into a strange but very formal agreement with representatives of the Emperor Napoleon. In sum, he gave free passage up and down the James River to French warships and French-chartered merchant vessels, that they might haul the tobacco from the Richmond warehouses and transport it to wherever the emperor wanted it dispatched. As a result, there were the French, with Seward's blessing, not only cluttering up the river in the midst of a major military move, but also making tatters of security measures designed to protect the Union forces.

Early on, Butler had informed Seward that the tobacco involved had not been bought by the French before the war began, but that it represented current transactions of great financial benefit to the Confederacy. Now he protested that in any case, whether the purchases were prewar or current, there was no justification for issuing an official permit to the French to run the blockade as Seward had authorized—up front, in open daylight, with a convoy of French warships.

With small hope of influencing Washington one whit, Butler complained to Stanton that he was "much embarrassed" by Seward and his tobacco deal. The move authorized by the secretary of state, said Butler, would inform the rebels of Union movements as effectively as if Butler himself reported them all to Seddon, the Confederate secretary of war.

The navy was similarly disturbed. Adm. S. P. Lee, commanding the blockading forces, informed Secretary Welles in some perplexity that the French ships had arrived at the Roads. Lee asked for instructions. Welles thereupon tried to take up the matter with Lincoln, but the president ducked all discussion with him. In his diary Welles noted:

> He was annoyed, I saw, when I introduced the topic. . . . He knew full well my opposition to this whole proceeding, which I had fought off two or three times, until he finally gave in to Seward. When,

therefore, some of the difficulties which I had suggested began to arise, the President preferred not to see me. It will not surprise me if this is but the beginning of the trouble we shall experience.

In the end Seward got his way, even Grant's heavy presence being insufficient to change the arrangement. The best Grant could do was to insist that the French conclude their business at Richmond by April 23, when the Seward agreement was to expire. Even this was perilously close to the day set for the general advance of all Union armies as planned.

Amid all difficulties, usual and extraordinary alike, Butler and his staff attended to the details of concentrating, equipping, feeding, and housing the troops that would compose the Army of the James.

There was the matter of coordinating army-navy collaboration and of assigning duties to Butler's own homemade navy, his little fleet of army gunboats and their complement of specialist troops trained for mobile waterborne operations—Butler's Marine Brigade. The navy command tended to be fidgety about Confederate "torpedoes," an 1864 version of latter-day mines, and was especially pleased that Butler's light draft boats would precede the navy's vessels in upriver sweeps to deal with torpedoes and also with rebel snipers along the banks.

Along with other problems, Butler was called upon to use his political contacts in behalf of General Gillmore, assigned as his X Corps commander. The Senate was balking at confirming Gillmore's commission as major general. Brig. Gen. John W. Turner, then chief of staff in the Department of the South, wrote Butler in behalf of Gillmore. If Gillmore was passed over for promotion, Turner said, command of X Corps would have to pass to one or another of Gillmore's juniors, creating both organizational and morale problems on the very eve of the grand offensive. In response, Butler promptly got his friends in the Senate to withhold contemplated action which would have scuttled Gillmore's promotion. Earlier, Grant had done as much for General Smith in order to protect Smith's assignment as XVIII Corps commander.

On April 28, at last, Butler received formal orders from Grant that set May 4 as the date for a coordinated move by all forces. Butler was directed to begin his operation on the night of the fourth, so as to be as far up the James River as he could get by the morning of the fifth. "Push with all your might for the accomplishment of the object before you," Grant telegraphed from his headquarters at Culpeper Court House.

In the following days all was ready in Butler's command except for the full arrival of all of Gillmore's units, some of which were inexplicably lagging despite Butler's repeated inquiries and warmly worded urgings. Gillmore himself had not yet put in an appearance, either, a circumstance that bothered Grant. As late as May 2, Grant was still uneasy about X Corps and its commander. "What is the latest news from General Gillmore?" Grant telegraphed Butler. "State what number of force is yet to arrive." In a follow-up telegram the same day, suggesting more than a little exasperation at Gillmore's performance, Grant directed full speed ahead with or without that general or his full complement of troops. "Start on the date given," Grant ordered Butler. "There will be no delay with this army."

Next morning Butler was able to reply that the tardy General Gillmore had just arrived but had not yet debarked. "We understand the order to be on Wednesday, the 4th, at 8:00 P.M., and it will be obeyed," he wired Grant.

The next word he received was brief. Grant had crossed the Rapidan. Now the Army of the James was free to begin the massive amphibious operation that Butler had planned and organized.

45

As he gathered in the scattered forces that were to compose the Army of the James, Butler posted them so as to suggest to watching Confederates that he meant to move north of the James, rather than south, and nearer to, rather than farther away from Grant's huge force at the Rapidan. Butler's white troops were concentrated around Yorktown and Gloucester Point. Black cavalry units were stationed at Williamsburg. Black infantry and artillery were encamped at Hampton. The white cavalry division under General Kautz, which did not figure in the deceptive element of Butler's plan, was to operate from the area of Norfolk.

On May 1, Union troops seized West Point, a railhead at the far upper reach of the York River, and began a great show of building wharves and fortifications there, suggesting that this was to be the base for a linkup with Grant. Confederate intelligence reports reflected this, and General Beauregard, under somewhat vague and ambiguous orders from Richmond as to his next assignment, thoughtfully requested maps covering the region north of the James.

By May 4, Butler was entirely ready for his expedition. Even the laggard Gillmore had arrived, although too late for a final briefing that the commanding general thought would be of benefit.

As a deceptive preliminary, Butler had sent a considerable showing of his armada up the York. But during the night all of his transports, escorts, and supply boats were moving toward their true objective, and Butler's special troops, those of his Marine Brigade, were knocking out the Confederate signal stations along the way. On the fifth, the light of morning disclosed a fleet of one hundred or more vessels of all classes and sizes moving up the James. Among them was Butler's command vessel, a fast new steamer, the *Greyhound*, which ranged up and down the fleet as the general urged his men on, acknowledging their answering cheers with a jaunty wave of his hat. Butler, with his special enthusiasm for fast waterborne troop movements, may have been the only Civil War general who could make an amphibious operation look like a cavalry charge.

Two far-ranging flanking movements were set in motion to round out the advance. To the south, from the Norfolk area, General Kautz led three thousand white troopers on a raid in force to tear up rails and burn bridges on the railroad lines leading into Petersburg. To the north, Col. Robert West led seventeen hundred black cavalrymen on a wide sweep up the York Peninsula and across the Chickahominy River as though to threaten Richmond.

As Butler's armada moved upriver, black infantry regiments of General Hinks's command seized two strong points along the way. These, on the north bank of the James, were potential battery sites that, if left unguarded, might be used by rebel gunners to cut the Federals' long waterborne supply line. With the remainder of his division, Hinks took City Point, at the confluence of the James and the Appomattox, and began fortifying it. City Point, on a small shoulder of land protruding into the James, was to be the navy's advance supply depot. White troops of X Corps and XVIII Corps moved in on Bermuda Hundred, and by 8:00 P.M. Butler had some ten thousand troops ashore there, along with their artillery, equipment, and supplies.

When the general himself landed at 5:00 P.M., he was met by one of his intelligence operatives bearing word from his spy in Richmond, Miss Van Lieu. Her word was that the city had been emptied of troops to reinforce Lee and that forces expected from North Carolina to defend the capital had not yet arrived. This strongly tempted Butler to make an immediate night march on Richmond with the troops he already had on hand. The landing at Bermuda Hundred had been a complete surprise to the Confederates, the night was bright and clear, and the Union troops would probably benefit from a stretch of the legs after their tight confinement aboard ship. In those terms he broached the idea to Gillmore and Smith, both of whom reacted in something like horror. Gillmore, in fact, said flatly that if he received such an order he would refuse to obey it. This was the beginning of severe difficulties Butler continued to have with both of these hesitant generals from this point on.

With his two corps commanders in a mood just this side of mutinous, Butler called on his faithful friend, Gen. Godfrey Weitzel, although by this time the hour was getting very late for any substantial move. Weitzel was willing, but dubious. He said he thought the march on Richmond could be hazardous, particularly with the cavalry occupied elsewhere and thus not available to screen the advance. Weitzel noted the political circumstance, always an important consideration in any matter affecting the Union high command. He said if the attempt failed, after both corps commanders had recommended so strongly against it, Butler would be ruined—an outcome that would surely please Smith and Gillmore, not to mention Butler's enemies in Washington. Moreover, Weitzel added, he was certain that, if he tried the move, both Smith and Gillmore would throw every possible obstacle in the way of it. Nevertheless, Weitzel said he was ready to go if Butler

William F. Smith
Photographic History of the Civil War

Quincy A. Gillmore
Battles and Leaders of the Civil War

August V. Kautz
Photographic History of the Civil War

Edward W. Hinks
Photographic History of the Civil War

still wanted to issue the order. Swayed by Weitzel's practical objections and earnest advice, Butler gave up the idea, much to his future regret.

Next day, May 6, all the remaining troops landed and took up positions in the line across the narrow neck of the Bermuda Hundred peninsula, which was quickly made all but invulnerable.

Butler turned immediately to the task of severing Richmond's rail network. He sent General Smith toward the key railroad line between Richmond and Petersburg, but for reasons best known to himself Smith did not attempt actually to reach it. On the following morning, Butler directly ordered Gillmore to advance and tear up that rail line, with particular attention to Chester Junction, where an important branch line joined it from the southwest. Gillmore, however, failed to move. His eventual response to Butler's order, incredibly enough, was to report that he did not do what he was told to do "for what I deem good and sufficient reasons." Neither then nor later did he amplify his report to state what his "good and sufficient" reasons were.

Smith, for his part, sniped at Gillmore. He finally explained that the brigade he had originally sent from X Corps would have destroyed the rail connection, but stiff enemy resistance had kept it from reaching the objective. If Gillmore had cooperated, Smith said, the mission would have been successful.

Butler, patiently enough, then put Smith directly in command of the assignment and directed Gillmore to detach several brigades of his best troops to operate under Smith's command. Gillmore's stubborn response was to insist that Butler issue a formal general order assigning the detached brigades to Smith. Butler drafted the order, Gillmore was brought to cooperate, and Smith finally made the contemplated move. At last the key rail line was torn up as Butler had ordered it done in the first place.

Grant was later to reminisce that he had saddled Butler with a pair of incompetents when he selected Gillmore and Smith as Butler's corps commanders. Smith's promotion to major general had been sponsored for confirmation in the Senate by Grant himself, a decision which he admitted he had cause to regret. Gillmore's Senate confirmation had been endorsed by Butler at the request of his friend, Brig. Gen. John W. Turner, and now Butler regretted that favor. Thoroughly alarmed by Gillmore's laxity and annoyed by his attitude, Butler wrote a warmly worded letter to Sen. Henry Wilson withdrawing his endorsement and requesting that Gillmore's promotion be denied. But in spite of Butler's indictment, the Senate neither approved Gillmore nor rejected him, but simply kept the matter of his confirmation buried in committee.

While Smith and Gillmore were moving sluggishly, Kautz's cavalry, at any rate, was showing signs of vigor. Kautz was busily striking key points on the rail network south and west of Petersburg, scattering the defenders, tearing up track, burning bridges. In his best such exploit, early on May 8, Kautz attacked the Confederate force guarding the railroad bridge across the Nottoway River. The bridge, a wooden structure more than two hundred feet long, was set ablaze and totally destroyed, its ruined remains falling into the river. This effectively cut the Petersburg and Weldon Railroad, since the Nottoway bridge, unlike the shorter and simpler structures common in the region, could not easily be replaced.

After Kautz's successful raid, supplies moving up the Petersburg & Weldon had to be unloaded below the long break, transferred to wagons, and then hauled some five miles to Stony Creek for reloading on freight trains there—a cumbersome procedure creating a quartermaster's nightmare. By destruction of the bridge, General Beauregard's troops were divided north and south of the break, with no quick and easy way to regroup.

Meanwhile Butler's decision to leave North Carolina outposts thinly held was proved correct. On May 9, the garrison at New Bern reported that Confederate forces attacking that position had given up the struggle after two days of fighting. The sluggish Confederate ram *Albermarle*, which had caused such havoc at Plymouth, had been hotly engaged by navy gunboats and sent limping up the Roanoke River. At this point, as Butler had anticipated, General Hoke abandoned his campaign against Union-held points in North Carolina and hurried off to reinforce Beauregard in the defense of Richmond.

Also on May 9, Butler began to receive a series of remarkably rosy reports from the War Department as to Grant's all-out drive for Richmond. "A bearer of dispatches from General Meade has just reached here by way of Fredericksburg," said Stanton's first message. "States that on Friday night Lee's army were in full retreat for Richmond, Grant pursuing with his army. . . ."

An hour or so later, Stanton telegraphed Butler: "A despatch from Gen. Grant has just been received. He is on the march with his whole army to form a junction with you, but has not determined his route. . . . "

In immediate response, Butler issued fresh orders to General Hinks, commanding the black infantry regiments. "We have very good news from the Army of the Potomac," Butler said. "This involves a change of plan. You will therefore not move on Petersburg. . . "

To Generals Smith and Gillmore, at the same time, Butler sent instructions also based on the "good news." "The information I have received from the Army of the Potomac convinces me that our demonstration should be toward Richmond," Butler said.

Butler ordered the corps commanders to withdraw as soon as possible from their southerly lines at Swift Creek, destroying rails and bridges as they moved, and to regroup for a drive up the James toward Richmond.

Next day, Stanton forwarded further intelligence: "Reports say that Lee is retreating and Grant pursuing with his whole army."

In point of fact, however, what had actually transpired from the very outset of Grant's offensive constituted anything but the splendid results Stanton was telegraphing to Butler. The word Stanton relayed was totally wrong in suggesting that anything like a linkup of Grant's forces with Butler's was contemplated or, for that matter, even possible.

For his grand campaign Grant had reorganized the unfortunate Army of the Potomac, keeping Meade in command but with Grant himself at Meade's elbow at all times. He added Burnside's IX Corps as part of that army and assigned the cavalry to a corps under Gen. Philip S. Sheridan.

To describe Grant's move as ponderous is to understate the case by a wide margin. On the march Grant's lavish supplies and impedimenta required a wagon train more than sixty miles long, and this was after he had trimmed it back in preparation for the campaign. The lieutenant general found himself with so much surplus artillery that it was an embarrassment, cluttering up the roads, consuming vast quantities of forage and stores, and generally getting in the way. Finally, he had elected to launch his offensive in the jungle-like terrain of the Wilderness, a country of thick second-growth forest, impenetrable brush and brambles, and deserted, overgrown, vine-clogged dirt roads that had been little more than tracks even when they had been in use. Numerous streams traversed the area, their abandoned crossing points marked by the wreckage of destroyed bridges. No worse country for campaigning could have been found on the continent.

Far from routing Lee and starting on his way to link up with Butler, Grant had begun one of the slowest and bloodiest campaigns of the war. Before he would finally join Butler—south of Richmond in the manner Butler had suggested in the first place—Grant would have withdrawn from Butler some seventeen thousand troops for his own reinforcement and lost three thousand of them as casualties.

While Butler, spurred by Stanton's telegrams, prepared to shift his total effort northward, the Confederate high command (aside from the absent Lee) floundered in a state of confusion. Gen. Braxton Bragg was now technically commander of the armies and military adviser to President Davis, a position that made him a kind of Confederate Halleck. James A. Seddon, secretary of war, felt that he, too, had a right to issue command directives. And as for General Beauregard, the principal field commander of Richmond's defenses, he was playing his favorite role of the haughty genius who, if not handled gently and with deference, would simply quit and go home. Lesser Confederate generals were coping with conflicting orders as best they could and waiting, meanwhile, for Beauregard to get around to telling them what to do.

Beauregard, in fact, produced a highly fanciful plan in which Butler would first be crushed and Grant soon thereafter, following which triumphant Confederate forces would dictate the peace in Washington. All it required was for Lee to disengage, retreat some sixty miles to the outer defenses of Richmond, and give up at least fifteen thousand of his troops for Beauregard to maneuver. Bragg, Davis, and Seddon united to veto this mad plan, and managed to do so with such courtly tact that Beauregard threatened only once to resign. Afterward he settled down to the more prosaic role assigned him, that of defending the southern approaches to Richmond with the resources already on hand.

Butler now received yet another "good news" bulletin from Stanton: "Advices from the front give reason to believe that General Grant's operations will prove a great success and complete victory." Lee's only hope, Stanton's message added, was in receiving heavy reinforcements from Beauregard.

With Beauregard in front of him, Butler correctly assessed that presumed hope of Lee's as slender indeed. He determined to advance northward at once, in accordance with the agreement he had reached with Grant at their first planning session. On Grant's original timetable, the linkup was to take place in ten days after the start of the spring campaign. As to cutting the Petersburg-Richmond rail link, Butler felt that mission could be accomplished just as well on the north side as on the south.

The Confederate defense to the north of Butler's lines was anchored on Drewry's Bluff, a naturally strong position on the James River about seven miles south of Richmond. Beauregard's concentration was based on this point, and it was where Butler directed his major advance. He chose to take command in the field on this operation, since he could not rely on Smith and Gillmore to cooperate with each other unless they were closely supervised. From the start of the campaign, as a matter of fact, Butler, a good horseman since his teen years, was in the saddle much of the time, and the exercise agreed with him. In a brief note sent back to Sarah at Fortress Monroe, he said he had never felt better in his life—and he asked her to send replacements for his badly used flannel pants, which his saddle had worn to shabby ruin.

Kautz's cavalrymen continued to beat up the Richmond rail lines, severing the capital's last two connections to the south, while X Corps and XVIII Corps advanced along the Richmond-Petersburg Turnpike to converge on Drewry's Bluff. There they assailed and overran the outer defense lines of the Confederate stronghold. Gillmore's X Corps now held the left of Butler's line, and Smith's XVIII Corps was solidly in place on the right.

General Weitzel, ever the engineer, devised a strange defensive use for the plentiful telegraph wire that accompanied the columns. Weitzel's idea was to string tangles of wire at shin level in front of the Union positions, running it from tree to tree and stump to stump. When the Confederates counterattacked at dawn on May 16 in a heavy ground fog, Weitzel's wire maze took them by surprise and slowed them down under murderous fire from the Union lines. Only where Brig. Gen. C. A. Heckman had failed to adopt the device did the Confederate attack succeed, throwing his brigade into confusion. The general himself was captured, along with some four hundred of his men. Otherwise, after much confused fighting, Beauregard's effort fizzled out. It had cost him twenty-five hundred casualties.

Beauregard had hoped to coordinate his attack with a northward movement of the forces at Petersburg, the object being to cut Butler off from his base at Bermuda Hundred and completely destroy the Union army in the field. But the Petersburg contingent never arrived, having hesitated before a small Federal force Butler had posted to observe and delay any Confederate movement from that direction.

By now, something of the truth about Grant's situation to the north had reached Butler in a rather dramatic way. Gen. Philip Sheridan, with ten thousand cavalrymen in a column thirteen miles long, had left the Army of the Potomac to undertake a massive raid that would reach the outskirts of Richmond. His primary mission was to draw off the Confederate cavalry, force a major engagement with it, and then, with his superior numbers and equipment, destroy it as a fighting force. But he was also to carry out the usual role of far-ranging cavalry: to wreak thorough destruction along the way. That assignment Sheridan's troopers carried out with enthusiasm and effect, notably at the rail center of Beaver Dam on the Virginia Central, where nearly a million rations of meat and half a million of bread went up in flames, along with Lee's medical supplies and about one hundred railroad cars.

Sheridan's horse soldiers finally penetrated the outer defenses of Richmond, met up with J.E.B. Stuart's cavalry in a clash in which the colorful Confederate commander was fatally wounded, and then withdrew in an easterly direction north of the James to refit in the security of Butler's domain. As a practical matter, however, the main purpose of Sheridan's raid had not been achieved. Although deprived of the inspired leadership of Jeb Stuart, the tough Confederate cavalry was still a highly effective force, still capable of operating against Grant.

After conferring with Sheridan it became clear to Butler that the original grand design of joining Grant's huge army with Butler's lesser force in order to surround and invest Richmond was now sheer fantasy. Far from sweeping all before him, as Stanton's telegrams had indicated, Grant was bogged down in a costly campaign of attrition and was sideslipping southeastward. Butler knew now that if there was to be a joining of the two Federal armies it had to occur right where he was, in solid position on the James—the alternative he had proposed in his initial conference with Grant.

Butler broke off contact with Beauregard's force, held the shoulders of his lines long enough to permit Kautz's cavalrymen to withdraw safely from their advanced position, and then pulled back into his defenses across the neck of Bermuda Hundred. According to Beauregard's own summary of Confederate strength, Butler had kept some twenty-five thousand of the rebel general's forces pinned below Richmond, plus perhaps an additional five thousand in the city itself and at river defense posts.

With Sheridan's strong cavalry force now on hand, the opportunity was ripe for a profitable reassessment of the situation south of Richmond. But now there occurred some of those remarkable moves in Washington that always seemed to take place whenever Butler's wary enemies thought the time was opportune to deflate his irksome popularity with voters in the North. Butler, after all, had been reasonably successful and markedly humane in his campaigning against Richmond, while Grant—the administration's man—was now being called a butcher because of the appalling losses resulting from his blind, brutal, and frequently stupid assaults against Lee's resilient forces. At this point nobody had been able even to get an accurate count of Grant's casualties in the Wilderness, but they were estimated at something over seventeen thousand—and all to no gain. Under Grant the ill-fated Army of the Potomac was undergoing yet another bloodbath that would end in depleting it of most of its veteran troops. How Stanton derived intelligence for his cheery telegrams to Butler remains a mystery.

At any rate, in the midst of these appalling events, the remarkably obtuse General Halleck chose to become preoccupied with a mission dear to his heart. Old Brains, at this tragic time, decided to concentrate on seeing to it that Butler did not get an appointment as major general in the Regular Army, two vacancies having occurred in that grade. Halleck, in his communications to Grant, did not concern himself with the ugly mess in the Wilderness, but rather sought to consult with Grant on how best to thwart Butler.

On May 16, at the height of the Wilderness carnage, Halleck wrote Grant a "My Dear General" letter, urging him to nominate Halleck's own candidates, Meade and Sherman, for permanent promotion. "I do not wish to see these vacancies left so long unfilled, lest outside political influences may cause the President to fill them by persons totally unworthy," Halleck wrote. And he added, oddly enough in view of Grant's bloody stalemate at the time, "After your splendid victories, almost anything you ask for will be granted. The case may be different if you meet with reverses. . . . "

In the upshot of this curious episode, President Lincoln, always a man to weigh the political odds, and with his reelection to consider, did nothing whatever about those appointments. He held them dangling, possibly with the thought they might prove useful someday if he wanted a heavy favor or two in return. Lincoln by now was paying little attention to Halleck, finding him useful merely as a figurehead and military clerk.

Ulysses S. Grant
The Great Rebellion

Henry W. Halleck
Battles and Leaders of the Civil War

Halleck kept busy, however, and somehow, flying in the face of facts, Grant was moved to write a letter to Halleck complaining that Butler had not held ten thousand men on the southern front. Halleck quickly responded by sending Quartermaster General Meigs and Gen. J. G. Barnard from Washington to inspect Butler's command. Among routine directions Halleck included the note, with emphasis added: "General Grant wishes particularly to know *what* is being done there, & what in your judgment it is advisable to do."

Earlier, Butler had asked Sheridan to bring his strong cavalry force across to Bermuda Hundred where, in cooperation, the two commands might have accomplished something quite useful. But Sheridan, coincidentally a protégé of Halleck's, had suddenly decided that, instead of waiting the eight days he thought he needed to refit, he was now ready to march off and rejoin Grant. And that is what he did.

Halleck's inspectors (Butler called them "a smelling committee") initially returned a remarkably favorable report to their chief. It estimated at twenty-five thousand to thirty thousand the number of rebel troops held in place confronting Butler, and noted that in four days Confederate prisoners from ten brigades had been brought in. The report said:

> General Butler's position is strong; can be defended, when works are complete, with 10,000 men, leaving 20,000 free to operate. We think it is already strong, and think if General Grant is engaged in decisive operations that General Butler should not remain on the defensive. We think that this force should not be diminished, and that a skillful use of it will aid General Grant more than the numbers which might be drawn from here. Supplies of all kinds are abundant; the troops in good spirits. . . .

What happened between the writing of this report and the writing of the next can only be surmised, but the inspectors' second report was something of a turnabout and tended to reflect rather strongly what Halleck had wanted to hear in the first place. In summary it recommended reorganization of the Army of the James under a field commander other than Butler or, alternatively, the detachment of twenty thousand of Butler's troops "for service elsewhere"—meaning moved north to be thrown into Grant's battle of attrition.

Orders quickly followed from Washington, stripping Butler's army to the bare minimum necessary to hold his position at the Bermuda Hundred stronghold. Butler was instructed to put Smith in command of all the rest of his troops and send them to make a landing at White House on the Pamunkey River, from which point they were to reinforce Grant. Butler moved promptly to comply but suggested to Halleck that the debarkation point be changed to West Point, some ten miles away downriver. Butler said the stretch of river from West Point to White House was narrow, tortuous, and heavily mined and that moreover there was no landing at White House. "At West Point the wharves were repaired under my direction," said Butler, "and the landing can be perfectly covered by gunboats and a safe depot made there if desirable."

Halleck's curt reply said, "General Grant's order was to White House. I cannot make any change."

And thus it went, Smith arriving finally at White House on May 30 to find no facilities for disembarking his troops, and floundering ashore as best he could. Once his troops had landed, confused orders from Grant's headquarters sent him marching off in the wrong direction. And Smith's departure from Butler's area was promptly followed by the transfer of Hoke's division from Richmond to reinforce Lee. In sum, the transfer accomplished little else than a useless bloodying of Butler's purloined troops. What was shaping up in Grant's theater at this time was the Battle of Cold Harbor, at the conclusion of which Grant's casualty list would finally total something over fifty-five thousand, with his best veteran troops all but wiped out.

After Cold Harbor Grant would have had enough of this costly slogging, which was raising a storm of anguished criticism in the war-weary North and creating considerable alarm in Washington, where Lincoln's reelection was looking to be in doubt. In the end, Grant at last would resolve to transfer operations to Butler's area on the James, where Butler's foresight and diligence—never admitted or acknowledged—had prepared a strong, safe, and efficiently supported base.

46

In his initial campaigning south of the James, Butler was not unaware of Petersburg's importance as the hub for key rail lines serving Richmond. But in obedience to Grant's directive he had moved northward toward Richmond, dealing meanwhile with Petersburg by making good use of Kautz's active cavalry division to destroy tracks, stations, and bridges. By this strategy he provided maximum strength for the northward move, held the maximum number of Confederate units in place, and deployed the Army of the James in the best position to effect the planned linkup with Grant's main force. If Grant had been successful north of the James, the taking of Petersburg would have become a secondary detail. Instead, as the campaign developed, Petersburg became the key to Lee's defense of the Confederate capital.

When it became apparent that Grant could not move his army after all to that planned joining of forces at Richmond, Butler proceeded logically to make Bermuda Hundred a secure base for Grant's massive sideslip south of the James. In falling back to his strong defense line, Butler also had in mind the possibility that Lee, relieved of pressure from the Army of the Potomac, might now free heavy forces to fall upon the Army of the James while Grant's change of base was in progress. Indeed this was one of Grant's worries as well as he prepared his massive move.

Having weighed all these factors, Butler proceeded to strengthen his field fortifications across the neck of the Bermuda peninsula and, incidentally, to ask Washington for better weaponry for at least part of his force. Butler wrote Stanton: "I most earnestly request that 3,000 Spencer rifles with appropriate ammunition be forwarded to this command. I think it would be more than equivalent to reinforcing us with that number of men. . . . "

Butler, as it happened, was one of the few Union generals who appreciated weapons technology, including the effectiveness of the breech-loading, lever-action repeating rifle, available since 1860, but shunned by the Union high command, largely on the theory that such fast-firing rifles would only encourage the troops to waste ammunition. Now, at this late stage of the

war, Federal cavalry units had begun to use the newer rifles, and Confederate soldiers dreaded to encounter troops so equipped. Confederate Brig.
Gen. E. Porter Alexander was later to comment in his memoirs that, if the
Federals had been equipped with breech-loaders in 1861, the war would
have been over within a year.

Butler also saw wide possibilities in the use of Richard J. Gatling's 1862
invention, the Gatling gun, and he was the only Union general to make use
of it. Butler managed to obtain seventeen of these weapons, which could
fire 250 rounds a minute, but the Union high command ignored the weapon
completely.

Butler's defense line was now solidly in place. It protected all of the
Bermuda Hundred peninsula within the loop of the James River plus an
additional area, across the Appomattox, covering the base at City Point. A
pontoon bridge provided communication between the areas north and
south of the Appomattox.

Since comparatively little manpower was needed to hold his enor-
mously strong position, Butler was now able at last to plan a serious move
against Petersburg. He assigned Smith's XVIII Corps to the task, but on the
very day Smith was to have begun his march the order had to be canceled.
Grant required that XVIII Corps be sent at once to his aid north of the
James—just in time, as it happened, to be bloodied at Cold Harbor.

Still, Butler resolved to try a move on Petersburg anyway, using the
resources left to him. A cavalry probe had verified that the city defenses
were very lightly held. Having little confidence in Gillmore, Butler assembled a group of his more trusted senior officers to plan the attack, with his
old friend Weitzel on hand to provide his usual sound counsel. As the plan
was developed, Butler proposed to rely heavily on Kautz's cavalry and on
the Negro troops of Generals Hinks and Wild. All was progressing nicely
until, to Butler's chagrin, Gillmore stumbled in on the meeting. In no time at
all Gillmore, with quite some enthusiasm, was planning right along with the
rest of them and asserting his right as senior general to command the
operation. Butler felt he had to agree, and almost from that instant the
enterprise became a stumbling fiasco.

In a quick note to Sarah, Butler confided his strong misgivings. "I have
ordered an attack on Petersburg. I had to put it under the command of
Gillmore. I think it will fail from that cause."

Initially, Gillmore proposed to provide three regiments. Later he
decided to commit five. Butler vetoed his idea of taking along a lot of
artillery, commenting, "This is not to be artillery work but a quick, decisive
push."

The move began in a night march to the assembly area, which was
across the pontoon bridge over the Appomattox. However, most of Gillmore's troops lost their way, wandered around through the swamps, and

only with difficulty at last found the bridge. When finally across the river, Gillmore reported back only to complain that the bridge had not been properly muffled with straw. He was sure that the Confederate defenders must have heard the cavalry and were now alerted.

Butler somewhat impatiently explained that the bridge had indeed been heavily muffled but that the passage of Gillmore's bedraggled troops had used up all the straw as the men tried to clean the mud and slime off their boots and trousers. In any case, he assured Gillmore, the Confederates at Petersburg were too far away to have heard anything.

In daylight Gillmore resumed his hesitant march, taking up a position to the northeast of Petersburg, athwart City Point Road and the City Point railroad line. Hinks, on Gillmore's left, moved along a converging line following the Jordan Point Road. The energetic Kautz launched his cavalry in a dash from the south along the Jerusalem Plank Road, also aiming toward the presumed area of attack.

In the upshot, only Kautz persisted. Gillmore halted everything else, including Hinks's troops, and would also have recalled Kautz except that the cavalry, moving vigorously into the outskirts of the city, was out of touch with him and waiting in vain for some sign of activity on his part. That indication never came because Gillmore had quit and headed for home.

Gillmore had withdrawn in the face of scanty resistance by a scratch force of Confederate militia. In the course of his futile march he had convinced himself, somehow, that Richmond had dispatched heavy reinforcements by train, although Butler's signal station had reported no rebel movement whatever on either the rail lines or the turnpike. Kautz, on the other hand, had charged the entrenchments, penetrated the town, and captured forty prisoners and four pieces of artillery. Left on his own, Kautz afterward worked some destruction on the Weldon-Petersburg railroad line, and finally withdrew at his leisure, carrying away his prisoners and the captured guns. Butler, furious with Gillmore, fired him on the spot and put Gen. Alfred H. Terry in command of X Corps, a decision later endorsed by Grant.

Next day Butler—still fuming, although managing to maintain an outward appearance of calm as usual—received word from Stanton that Abraham Lincoln and Andrew Johnson had been nominated as the Union party's choice for the November election. At this he allowed his bitterness to spill over, but only in a short note to Sarah: "Hurrah for Lincoln and Johnson! That's the ticket! This country has more vitality than any other on earth if it can stand this sort of administration for another four years."

On June 14 Robert E. Lee, in a report to Davis, indicated he was still a little uncertain whether Grant proposed to stay north of the James or south. But he suspected that Grant's troop movements meant a major change of

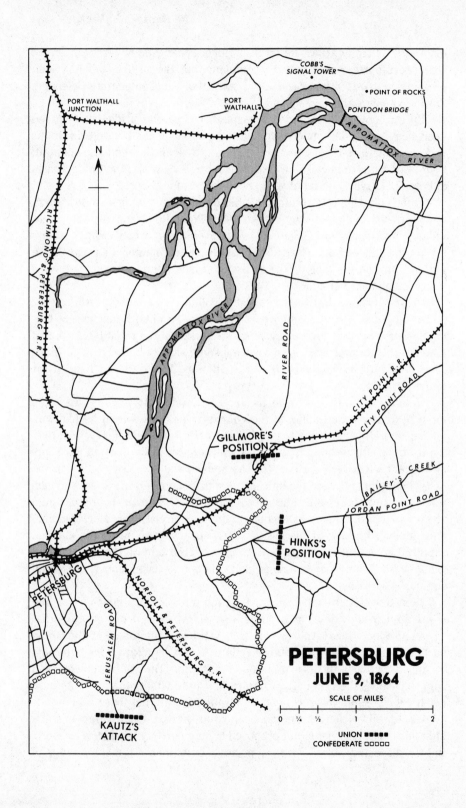

COBB'S
SIGNAL TOWER

•POINT OF ROCKS

PORT WALTHALL
JUNCTION

PORT
WALTHALL•

PONTOON BRIDGE

APPOMATTOX RIVER

N

RICHMOND & PETERSBURG R.R.

APPOMATTOX RIVER

RIVER ROAD

CITY POINT R.R.
CITY POINT ROAD

BAILEY'S CREEK

GILLMORE'S
POSITION

JORDAN POINT ROAD

HINKS'S
POSITION

PETERSBURG

NORFOLK & PETERSBURG R.R.

JERUSALEM ROAD

KAUTZ'S
ATTACK

PETERSBURG

JUNE 9, 1864

SCALE OF MILES

0   ¼   ½   1   2

UNION ■■■■■
CONFEDERATE ◻◻◻◻◻

front. Grant might be sending troops up the James for an attack at Petersburg, Lee warned, adding, "We ought therefore to be extremely watchful and guarded."

On the fourteenth, as a matter of fact, Smith's XVIII Corps was already landing in Butler's stronghold, and Smith himself, obviously shaken, was paying a courtesy call on Sarah at Fortress Monroe. She described the visit in a letter to her brother, Fisher Hildreth, with a hint that he might pass the information on to the journalist James Parton.

> He [Smith] is thoroughly disgusted with what they have made him do, and the conduct of the war generally in the details, which he puts upon Meade. He is inclined to shield Grant somewhat, but he evidently looks upon it from the beginning as a desperate butchery for us with comparatively little loss for the rebels. He says on the line of the Potomac alone we have lost seventy thousand men, and that this campaign will end it—if we are not successful now we can never raise another army. He hopes that [Senator] Wilson will institute an inquiry of those battles where he was engaged on the Potomac. He says it was absolute butchery, his Massachusetts men were piled in heaps without any results. . . . He says he was of no use on the Potomac. They had men enough already for the slaughter. . . .

Butler's spirits were lifted as Smith's men began landing. He took time for a quick note to Sarah: "All is busy and moving. My plan has triumphed after all. We could have landed here without all this loss, and fought the enemy at the gates of Richmond. All will be done here yet. . . ."

If there was an irony in these circumstances, it was to be found in the fact that Smith, even before his troops had landed, was now under orders from Grant to move at once on Petersburg, where Butler had been about to send him in the first place, just before Grant and Halleck snatched XVIII Corps away for its fruitless mission north of the James.

In a remarkable dispatch to Halleck, Grant provided the official party line to justify his massive move to the south of the James. Grant explained that, in moving sideways while attempting to get around Lee's army, he had got the Army of the Potomac in a position where it could neither advance on the swampy grounds in front of it nor protect its supply line, which was dependent on the Fredericksburg Railroad.

In the message to Halleck, Butler's strategy was now transformed into Grant's strategy. "My idea from the start," Grant wrote, "has been to beat Lee's army if possible north of Richmond; then after destroying his lines of communication on the north side of the James River to transfer the army to the south side and besiege Lee in Richmond, or follow him south if he should retreat."

To explain the costly deadlock north of the James, Grant complained, curiously enough, that the Confederates were taking advantage of field fortifications and entrenchments, digging in and decimating the attacking Federals. Grant's concluding paragraph in his report to Halleck was remarkable for its sheer stupidity: "The feeling of the two armies now seems to be that the rebels can protect themselves only by strong entrenchments," Grant wrote, "whilst our army is not only confident of protecting itself without entrenchments, but that it can beat the enemy wherever and whenever he can be found without this protection."

This statement, in mid-1864, after artillery firing grapeshot and canister had long since proved to be the deadliest weaponry of the war against unprotected troops, more than suggests that Grant had either learned nothing or was operating in a kind of mental vacuum after Cold Harbor. As for the confidence of his troops and their asserted scorn for entrenchment, the sorry truth was that the morale of the Army of the Potomac had never been lower than when this dispatch was written. And any hope of catching Lee's men standing in unprotected ranks was sheerest fantasy. Lee, after all, was a general whose insistence on entrenchments had once caused his troops to dub him The King of Spades.

Having made his decision, Grant's sideslip to the safety of Butler's impregnable base was rapid and successful. It was made possible by an engineering achievement which, perhaps because it was Butler's achievement, went entirely without notice in the dispatches between Grant and Halleck. In a single night Butler and his engineers constructed a twenty-one-hundred–foot pontoon bridge that eventually went into military engineering annals as the most extraordinary such structure ever emplaced. Six sawmills that Butler had built to provide timbers for hospital construction now provided planking for the bridge—planking that was replaced three times while the bridge was in use. To solve the problem posed by the thrust of four-foot tides and strong tidal currents, Butler anchored a small flotilla of schooners in such a way as to brace the bridge against forces that would otherwise have swept it away. Butler obtained the schooners in a typically Butlerian way: he simply dispatched his provost guards to seize them without ceremony from the sutlers who had been conducting their operations from the vessels.

Butler now had Grant at his elbow, and Meade as well. As he had done with Meade's Army of the Potomac, Grant continued to retain the Army of the James intact as a separate entity, Butler in command. And also as he did with subordinates in Meade's army, Grant issued direct orders to elements of Butler's army whenever the spirit moved him. It was perhaps to Grant's credit that he never became unduly concerned with a finicky regard to the chain of command or burdened himself with excessive attention to administrative red tape and the niceties of military courtesy.

What folk in the North came to describe as The Great Rebellion was now in its twilight months. Lee was running out of resources, even complaining that recruiting officers outnumbered the recruits they were gathering, and suggesting to Davis that they be called in from the field and put in the line. Sherman, the relentless destroyer whose tactics were not to be seen again until German armor in World War II adopted and perfected them, was killing the Confederacy. Lee's defense of Richmond, in fact, was now a sideshow—a stubborn holding action whose only purpose, if it had any at all, was to delay the finale until the war-weary North held its election, possibly rejected Lincoln, and accepted a compromise peace.

In this atmosphere, with Grant making all the important decisions, Butler was left with time on his hands to amuse himself at the front. One of his diversions was to ride out daily to the two-hundred–foot signal tower he had erected on Cobb's Hill, near the Appomattox. The tower was a semipyramidal structure built of timbers and braced like a railroad bridge. Atop the tower was a breezy platform nine feet square, from which observers with telescopes could spot any enemy activity within an area of more than three square miles and, by using signal flags, send appropriate word to other signal stations along the line. Observers were lifted to the top platform by means of a large wicker basket drawn up by a winch-operated rope.

Butler rather delighted in having himself hauled to the top of this structure, where he would spend an hour or so every day, scanning the countryside through his telescope. One fine June day, having amused himself in this way for a time, Butler was about to be lowered back down again when he was riveted in place by the distinctive shriek of a Whitworth projectile passing close overhead.

Lee's Army of Northern Virginia had but two of these oddly designed long-range guns, smuggled through the blockade from Britain. They fired a long hexagonal projectile that weighed twelve pounds and carried an explosive charge of nearly two pounds of powder. The design of the gun gave a remarkable spin to the shell, which contributed to the screech the shell made in flight. The Whitworth was designed for accurate long-range fire, but it was difficult to transport and loading it was a slow and tedious process, so the Confederates had made little use of their pair.

In this case the Whitworth had been hauled out of the Richmond arsenal for the specific purpose of knocking out that annoying signal tower. The Confederate gunners had placed their gun on a high bluff on the rebel-held side of the deep ravine that ran between the signal station and the Confederate lines. The high site was approximately on a level with the top of Butler's tower. That the commanding general of the Army of the James was on the tower at the moment was a bonus the Confederates had not counted on.

The explosion of the Whitworth shell brought Butler's soldiers on the

Lookout and signal station, Cobb's Hill, Butler's front, Army of the James
Butler's Book

The Whitworth gun. Lee's army had two of these. One took Butler under fire at this signal tower near the James. Union counterfire silenced the Whitworth.
Photographic History of the Civil War

run, yelling to the general to get himself down from his perch. Butler, although "considerably frightened" as he afterward put it, instead had his signal officer transmit an order for two artillery batteries to get into line at once at the breastworks to the right of the tower. As this was being done the rebel gunners got off another round, which passed high overhead.

Butler then proceeded to direct the counterfire of his own artillery, which he ordered to fire slowly and "by the numbers." Number 1 gun fired low by fifty feet. Number 2 gun was off target to the left. Number 3 gun was off to the right. And so it went until Butler had ranged in on the Whitworth, which in the meantime had managed to get off another round, this one also high. Finally, having zeroed in on the range, Butler ordered all twelve of his guns fired. In a matter of five seconds, twelve ten-pound shells were exploding around the Confederate emplacement. Two more rapid volleys were fired, and through his glass Butler could discern the Confederate gunners running for cover. The Union gunners scored direct hits on the Whitworth gun itself, putting it out of action.

"One more volley, and cease firing," ordered Butler. And that ended the episode, the Whitworth never being seen again in action. To the cheers of his men, Butler descended in full dignity from his aerie.

On the broader front, of course, there remained the strategic objective, Petersburg, where the struggle was to deteriorate into weary siege warfare in the long months ahead. To that task Grant finally would bend his best talents, those of dogged patience and endurance backed by the last outpouring of the blood and wealth of the weary North. But in this initial stage of the Petersburg campaign, direct assault was ordered. And in this attack General Smith, operating under Butler's command, was to falter and fail in perhaps the most spectacular series of fumbles of the entire campaign south of Richmond.

47

Where once Butler had a plague of brigadiers to contend with, now he had in his department a plethora of major generals, all of them orbiting around Grant, the lieutenant general himself. After the arrival of all these stars, the command structure south of the James, never a model of clarity, became even more blurred. This contributed in no small measure to the failure of the second direct assault on the defenses of Petersburg.

Butler's earlier and more modest attempt on the rail center had degenerated into a mere cavalry raid when the commander of the infantry units decided, on his own and at the last moment, not to take part after all. Now it was Grant's ponderous force that was to dissolve in confusion before Petersburg's defenses. Where one sound general with a third of the force might have got the job done, half a dozen generals up to their epaulets in men and equipment milled around—mostly getting in each other's way.

While Butler and the rest of the high brass were afterward more than content to blame Gen. William F. Smith for the debacle that occurred, this was an easy judgment, and it was by no means entirely fair. Smith's failures were obvious, but they were not irredeemable as other commanders and their troops arrived on the scene. When the smoke finally cleared there was, in fact, more than enough reproach to share around in the high command. However, in both the Federal and Confederate armies, scapegoating was an activity to which those in the upper echelons devoted much energetic attention.

Up to the moment he recrossed the James, Smith had fought a long, hard, active war and had seen much slaughter: Antietam, Gettysburg, Fredericksburg, and now, just days before, Cold Harbor. Smith's bitter conversation with Sarah Butler when he arrived at Fortress Monroe was that of a weary, worn-out, nerve-frazzled man badly in need of rest and recuperation. Instead he was wound up and set in immediate motion for the entrenched and fortified lines guarding Petersburg. There, as the assault developed, he was to find himself acting under directions or suggestions from Grant, Butler, Meade, and yet another senior, Gen. Winfield S. Hancock.

To open the proceedings Butler sent Smith off on a night march with his XVIII Corps supported by six thousand reinforcements, including Kautz's cavalry division and Hinks's Negro infantry. Smith was directed to move up to the Confederate defense positions and make preparation for an attack to be made at dawn. The Petersburg line, however, was no mere improvisation. Carefully engineered, it was anchored on a series of redans, triangular artillery emplacements designed to provide overlapping fields of fire. Linking the redans was a line of entrenchments. Approaches to the line were obstructed by ditches, brush, and a tangle of fallen trees. An attack on this defense system without some rather careful inspection and preparation was not the prudent course of action—nor was it Smith's way.

Butler kept nipping at his heels, but Smith ignored all querulous messages from headquarters, electing to spend a full day examining the position. Whatever other effect this delay may have had, it at least gave most of his marched-out, fought-out, and generally worn-out troops a chance to get some rest. Around 7:00 P.M. Smith finally attacked, sending his freshest troops, the black regiments under Hinks, against the center of the Confederate line. Moving briskly, these troops were shortly in possession of five of the redans and their guns. They had captured a number of prisoners and were holding about a mile of the broken Confederate position.

Smith, proceeding with a caution that was now clearly excessive, failed to exploit this success, for reasons that neither then nor later were susceptible to any explanation other than Smith's weariness and nervous exhaustion. Hancock, who outranked him, was close at hand and on his way. Quite possibly, Smith was simply looking forward to the moment when somebody other than himself would assume the burden of command. No military logic could explain his sudden suspension of the attack at the very point when Petersburg was his for the taking.

Butler continued to nag Smith, sending him increasingly urgent messages hand-carried by Lt. John I. Davenport, one of Butler's staff aides. Davenport rode back and forth repeatedly from Butler's field headquarters, but to little practical effect. On his second such gallop, Davenport found Hancock present and from Smith got only the comment that Hancock was now the senior general on the field, meaning perhaps that Butler should either relax and shut up or else direct his complaints to Hancock. After this short remark Smith turned on his heel and walked away.

Sent back by Butler a third time, now long after midnight, Davenport was unable to find Smith anywhere in his command post, nor did any of Smith's officers profess to know where he had gone. Perhaps, some of them said, he had gone off to talk with Hancock. The stubborn lieutenant waited until daylight and finally found Smith emerging from sleep in a tent that had been pitched among those of the servants and orderlies of the headquarters staff.

General Butler and his staff in camp near the James

Taken somewhat aback, Smith apparently felt he ought to explain why he had hidden himself away. "I was very tired," he said. As to Butler's peremptory order to continue the attack, Smith shrugged it off. He would look things over, he said, and then see about preparing his troops for an advance.

Meanwhile there was activity to the north. Beauregard, without hesitation, had withdrawn his forces from their entrenchments opposite Butler's position at Bermuda Hundred and rushed them into the Petersburg defenses, leaving it up to Richmond to plug the gap he had left behind. On discovering this, Butler sent his troops forward, bagged those few Confederate pickets who had been left to cover the withdrawal, and sent a force to cut the Petersburg-Richmond rail line and turnpike.

At 8:00 A.M. on the sixteenth, Butler sent a dispatch to Grant telling him what had occurred and suggesting that reinforcements from Grant's reserve, if sent now to Bermuda Hundred, might enable him to accomplish more. "We could I think advance on the railroad and isolate Petersburg, and as only a part of Lee's army has passed down, cut it in two and hold it cut," said Butler. "At least we should hold an opening from which to envelop Richmond on the south side, and save marching."

Almost timidly, Butler added: "The suggestion is a crude one, and is most respectfully submitted."

Grant's response was prompt. "Whilst the body of the troops are engaged at Petersburg I do not think it advisable to make an attack in the center of the enemy's lines," Grant said. "Their troops are now moving from Richmond to Petersburg, and at any time enough could be stopped opposite you to hold their strong works."

The move Butler suggested would indeed keep Confederate forces away from the Petersburg front, Grant added, "but would attract attention to a point where we may want to make a real attack some day hence."

What Butler had in mind was a "real" attack, but Butler's idea did not become Grant's idea until the next day, when the lieutenant general sent a staff officer to look over the situation. His next dispatch to Butler said, "It seems to me important that we should . . . maintain a position commanding the road between Petersburg and Richmond. With such advantage, it seems to me, we can always force a heavy column between the two cities, and force the enemy to abandon one or the other."

Grant's staff officer, Col. O. E. Babcock, reported that the proposed move was feasible. Grant ordered the attack to go forward. Butler issued the necessary orders. Then one of the debating teams so common in the upper levels of the Union army met to find reasons why not. Generals Wright and Terry, seconded by Col. Henry L. Abbot, huddled over their maps and finally decided they would rather not carry out the attack Butler had ordered at Grant's direction. Once again the loose command structure under Grant was failing badly, and Grant as usual seemed remarkably com-placent about it. When Butler again ordered the attack, again emphasized it was at Grant's command, and this time demanded compliance, Grant undid everything by abruptly canceling the operation.

The Petersburg assault was now being managed in a tangle of direc-tives from Grant, Meade, and Hancock, and it was slackening into feeble confusion. In sharp contrast, the Confederate forces, although severely lim-ited in numbers, were being competently managed by Beauregard, with the full assistance of Lee and the Richmond high command. The Federal attack, for all its overwhelming strength in manpower and equipment, was to dwindle away without decisive result, degenerating almost at once into a prolonged siege that would go on for ten weary months. Grant had fought and marched his troops into a state of exhaustion.

General Smith and his XVIII Corps were now taken out of the line and returned to Butler at Bermuda Hundred, where Smith continued to sim-mer—in chagrin at the Petersburg fiasco and also with rising resentment of his status as subordinate to Butler. This state of mind reached the boiling point some weeks later when Butler, at Grant's direction, was called upon to post Smith's corps once again in the Petersburg line. What followed was an episode that blossomed into something bordering on sheer insanity.

Butler issued a routine march order. With the dry summer tempera-tures now ranging in the high nineties, he had directed Smith to have his troops in motion at dawn in order to avoid the parching midday heat. When Smith did not do so, and in fact did not start his march until very late in the morning, Butler sent him a chiding message. He was tactless enough to remind Smith that he had relieved Gillmore of command for the same kind of tardiness.

Smith seized on Butler's abrasive reprimand to fire back a hot and insubordinate reply:

> In giving to your rank and position all the respect which is their due, I must call your attention to the fact that a reprimand can only come from the sentence of a court-martial, and I shall accept nothing else as such. You will also pardon me for observing that I have some years been engaged in marching troops, and I think in experience of that kind, at least, I am your superior.
>
> Your accusation of dilatoriness on my part this morning or at any other time since I have been under your orders is not founded on fact and your threat of relieving me does not frighten me in the least.

Butler promptly sent Smith a soothing message marked "Unofficial." In truth, especially urged by the ever-counseling Sarah, Butler had continually gone out of his way to cultivate Smith's good will and cooperation, and he

had made a point of issuing no judgment as to Smith's lamentable performance in the Petersburg assault. Now he realized that his sharp note had
nearly undone all his efforts at diplomacy, and he hastened to attempt
repairs.

"When a friend writes you a note, is it not best to read it twice before
you answer it unkindly?" Butler wrote. "If you will look again you will find
that it contains neither an accusation nor a threat. . . . Read the note again
and see if you cannot wish the reply were not sent."

Butler was even conciliatory enough to scrap the usual military protocol
and sign the note, "Truly your friend, Benj. Butler."

But Smith was by this time determined to nurse his grudge and push the
quarrel he had begun to its ultimate limits. He forwarded copies of the two
official notes to Gen. John A. Rawlins, Grant's chief of staff, but omitted the
personal one Butler had sent him. Without making any comment on the
notes as such, Smith requested to be relieved of duty in Butler's department.

Grant, however, was in no particular hurry to deal with Smith's problem.
Routinely, two days later, he told Butler to send reinforcements to Smith and
to instruct him to relieve Burnside's IX Corps on the Petersburg front.

Smith's performance as a commander continued to be erratic. He suggested to Grant a minor attack on a certain advanced Confederate post, got
approval for it, set a date, and then canceled the operation, saying he had
fewer men than he thought he had. Grant questioned Butler about this,
who passed along the query to Smith, whereupon Smith replied that he
now thought the Confederate outpost was too strong to attack and had
called off the move entirely.

Smith now began to complain about the Negro troops in his corps,
reporting to Grant that they were inefficient, not properly trained, and
generally ineffective. He asked that they be replaced with white troops.
General Hinks had been badly wounded in action with his black soldiers,
and now Smith wanted to disband Hinks's division altogether and scatter
his men to the rear for further training. This brought Smith into sharp
collision with Butler, who contradicted all of Smith's allegations vehemently
and in detail. Butler was not only proud of the black troops in his command, he had asked the War Department to send him additional black
regiments—some from the North and some from the Department of the
Gulf where, Butler charged, they were being badly used and ill treated.

Smith now began to press for a leave of absence, complaining of health
problems he said were acerbated by the hot summer sun. "One of my
troubles, that of my head, has three times driven me from a southern climate," he wrote Grant, "and I really feel quite helpless here, unable to go
out in the heat of the day even to visit my lines. . ."

Grant's response, kindly enough, was to suggest that he stay under
cover in the heat of the day. He offered to send him an assistant corps

commander to help him past his difficulty. But Grant could no longer ignore the tensions between Smith and Butler. Temporizing, he consulted with Halleck, who was delighted when he perceived in this a splendid opportunity to scuttle Butler.

Halleck's feline move was to prepare a general order giving Smith the command of all Butler's troops in the field and retiring Butler to shuffle papers at Fortress Monroe. With Stanton's bemused approval, Halleck got Lincoln to sign the order. However, Grant himself spiked it and saw to it that it was never issued. Instead of benching Butler, Grant relieved Smith of his command and sent him north to New York.

Now the strangest development in this ongoing controversy occurred. Grant and Butler had visited Smith at the latter's headquarters while Grant was continuing to try to mend the rift. Smith, writing now from New York, gave a bizarre account of this visit in a letter to Sen. J. M. Foote of Vermont. In his letter he sought to raise the issue of Grant's well-known reputation for drunkenness, hinting that Butler had special knowledge of some kind about Grant's drinking and was using this to bend the lieutenant general to his will.

Smith's letter quoted Grant as saying to Butler as they entered his tent, "General, that drink of whiskey I took has done me good." According to Smith, Grant then asked for another drink, which Smith supplied, and after a while demanded yet another.

"Shortly after his voice showed plainly that the liquor had affected him," Smith wrote, "and after a little time he left. I went to see him upon his horse, and as I returned to my tent, I said to a staff officer of mine, who had witnessed the departure: 'General Grant has gone away drunk; General Butler has seen it and will never fail to use the weapon that has been put in his hands.' "

Smith concluded his long, rambling letter to Senator Foote by charging that Butler not only had threatened to expose Grant's drinking, but moreover had threatened to "make something public that would prevent the President's reelection." A clear implication from Smith's curiously pathetic letter was that his long, hard war had finally brought him close to the breaking point.

In the finale of all this, Grant not only retained Butler in full command of the Army of the James, but added another army corps to Butler's command. Thereafter, Grant doggedly began pushing both armies forward, left, and right, wearing Lee down. Butler's "Bottle" at Bermuda Hundred (as it was termed in the hostile press) proved to be the impregnable and flexible base Butler said it would be, with fully supplied and well-equipped forces moving easily out of it on either side for operations north and south of the winding James.

48

The war was winding down, although this appeared to be more evident to the men in the ranks than to the generals and politicians. In both the Union and Confederate armies, desertions became commonplace. Among Confederate troops, particularly, many soldiers began to perceive a higher loyalty to their distressed families, who encouraged them to chuck it in and return home. Letters from kinfolk assured them that they would be safe from arrest, since there were already so many fully armed deserters in the home areas that provost guards were outnumbered and outgunned. Closer at hand, on the Petersburg front, many discouraged and hungry rebels were deserting to the Union lines for survival, safety, and a square meal.

In the Union army, motivations of deserters were somewhat different. Lincoln's draft had gathered in large numbers of reluctant recruits as well as profit-minded substitutes and bounty jumpers. Many of the latter were known to vanish into the night as soon as they had collected their money and drawn their equipment. In any case, patriotic slogans on both sides of the line had lost their sheen. Even the veterans who remained faithful enough to reenlist were bone weary, concerned now less with winning whatever the generals had in mind to win than with simply enduring to survive the waning war.

Against this background the nimble Lee himself finally had occasion to pay tribute to the strategic value of "Butler's Bottle." In a letter to President Davis, Lee reported:

> The enemy's position enables him to move his troops to the right or left without our knowledge, until he has reached the point at which he aims, and we are compelled to hurry our men to meet him, incurring the risk of being too late to check his progress and the additional risk of the advantage he may derive from their absence. . . . These rapid and distant movements also fatigue and exhaust our men, greatly impairing their efficiency in battle.

Butler, alone among Federal generals with the possible exception of McClellan, also had a keen understanding of the mobility afforded by the Union's profusion of gunboats, supply craft, and troop transports. When he first urged Grant to concentrate at Bermuda Hundred, Butler had argued that the Union's ability to make free use of the waterways rendered Washington perfectly safe. Lee, he had said, could not move units overland faster than Grant could move them by sea and river.

This thesis was now put to the test when Confederate Gen. Jubal A. Early, in mid-June, took ten thousand infantry plus another four thousand of cavalry and artillery on a sweeping march up the Shenandoah Valley. It is a telling commentary on the economics of the war that fully half of Jube Early's infantrymen were without shoes when they began their long hike, and that this lack of footgear was not made right until July 6, when Early's column finally crossed the Maryland border and paused for diligent plunder. By July 11, Old Jube had reached the outskirts of Washington, was studying the elaborate fortifications there, and was assessing his chances to capture the city.

But Federal sea power, as Butler had predicted, proved decisive. From Meade's army, transports carried VI Corps north, and Early found those divisions manning the Washington defenses. In addition XIX Corps, which had arrived at Fortress Monroe from New Orleans, was kept aboard ship and dispatched north, reaching Washington at nearly the same time as VI Corps. Early now had no choice but to retreat back down the Valley, marauding as he went. This process was made easier for him by the nervous and confusing orders issued to Federal forces by Halleck and Stanton, in a command crisis that was not resolved until Grant himself finally went north to untangle the mess.

Back at Petersburg—while Early was making his raid up the Valley—Grant, Meade, and Burnside were collaborating on an attack to be launched after the explosion of an enormous mine under a section of the Confederate line. Butler's part in this was peripheral, but it once again demonstrated the flexibility of his Bermuda Hundred base. He was to coordinate the movement of a force of infantry and cavalry across the pontoon bridge he had constructed to reach the north bank of the James at Deep Bottom, some ten miles southeast of Richmond. This bridge, backed by the presence of Federal gunboats, enabled easy movement of troops to menace the Richmond defenses north of the James. Union lines on the north bank were lightly held, readily supplied, easily reinforced, and at all times a threat.

The move across the James was designed to draw as many troops as possible from Lee's defenses at Petersburg, so that the attack there—when the massive mine exploded—would meet the least possible resistance. Thus Grant took no special pains to conceal the march, which was rather cannily planned merely to give the appearance of secrecy. Lee was expected to discover the operation and take heroic measures to counter it. This Lee did, dispatching four depleted divisions of infantry and two of cavalry to the presumed danger point, all at some cost in fatigue to his worn-out troops.

Burnside's Pennsylvania miners, who had excavated an enormous gallery directly under a Confederate fortification, at last placed four tons of powder in the mine and attached a network of fuses. After quite some delay as Meade's headquarters shuffled troop assignments, the hour was set for the explosion. At dawn on July 30, finally, the mine was exploded, killing more than 250 Confederate soldiers who had been holding the strong point directly above the blast.

After that all Federal plans quickly went awry. Brig. Gen. James Ledlie, who was to have led the follow-up attack, instead hid himself away in a bomb-proof dugout where, with a bottle of brandy, he was putting the finishing touches on a first-class drunk. Federal troops rushing into the crater left by the explosion found themselves in a trap. Confederates on the rim of the crater poured a heavy fire into the milling mass below them. By the time the debacle was complete, 3,500 Union soldiers had been killed or wounded and 1,500 were prisoners. Confederate losses totaled 1,500. Their defense line was intact.

Grant telegraphed Halleck: "It was the saddest affair I have witnessed in the war. . . . "

Now the struggle around Petersburg became once again a matter of digging in and exchanging artillery fire, although Union raiders continued to hit the railway lines. As this went on, Grant's casualty lists lengthened.

In Butler's area the troops that had crossed the river on their diversionary movement had been recalled according to plan, so as to be held in reserve to exploit the expected breakthrough at Petersburg. Their dash across Butler's bridge had served Grant's initial purpose, drawing off Confederate defenders from Petersburg. But with the Petersburg mine fiasco, this strong Union force now had no further role. It was back where it had started, in a classic demonstration of the old army maneuver known as Hurry Up and Wait.

Grant now turned Sheridan loose with strong reinforcements to drive Jube Early out of the Valley and ensure, once and for all, that it would no longer serve as a granary for Lee's hard-pressed army. In personally supervising this move, Grant was careful to bypass Halleck and the War Department by keeping to the field and avoiding Washington entirely.

Butler, in command at Bermuda Hundred but cautioned by Grant to attempt nothing ambitious, whiled away a dreary time by reading the inside political news his numerous contacts forwarded to him and also by indulging in tinkering, Yankee-style.

One thing he had discovered was that as a major general he had but to sign requisitions and the ponderous Federal rear echelon would process

General Butler in the field with the Army of the James, 1864
Battles and Leaders of the Civil War

them, sometimes to actual effect. His requisition for 1,000 horses had got him not horse one, nor had his order for 3,000 Spencer rifles produced any firearms. But when a chit from Butler demanded kite string, 10,000 yards of kite string appeared as though by magic. There may have been some head scratching back at the supply depot, but the general got his string and put it to use in flying large kites over enemy-held territory, the kites being rigged to drop propaganda leaflets. In a more serious mood, but still tinkering, Butler ordered up a specially cast long-range cannon and mounted it on an armored railway flatcar of his own design, the better to bombard Petersburg.

Butler had already counted himself out of all overt political activity while the war should last, but this did not keep him from studying the Lincoln-McClellan campaign closely. Nor did he go out of his way to discourage those movers and opinion makers who urged him to endorse a Butler-for-president drive. Even Lincoln's supporters, many of them, felt that the president's chances for reelection depended on his making a clean sweep of his cabinet. If the general would not agree to run against Lincoln, they insisted, he surely ought to get from Lincoln a solid commitment to fire Stanton and put Butler in as secretary of war.

Lincoln, quite as politically canny as Butler, was careful not to alienate him—not when the votes had yet to be counted. However, Butler never demanded a cabinet post, nor did Lincoln offer one as a condition of support. All Butler wanted was to be left undisturbed in his command, with some reasonable assurance there would be no repetition of the New Orleans knife thrust. Butler's roving correspondent, Col. J. W. Shaffer, called on the president and made a point of getting Lincoln's reassurances in writing. Shaffer forwarded the statement which Lincoln had written and signed:

> Colonel Shaffer has been conversing with me, and I have said to him that General Butler has my confidence in his ability and fidelity to the country and to me. And I wish him sustained in all his efforts in our great common cause, subject only to the same supervision which the Government must take with all Department Commanders.

Across this document Lawyer Butler eyed Lawyer Lincoln narrowly. Plainly enough it wasn't much, but it would have to suffice.

In August Sarah had to leave Fortress Monroe and return home to Lowell on receiving urgent news that her sister Harriet had fallen seriously ill. That illness saddened Ben deeply, since Harriet was his favorite sister-in-law. It was diagnosed as inoperable and terminal breast cancer. In a series of highly emotional letters, Sarah begged Ben to come home and to bring Dr. McCormick, his medical director, with him. She was not willing to accept the verdict of Harriet's physicians, hoping against hope that they were wrong.

"I hate doctors, they say horrible things in the most indifferent way, and go away without doing anything," Sarah wrote. "Dr. McCormick is better than that. He will try many things, and never gives up. . . . Oh dear, I shall die, with catching at straws! . . . You give me a little hope that you will come. I have a firm belief that circumstances will make it necessary."

At this time, however, Butler's full attention had to be focussed on a new trans-James assault ordered by Grant, making use of the pontoon bridge at Deep Bottom for the crossing of cavalry and artillery. Grant proposed to send the infantry of II Corps upstream from City Point on transports. Butler was to follow the cavalry and artillery across the bridge with whatever force he could spare from his defenses, and for this assignment he designated his X Corps under Gen. David B. Birney. The movement was to be made at midnight of August 13.

Meade, meanwhile, was instructed to watch the Confederate lines at Petersburg for any sign that the movement to the north was drawing off troops from his front. He was to attack without further orders if he saw an opportunity to do so.

In any case Grant's real purpose in ordering the attack was strategic rather than tactical. His main concern was with Sheridan, operating in the Valley, and his object was to hold Lee in position, preventing him from sending reinforcements to Jube Early. His orders to the forces on the James, therefore, were somewhat equivocal. They were not to be committed to a major battle unless an opportunity developed for a sure win.

Butler welcomed the break in monotony. As the attack got under way, he rode to the front and spent the day with X Corps in the field. Birney's troops moved forward smartly, capturing 150 prisoners and four guns. Hancock's II Corps, somewhat less successful, became heavily engaged, with a loss of prisoners on both sides. Further inconclusive fighting served Grant's purpose in that Lee was unable to send troops to reinforce Early while Richmond was being threatened by this operation at the James. But, having accomplished that much, the Federal forces were ordered to withdraw back across the river on the night of the twentieth.

In the final outcome the attack out of Butler's Bermuda Hundred stronghold served yet another purpose besides that of relieving pressure on Sheridan. It had required Lee to withdraw troops from his entrenchments guarding the Weldon Railroad. Seizing this opportunity, Federal troops finally gained full control of that important rail line, which Lee had been desperately trying to hold from the outset of the Petersburg campaign. Lee was unsuccessful in two desperate attempts to regain what he had lost, and the effort cost him heavily in casualties.

In the comparatively quiet period after his adventure across the James,

Butler finally took a short leave of absence. The only military project that occupied his attention at the time was the digging of a canal at Dutch Gap, designed to open the upper James to easy passage of Union gunboats. That work was well along and did not need his further attention.

Butler went first to New York on August 25, where he attended to the probate of Andrew Butler's estate and also talked politics with a number of his partisan cronies. Two days later he headed home to Lowell for a brief reunion with his family. Sarah, always high-strung, was more tense than usual—worried literally sick about her sister Harriet, worried about the many intrigues directed against Ben, worried about the course of the war, and weary of it all. Not encouraged by any of this to prolong his leave, Butler was back at Fortress Monroe by September 8 and feeling low. Ben wrote:

> My Dear Sarah, I am back in camp again, and oh! so lonely after all! Why should I stay here fretting and laboring? Who will thank him who does it? I am sure I would not do this if I did not really think I could do my work better than any man in the country. Events have settled it better than any other way that Lincoln is to be run again, and again elected, perhaps. I have therefore nothing to hope or to fear. . . .
>
> You will kiss the boys for me, and tell them their father loves them very much, and is very proud of them as good boys, and that they must study so as to grow up and fill his place and more too. I am writing this in the morning, and the mail calls. Yours, dearest, Benj.

Two days later Butler was even gloomier. "My dearest wife, suppose you and I go home together, and stay there and not go away again," he wrote. "I believe that would be best. I am sick and tired of it all."

A few days later Butler became physically sick, racked with chills, fever, nausea, and an assortment of generalized aches and pains. At first he toughed it out, but finally he was bundled off to bed at his Fortress Monroe quarters by Dr. McCormick, who prescribed a hot bath, a hot toddy, some pills, and a heavy sweat under six blankets, with two hot-water bottles at his feet.

"Not a wink of sleep did I get," Ben reported ruefully to Sarah. "The doctor's opiate was so strong that it kept me broad awake."

Next day Butler's aches and pains were mostly gone, and this was fortunate because Grant had chosen this time to join Sheridan in the Valley, leaving Butler in command of both armies on the Petersburg-Richmond front. Weak on his feet, Butler took over, cheered by a warm and loving letter from Sarah which, besides its endearments, contained the elements of a fine chuckle. The latter had to do with the arrival of a horse Butler had bought and sent north to his stable. Their hired man, Frazer, did not know what to make of the beast.

"I must take room to write you about a horse, sent here yesterday," Sarah wrote as a kind of postscript.

A boy brought him with a bill of expenses, three dollars, from Boston. Frazer says he was sent from New York. Have you ordered one home from the Fort? Frazer says he is wholly worthless. Blind, poor, and has the heaves. He is afraid to put him with the other horses, and will turn him into the field. Did you send a horse, or is this a practical joke?

"My Dear Wife," Ben replied.

I will kiss you this minute, once, twice, three times, and make up. As to the horse, tell Frazer to feed him very well, keep him well groomed, and fetch him up. Why, he is as good blood as Godolphin, only he has been abused. I am afraid you don't know about horses. He is worth, I don't know how many thousands of dollars. He is Frantz Cheatham's thoroughbred, and sire to a long line of illustrious sons. He is like old china . . . which nobody can see the value of but the owner, and those that fancy it. Practical joke! Indeed, is it possible that this famous horse has come to that!

The horse, privately dubbed Old Wall-eye, became a standing joke between Ben and Sarah. Recovering quickly, her next letter said, "It is funny about that horse. Do you know, I told Frazer the creature was rather smooth-looking. . . ."

But as for Frazer, the Yankee handyman was unmoved in his opinion. He did as he was told, but not without grousing. "If that animal ain't worthless, then I'm no judge of horses," he said.

With one important exception things remained quiet on the Richmond-Petersburg front. On September 16 three brigades of hungry, hard-riding Confederate cavalry raided deep into Federal lines and made off with two thousand head of cattle from a rear-area corral below Grant's headquarters at City Point. Butler estimated that in this one stroke the rebels had more than made up for their loss of the Weldon Railroad supply line and the tightening of rations that it had cost them.

Sheridan's Valley campaign ended in triumph, meanwhile, and Grant ordered a 100-gun salute fired to celebrate the victory. It was not an empty gesture. Shells from the 100 guns were directed against the battered Petersburg lines.

Now Butler's attention was about to be fixed on an assault in earnest on the Richmond defenses north of the James. Grant at last proposed to turn him loose in command of a major offensive.

49

As September dragged to a close, even the resilient Butler began to show signs of depression and war-weariness. Seward came down to visit. He made it very clear that whatever speculation might be circulating about wholesale changes in Lincoln's cabinet, the secretary of state was firmly fixed in his post, and Stanton likewise. Advice from Washington suggested that the Lincoln administration expected the Army of the James to vote "right" in the upcoming election, and that it would be a good move if Butler were to pass this word along to his brigadiers. Republican groups asked him to make speeches seconding Lincoln's renomination. Ben declined, pleading the press of duty, but he did address letters of endorsement to various organizations. On request he even wrote some kind and quotable words to help the re-election campaign of his political enemy, Governor Andrew of Massachusetts.

Days had gone by without a letter from Sarah. Butler wrote home asking her to have his tailor send him a new uniform. "I am in absolute rags," he said.

"Where we shall be or what is the future for us God only knows," Ben wrote his wife.

> It is all a blank, and I think of not much consequence. There is not much worth living for to a man of forty-five. We have seen it all. How tame is life now in comparison to what it was! All's known. Why drag out a few more years to reiterate the same routine? Alas! for the enthusiasm of youth!

Butler hastened to add: "Not that I am sad or hypochondriac, but solely that it does not seem of consequence as to what becomes of the future."

To shake off his black mood, the general turned his mind to thoughts of home and, for a paragraph, became the brisk householder.

> Tell Frazer to look out for the pear trees—see that they are dug around this fall and manured, the raspberries and strawberries

protected. Also let him look to the lawn and rake in some grass seed where there are bare spots. Send to Boston and buy a large lot of hyacinths and bulbs, such as tulips and narcissus and the like, and plant them in the flower beds. Renew the stock of roses if possible. Take care of the grape border near the green-house, and cover it up with a coating of manure, and see if we can't have some grapes next year. . . . Let him take pains with the green-house, and have a fine show of flowers which he may sell if he chooses. In fine, if he will take care of the place I will see that he is handsomely rewarded.

Ben apologized obliquely for dwelling on all these details. "And yet," he wrote, "I have room to say I love you much, dearest, and wish you were with me. . . . "

Butler's dark mood was all the more strange in that he had just been given the assignment he had wanted for so long. Grant, a few days before, had verbally approved his plan for a serious drive on Richmond, to be carried out on the north bank of the James, with Butler in command. Once this would have had him brimming with enthusiasm. Now he was merely the diligent technician, drawing up a meticulous operational order so complete in detail that it might have served as a textbook exercise.

Thoughts of his own mortality may have been lurking in Butler's mind as well. There was one special part of the offensive that he intended to supervise in the field and in person. Butler's black troops had been getting scant respect from Grant's other generals, who doubted the Negro's capacity for combat. Not even the successful assault by U.S. Colored battalions on the Petersburg entrenchments, in the first of the Federal attacks, had convinced Grant's commanders that black soldiers were brave and effective fighters. Now Butler proposed to gather his black regiments together as a striking force and oversee their assault on a key section of the fortified Confederate line. For once and for all, he meant to put all doubts about their abilities to rest.

On September 27 Grant issued a formal order for the movement, the details of which were to be outlined in Butler's own directive to his generals. Grant's order was bold and buoyant in tone and in odd contrast to the caution and hesitation he was to show later as the offensive developed. Grant called for bypassing strong points held by the Confederates, and even for Butler to accept being cut off entirely from his supply line, should the drive on Richmond require it.

"Should you succeed in getting to Richmond, the interposition of the whole army (rebel) between you and your supplies need cause no alarm," said Grant.

Butler was instructed to subsist on whatever he could find in Richmond while Grant and Meade would undertake to push through and join him in the Confederate capital.

On the next day Butler issued his operational order to Gen. Edward O. C. Ord (XVIII Corps), Gen. David B. Birney (X Corps), and to Gen. August V. Kautz, commanding the cavalry division.

Butler's engineers were directed to emplace a second pontoon bridge to the north of the existing one at Deep Bottom, the work to be done under cover of darkness and completed by midnight. The north bank bridgehead was to be in the vicinity of Varina, giving access to the Varina Road leading to Richmond. Ord's XVIII Corps was to move across the new bridge while X Corps crossed at Deep Bottom.

Always attentive to military intelligence, Butler had gathered from deserters and prisoners a reasonably complete roster of Confederate forces north of the James. These he listed, unit by unit, together with an estimate of their strength and the nature of whatever fortifications they were holding. This information was so detailed and accurate, he reminded his generals, that they need not waste any time dithering with reconnaissance before getting their attack under way.

The Confederate position at the James River itself was based firmly on fortifications at Drewry's Bluff, on the southerly side, and at Chaffin's Bluff, directly across the river. A pontoon bridge provided communication between these two strong points and would be a primary route for Confederate reinforcements moving north. Confederate gunboats ranged this section of the river.

Ord was to advance up the Varina Road. Birney was to direct his attack toward the New Market Road. Both generals were to set their forces in motion at 4:30 A.M., just before daybreak. Kautz's cavalry was to move across the pontoon bridge at Deep Bottom, pushing off at the sound of the guns to begin an enveloping movement across the New Market Road. Their assignment was to turn the left of the Confederate line without getting bogged down in an engagement. Kautz was to strike directly toward Richmond on either the Darbytown Road or the Charles City Road, on whichever he met the least resistance.

For all the troops involved, Richmond was the objective. If some units reached the city while others were under heavy pressure outside the city, the latter were instructed to withdraw into Richmond, not away from it. This was in full accordance with Grant's idea about cutting loose from supply lines if necessary. In a typically expansive gesture, Butler concluded his formal directive by promising a bonus of six months' pay and promotions to all officers and men of the unit that first secured a lodgment in the city.

Butler checked the staging area in person just before sunset. He was pleased to see that there was no indication on the riverfront that anything unusual was in motion. As soon as darkness set in, his engineers went to work. At midnight almost precisely to the minute, Ord's column reached the newly installed bridge and his troops began the crossing, their tread muffled by the thick layer of straw that covered the planking.

At exactly the same time, Birney's column started to cross on the lower pontoon bridge. Birney sent word that his troops, including the Negro regiments, would bivouac for the night, and that he would be on the march at daybreak, at which time he expected Butler himself to assume direct supervision of the Negro regiments.

Butler, satisfied that all was in order, returned to his tent to sleep for an hour or so. At 3:00 A.M. he was awakened by an orderly, who brought him some coffee, and by 4:00 A.M. he was crossing the lower pontoon bridge. He found the black infantry division, three thousand strong, already formed up and ready to move. Butler rode among the men, speaking to them as he went: a few words of encouragement, a few general directions.

The black troops had been encamped on the reverse slope of a hill, where they were concealed from the Confederates' fortified line that lay ahead. At the foot of this hill, on the side facing the rebels, there was a small brook bordering a meadow, and to the left of the meadow was a section of marshy land. On their attack the troops would first have to climb the hill, descend the other side, splash through the brook, cross the meadow, and then attack uphill against the Confederate position. The key point of that stronghold was a square redoubt with artillery emplaced to cover the steep slope to its front. The enemy line was protected by two rows of abatis. The first row was one hundred fifty yards to the front of the rebel position; the second was one hundred yards behind the first row. The position was held by about one thousand men.

Butler planned the attack to go forward in a rush—no skirmishers out front, no pausing to fire—because he knew that the outcome depended on coming to close quarters as quickly as possible. In preparation he ordered the percussion caps removed from all muskets, to make sure there would be no temptation to halt the forward progress of the charge.

When the order to move out was given, the troops marched up the hill as though on parade. As they reached the crest and started downward, most of the men splashed through the brook and stayed on solid ground. But some mistakenly angled off to the left a little and had to contend with the watery marsh, which they traversed waist deep in places, holding their rifles above their heads to keep them dry. From the fort the Confederates began firing heavily, at first to little effect, their aim being high. In the ensuing uproar the Federal attack broke into some confusion when shouted commands could not be heard.

The clear notes of a bugle sounding the rally call finally restored order, and the men formed up again, moving forward at a run to the first line of abatis, which they cleared out of the way with axes, as Confederate fire began to take a heavy toll. With a loud yell the Federal troops reached the second line of abatis and cleared that out of the way. And now, in a hail of fire from the fort, they charged uphill that last fifty yards. Then suddenly it was over. The Confederates fled, having suffered few casualties. But the headlong charge through the two lines of obstacles had cost the black Union soldiers 365 dead and dying.

Butler was shaken as he slowly rode up the slope, guiding his horse first to the left and then to the right to make his way past the bodies of the fallen without disturbing them where they lay. Writing to Sarah a few days later, he tried to describe the deep emotion he felt on seeing the features of the dead still frozen, as Butler put it, "in their expression of determination, which never dies out of brave men's faces who die instantly in a charge. . . ."

With great feeling Butler's letter continued:

> Poor fellows, they seem to have so little to fight for in this contest, with the weight of prejudice loaded upon them, their lives given to a country which has given them not yet justice, not to say fostering care. To us, there is patriotism, fame, love of country, pride, ambition, all to spur us on, but to the Negro none of all this. . . . But there is one boon they love to fight for, freedom for themselves and their race forever, and "may my right hand forget her cunning" but they shall have that.

Butler would recall the stark scene with these same deep feelings in all the long years ahead as, in speeches and writings, in legislation and campaigning, he faithfully carried out the vow he made. It is a footnote in military history that fourteen black soldiers and two of their officers won the Medal of Honor in the fighting to secure New Market Heights. United States Colored Troops, soon popularly known as the USCT, came to number nearly 179,000 by the war's end, and of that number 36,847 died in the service. After New Market Heights there was no reluctance on the part of white troops or their generals in the Armies of the James and the Potomac to put their trust in the USCT.

Elsewhere on Butler's front, a more important gain was made with the capture of Fort Harrison, the powerful central position upon which the Confederate defense line was anchored. Troops of Ord's XVIII Corps stormed and occupied the fort and its adjacent entrenchments, capturing fifteen artillery pieces. But Ord himself was painfully wounded when a sharpshooter's bullet shattered his ankle. Weitzel assumed command of the corps and prepared to hold the fort against a counterattack that was not long in developing.

Capture of Fort Harrison set alarm bells ringing in Richmond. Lee telegraphed to Bragg, directing him to call out all available reserves in the city and rush them to Gen. Richard S. Ewell, commanding north of the James. Lee ordered Gen. George Pickett to send a brigade north from the Petersburg line, and Lee himself moved his headquarters to Chaffin's Bluff to oversee operations. Ewell was ordered to move against Fort Harrison at once, without waiting for reinforcements, but this proved futile. The Federals were not to be that easily dislodged.

Under Lee's direction a heavy force was launched against Fort Harrison on September 30, employing Pickett's brigade, two infantry divisions, a cavalry division, and an artillery unit that Lee reinforced by the addition of twenty-four guns. After a poorly coordinated attack in which both his infantry divisions were driven off, Lee unaccountably fed one of them, Gen. Robert F. Hoke's North Carolina Division, back into the assault not once, but twice. After failing in their final charge, the third they had attempted that day, Hoke's badly mauled division literally fled the field, seeking cover. One of Hoke's regiments was all but annihilated; when the attack was over it mustered only twenty-five men, these under the command of the senior surviving officer, a lieutenant.

Lee's report to Richmond was terse, and in view of the facts, more than somewhat misleading. His telegram said, "An attempt was made this afternoon to retake Battery Harrison which, though partly successful, failed." There was no success, partial or otherwise. And the disintegration of Hoke's division was nothing less than disaster.

In the following days Butler's troops established a stable forward line. He suggested to Grant that if a corps could be shifted from the south, to do no more than hold his base securely, the troops he already had could make a final advance on Richmond. Grant, however, was not responsive to this. Probably as war weary as anybody in his command, Grant was now thinking of postponing any further heavy fighting while he drew in massive reinforcements from Washington and points north. Grant's orders began to contain specific warnings against attacking entrenched and fortified positions. He appeared to be anticipating, quite correctly, the complete collapse of the Confederacy as he methodically went about the business of severing all of Lee's remaining lines of supply.

The Federal line north of the James gradually stabilized, while Lee, in full agreement with Grant's estimate of the situation, called Richmond's attention to the growing disparity in numbers between the contending forces. Aside from battle losses among the rank and file, Lee's higher command was suffering severe attrition. In one short period he had lost the services of nine of his generals—some killed, others retiring sick and exhausted.

There was occasional heavy skirmishing. Kautz's cavalry got into difficulties on the far right of the Federal line and was driven back with the loss

The honor medal awarded by Butler
to heroic members of the USCT
Butler's Book

Godfrey Weitzel
Battles and Leaders of the Civil War

of his artillery. Infantry support, however, quickly stabilized that section of the front. Butler set up relatively comfortable headquarters on the grounds of an abandoned plantation house. Under Grant's direction his troops probed the rebel lines, which were now manned by a thinning force of veterans supplemented by the willing but bewildered Richmond reserves— clerks from the Navy Department, clerks from various express companies, and most of the Richmond police.

To the south, likewise, Grant continued to press ponderously, again avoiding pitched battle or any assault against heavily prepared positions.

Butler, now not too heavily engaged, found time to design and have cast in bronze a special medal for those of his U.S. Colored Troops who had distinguished themselves. He awarded some two hundred of these. From time to time in years long after the war, he would encounter one of his veterans wearing the medal, much to his great pleasure. "Distinguished for Courage," the reverse side read, and on the face the motto *Ferro iis libertas perveniet.*

As military affairs settled down to routine, the Lincoln administration had one further chore for Butler to perform. There were rumors that Copperhead conspirators and rebel spies proposed to disrupt the election balloting in New York, so Butler was dispatched there with five thousand troops to keep the peace. This he did without difficulty or incident, aside from a number of assassination threats, which Butler ignored and which came to nothing. New York conducted the quietest election in its history, so that even the most timid of Lincoln's supporters found no excuse to stay away from the polls. Butler had fully kept all of his commitment to Honest Abe, but as for Honest Abe's written endorsement of Butler—well, with Honest Abe's reelection that had now become just another scrap of paper.

50

With Lincoln safely reelected and no longer needing troops in New York to maintain public order, Butler returned to the Army of the James, still keeping to his word that personal political ambitions would be put aside so long as the war continued. Before he left New York, however, he was given a reception and banquet at the Fifth Avenue Hotel, at which the Reverend Henry Ward Beecher, to ringing cheers, put Butler forward as the logical candidate for the presidency in 1868. Ben, taking note of all the champagne that had been consumed, merely smiled and said nothing. But this, he was to reminisce late in life, turned out to be "one of the most unhappy and unfortunate occurrences of my life." If Butler did not take the Reverend Beecher's speech seriously, others did, and the general's military career was not long in suffering for it.

Recalling the incident ruefully, Butler said that, if he had been alert enough, he would have risen to name Grant as the rightful candidate in prospect for 1868. "If I had had brains enough to say that, the sting would have been taken out of the whole affair," Butler wrote in his memoirs. "Nay more, I could have been put in command of the Army of the Potomac if I wished."

Thus in hindsight did Butler recall how Grant's previously friendly attitude toward him rather suddenly hardened. This was to the evident delight of that preeminent maker of mischief, Henry Halleck, who redoubled his efforts to ruin the Yankee general. Grant, oddly enough, was unaware until well after the war that Halleck had once used the very same tactics in trying to get Grant himself fired, accusing him in reports to Washington (in the days before Vicksburg) of drunkenness, incompetence, and inattention to duty.

At this time Butler also became snarled in the inner circle maneuverings of Lincoln's cabinet. The death of Chief Justice Taney at the age of eighty-seven had finally opened his high office to an appointment by Lincoln. Stanton wanted it and, as a matter of fact, needed it. If he were to be named to the high court, that would make it possible for Lincoln to install

Butler as secretary of war, a move long urged by many prominent advocates but always disavowed by Butler himself.

To complicate the picture, Butler's old childhood friend, Gustavus Fox, was opposing Stanton's promotion. He wrote Butler asking for his help in getting the court appointment for Montgomery Blair. He quite frankly put it on the basis of quid pro quo, noting that Butler was indebted for help he had received at a critical time from Blair and from Fox himself, when the New Orleans expedition was in the planning stage.

Butler did his best to stay out of the gathering intrigues. He explained to his well-wishers that in no case would he seek the cabinet appointment while Stanton still held the position. And he added that in any case the troubles Stanton had experienced with the professionals from West Point would be as nothing compared with the grief they would lavish on Butler in that key post. As for the request from Fox, he fended that off as best he could in a private conversation with his old friend when the latter visited him at Fortress Monroe. At this point, anyway, he reckoned his influence with Lincoln at a value hovering close to zero; the probability that Honest Abe would consult him about the Court vacancy was even smaller.

All of this was resolved when Lincoln, more than somewhat reluctantly, paid off Salmon P. Chase for his support in the recent campaign by naming that lawyer of indifferent talent to be the new chief justice. Stanton dutifully stayed in place as secretary of war, although this was a sacrifice for him. His wartime service in the cabinet was all but ruining him financially, since he had no great fortune to rely upon and in the midst of massive corruption had stayed stubbornly honest.

In the heated economy of wartime the Lincoln administration, in fact, had become the most corrupt in the nation's history, only to be exceeded in that respect when the politically naive Grant finally acceded to the office. It was a time when crooked contractors and busy lobbyists were a plague on the land. The spoils system was in full sway, and Federal appointments from rural postmasterships to supervisory jobs in the shipyards were political plums to be marketed. Testy Gideon Welles was moved to despair by the frauds and swindles perpetrated in shipbuilding and supply contracts. He was outraged when Republican fund-raisers took to appearing routinely on payday at the shipyards to deduct a party "donation" from each worker's pay. With even less restraint than Welles was able to impose, similar abuses flourished in all the governmental departments.

With all this going on, important segments of the equally corrupt press—content to ignore genuine and massive incidents of graft and thievery—now chose instead to fasten on the ridiculous story that General Butler had enriched himself at New Orleans by making off with some silver spoons. The truth of this, which the press lords ignored, had to do with tableware seized as contraband by a provost guard and impounded. It was among the properties receipted for when General Banks took over from Butler. But the records kept by the officer in charge under Banks listed this property under the wrong name, and the indignant owner got lost in the shuffle. It was all resolved properly, after much official correspondence, but the editors were much too content with the legend they had created to spoil it with anything so dull as an infusion of truth. Butler, as usual, remained aloof, not deigning to complain and considering, as a reasonable man, that the whole thing was too ridiculous for anyone to believe.

More serious was an equally false allegation that he had made off with $50,000 in gold that he had ordered seized from a rebel banker, Samuel Smith. This gold, contained in two kegs concealed behind a brick wall, had been uncovered by Butler's men when they were tracking down the assets stripped from the United States Mint as the Federal fleet approached the city. Butler's attention had been drawn to certain peculiar entries, made over erasures in the bank's books. One purported to record $50,000 worth of lead, another $50,000 worth of tin. Smith remained obdurate when questioned about these entries, but after being placed under arrest and jailed he decided to cooperate. He finally led the investigators to the hidden cache in the wall behind the bank's vault. Other coin uncovered was returned to the bank as a legitimate asset. But the gold, in Butler's opinion, clearly represented part of the loot taken from the Mint.

After seizing the gold, Butler used it to make up part of a deficiency in paymaster funds sent to pay his troops. Afterward, Stanton credited the $50,000 to Butler's account, with a hazy explanation that the War Department would deal with the matter later. All Butler wanted was a receipt for it, but that was not forthcoming. The fund remained dormant, and so did Butler's full and official report on the affair.

Now an old voice from the past was heard again: Reverdy Johnson, the prorebel lawyer with close ties to Lincoln, popped up as attorney for the rebel banker, Smith, who now had been transformed by an oath-taking into a fervent and dedicated Yankee—complete with a Yankee address in Saratoga County, New York. Johnson, who well knew which Washington buttons to press, prudently arranged for Attorney Edwards Pierrepont, a close friend of Stanton, to represent Banker Smith in a lawsuit against Butler. The suit was filed in New York, neatly timed to coincide with Butler's appearance there in command of the peace-keeping force.

Butler once again asked Washington to take control of the orphan $50,000 and deal directly with Pierrepont to whatever outcome seemed right. He submitted another full report on the matter and asked for permission to publish it, since the inimical press was having a field day with the story. But now Pierrepont's friend, Stanton, developed a curious disinterest. He refused to have the War Department admit responsibility for the money; instead he referred the matter to the department's solicitor general. The latter, equally aloof, promptly told Butler to go defend himself against Smith's lawsuit. To complete Butler's isolation, Stanton at this time ignored Butler's request for permission to publish his official report. Quite clearly, the Lincoln election campaign was over.

While all these troubles were plaguing the general, yet another incident occurred to cause him grief. His swift and much-prized command vessel, *Greyhound*, caught fire and was totally destroyed. The fire started while Butler himself was on board. For some unexplainable reason the firebox door blew open, scattered live coals throughout the fire room, and set the steamer ablaze. Butler stood by while the crew fought the flames until finally, with the fire out of control, all abandoned ship.

Two days later a hometown well-wisher, Peter Lawson, relayed an account of his conversation with the purser of a Cunard steamer in Boston, strongly hinting at sabotage. The purser, Lawson said, had been told six weeks previously in Liverpool that the boilers of the *Greyhound* would be rigged to set off a fire. The plot was widely known in Liverpool, the purser told Lawson, having been bruited about by a passenger who had boarded the liner at Halifax. The presence of rebel saboteurs and arsonists operating out of Canada perhaps lent some credence to the story. But no evidence of a plot was obviously apparent, and Butler showed no inclination to pursue the matter. In any case the general's mind, amid all the distractions, was fully occupied now with details of an expedition to capture Fort Fisher and close the port of Wilmington, the last haven of Confederate blockade-runners.

51

On November 15, 1864, having fought, looted, burned, and vandalized his way through the heartland of the Confederacy, Gen. William Tecumseh Sherman set his army on its great march to the sea. By December 10, Sherman had reached Savannah. Five days later, Federal troops under Gen. George H. Thomas routed a Confederate army at Nashville. A week after that, Savannah fell to the Federals. All this occurred while Grant's overwhelming forces held Robert E. Lee's dwindling remnants fixed in place at Petersburg and Richmond—cold, hungry, sick, exhausted. Clearly the war was in its final stages.

In the United States Navy Department, however, planning went on as though it were still 1863. In that year the navy had begun working on plans for a proposed army-navy expedition to seal off the port of Wilmington, North Carolina, where the North Atlantic fleet had been least successful in coping with the activities of blockade-runners. Now, with the Confederacy about to collapse, the navy revived the proposal.

Butler had his own ideas about the importance of Wilmington to the navy officers who had been conducting that leaky blockade. He had noticed that far fewer blockade-runners were captured on their way into Wilmington than were captured on the outbound run. Inbound the adventurers carried goods that were scarce in the Confederacy and commanded high trade value at Wilmington. Those same goods, at New York prices, were relatively cheap. Outbound, however, the blockade-runners carried cargoes that commanded premium prices in the North. Prize money for captured outbound vessels was therefore much higher, and in Butler's view this accounted for the remarkably uneven statistics.

Now Grant agreed to the navy's proposal, and Butler, to his eventual regret, assumed direct command of the army force that would carry out the Fort Fisher assault. Only Sherman, with his sound sense of strategy, considered the Fort Fisher plan to be basically flawed. He said Wilmington would readily fall to his own troops anyway as he marched them northward through the Carolinas. Furthermore, he said he would much prefer that

Confederate forces guarding Wilmington be held there, threatened but not displaced, since this would keep them from "piling up," as he phrased it, on the line of his own advance.

Navy Secretary Welles wanted to assign Farragut to command the assault fleet. Farragut was the admiral he most trusted and who indeed seemed much of the time to be the only admiral he trusted. But Farragut took sick and required extensive shore leave at this time, leaving Welles in a quandary. After ticking off the names of all available admirals and discarding them one by one for reasons ranging from lack of initiative to lack of brains, Welles settled reluctantly on David D. Porter.

Fort Fisher was the strongest system of bastions, ramparts, parapets, and bombproofs to be found anywhere on the continent. To attack this formidable position, Porter was assigned the biggest fleet ever assembled in the entire history of naval warfare up to that time. In addition, Butler and Porter, both enthusiastic innovators, collaborated on an imaginative gimmick. The assault on Fort Fisher was to open with the planned explosion of an entire ship packed from stem to stern with gunpowder.

The powder ship was Butler's idea. He had read of an enormous gunpowder accident that had all but destroyed an English town. Closer at hand, an ammunition ship had blown up at City Point only a short time ago, causing great destruction. From these musings it was but a step to planning the fabrication of the greatest "torpedo" in the history of warfare. All that Butler supplied was the suggestion. Porter and his ordnance people undertook the task of preparing the powder vessel.

Grant had assigned the army's part in the expedition to General Weitzel. Butler was concerned about Weitzel's assuming this responsibility, however, since it put Weitzel's entire career at stake, and the army was the young officer's only occupation. His promotion was before the Senate for confirmation. If anything went wrong—and, with the devious Porter commanding the naval forces, that possibility loomed large—Butler felt that he could shrug off the blame that otherwise might well destroy his loyal friend. Weitzel himself explained these circumstances to Grant, who consented to let Butler oversee the operation.

The navy ordnance experts now set about gathering the three hundred tons of explosives with which the powder vessel would be packed. Navy technicians put in charge of preparing the ship, the explosives, and the clockwork detonating devices fell to their task with enthusiasm. Porter himself issued a general fleet warning that it would be a good idea to stand off about twenty-five miles when the time came to explode the vessel.

Coordinating the preparation of the powder vessel, the movement of Butler's troopships, and the movement of Porter's enormous fleet proved to be difficult, and Grant grew increasingly irritated at the many delays. Somewhat naively, in view of the size of the expedition and the alertness of

Confederate spies and coast watchers, Grant had hoped somehow to surprise the garrison at Fort Fisher. But as time passed and word of the movement became rather general knowledge, Lee promptly shifted a division
from the Richmond defenses to reinforce Wilmington.

Butler was allotted some sixty-five hundred men to carry Fort Fisher by
assault. These consisted of a division of XXIV Corps under Gen. Adelbert
Ames and a division of U.S. Colored Troops drawn from XXV Corps and
placed under Weitzel's direct command. On December 9, finally, Butler
advised Porter that the troops were at Fortress Monroe, ready to go. Three
days later, Porter said he was about ready, too, and would sail on the thirteenth, but that he had to lay over in Beaufort to take on ammunition.

In a rather pointless effort at deception, Butler put his transports in
motion before dawn on the thirteenth, with orders to make their way up
Chesapeake Bay and the Potomac in daylight for the benefit of Confederate
watchers. The ships came about in hours of darkness and made for the
point of rendezvous. On the evening of the fifteenth Butler's vessels were at
New Inlet, where they were supposed to join up with Porter's armada. The
perverse weather of this region provided Butler with three splendid days of
smooth seas and sunshine while he waited for Porter. But when the admiral
finally hove into view on the evening of the eighteenth, his arrival was
promptly greeted by rising winds and heavy seas, which ruled out any
hope of landing troops through the tumultuous surf.

By now the transport fleet—except for the *Baltic*, with General Ames
and a brigade aboard—had run low on coal and water. Leaving the *Baltic*
and her twelve hundred men behind on station, the rest of Butler's transports put back to Beaufort for fuel and supplies. The fine fair weather now
had given way to a full-force gale.

After refueling and resupplying, Butler sent a fast dispatch boat ahead
to inform Porter that his transports would be back at New Inlet on the
twenty-fourth. But when he arrived as promised on the afternoon of that
day, he found that Porter had already exploded the powder boat and begun
a bombardment of the fort.

The powder boat was a failure. Porter and the fleet drew off some
eighteen miles to watch, but they need not have bothered to go so far.
Timing devices set by the navy technicians failed to function, and what
finally touched off the explosion was a fire of oily kindling set ablaze as a
backup measure by the detail assigned to the job. These bold volunteers set
the timers, lit the blaze, and made off in all prudent haste to put miles
between them and the floating bomb. But instead of producing one coordinated bang, some of the charge blew, some burned, and some was merely
thrown high into the air. At Fort Fisher the garrison heard a considerable
roar and assumed only that a Yankee ship had blown its boilers. The explosion of the powder vessel had no effect whatever on the fort.

Fort Fisher had been elaborately constructed on the tip of a narrow peninsula flanked on one side by Cape Fear River and on the other by the open Atlantic. The land face, traversing the peninsula, featured an outer slope some twenty feet high, topped by a parapet twenty-five feet thick. On the side facing the sea, the same heavy construction extended a full mile. To guard against infantry attack, the Confederates had contrived that day's equivalent of a mine field on the approach to the land face. It consisted of a carpet of buried "torpedoes," all individually wired. Backing the mine field was a nine-foot-high palisade of sharpened logs, which extended all the way from the river to the seashore. This palisade was pierced to permit rifle fire on an advancing enemy and was curved inward so that fire could be concentrated toward the center. At the midpoint of the palisade was a redoubt housing two heavy guns that could be run out as needed.

Porter was prompt to send enthusiastic and totally false word to Navy Secretary Welles on the twenty-fourth: he said he had just about destroyed the Confederate fort.

"After getting the ships in position we silenced it in about an hour and a half, there being no troops here to take possession," Porter reported. "I am merely firing now to keep up practice."

In truth Porter's bombardment had done little or no damage to the massive works or to the fort's heavy armament. His statement that there were no Union troops present overlooked the fact that Ames was on hand with twelve hundred infantrymen aboard the *Baltic* and that Butler was due to arrive with the rest of the army contingent in a matter of hours. Porter's strange conduct continued on Christmas Day when, for reasons known only to himself, he directed his ships to fire in a desultory fashion rather than for effect.

"The firing this day was slow," he reported to Welles, "only sufficient to amuse the enemy while the army landed."

After getting off that dispatch, Porter sent word to Butler that the Confederate guns had been silenced, whereupon a landing some two miles north of the fort began. Two small outlying batteries on the sand dunes were quickly taken, along with 228 prisoners. The only Federal casualties were caused by misdirected fire from Porter's ships, which wounded ten men.

Now Weitzel, going forward to reconnoiter, found not only that Fort Fisher itself was essentially undamaged, but that the log palisade was still solidly in place. It was his estimate as an expert military engineer that there was no chance whatever of mounting a successful attack. General Curtis, commanding one of Ames's brigades, had been authorized by Ames to try an assault if he thought it could succeed, but Curtis agreed with Weitzel that the attempt would be suicidal. Confederate prisoners captured in the landing, meanwhile, said advance elements of a division under General Hoke

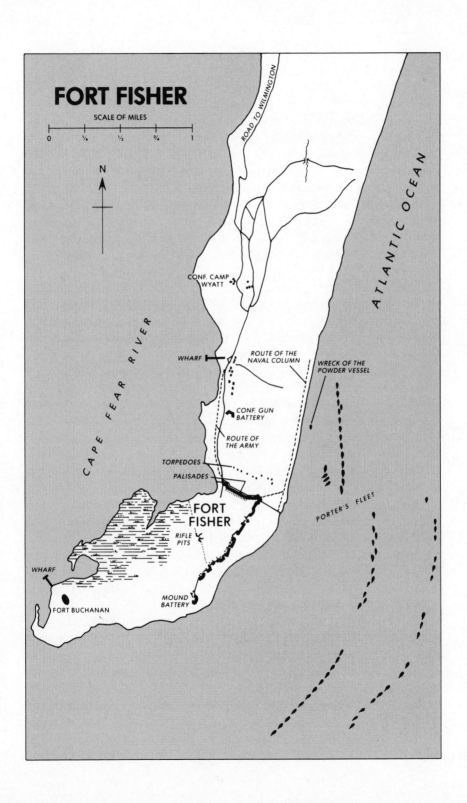

FORT FISHER

SCALE OF MILES

0   ¼   ½   ¾   1

N

ROAD TO WILMINGTON

ATLANTIC OCEAN

CAPE FEAR RIVER

CONF. CAMP WYATT

WHARF

ROUTE OF THE NAVAL COLUMN

WRECK OF THE POWDER VESSEL

CONF. GUN BATTERY

ROUTE OF THE ARMY

TORPEDOES

PALISADES

PORTER'S FLEET

FORT FISHER

RIFLE PITS

WHARF

FORT BUCHANAN

MOUND BATTERY

were already on the march to relieve the fort and that the rest of Hoke's troops were following close behind.

With the Confederates' strongest fort in front of him undamaged and Hoke's division behind him, Butler concluded to take Weitzel's well-considered advice and withdraw from the beach before disaster ensued. This he did, carrying off some three hundred prisoners as well as some captured artillery pieces. Besides the ten men wounded by naval gunfire, the expedition cost Butler two men: one man drowned in the heavy surf and one officer lost his way and was captured.

By now a severe storm was setting in, and the navy was running short of ammunition for its heavier guns. After further reconnaissance fully confirmed Weitzel's report, Butler was amply convinced that no further effort was justified. Thereupon he abandoned the enterprise and took his men and their prisoners back to base.

Porter, resupplying at Beaufort, at once began sending back a frantic stream of reports. Writing to Gideon Welles, Porter said of Fort Fisher, "It could have been taken on Christmas Day with 500 men, without losing a soldier; there were not twenty men in the forts, and those were poor, miserable, panic-stricken people, cowering there with fear. . . ."

Porter did not explain the extraordinary vision that enabled him, miles offshore, to count twenty rebels inside the fort and perceive that they were shaking with fright, nor did Welles blink at this estimate of the situation. Significantly enough, in view of immediate political developments that followed, Porter added: "If this temporary failure succeeds in sending General Butler into private life, it is not to be regretted, for it cost only a certain amount of shells, which I would have expended in a month's target practice anyhow."

Butler was indeed relieved of command right after the Fort Fisher episode. The circumstances suggest that this may well have been done through quick and improvised action on the part of his enemies rather than as the last step of a conspiracy among them. Porter's false reports, followed by that oddly knowing letter to Welles, provide only a dark hint of something deeper. What really went on in Porter's mind as he directed his fleet in that first bombardment is beyond anybody's guess.

Did Butler sail into a setup? Porter's fire support for Butler had been remarkably ineffective. But his second such effort, in the next assault on Fort Fisher under a different ground-forces commander, was little less than awesome. Porter's mad letters and reports critical of Butler were released right away to the press, while Butler's own report was withheld from publication, somehow managing to go astray for some time in a Washington shuffle. The failure of the powder boat was laid at Butler's door, although the navy had been in charge of preparing it, siting it, and detonating its explosives. And as though by program, Grant did move immediately on

David D. Porter
Battles and Leaders of the Civil War

Gideon Welles
Battles and Leaders of the Civil War

Butler's return to have him relieved of his command and sent home to sit out the rest of the war in Lowell. The order was promptly issued "by direction of the President," and it was drawn and signed by Halleck. The entire package could not have been wrapped more neatly.

Although Porter's strange conduct in the assault commanded by Butler appears beyond any satisfactory explanation, the fact that it was strange is beyond dispute. Col. William Lamb, the Confederate officer directing the defense of Fort Fisher, testified later that "the fire of the fleet had been diffuse, not calculated to effect any particular damage, and so wild that at least one third of the missiles fell in the river or beyond the fort or in the bordering marshes."

Colonel Lamb entirely agreed with Weitzel's report. "When Butler's skirmishers approached I purposely withheld the fire of infantry and artillery until an attack should be made in force," Lamb testified. "Only one gun on the land face had been disabled, and I could have opened a fire of grape and canister on the narrow beach, which no troops could have survived."

Against Lamb's strength returns (over fourteen hundred men in the garrison, most of them veterans) Porter's vision of twenty cowering Confederates was sheer fantasy. But Lamb's testimony was not yet in the record. In the meantime Porter's assessment was given credence and accomplished the purpose he intended. It was not until months later, after holding extensive hearings and collecting reams of testimony, that the Committee on the Conduct of the War officially declared that Butler's action at Fort Fisher had been entirely correct. By that time, of course, it came as cold comfort indeed to the general.

Upon removing Butler from command, Grant put General Terry in charge of a beefed-up force assembled for a second assault upon Fort Fisher. Moreover he wrote Porter, offering a blank check: "A division of troops numbering from 4,000 to 5,000 men will be in readiness to sail to you at an hour's notice. In addition to this, if it becomes necessary, I will send all the men that can be used."

On January 8, with wild weather still prevailing, the second army force joined Porter. By now the admiral was telling General Terry that the Confederates had actually abandoned Fort Fisher on Christmas Day. However, to attack what Porter was describing as an empty fort, Terry five days later was asking Grant to send reinforcements, even as he landed his eighty-five hundred troops for the first assault.

Now that remarkable change in Porter's tactics was clearly to be seen. This time there was no more desultory fire intended only to "amuse the enemy." All day and all night on the thirteenth and fourteenth and until 3:30 in the afternoon of the fifteenth, Porter's guns blasted the rebel ramparts.

Terry's troops landed two miles north of the fort. Their first assignment

Adelbert Ames
Sophia Smith Collection

William T. Sherman
Frank Leslie's Illustrated History
of the Civil War

was to prepare a rear defense line facing north to guard against possible attack by Confederate forces moving down from Wilmington. To their front, however, that formidable palisade of pointed logs was still in place undamaged. Terry saw that no attack was possible against that barrier, so he asked Porter if he would redirect his fire to destroy it. Porter at once cooperated by shifting his heavier vessels so that their guns were brought to bear on the stockade. Naval gunfire made some openings in the palisade, but it remained for infantrymen wielding axes to cut enough holes to make an assault possible. The division commanded by General Ames finally moved to the attack, incurring casualties not only from Confederate artillery and musketry but also from the shells fired by Porter's fleet.

Porter himself, entering into the spirit of things, sent two thousand sailors and marines ashore armed only with cutlasses and pistols to attack the looming mass of the fortifications that faced the sea. Porter's remarkable order was that his men were to "board the fort on the run in a seamanlike way." Few of the naval detachment even reached the fort in this suicidal charge. Some three hundred sailors fell in the assault, and the survivors who were able to do so sensibly fled in disorder. Porter later said in an offhand way, giving testimony to Congress, "I suppose the whole thing was over in fifteen minutes, as far as the sailors were concerned, for they were cut down like sheep."

In seven hours of heavy fighting, much of it after dark, Ames's men secured the land face of the fort, after which the Confederates surrendered. The attack had cost Ames's division some five hundred sixty casualties, and next morning the casualty list was lengthened when the fort's main magazine exploded, killing or wounding another one hundred thirty Union soldiers. The Confederates lost some four hundred casualties out of a defending force of twenty-six hundred. A few of the defenders escaped across the river, but most of the surviving garrison became prisoners.

Somehow the totally destroyed and empty fort described by Porter had put up fierce resistance. But it had fallen at last, and now came a time when Porter's reports would be assessed for what they were worth. A very angry Confederate leader, Gen. W.H.C. Whiting, wounded and taken prisoner at Fort Fisher, provided written testimony. Like Colonel Lamb, General Whiting said that Porter's bombardment in the first attempt against the fort had caused few casualties and inflicted negligible damage. His anger was directed against General Bragg. Whiting said Bragg was close by with ample troops and could have bagged the entire Federal landing force if he had moved forward instead of standing aloof. Not only that, Whiting said Bragg's continuing inaction at the time of the second assault was the cause of the Confederate defeat.

As for Porter himself, he now professed to see the fort in a different light. No longer was it a deserted pile of wreckage manned by twenty

W. H.C. Whiting
Battles and Leaders of the Civil War

Braxton Bragg
Battles and Leaders of the Civil War

William Lamb
Battles and Leaders of the Civil War

Alfred H. Terry
The Great Rebellion

cowering men. "I have since visited Fort Fisher and the adjoining works," he wrote Welles on January 17, "and I find their strength greatly beyond what I had conceived. An engineer might be excusable in saying that they could not be captured except by regular siege. I wonder even now how it was done. . . . "

And only one week later Porter was writing Welles another rambling screed, this time bitterly complaining that Grant was hogging all the credit for the Fort Fisher victory. The navy alone deserved the glory, said Porter. Grant sent too few men. Without the help of the navy, Grant would never have become a lieutenant general in the first place. And Porter was seeing phantoms: "I am uneasy now for fear that the enemy may turn all their force this way, and throw forty thousand men into the peninsula. They would retake Fort Fisher, even with the gunboats we have here, and turn the guns of the fort on us."

Grant knew little about Fort Fisher and cared even less, Porter complained, since he was leaving it with only about seven thousand men to hold it.

Why the level-headed Welles retained confidence in Porter, after receiving constant floods of wild messages like these, remains mostly a mystery. There is one clue, however, in a typical Porter paragraph addressed to the navy secretary. Porter leaves off castigating Grant long enough to say: "I tell it to you for your own personal satisfaction, that you may know and feel that you are entitled to the entire credit for getting this expedition off, and for its success. I am merely the agent. . . . No country under the sun ever raised a navy as you have done in the same time. . . ." And so forth, Porter the courtier, in full voice.

Welles noted in his diary on January 14 that there was much speculation concerning Butler's removal. While he was no admirer of the general and was pleased to see him relieved of his command, Welles had his own ideas on why Grant had taken the action: "The quidnuncs and indeed most of the public impute [Butler's] dismissal . . . to the Wilmington failure," Welles wrote. "But it will soon be known that General Grant desired to get rid of him. Butler's greater intellect overshadowed Grant, and annoyed and embarrassed the General-in-Chief. . . . Of course the Rebels and Copperheads will be gratified, and do not conceal their joy. . . ."

Welles was oversimplifying. True, Fort Fisher was the excuse, not the reason, for Butler's sudden removal from command. The move neatly suited the Byzantine politics of the Lincoln administration. Stanton had reacted sharply to Capitol Hill talk that Butler should and would replace him as war secretary. Seward was inimical. Halleck, whose hatred of Butler was as intense as it was unjustified, was sniping at all times. And, above all, Lincoln had been reelected and no longer needed Butler's help and support.

Butler's war career was over, but the closing months of the conflict were to bring him a certain modicum of satisfaction. A desperate Confederate attack on the strong line he had established north of the James turned into a rebel disaster. Butler's black regiments, commanded by his friend Weitzel, marched from that line to take over Richmond. Butler's black regiments also, to the great anger of General Ord, were the first to detect the Confederate abandonment of Petersburg, and without ado (or Ord's permission) were the first to enter that fallen city. Butler had been denied a share in the final victory, but with what he had done while in command of the Army of the James he was forever well content.

52

Butler now had to complete only two formalities in order to sever his connection with the United States Army: he had to settle his financial accounts with the War Department, and he had to resign his commission. Professional testimony from both Union and Confederate participants had confirmed his judgment in refusing to court bloodbath and disaster at Fort Fisher. Proud of his military record but with no further useful service to perform, Butler looked forward to resuming his law practice. Most of all he relished the prospect of being his own man again, no longer under the chafing restraints of a discipline that required him to obey orders and directives from superiors, many of whom he clearly regarded as dullards, and some as not only stupid but entirely devoid of scruples.

Butler's state of mind was revealed in a lengthy letter he wrote at this troubled time to a stranger. Eugene H. Gilbert, a young man from Waukegan, Illinois, had written him to ask if he could study law as a clerk in his office. Butler tactfully refused the request, but he provided counsel and added some thoughtful commentary.

> I hope your father will permit you to study the law, and would advise you that I would take two years' study (and, my young friend, it must be hard and efficient study to do any good) at Cambridge Law School. I would then advise going into an office of some good lawyer of large practice in the state where you propose to make your home, and then take a full year of study and hard study and drudgery at the practice to learn the details, and then I think you will be a *lawyer*, and there is, in my belief, no higher title.

As he concluded his letter, Butler's suppressed resentments spilled over.

> Never hold office. Hold yourself above it. An officer is a servant. I never held [an office] till the one I hold in the Army, and that made me a slave to the caprices of other people, whom I neither loved nor

respected. Be in the high position which every good lawyer can easily hold. Call no man master, make yourself felt. Be independent.

Eager to surrender his commission and return to civilian life, Butler telegraphed Halleck asking formal permission to go to Washington to settle his accounts. Halleck replied by mail with a brusque paragraph: permission denied. Butler, however, had already left for the capital before Halleck's letter reached Lowell. Not that he was paying much attention now to Halleck anyway, a man whom he openly termed "a lying, treacherous, hypocritical scoundrel with no moral sense."

The War Department accounts were settled—Butler always got receipts for everything—but he remained a major general a few months longer. Washington thought that he might have just one more duty to perform as a general and as a lawyer, that of prosecuting Jefferson Davis, should the Confederate leader be tried before a military commission. Davis was presiding in bitterness at this time over nothing more than the remnants of the fast-dissolving Confederacy.

In March, as overwhelming Federal forces were closing in on the last brave tatters of the Confederate armies, Butler directed his energies toward ensuring that the peace which was about to come would be worth all the blood and treasure that had been poured out to obtain it. To Butler and the Radical wing of the Republican party, this meant that several key aims had to be realized: guaranteed civil rights for the freed slaves, trial and punishment of the Confederate leaders, and armed supervision of the rebel states until they earned the right to rejoin the Union. Butler's plan for dealing with the conquered states was, in fact, the most radical of all. He proposed that they should be wiped off the map, their old boundaries obliterated, and their territories reconstituted into districts which, in time, would be admitted into the Union as entirely new states.

The Radicals had some hope of gaining influence with Lincoln as he entered upon his second term. Butler and his powerful associates had reason to believe that he would appoint a Radical to a major cabinet post, and among themselves they agreed that the appointment should go to Butler. The Radicals hoped to see him named secretary of state.

Butler himself met with the president on April 11. And then, just three days later, the assassin John Wilkes Booth capped the tragedy of civil war with the murder of Lincoln, while another conspirator, Lewis Paine, severely wounded Seward in an attempted assassination. For a brief moment, at least, political maneuvering was put aside as the North went into mourning.

Ben and Sarah were on their way from Washington to New York and had got as far as New Jersey when word of the assassination reached them. They immediately turned back to the capital. Butler was not certain what he might be called upon to do in the crisis, but he felt he should make himself available. He was, after all, still technically the army's ranking major general. Butler reported to Stanton who, in this emergency, found himself practically in charge of the federal government. The general also conferred with a bewildered Andrew Johnson, outlining for the new president the course the Radicals would expect of him.

Although strongly supported in both the House and Senate, Butler's proposed appointment to the cabinet did not occur. Toward midsummer, as Johnson's policies veered from the course demanded by the Radicals, Butler told his backers he no longer wanted any part in the Johnson administration. "All is wrong," he wrote Sen. Ben Wade. "We are losing the just results of this four years' struggle."

Johnson, however, did call upon him for advice as to how the government should deal with Jefferson Davis, who was now a prisoner at Fortress Monroe, and Butler was quick to respond. He proposed that Davis be tried for treason by a military commission to be made up of an odd number of major generals, with Butler himself presiding as the senior general. He assumed that the commission would find Davis guilty. Thereafter, he said, the case could be taken up on appeal to the Supreme Court, ensuring that Davis would have every remedy available to him to secure full and fair trial. Johnson, however, was in no frame of mind to act in haste on the Davis case or anything else. Eventually, after Davis had endured two years in close confinement and two more years under civil indictment, all charges against him were dropped.

Summer of 1865 was a relaxed and pleasant time for Butler. War and politics were put at least partly aside while he enjoyed the company of his family and friends at Bay View, the seaside property near Gloucester which he had bought while sitting out his exile from New Orleans. Butler and his sons, Paul and Little Benny, camped out under canvas on the beach, while Sarah and Blanche stayed at a nearby farmhouse. Later Butler would build a substantial summer home on the property. But for now the forty-seven acres of sand and scrub served as base for a lazy summer of fishing, swimming, sailing, and lying about on the beach.

The beachfront property soon served yet another purpose when Butler took it in his head to run for Congress. He had no wish to disturb the tenure of the congressman representing his Lowell district so, in the fall elections of 1866, he declared the Bay View tent his home and ran to represent the Essex District in Congress. He was overwhelmingly elected. Despite frantic cries of his opponent that the whole procedure was illegal, Butler's election was formally certified, and he took his place in the House for what was to be the first of four consecutive terms.

Butler and the Radicals watched in rising anger as President Johnson veered ever farther from the strict course of reconstruction demanded by an overwhelming majority in the Congress. Finally the conflict resulted in Johnson's impeachment. The Radicals were determined that Congress should control the military occupation of the South; Johnson, equally stubborn, insisted on his powers as commander in chief to install military governors of his own choosing. In defiance of Congress, Johnson attempted to fire War Secretary Stanton and removed hard-line generals like Phil Sheridan from occupation duties.

The break soon came. The House voted to impeach Johnson, and Butler was chosen to be the lead speaker in presenting the case when it came to be tried before the Senate. In three days of nonstop work, scarcely pausing to eat or sleep, Butler prepared a detailed and lawyerlike indictment. His two-hour speech, setting forth the charges, opened the proceedings. Forty thousand copies of it were printed and distributed.

Johnson, finally, was sustained in the Senate. The two-thirds majority needed to remove him from office fell short by only a single vote, but the narrow margin was deceptive. Indications were that other senators were prepared to rescue the president if called upon—they having voted "for the record" only, with no intention of seeing Johnson actually deposed. The more-or-less hidden issue had to do with the succession. Ben Wade of Ohio—president pro-tem of the Senate, but by no means a universal choice among his colleagues—would have become president if Johnson had been convicted. Wade's opponents had no intention of letting that happen.

After the impeachment drama, Butler's continuing effort in Congress centered on currency reform. Like Senator Wade, Butler was a Greenbacker, preaching a heresy hated and feared by the banking community, the monopolies, and big business generally. Butler, anticipating modern government financing by half a century or more, held that a simple government note was amply secured by the wealth and taxing power of the government and needed no equivalency in gold or silver to be universally accepted as money. Throughout his legislative career Ben never ceased to advocate the calculated issuance of paper money in response to supply and demand.

On balance the early postwar years were happy ones for the Butler family. Ben himself, ever restless, practiced law in Boston, New York, and Washington. He added to his financial interest in the textile mills and even launched an entirely new one, the first American mill to produce flags and bunting. He spotted a likely outcropping of granite while sunning himself at Bay View, bought the site, and set up a quarry. He made money in railroad stock. He bought up farmlands and installed Negro families to work the farms on shares. He built a fine new house in Washington. He replaced that tent at Bay View, which once had served him so well, with a solid stone residence overlooking Ipswich Bay. Sarah, as always, was at his side.

Butler campaigned for monetary reform, for fair labor practices and

safe working conditions, for the dismantling of monopolies, and even for—
of all horrid notions—extending to women the right to vote. All of these
things were anathema to the rich and powerful and their paid press, with
the result that Butler was forever the subject of an endless torrent of editorial abuse, cruel caricature, and outright libel.

Butler, as always, relished the challenge of pitting wit and solid argument
against the sheer money power of his political enemies. In his first campaign
for reelection to Congress, he was opposed by Richard Henry Dana Jr., the
distinguished attorney who had won early fame as the author of *Two Years
Before the Mast*. Dana's campaign was well financed by the banking and
business interests. But the elegant candidate's effort to woo ordinary voters
became a joke when he told an audience of working men that once, when he
was a sailor, "I was as dirty as any of you." After that widely quoted howler,
Dana got less than 10 percent of the votes cast in the election.

In the fall of 1869, after much soul-searching, Ben and Sarah sent their
boys, Paul and Bennie, to spend two years with Sarah's sister Susan in Frank-
furt, where her husband, William Prentiss Webster, was the United States
consul general. Two years of schooling in Germany, they felt, would be of
great value to the boys. But Sarah was desperately lonely at the parting.

"The children are out at sea," she wrote Blanche. "The wind is blowing
freely from the northwest, the rain is beating against the windows. . . ."

She pictured the shipboard scene as she imagined it in the heavy
weather:

Poor little Benny is cowering in his berth, sick and wretched. Paul
I hope is well and able to take care of him. It is not promising to start
off in a storm. Poor boys. They will feel lonely tonight. . . . We have
left them so many times, after the war began, always with reluctance
and sadness; now they have left us and gone so far away. . . .

Blanche, now a bright, competent, and beautiful young woman of
twenty-two, was managing her father's household in the capital and taking
her place in Washington society. There was no dearth of suitors, but she
was attracted especially to young Gen. Adelbert Ames, now a United States
senator from the semireconstructed state of Mississippi. In April 1870 their
engagement was announced. On July 21 of that year they were married in
Saint Anne's Church in Lowell, with the Reverend Dr. Edson, Butler's old
friend, performing the ceremony. It was an event.

"Ten thousand persons cheered loudly when the bridal party entered
the church," said one newspaper account. "There were about six hundred
persons admitted into the church by cards of invitation."

Butler and his new son-in-law had quickly become cronies in Washington, exchanging notes, planning political moves, breakfasting and dining

General Butler's yacht, *America*

together, and competing vigorously at the billiard table. Blanche, also a billiards enthusiast, could beat them both except, as she complained, when her father cheated. Ames admired the older man's intellect and accomplishments and constantly sought his counsel. This was a marriage with which both Ben and Sarah were well pleased.

In 1871 Butler began what was to become a long and stubborn campaign to become governor of Massachusetts, losing out in a struggle for the Republican nomination. In 1872 he challenged the Republican governor for the nomination and lost again.

Perhaps to console himself, Butler turned to his avocation as a seafaring man and bought the splendid racing yacht *America*. This was the yacht that, in 1851, had won the challenge race around the Isle of Wight sponsored by the Royal Yacht Squadron of England, capturing the trophy which ever thereafter was to be known as the America's Cup. The *America* would be a prized family possession for the next thirty years.

The years flew by, not without their portion of grief. Sarah's sister Harriet, Butler's favorite, died in 1866. In the autumn of 1870, Butler's mother died and was laid to rest beside Andrew in the family plot. "All there is good in me I owe to her," wrote Butler as he informed his sons in Germany of their grandmother's passing. In July of 1873 Sarah's brother and Ben's lifelong friend, Fisher Hildreth, died after a long and agonizing illness. By this time Sarah herself was in failing health.

Butler fought his last lonely battle in Congress in February of 1875, as he tried to achieve passage of a long-pending civil rights act broadly outlawing racial discrimination. In the interval between 1865 and 1875, largely by force of organized terrorism, outright slavery had been effectively replaced in the South by de facto slavery, and the forces of reform were in full retreat. Unwisely, Butler had thought his congressional seat was secure enough to permit him to campaign outside the state in behalf of the Republican party. A Democratic resurgence in Massachusetts, however, had cost him the election. Now he was a lame duck, serving out the last two months of his term. It was a telling commentary on the course of the postwar years that Butler's principal opponent in the civil rights debate was Congressman Alexander H. Stevenson of Georgia—the former vice president of the Confederacy.

In the end Butler achieved only a hollow victory. The bill was passed, but only after significant amendments, including the excision of a section calling for integrated schools. There was no provision for enforcing even what remained, except that it authorized blacks to bring lawsuits in federal courts to redress individual acts of discrimination. Finally, although not immediately challenged, the much-mangled Civil Rights Act would be declared unconstitutional by the Supreme Court in 1883.

During this time Sarah had been troubled by a persistent inflammation

Darius Cobb's painting of Butler, 1890
Butler's Book

Butler was seventy-two when Darius Cobb painted this portrait. The flower in Butler's lapel has sentimental significance as a quiet tribute to his late wife. He always wore a boutonniere each day, just as he had in happier times, when Sarah never failed to supply him with a fresh posy from their gardens.

of the throat, which now and again grew serious enough to cause her difficulty in breathing. In the summer months of 1875, the condition grew worse. A Washington specialist, after examining her throat in March of 1876, pronounced her illness merely a minor inflammation and prescribed some medication, mostly for Sarah's taut nerves. But now Sarah wanted to go home to Massachusetts, where she could consult with her own doctors. She had a despairing suspicion that the problem required surgery.

The end came suddenly. Ben and Sarah headed home on April 3. Three days later she was admitted to Massachusetts General Hospital in Boston, where surgeons found the growth in her throat to be cancerous and inoperable. A tracheotomy was performed to ease her breathing. On April 8 Sarah died quietly and without pain. She was fifty-eight.

All the world knew Butler's formidable strengths and skills; only Sarah was admitted behind the walls of Yankee granite to that secret place where Butler hid a sensitive and compassionate heart. Prideful Boston Brahmins, vituperative journalists, diehard white supremacists, anonymous writers of poison-pen letters—all were convinced after serious and unrelenting effort that Butler was too tough to be hurt. Sarah knew better, and when he was wounded she bled also. But neither let the world know. Nor did Ben let the world in now to observe the depth of his grief. With almost ponderous force, he returned to his law practice and to politics, finding solace in hard work. From Washington he wrote Blanche: "I am well, but very lonely at the table, and when I am alone. . . ."

In 1878 Butler turned again to the notion of becoming governor of Massachusetts. By now it was clear that the commonwealth's tightly controlled party machine would never let him win the Republican nomination, so Butler ran as an independent candidate. But even with some Democratic support, he lost. The following year he ran as the regular Democratic nominee, only to lose again as the Democrats, divided as ever, quarreled among themselves.

Ben's boys, Paul and Ben Israel, were now young men of consequence. Paul, with a talent for business, was in charge of one of the family enterprises, the United States Cartridge Company, which was prospering under his management. Ben Israel, the erstwhile "poor little Benny" so favored by Sarah, had graduated from West Point and served his stint on the western frontier. Afterward he had studied law at Columbia, and passed his bar examination and now, in the autumn of 1881, was preparing to become his father's law partner.

That September Butler headed northward on the *America* for a vacation cruise. Benny, rounding out a pleasant summer at Bay View with Blanche and her family, had planned to go along on the cruise with his father but, feeling feverish and ill, he elected to stay behind. To Blanche's dismay Benny's condition, now diagnosed as Bright's disease, worsened.

Ben Israel Butler
Sophia Smith Collection

Paul Butler
Sophia Smith Collection

Benjamin F. Butler as governor of Massachusetts, 1882-84

She managed to get word to her father, who immediately set course for home, crowding on all the sail the fast yacht could carry. As the *America* rounded toward Bay View, Ben's heart sank: the flag at the family home was flying at half mast. Young Ben, Sarah's beloved "poor little Benny," had died that very morning.

Now Butler drew even closer to Paul, who shared his keen interest in business affairs as Benny had not. The antidote for sorrow was now a familiar one: work, more work, and politics. Running in 1882 as the candidate of a united Democratic party, Butler won the election and took office as the governor of his state. As governor of Massachusetts he cleaned up graft and corruption, most notably at the Tewksbury Almshouse, a state institution for paupers, where his investigation found that officials far gone in depravity were even selling the bodies of indigents to medical schools. He brought some order to the administration of the state's affairs, reorganizing budget and purchasing procedures. As he had in Congress, Butler crusaded for extending the franchise to women, much to the dismay of old-line politicians. He called for mandatory shorter working hours and better pay for workers.

Butler did not neglect to exercise his sardonic sense of humor in setting snares for his political enemies, as when he issued the traditional Fast Day Proclamation in 1883, calling for the customary "day of public humiliation, fasting, and prayer." Ben fully expected that even this pious exercise would be assailed—as was everything else he did as governor—in every Tory pulpit in Boston. So he took a certain delight in exhuming a long-forgotten proclamation that had been composed by the devout and much revered Gov. Christopher Gore in 1810. Butler signed and issued it as his own, adding only a partial paragraph. As Butler had expected, the Fast Day sermons lambasted the proclamation, as did many of the establishment newspapers. When, finally, the press called upon Butler to respond to his critics, Ben blandly admitted the source of "his" proclamation, and the whole state enjoyed a chuckle.

In more serious political pioneering, Butler appointed a highly qualified Negro lawyer, George L. Ruffin, to the bench—the state's first black judge. No Irish Catholic had ever been appointed to judicial office, either, until Butler named Michael J. McCafferty to the bench. Both served with distinction for the rest of their lives.

None of this, not even the Tewksbury exposé, sat well with the Boston establishment. They showed their resentment in a remarkably petty way when it became time for the governor, as custom dictated, to appear at Harvard's annual commencement exercises. Led by Butler's ancient adversary, Ebenezer Rockwood Hoar, the Harvard Board of Overseers voted to withhold from Butler the usual honorary degree which Massachusetts governors had always received at these ceremonies. In taking this action they overruled the Harvard faculty, which had voted to award Butler the customary degree.

Inwardly seething, Butler arrived at Harvard in high ceremonial style, formally dressed in civilian attire but accompanied by an honor guard of the military in full-dress uniform. The governor's open carriage was drawn by a team of six matched horses; his mounted guard of honor followed in close formation behind.

Butler had with him a white-hot speech he had written for the occasion, but he never gave it. Charles William Eliot, the renowned Harvard president, much embarrassed by the churlish action of Hoar and the Overseers, was his host at a faculty luncheon. Dr. Eliot and the faculty members took pains to make Butler welcome and to disown, as far as they could, the snub. Butler, responding to their warmth, improvised a speech. It was light and friendly in tone to match his hospitable reception by the faculty. Except as a courteous gesture, the degree meant little to Butler anyway. He already held the LL.D., which Williams College had given him several years before.

Defeated for reelection by a resurgent Republican party the following year, Butler turned his attention to presidential politics. As a delegate to the Democratic convention of 1884, he opposed the nomination of Grover Cleveland. Democrat Butler favored a strong tariff to protect American industry and American jobs—a position that was more in harmony with Republican doctrine—and he considered Cleveland weak on this issue. After Cleveland won the nomination, Butler attempted to marshal his Greenbackers, antimonopolists, and labor groups in forming a third party: the People's party. As the candidate of this coalition, Butler received few votes in the November balloting, and failed to block Cleveland's election in the Electoral College, as he had hoped to do.

Now, at sixty-six, finding little hope or comfort in either the Republican or Democratic party, Butler considered that his active participation in politics had better be put behind him. He devoted himself ever more actively to the practice of law, spending much of his time in Washington, where he frequently had several cases at a time pending before the Supreme Court.

On a raw, cold January day in 1893, Butler stood bareheaded in the rain while yet another old friend was laid to rest. These occasions were getting ever more frequent as the general entered his seventy-third year, but Ben never shirked the duty, however infirm his health or however inclement the blustery New England weather. This time he already had a bad cold, and by the time he returned home, soaked to the skin, he was feeling feverish and congested.

Butler never shirked his duty to his clients, either, so despite the urgent pleas of his family he set off that night for Washington, where he had an appeal pending before the Supreme Court. Accompanied only by his valet,

Governor Butler and escort on the way to graduation exercises at Harvard, 1883

Albert West, Butler "took the cars," as railroad travelers termed it in those days, for the long, tedious journey to the capital.

Ben's cold grew worse. At the Butler residence in Washington, around midnight on January 11, Butler's valet, sleeping in an adjoining room, was awakened when he heard the general coughing violently. West quickly went to Butler, who brusquely informed him he was all right and told him to go back to bed. West, who knew better, awoke the household, and a doctor was called. Somewhat after 1:00, comatose, Butler breathed his last, succumbing to the severe pneumonia that had taxed his heart beyond its ability to sustain the fight.

As the family assembled in Lowell, Butler's body was accompanied on the long journey home by an honor guard of the Grand Army of the Republic. Two members of the eight-man guard were veterans of the U.S. Colored Troops, and one of them wore the medal of honor that Butler had awarded him for valor in the campaigning for Richmond and Petersburg.

At Lowell it immediately became apparent that the Butler residence could not begin to accommodate the throngs of mourners who wanted to pay their last respects to the general. Butler, therefore, lay in state in commodious Huntington Hall on Merrimack Street, close by Saint Anne's Church. There some thirty thousand of his fellow citizens passed by the bier. The *Lowell Daily Courier* described the scene:

> The long line in double file moved steadily by the casket and around to the flowers hour after hour. Officers all along the room told the people quietly to keep in motion. There was not a sound but the quiet tramp of feet, and the mellow light in the midst of the dense folds of black made a scene never to be forgotten. It was a hall no longer, but the tent of a dead brigadier general, with his sad soldiers on guard for the last time.

At 5:30 P.M. the hall was cleared, and Paul and Blanche went in to look for the last time on the face of their father. There were still throngs outside the building, so the doors were opened again from 6:30 until 10:00, and the mourners continued their sad, slow procession past the casket. The *Courier* reporter observed one war veteran who broke into sobbing tears. Another mourner, an old Irish woman, paused to blow three sad kisses toward the general's coffin.

Butler's home city honored him with a funeral that would have been appropriate for an emperor. All commerce was shut down for the day by proclamation of the mayor. Facades of the downtown buildings were draped in black. Many thousands lined the streets to stand in silence as the funeral procession, more than a mile and a half long, made its way through the heart of the city.

Butler's funeral procession

Butler's body was borne in a hearse drawn by six black horses, accompanied by a troop of cavalry, a battery of artillery, the infantry of the 6th Massachusetts, and the Lowell High School Battalion. In this long, last march, military bands played dirges, while the bells—those solemn, deep-toned, brazen bells of Lowell—tolled from all the mill towers, the schoolhouses, the church belfries. At several intersections the grieving throngs pressing forward brought the procession to a halt.

After the services at Saint Anne's Church, Butler went to his final rest in the old Hildreth Burying Ground, the artillery thundering a last salute, and the firing party of infantry a final volley. The general was home for eternity, at last again beside his beloved Sarah. And there his family erected his monument, on which the inscription reads:

BENJAMIN FRANKLIN
BUTLER
JURIST   SOLDIER   STATESMAN
HIS TALENTS WERE DEVOTED TO
THE SERVICE OF HIS COUNTRY
AND THE ADVANCEMENT OF HIS
FELLOW MEN

The engraving on stone covers all of Butler's many-faceted career. But for Butler the soldier, the general himself wrote his own best epitaph:

"In all military movements I never met with disaster, nor uselessly sacrificed the lives of my men."

53

Exeunt Omnes

Adelbert Ames became governor of Mississippi in 1873. There he fought a lone, losing struggle against the Ku Klux Klan and other resurgent rebel terrorists. His white supremacist opponents—after a campaign of lynchings, shootings, and arson—gained overwhelming control of the legislature in 1875 and forced him to resign under threat of impeachment. Afterward he became a successful businessman and inventor. He patented a number of inventions, ranging from flour-mill machinery to an ingenious pencil sharpener. After service in the Spanish-American War, he lived to become the oldest surviving Civil War general. Ames died in 1933.

Blanche Butler Ames became a painter and sculptor of some talent while raising the six Ames children: Butler, Edith, Sarah, Blanche, Adelbert, and Jessie. The oldest, Butler, entered West Point as the nominee of his grandfather, Ben Butler, and won his commission.

John Albion Andrew, 1818-1867, was governor of Massachusetts through 1866. After peace came he was an outspoken advocate of a soft policy toward the South.

Pierre Gustave Toutant Beauregard became a railroad president after the war, was adjutant general of Louisiana, manager of the Louisiana lottery, and superintendent of public works in New Orleans.

John C. Breckinridge fled to Cuba when the war ended and later lived as an exile in Europe. In 1869 he returned to his home in Lexington, Kentucky.

Simon Cameron became a rich industrialist and founded a Republican political machine in Pennsylvania that endured almost unchallenged until the 1930s. At age seventy-eight he figured in a lively scandal when he was sued for breach of promise by Mrs. Mary Oliver, a forty-year-old clerk in the War Department. Cameron won the lawsuit. His attorney was Benjamin F. Butler.

David Glasgow Farragut became Admiral of the Navy in 1866, the first to hold that rank. His attorney, Benjamin F. Butler, helped him settle

Blanche and Adelbert Ames and their children (l to r): Blanche, Butler, Jessie, Sarah, Adelbert, Edith

his claims for prize money won through the capture of Confederate vessels during the war. Farragut died in 1870.

Gustavus Vasa Fox retired in 1866 as assistant secretary of the navy (a post that had been created specifically for him) and became one of the richest men in New England. Fox died in 1883.

Henry W. Halleck at war's end assumed command of the Division of the James, with headquarters at Richmond. Later he was in command of the Military Division of the Pacific until 1869, when he became commander of the Military Division of the South, a post he held until his death in 1872.

Reverdy Johnson became minister to Great Britain in 1868 at the age of seventy-two and enjoyed a lively social life in London in the company of his ex-Confederate friends there. He initiated negotiations that eventuated in a trifling "bargain sale" settlement of American claims against Britain for the enormous losses incurred through British aid to the Confederacy. While Charles Sumner and Ben Butler, among many others, thought ceding all of Canada would scarcely redress the wrong, Britain finally got off with a payment of $15.5 million.

John Bankhead Magruder, "Prince John," fled to Mexico where he became a major general in the army of the Emperor Maximilian. After Maximilian's overthrow and execution, he returned to the United States and went on the lecture circuit with a dramatic presentation of his adventures in Mexico.

David D. Porter became superintendent of the U.S. Naval Academy and later was named Admiral of the Navy after the death of Farragut.

William Henry Seward capped his career with the purchase of Alaska from Russia for $7.2 million, of which $200,000 somehow "disappeared" as uncataloged expenses.

Edwin McMasters Stanton resigned as secretary of war after President Johnson's impeachment failed in the Senate. In December 1869 President Grant appointed him to the Supreme Court, but he died before taking office.

Godfrey Weitzel was transferred after the war to an obscure post in Texas, where his chief worry was the widespread scurvy that afflicted his troops for lack of fresh vegetables. He was confirmed as a brigadier general in the Regulars.

Gideon Welles left office with President Johnson on March 4, 1869. As a noted journalist he wrote extensively for the *Atlantic Monthly*, among other publications. Welles continued to resent the Seward-Porter conspiracy, which had scuttled his efforts to relieve Fort Sumter, and in 1874 wrote a slender book (*Seward and Lincoln*) in which he discoursed on the subject. Welles died in 1878. His famous diary was first published in successive issues of the *Atlantic* in 1909.

Appendix 1

[Butler's Civil Code]

Proclamation of General Butler
Headquarters, Department of the Gulf, May 1, 1862

The city of New Orleans and its environs, with all its interior and exterior defenses, having surrendered to the combined naval and land forces of the United States, who have come to restore order, maintain public tranquility, and enforce peace and quiet under the laws and constitution of the United States, the major-general commanding hereby proclaims the object and purposes of the government of the United States in thus taking possession of New Orleans and the state of Louisiana, and the rules and regulations by which the laws of the United States will be for the present, and during the state of war, enforced and maintained, for the plain guidance of all good citizens of the United States, as well as others who may have heretofore been in rebellion against their authority.

Thrice before has the city of New Orleans been rescued from the hands of a foreign government, and still more calamitous domestic insurrection, by the money and arms of the United States. It has of late been under the military control of the rebel forces, and at each time, in the judgment of the commanders of the military forces holding it, it has been found necessary to preserve order and maintain quiet by an administration of martial law. Even during the interim from its evacuation by the rebel soldiers and its actual possession by the soldiers of the United States, the civil authorities have found it necessary to call for the intervention of an armed body known as the European Legion, to preserve the public tranquility. The commanding general, therefore, will cause the city to be guarded, until the restoration of the United States authority and his further orders, by martial law.

All persons in arms against the United States are required to surrender themselves, with their arms, equipments, and munitions of war. The body known as the European Legion, not being understood to be in arms against the United States, but organized to protect the lives and property of the citizens, are invited to still co-operate with the forces of the United States to that end, and, so acting, will not be included in the terms of this order, but will report to these headquarters.

All ensigns, flags, devices, tending to uphold any authority whatever, save the flags of the United States and those of foreign consulates, must not be exhibited, but suppressed. The American ensign, the emblem of the United States, must be treated with the utmost deference and respect by all persons, under pain of severe punishment.

All persons well disposed towards the government of the United States, who shall renew the oath of allegiance, will receive a safeguard of protection to their persons and property from the army of the United States, and the violation of such safeguard will be punishable with death. All persons still holding allegiance to the Confederate States will be deemed rebels against the government of the United States, and regarded and treated as enemies thereof. All foreigners, not naturalized and claiming allegiance to their respective governments, and not having made oath of allegiance to the governments of the Confederate States, will be protected in their persons and property, as heretofore, under the laws of the United States. All persons who may have heretofore given adherence to the supposed government of the Confederate States, or been in their service, who shall lay down or deliver up their arms, return to peaceful occupations, and preserve quiet and order, holding no farther correspondence nor giving aid and comfort to enemies of the United States, will not be disturbed in their persons or property, except so far, under the orders of the commanding general, as the exigencies of the public service may render necessary.

Keepers of all public property, whether state, national, or confederate, such as collections of art, libraries and museums, as well as all public buildings, all munitions of war and armed vessels, will at once make full returns thereof to these headquarters. All manufacturers of arms and munitions of war will report to these headquarters their kind and places of business. All rights of property, of whatever kind, will be held inviolate, subject only to the laws of the United States. All the inhabitants are enjoined to pursue their usual avocations. All shops and places of amusement are to be kept open in the accustomed manner, and services are to be held in the churches and religious houses, as in times of profound peace.

Keepers of all public houses and drinking saloons are to report their names and numbers to the office of the provost-marshal, and they will then receive a license, and be held responsible for all disorders and disturbances arising in their respective places.

Sufficient force will be kept in the city to preserve order and maintain the laws. The killing of American soldiers by any disorderly person or mob is simply assassination and murder, and not war, and will be so regarded and punished. The owner of any house in which such murder shall be committed will be held responsible therefor, and the house be liable to be destroyed by the military authority. All disorders, disturbances of the peace, and crimes of an aggravated nature, interfering with the forces or laws of the United States, will be referred to a military court for trial and punishment. Other misdemeanors will be subject to the municipal authority, if it desires to act.

Civil causes between party and party will be referred to the ordinary tribunals.

The levy and collection of taxes, save those imposed by the laws of the United States, are suppressed, except those for keeping in repair and lighting the streets, and for sanitary purposes. These are to be collected in the usual manner.

The circulation of Confederate bonds, evidences of debt (except notes in the similitude of bank-notes) issued by the Confederate States, or scrip, or any trade in the same, is forbidden. It has been represented to the commanding general by the civil authorities that these Confederate notes, in the form of bank-notes, in a great measure, are the only substitutes for money which the people have been allowed to have, and that great distress would ensue among the poorer classes if the circulation of such notes should be suppressed. Such circulation, therefore, will be permitted so long as any one will be inconsiderate enough to receive them, until farther orders.

No publication of newspapers, pamphlets, or hand-bills, giving accounts of the movements of the soldiers of the United States within this department, reflecting in any way upon the United States, intended in any way to influence the public mind against the United States, will be permitted, and all articles on war news, editorial comments, or correspondence making comments upon the movements of the armies of the United States, must be submitted to the examination of an officer who will be detailed for that purpose from these headquarters. The transmission of all communications by telegraph will be under the charge of an officer detailed from these headquarters.

The armies of the United States came here not to destroy, but to restore order out of chaos, to uphold the government and the laws in the place of the passions of men. To this end, therefore, the efforts of all well-disposed are invited, to have every species of disorder quelled.

If any soldier of the United States should so far forget his duty or his flag as to commit outrage upon any person or property, the commanding general requests his name to be instantly reported to the provost guard so that he may be punished and his wrong act redressed. The municipal authority, so far as the police of the city and environs are concerned, is to extend as before indicated, until suspended.

All assemblages of persons in the streets, either by day or night, tend to disaster, and are forbidden. The various companies composing the Fire Department of New Orleans will be permitted to retain their organizations, and are to report to the provost-marshal, so that they may be known, and not interfered with in their duties.

And, finally, it may be sufficient to add, without farther enumeration, that all the requirements of martial law will be imposed as long as, in the judgment of the United States authorities, it may be necessary; and while it is desired by these authorities to exercise this government mildly, and after the usages of the past, it must not be supposed that it will not be rigorously and firmly administered as the occasion calls for it.

By command of Major-General Butler

Geo. C. Strong, A.A.G., Chief of Staff

Appendix 2

[Butler's Civil Rights Code]

By General Butler
Hdqrs. Eighteenth Army Corps
Dept. of Virginia and North Carolina, FORT MONROE, VA.
December 5, 1863
GENERAL ORDERS No. 46

The recruitment of colored troops has become the settled purpose of the Government. It is therefore the duty of every officer and soldier to aid in carrying out that purpose, by every proper means irrespective of personal predilection. To do this effectually the former condition of the blacks, their change of relation, the new rights acquired by them, the new obligations imposed upon them, the duty of the Government to them, the great stake they have in the war, and the claims their ignorance and the helplessness of their women and children make upon each of us who hold a higher grade in social and political life, must all be carefully considered.

It will also be taken into account that the colored soldiers have none of the machinery of "State aid" for the support of their families while fighting our battles, so liberally provided for the white soldiers, not the generous bounties given by the State and National Governments in the loyal States, although this last is far more than compensated to the black man by the great boon awarded to him, the result of the war—freedom for himself and his race forever!

To deal with these several aspects of this subject so that as few of the negroes as possible shall become chargeable either upon the bounty of Government or the charities of the benevolent, and at the same time to do justice to those who shall enlist, to encourage enlistment, and to cause all capable of working to employ themselves for their support and that of their families, either in arms or other sevice, and that the rights of negroes and the Government may both be protected, it is ordered:

I. In this department, after the 1st day of December, instant, and until otherwise ordered, every able-bodied colored man who shall enlist and be mustered into the service of the United States for three years or during the war shall be paid as bounty, to supply his immediate wants, the sum of $10. And it shall be the duty of each mustering officer to return to these head-quarters duplicate rolls of recruits so enlisted and mustered into the service on the 10th, 20th, and last days of each month, so that the bounty may be promptly paid and accounted for.

II. To the family of each colored soldier so enlisted and mustered, so long as he shall remain in the service and behave well, shall be furnished suitable subsistence, under the direction of the superintendents of negro affairs or their assistants; and each soldier shall be furnished with a certificate of subsistence for his family as soon as he is mustered; and any soldier deserting, or whose pay and allowances are forfeited by court-martial, shall be reported by his captain to the superintendent of the district where his family lives, and the subsistence may be stopped, provided that such subsistence shall be continued for at least six months to the family of any colored soldier who shall die in the service by disease, wounds, or battle.

III. Every enlisted colored man shall have the same uniform, clothing, arms, equipments, camp equipage, rations, medical and hospital treatment as are furnished to the U.S. soldiers of a like arm of the service, unless, upon request, some modification thereof shall be granted from these headquarters.

IV. The pay of the colored soldiers shall be $10 per month, $3 of which may be retained for clothing. But the non-commissioned officers, whether colored or white, shall have the same addition to their pay as other non-commissioned officers. It is, however, hoped and believed by the commanding general that Congress, as an act of justice, will increase the pay of the colored troops to a uniform rate with other troops of the United States. He can see no reason why a colored soldier should be asked to fight upon less pay than any other. The colored man fills an equal space in ranks while he lives, and an equal grave when he falls.

V. It appears by returns from the several recruiting officers that enlistments are discouraged, and the Government is competing against itself, because of the payment of sums larger than the pay of the colored soldiers to the colored employés in the several staff departments, and that, too, while the charities of the Government and individuals are supporting the families of the laborer. It is further ordered, That no officer or other person on behalf of the Government, or to be paid by the Government, on land in this department, shall employ or hire any colored man for a greater rate of wages than $10 per month, or the pay of a colored soldier and rations, or $15 per month without rations, except that mechanics and skilled laborers may be employed at other rates, regard being had, however, to the pay of the soldier in fixing such rates.

VI. The best use during the war for an able-bodied colored man, as well for himself as the country, is to be a soldier: It is therefore further ordered, That no colored man, between the ages of eighteen and forty-five, who can pass the surgeon's examination for a soldier, shall be employed on land by any person in behalf of the Government (mechanics and skilled laborers alone excepted). And it shall be the duty of each officer or other person employing colored labor in this department, to be paid by or on behalf of the Government, to cause each laborer to be examined by the surgeons detailed to examine colored recruits, who shall furnish the laborer with a certificate of disability or ability, as the case may be, and after the 1st day of January next no emploment rolls of colored laborers will be certified or passed at these headquarters wherein this order has not been complied with, and are not vouched for by such certificate of disability of the employs. And whenever hereafter a colored employé of the Government shall not be paid within sixty days after his wages shall become due and payable, the officer or other person having the funds to make such payment shall be dismissed the service, subject to the approval of the President.

VII. Promptness of payment of labor, and the facilities furnished by the Government and the benevolent, will enable colored laborers in the service of the Government to be supported from the proceeds of their labor; therefore no subsistence will be funished to the families of those employed by the Government at labor, but the superintendent of negro affairs may issue subsistence to those so employed and charge the amount against their wages, and furnish the officer in charge of payment of such laborers with the amounts so issued, on the first day of each month, or be himself chargeable with the amount so issued.

VIII. Political freedom rightly defined is liberty to work, and to be protected in the full enjoyment of the fruits of labor; and no one with ability to work should enjoy the fruits of another's labor, therefore no subsistence will be permitted to any negro or his family, with whom he lives, who is able to work and does not work. It is, therefore, the duty of the superintendent of negro affairs to furnish employment to all the negroes able to labor, and see that their families are supplied with the necessaries of life. Any negro who refuses to work when able, and neglects his family, will be arrested and reported to these headquarters to be sent to labor on the fortifications, where he will be made to work. No negro will be required to labor on the Sabbath unless upon the most urgent necessity.

IX. The commanding general is informed that officers and soldiers in the department have, by impressment and force, compelled the labor of negroes sometimes for private use, and often without any imperative necessity.

Negroes have rights so long as they fulfill their duties: Therefore it is ordered, That no officer or soldier shall impress or force to labor for any private purpose whatever any negro; and negro labor shall not be impressed or forced for any public purpose unless under orders from these headquarters, or because of imperative military necessity, and where the labor of white citizens would be compelled if present. And any orders of any officer compelling any labor by negroes or white citizens shall forthwith be reported to these headquarters, and the reasons which called for the necessity for such order be fully set forth.

In case of a necessity compelling negro or white labor for the purpose of building fortifications, bridges, roads, or aiding transportation or other military purpose, it shall be the duty of the superintendent of negroes in that district to cause employment rolls to be made of those so compelled to labor, and to present said rolls as soon as the necessity ceases to the assistant quartermaster of the district that the laborers may be paid; and the superintendent shall see that those that labor shall have proper subsistence, and may draw from the commissary of subsistence rations therefor. Any officer offending willfully against the provisions of this order will be dismissed the service, subject to the approval of the President.

And no negro shall be impressed into military service of the United States except under orders from these headquarters—by a draft which shall equally apply to the white and colored citizen.

X. The theory upon which negroes are received into the Union lines and employed, either as laborers or soldiers, is that every negro able to work who leaves the rebel lines diminishes by so much the producing power of the rebellion to supply itself with food and labor necessary to be done outside of military operations to sustain its armies, and the United States thereby gains either a soldier or a producer. Women and children are received because it would be manifestly iniquitous and unjust to take the husband and father and leave the wife and child to ill-treatment and starvation. Women and children are also received when unaccompanied by the husband and father, because the negro has the domestic affections in as strong a degree as the white man, and however far South his master may drive him he will sooner or later return to his family.

Therefore it is ordered, That every officer and soldier of this command shall aid by every means in his power the coming of all colored people within the Union lines; that all officers commanding expeditions and raids shall bring in with them all the negroes possible, affording them transportation, aid, protection, and encouragement. Any officer bringing or admitting negroes within his lines shall forthwith report the same to the superintendent of negro affairs within his district so they may be cared for and protected, enlisted, or set to work. Any officer, soldier, or citizen who shall dissuade, hinder, prevent, or endeavor to prevent or hinder any negro from coming within the Union lines; or shall dissuade, hinder, prevent, or endeavor to prevent or hinder any negro from enlisting; or who shall insult, abuse, ridicule, or interfere with, for the purpose of casting ridicule or contempt upon colored troops or individual soldiers, because they are colored, shall be deemed to be and held liable under the several acts of Congress applicable to this subject, and be punished with military severity for obstructing recruiting.

XI. In consideration of the ignorance and helplessness of the negroes, arising from the condition in which they have been heretofore held, it becomes necessary that the Government should exercise more and peculiar care and protection over them than over its white citizens, accustomed to self-control and self-support, so that their sustenance may be assured, their rights respected, their helplessness protected, and their wrongs redressed; and that there be one system of management of negro affairs: It is ordered, that Lieut. Col. J. Burnham Kinsman, aide-de-camp, be detailed at these headquarters as general superintendent of negro affairs in this department, to whom all reports and communications relating thereto, required to be sent to these headquarters, shall be addressed. He shall have a general superintendence over all the colored people of this department; and all other superintendents of negro affairs shall report to Lieutenant-Colonel Kinsman, who is acting for the commanding general in this behalf.

All the territory of Virginia south of the James River shall be under the superintendence of Capt. Orlando Brown, assistant quartermaster. All the territory north of James River shall be under the superintendence of Capt. Charles B. Wilder, assistant quartermaster. The District of North Carolina shall be under the superintendence of the Rev. Horace James, chaplain.

Each superintendent shall have the power to select and appoint such assistant superintendents for such sub-districts in his district as may be necessary, to be approved by the commanding general, such appointments to be confirmed by the commanding general.

The pay of such assistant, if a civilian, shall in no case exceed the pay of a first-class clerk in the Quartermaster's Department.

It shall be the duty of each superintendent, under the direction of the general superintendent, to take care of the colored inhabitants of his district, not slaves, under the actual control of a loyal master in his district (and in all questions arising as to freedom or slavery of any colored person, the presumption shall be that the man, woman, or child is free or has claimed protection of the military authorities of the United States, which entitles the claimant to freedom); to cause an accurate census to be taken of colored inhabitants in his district and their employments; to cause all to be provided with necessary shelter, clothing, food, and medicines; to see that all able to work shall have some employment, and that such employment shall be industriously pursued; to see that in all contracts for labor or other things made by the negroes with white persons the negro is not defrauded, and to annul all contracts made by the negro which are unconscionable and injurious, and that such contracts as are fulfilled by the negro shall be paid; to take charge of all lands and all property allotted, turned over, or given to the use of the negro, whether by Government or by charity; to keep accurate accounts of the same and of all expenditure; to audit all accounts of the negroes against Government, and to have all proper allowances made as well to the negro as the Government; to keep accurate accounts of all expenses of the negro to the Government, and of his earnings for the Government; to see that the negroes who have wrought on land furnished by the Government on shares shall have their just portion, and to aid in disposing of the same for the best good of the negro and Government; to make quarterly returns and exhibits of all accounts of matters committed to them; and to hold all moneys arising from the surplus earnings of the negro over the expenditures by the United States, for the use and benefit of the negroes, under orders from these headquarters.

XII. It appearing to the commanding general that some of the labor done by the negroes in this department remains unpaid—some for the space of more than two years, although contracts were duly made by the proper officers of the Government for the payment thereof—whereby the faith of the negro in the justice of the Government is impaired and the trust in its protection is weakened: It is ordered, That each superintendent shall be a commissioner, to audit all such accounts, procure evidence of their validity, make out accurate pay-rolls and return the same, so that they may be presented for adjustment of the proper Departments: *Provided, however,* That no sale of any such claim against the Government shall be valid, and no payment shall be made of any such claim except in hand to the person actually earning it—if he is within this department—or to his legal representative, if the person earning it be deceased.

XIII. Religious, benevolent, and humane persons have come into this department for the charitable purpose of giving to the negroes secular and religious instructions; and this, too, without any adequate pay or material reward. It is therefore ordered, That every officer and soldier shall treat all such persons with the utmost respect; shall aid them by all proper means in their laudable avocations; and that transportation be furnished them whenever it may be necessary in pursuit of their business.

XIV. As it is necessary to preserve uniformity of system, and that information shall be had as to the needs and the supplies for the negro; and as certain authorizations are had to raise troops in the department, a practice has grown up of corresponding directly with the War and other Departments of the Government, to the manifest injury of the service: It is therefore ordered, That all correspondence in relation to the raising or recruitment of colored troops, and relating to the care and control of the negroes in this department, with any official organized body or society, or any Department or Bureau of the Government, must be transmitted through these headquarters, as by regulation all other military correspondence is required to be done.

XV. Courts-martial and courts of inquiry in relation to all offenses committed by or against any of the colored troops, or any person in the service of the United States connected with the care, or serving with the colored troops, shall have a majority of its members composed of officers in command of colored troops, when such can be detailed without manifest injury to the service.

All offenses by citizens against the negroes, or by the negroes against citizens—except of a high and aggravated nature—shall be heard and tried before the provost court.

XVI. This order shall be published and furnished to each regiment and detached post within the department—a copy for every commanding officer thereof—and every commander of a company, or detachment less than a company, shall cause the same to be read once, at least, to his company or detachment; and this order shall be printed for the information of the citizens, once at least, in each newspaper published in the department.

By command of MAJOR GENERAL BUTLER
R. S. DAVIS, *Major and Assistant Adjutant-General*

Notes

Information about the subjects noted under each chapter number was found in the source or sources indicated. The full title of each source and other bibliographic information is found in the bibliography of this book.

Chapter 1
  1. Butler's ancestry and childhood: *Butler's Book, General Butler in New Orleans* (by James Parton), cited hereafter in this section as Parton
Chapter 2
  1. Butler's childhood: *Butler's Book*, Parton
Chapter 3
  1. Butler at Deerfield Academy and Exeter: *Butler's Book*, Parton
  2. Working conditions in the textile mills: *Butler's Book, The Merrimack*
Chapter 4
  1. The development of textile industry in Lowell: *The Merrimack*
  2. The Boott-Edson controversy over school construction: *Butler's Book*
Chapter 5
  1. Butler at Waterville College: *Butler's Book*
Chapter 6
  1. Butler's first sea voyage: *Butler's Book*
Chapter 7
  1. Butler's law studies and his courtship of and marriage to Sarah Hildreth: *Butler's Book*
Chapter 8
  1. Butler and the politics of 1840: *A History of Presidential Elections, Butler's Book, Anti-intellectualism in American Life, A History of the Southern Confederacy, Lowell Courier*
Chapter 9
  1. Sutter's lawsuit (*Sutter v. the United States*): *Butler's Book, West of the West*
Chapter 10
  1. Butler's military training in the militia: *Butler's Book*

2. The political strife in the early 1850s: *A History of Presidential Elections, Butler's Book, Anti-intellectualism in American Life*

Chapter 11

1. The politics of 1856: *Butler's Book, A History of Presidential Elections*

2. The Dred Scott decision: *Scott v. Sandford, A History of American Law, Stanton: The Life and Times of Lincoln's Secretary of War*, cited hereafter in this section as *Stanton Life and Times*

3. Butler's votes for Jefferson Davis at the 1860 Democratic Convention: *Butler's Book*, Parton

Chapter 12

1. The proceedings of the Republican Convention that nominated Lincoln: *A History of Presidential Elections, Butler's Book, William Henry Seward*

2. Butler's proposal to try Southern commissioners for treason: *Butler's Book, Private and Official Correspondence of Gen. Benjamin F. Butler during the Period of the Civil War*, cited hereafter in this section as *Private and Official Correspondence*

Chapter 13

1. Massachusetts alerts the militia: *Butler's Book, Private and Official Correspondence*

2. South Carolina moves toward civil war: *The Great Rebellion, A History of the Southern Confederacy*

3. Equipping the Massachusetts Militia: *Butler's Book, Private and Official Correspondence*

Chapter 14

1. Stanton's "leak" of Buchanan cabinet proceedings: *Stanton Life and Times, Diary of Gideon Welles*, cited hereafter in this section as *Welles Diary*

2. Fort Sumter defenses: Abner Doubleday's account in *Battles and Leaders of the Civil War*, cited hereafter in this section as *Battles and Leaders*

3. The conspiracy to cripple the attempt to relieve Fort Sumter: *Welles Diary, Lincoln and Seward*

4. The attack on Fort Sumter: *Lee's Lieutenants, Battles and Leaders*

5. Butler's maneuvers to command the Massachusetts brigade being sent to the relief of Washington: *Butler's Book, Private and Official Correspondence*

Chapter 15

1. The Baltimore mob attack on the Massachusetts 6th Regiment: *Butler's Book, Private and Official Correspondence, The Great Rebellion, Battles and Leaders*

2. Butler's troop movement to Annapolis: *Butler's Book, Private and Official Correspondence*

3. The seizure of Annapolis and rescue of Old Ironsides: *Butler's Book, Private and Official Correspondence*, Sandburg's *Abraham Lincoln, Reveille in Washington, 1860–1865*

Chapter 16
1. The New York 7th at Annapolis: *Private and Official Correspondence*
2. The arrival of Massachusetts and New York regiments in Washington: *Private and Official Correspondence, Reveille in Washington, 1860–1865*

Chapter 17
1. The relations between Butler and Governor Hicks: *Butler's Book, Private and Official Correspondence*
2. Butler's disregarded warning of the pressing need to reinforce Federal troops holding Manassas Junction: *Private and Official Correspondence*
3. Butler's seizure and occupation of Baltimore: *Private and Official Correspondence, Battles and Leaders*
4. The arrest of millionaire secessionist Winans: *Butler's Book, Private and Official Correspondence, Welles Diary*

Chapter 18
1. The conflict between Butler and General Scott: *Private and Official Correspondence, Reveille in Washington, 1860–1865, Welles Diary*
2. Reverdy Johnson and the release of Winans: *Private and Official Correspondence, Abraham Lincoln, Welles Diary*

Chapter 19
1. Butler at Fortress Monroe: *Private and Official Correspondence*
2. Butler's "contrabands of war" edict: *Butler's Book, Private and Official Correspondence, From Plantation to Ghetto*
3. Lincoln's equivocal position regarding emancipation: *Complete Works of Abraham Lincoln*

Chapter 20
1. The Big Bethel skirmish: *Private and Official Correspondence, Lee's Lieutenants, Mary Chesnut's Civil War, Battles and Leaders*
2. General Scott's continuing feud with Butler: *Private and Official Correspondence*
3. The Hatteras expedition: *Butler's Book, Private and Official Correspondence, Abraham Lincoln*

Chapter 21
1. Recruiting New England troops: *Private and Official Correspondence*

Chapter 22
1. The Trent Affair and tension with Britain: *William Henry Seward, Welles Diary, When the Guns Roared, Mary Chesnut's Civil War*
2. Prince Albert and the Trent Affair: *The Oxford Book of Royal Anecdotes*
3. Stanton and Cameron: *Stanton Life and Times*
4. The New Orleans expedition: *Butler's Book, Private and Official Correspondence, Welles Diary, Stanton Life and Times*

Chapter 23
1. Butler and McClellan: *Private and Official Correspondence*

Chapter 24

1. The hard-luck steamer *Mississippi*: *Butler's Book*, *Private and Official Correspondence*

Chapter 25

1. The arrival at Ship Island: *Butler's Book*, *Private and Official Correspondence*

2. The rescue of shipwrecked child: *Butler's Book*

3. The word portrait of Butler: *A Volunteer's Adventures*

4. Butler and David Farragut: *Private and Official Correspondence*

Chapter 26

1. The characterization of David D. Porter: *Welles Diary*, *Lincoln and Seward*

2. Farragut's passage of the Mississippi forts: *The Great Rebellion*, Porter's account in *Battles and Leaders*, *Private and Official Correspondence*

3. The capture and occupation of Mississippi forts: *Private and Official Correspondence*, *Battles and Leaders*, *Confidential Correspondence of Gustavus Vasa Fox*, Parton

Chapter 27

1. Butler-Porter controversy over New Orleans forts: *Private and Official Correspondence*, *Confidential Correspondence of Gustavus Vasa Fox*, *Battles and Leaders*, *David Glasgow Farragut: Our First Admiral*, cited hereafter in this section as *Farragut*

Chapter 28

1. The occupation of New Orleans: *Private and Official Correspondence*, *A Volunteer's Adventures*, Parton

Chapter 29

1. Farragut raises the flag over New Orleans: *Battles and Leaders*

2. The capture and hanging of William Mumford: *Battles and Leaders*, *Butler's Book*, *Private and Official Correspondence*, *Farragut*

Chapter 30

1. Yellow Fever: *Butler's Book*, Parton, *Manson's Tropical Diseases*, *Private and Official Correspondence*

Chapter 31

1. Butler's police and intelligence services in New Orleans: *Butler's Book*, *Welles Diary*, Parton, *Private and Official Correspondence*

Chapter 32

1. Feeding the hungry in New Orleans: Parton, *Private and Official Correspondence*, *Reconstruction*

Chapter 33

1. The Woman Order: *Private and Official Correspondence*, Parton, *Patriotic Gore*, *When the Guns Roared*, *William Henry Seward*

Chapter 34

1. Butler and the foreign consuls in New Orleans: *Private and Official Cor-*

respondence, Parton, *William Henry Seward*

Chapter 35

1. Butler and the blacks in Louisiana: *Butler's Book, Private and Official Correspondence, Reconstruction*, Parton, *Complete Works of Abraham Lincoln, From Plantation to Ghetto*

Chapter 36

1. Financing the occupation of New Orleans: *Butler's Book*, Parton, *Private and Official Correspondence*

Chapter 37

1. Butler's defensive measures at New Orleans: *Butler's Book*, Parton, *Private and Official Correspondence, William Henry Seward*

2. The first attempts to capture Vicksburg: *Private and Official Correspondence, Memoirs of General William T. Sherman, Battles and Leaders, Personal Memoirs of U. S. Grant*

Chapter 38

1. The confederate attack on Baton Rouge: *Private and Official Correspondence, Photographic History of the Civil War, The Great Rebellion, Battles and Leaders, Welles Diary*

2. Butler's military moves west of the Mississippi: *Butler's Book, Private and Official Correspondence, Battles and Leaders*

3. The reports that Banks would supersede Butler: *Private and Official Correspondence*

Chapter 39

1. Butler leaves New Orleans: *Butler's Book*

Chapter 40

1. Butler's removal from command at New Orleans: *Private and Official Correspondence, Welles Diary, William Henry Seward*

2. Banks's military setbacks after superseding Butler: *Battles and Leaders, The Civil War, Memoirs of General William T. Sherman, Personal Memoirs of U. S. Grant*

Chapter 41

1. Butler at Fortress Monroe: *Private and Official Correspondence*

Chapter 42

1. Butler and Halleck: *Private and Official Correspondence, Stanton Life and Times, Personal Memoirs of U. S. Grant, Battles and Leaders*

2. General Wild's sweep of guerrilla encampments: *Private and Official Correspondence*

3. Butler's agents in Richmond: *Private and Official Correspondence*

4. The attempted raid to rescue Union prisoners in Richmond: *Private and Official Correspondence, Battles and Leaders*

Chapter 43

1. Prisoner exchange: *Butler's Book, Private and Official Correspondence, Personal Memoirs of U. S. Grant*

Chapter 44

1. Lincoln's equivocal position regarding the slaves: *Complete Works of Abraham Lincoln*

2. Amity between Butler and Grant: *Personal Memoirs of U. S. Grant, Butler's Book, Private and Official Correspondence*

3. Banks and the Red River campaign: *Battles and Leaders, Personal Memoirs of U. S. Grant, Private and Official Correspondence, Welles Diary*

4. Butler's role in Lincoln's reelection campaign: *Private and Official Correspondence, Butler's Book*

5. Seward and the French tobacco: *Welles Diary*

Chapter 45

1. The move to Bermuda Hundred: *Private and Official Correspondence, Personal Memoirs of U. S. Grant*

2. Grant's Wilderness campaign; its effect on Butler's operations: *Battles and Leaders, West Point Atlas of American Wars, Personal Memoirs of U. S. Grant, Private and Official Correspondence, Wartime Papers of R. E. Lee*

3. The detachment of Smith's XVIII Corps to reinforce Grant: *Private and Official Correspondence, Personal Memoirs of U. S. Grant, West Point Atlas of American Wars*

4. Smith's difficulties in landing his corps at White House on Halleck's orders, rather than at West Point, where Butler suggested, and where there were proper landing facilities: In *Lee's Lieutenants*, Freeman comments that the Confederates held their flank at Cold Harbor by a stroke of luck: "General Smith's inability to get his troops ashore quickly at White House where dockage was almost non-existent."

Chapter 46

1. Butler and weapons technology: *Private and Official Correspondence, A History of the Southern Confederacy*

2. The initial attempt on Petersburg: *Butler's Book, Private and Official Correspondence, Battles and Leaders, Lee's Lieutenants, Personal Memoirs of U. S. Grant*

3. Grant's shift to Bermuda Hundred: *Personal Memoirs of U. S. Grant, Private and Official Correspondence, Wartime Papers of R. E. Lee*

4. An appreciation of Sherman's tactics: *Strategy*

5. The artillery duel with Confederate Whitworth battery: *Butler's Book.* Photos and technical data on the Whitworth gun and its projectile may be found in *Photographic History of the Civil War, Vol. 5*

Chapter 47

1. General Smith's attempt against Petersburg: *Battles and Leaders, Personal Memoirs of U. S. Grant, Private and Official Correspondence*

2. Smith's removal from command: *Private and Official Correspondence, Personal Memoirs of U. S. Grant, Battles and Leaders*

Chapter 48

1. War weariness and desertions: *Wartime Papers of R. E. Lee, Personal Memoirs of U. S. Grant*

2. Lee's assessment of the high strategic value of Butler's base: *Wartime Papers of R. E. Lee*

3. Sea power as decisive in the defense of Washington: *Butler's Book, Lee's Lieutenants*

4. The battle of the Crater at Petersburg: *Inferno at Petersburg, Private and Official Correspondence*

5. Butler's neutrality in the presidential election: *Butler's Book, Private and Official Correspondence*

Chapter 49

1. Offensive operations north of the James: *Personal Memoirs of U. S. Grant, Private and Official Correspondence, The Negro as a Soldier, Battles and Leaders, Wartime Papers of R. E. Lee*

Chapter 50

1. Grant's change of attitude toward Butler: *Butler's Book*

2. The internal politics of Lincoln's cabinet: *Private and Official Correspondence, Stanton Life and Times, Welles Diary*

3. Corruption in the Lincoln administration: *Welles Diary*

4. Gold, silver, and spoons: *Butler's Book, Private and Official Correspondence, Stanton Life and Times*

Chapter 51

1. Sherman's march to the sea: *Battles and Leaders, Memoirs of General William T. Sherman, Wartime Papers of R. E. Lee*

2. Sherman's views on the Fort Fisher expedition: *Memoirs of General William T. Sherman*

3. Planning the Fort Fisher expedition: *Welles Diary, Private and Official Correspondence*

4. Fort Fisher defenses: *Battles and Leaders, Capture of Fort Fisher, Private and Official Correspondence*

5. The first assault on Fort Fisher: *Battles and Leaders, Private and Official Correspondence, Welles Diary, Capture of Fort Fisher*

6. The second assault on Fort Fisher: *Capture of Fort Fisher, Battles and Leaders, Welles Diary, Private and Official Correspondence, Personal Memoirs of U. S. Grant, Memoirs of General William T. Sherman*

Chapter 52

1. Butler's return to civilian life: *Butler's Book, Private and Official Correspondence, Chronicles from the Nineteenth Century, Adelbert Ames*

2. The death of General Butler: From contemporary newspapers accounts, notably the *Lowell Courier* and the *Lowell Sun*

Bibliography

Books

Ames, Adelbert. *Capture of Fort Fisher, North Carolina, Jan. 15, 1865* (privately published).

Ames, Blanche Butler. *Adelbert Ames, 1835–1933* (New York: Argosy-Antiquarian), 1964.

Ames, Blanche Butler (ed.). *Chronicles from the Nineteenth Century: Family Letters of Blanche Butler and Adelbert Ames*, 2 vols. (privately published), 1957.

Bailyn, Bernard; Davis, David Brion; Donald, David Herbert; Thomas, John L.; Wiebe, Robert H.; and Wood, Gordon S. *The Great Republic* (Boston: Little, Brown), 1977.

Beale, Howard K. (ed.). *Diary of Gideon Welles*, 3 vols. (New York: Norton), 1960.

Butler, Benjamin F. *Butler's Book* (Boston: Thayer), 1892.

Catton, Bruce. *Grant Takes Command* (Boston: Little, Brown), 1968.

Churchill, Sir Winston. *The American Civil War* (New York: Dodd, Mead), 1958.

Davis, Maj. George B., et al. *Atlas to Accompany the Official Records of the Union and Confederate Armies* (Washington, D.C.: Government Printing Office), 1891–1895.

De Forest, John William. *A Volunteer's Adventures* (New Haven, Conn.: Yale University Press), 1946.

Donald, David. *Lincoln Reconsidered* (New York: Knopf), 1947.

Dowdey, Clifford, and Manarin, Louis H. (ed.). *The Wartime Papers of R. E. Lee* (Boston: Little, Brown), 1961.

Eaton, Clement. *A History of the Southern Confederacy* (New York: Free Press), 1954.

Eggenberger, David. *A Dictionary of Battles* (New York: Crowell), 1967.

Eisenschiml, Otto, and Newman, Ralph. *The American Iliad* (Indianapolis: Bobbs-Merrill), 1947.

Esposito, Col. Vincent J. (ed.). *The West Point Atlas of American Wars*, Vol. 1 (New York: Praeger), 1959.

Fleetwood, Christian A. *The Negro as a Soldier* (Washington, D.C.: Professor G. W. Cook), 1895.

Foner, Eric. *Reconstruction: America's Unfinished Revolution, 1863–1877* (New York: Harper), 1988.

Foote, Shelby. *The Civil War: A Narrative*, 3 vols. (New York: Random House), 1986.

Freeman, Douglas Southall. *Lee's Lieutenants: A Study in Command*, 3 vols. (New York: Scribner), 1942.

Friedman, Lawrence M. *A History of American Law* (New York: Simon & Schuster), 1973.

Grant, Ulysses S. *Personal Memoirs of U. S. Grant*, 2 vols. (New York: Webster), 1886.

Hart, B. H. Liddell. *Sherman: Soldier, Realist, American* (New York: Praeger), 1960.

Hart, B. H. Liddell. *Strategy* (New York: Praeger), 1954.

Headley, J. T. *The Great Rebellion: A History of the Civil War in the United States*, 2 vols. (Hartford: Hurlbut, Williams), 1863.

Henderson, Col. G.F.R. *The Civil War: A Soldier's View*, ed. Jay Luvaas (Chicago: University of Chicago Press), 1958.

Hofstadter, Richard. *Anti-intellectualism in American Life* (New York: Knopf), 1963.

Holden, Raymond P. *The Merrimack* (New York: Rinehart), 1958.

Howe, Mark DeWolfe (ed.). *Touched with Fire: Civil War Letters and Diary of Oliver Wendell Holmes, Jr., 1861–1864* (Cambridge, Mass.: Harvard University Press), 1947.

Hughes, Quentin. *Military Architecture* (New York: St. Martin's Press), 1974.

Johnson, Robert Underwood, and Buel, Clarence Clough. *Battles and Leaders of the Civil War*, 4 vols. (New York: The Century Co.), 1887.

Kennedy, Frances H. (ed.). *The Civil War Battlefield Guide* (Boston: Houghton Mifflin), 1990.

Kennedy, Paul. *The Rise and Fall of the Great Powers* (New York: Random House), 1987.

Kirsch, Robert, and Murphy, William S. *West of the West* (New York: Dutton), 1967.

Leech, Margaret. *Reveille in Washington, 1860–1865* (New York: Harper), 1941.

Lewis, Charles Lee. *David Glasgow Farragut: Admiral in the Making*, 2 vols. (Annapolis: United States Naval Institute), 1941.

Longford, Elizabeth (ed.). *The Oxford Book of Royal Anecdotes* (Oxford: Oxford University Press), 1989.

Manson-Bahr, Philip (ed.). *Manson's Tropical Diseases: A Manual of the*

Diseases of Warm Climates (London: Cassell), 1942.

Marshall, Jessie Ames (ed.). *Private and Official Correspondence of Gen. Benjamin F. Butler during the Period of the Civil War*, 5 vols. (privately published), 1917.

McDonough, James Lee. *Chattanooga—A Death Grip on the Confederacy* (Knoxville: University of Tennessee Press), 1984.

McPherson, James M. *Battle Cry of Freedom* (New York: Oxford University Press), 1988.

Meier, August, and Rudwick, Elliott M. *From Plantation to Ghetto* (New York: Hill and Wang), 1966.

Miller, Francis Trevelyan (ed.). *Photographic History of the Civil War*, 10 vols. (New York: Review of Reviews), 1911.

Moat, Louis Shepheard. *Frank Leslie's Illustrated History of the Civil War* (New York: Mrs. Frank Leslie), 1895.

Nevins, Allan. *The War for the Union* (New York: Scribner), 1960.

Nicolay, John G., and Hay, John (ed.). *Complete Works of Abraham Lincoln*, 12 vols. (New York: Lamb), 1894.

Parton, James. *General Butler in New Orleans* (New York: Mason Brothers), 1864.

Pleasants, Henry, Jr., M.D., and Straley, George H. *Inferno at Petersburg* (Philadelphia: Chilton), 1961.

Roseboom, Eugene H. *A History of Presidential Elections* (New York: Macmillan), 1959.

Sandburg, Carl. *Abraham Lincoln: The War Years*, 4 vols. (New York: Harcourt Brace), 1939.

Sears, Stephen W. *George B. McClellan: The Young Napoleon* (New York: Ticknor and Fields), 1988.

Seward, Frederick W. *Seward at Washington as Senator and Secretary of State* (New York: Derby and Miller), 1891.

Sherman, William T. *Memoirs of General William T. Sherman*, 2 vols. (New York: Appleton), 1875.

Steiner, Bernard C. *Life of Reverdy Johnson* (Baltimore: Norman, Remington), 1914.

Stern, Philip Van Doren. *Soldier Life in the Union and Confederate Armies* (Greenwich, Conn.: Fawcett), 1961.

Stern, Philip Van Doren. *When the Guns Roared* (New York: Doubleday), 1965.

Thomas, Benjamin P., and Hyman, Harold M. *Stanton: The Life and Times of Lincoln's Secretary of War* (New York: Knopf), 1962.

Thompson, Robert Means, and Wainwright, Richard. *Publications of the Naval History Society*, Vols. 9 and 10: *Confidential Correspondence of Gustavus Vasa Fox* (New York: Naval History Society), 1918.

Van Deusen, Glyndon G. *William Henry Seward* (New York: Oxford University Press), 1967.

Warren, Robert Penn. *The Legacy of the Civil War* (New York: Random House), 1961.

Welles, Gideon. *Lincoln and Seward* (Freeport, N.Y.: Books for Libraries Press), 1874.

West, Richard S., Jr. *Lincoln's Scapegoat General: A Life of Benjamin F. Butler, 1818–1893* (Boston: Houghton Mifflin), 1965.

Williams, Kenneth P. *Lincoln Finds A General: A Military Study of the Civil War* (New York: Macmillan), 1949.

Williams, T. Harry. *Lincoln and His Generals* (New York: Grosset & Dunlap), 1952.

Wilson, Edmund. *Patriotic Gore: Studies in the Literature of the American Civil War* (New York: Oxford University Press), 1962.

Woodward, C. Vann (ed.). *Mary Chesnut's Civil War* (New Haven, Conn.: Yale University Press), 1981.

Van Creveld, Martin. *Technology and War* (New York: Macmillan), 1989.

Newspapers

Lowell Courier
Lowell Sun
Saturday Vox Populi (Lowell, Massachusetts)

Index